RAF Bomber Command Squadron Profiles

106 Squadron

RAF Bomber Command Squadron Profiles

106 Squadron

by Chris Ward

with Herman Bijlard

Bomber Command Books
from

MENTION THE WAR PUBLICATIONS

This edition first published 2016 by Mention the War Ltd., 32 Croft Street, Farsley, Yorkshire, LS28 5HA.

Cover design: Topics - The Creative Partnership www.topicsdesign.co.uk

A CIP catalogue reference for this book is available from the British Library.

ISBN 978-1-911255-04-8

Also by Chris Ward:

Dambusters. Forging of a Legend
by Chris Ward, published 2009 by Pen & Sword.

RAF Bomber Command Squadron Profiles –
617 Squadron
103 Squadron (with David Fell)
by Chris Ward, published 2015 by Mention the War Ltd.

Dambusters- The Definitive History of 617 Squadron at War 1943-1945
by Chris Ward, Andy Lee and Andreas Wachtel, published 2003 by Red Kite.

Dambuster Crash Sites
by Chris Ward and Andreas Wachtel, published 2007 by Pen and Sword Aviation.

Images of War: 617 Dambuster Squadron at War
by Chris Ward and Andy Lee, published 2009 by Pen and Sword Aviation.

1 Group Bomber Command. An Operational History
by Chris Ward with Greg Harrison and Grzegorz Korcz, published 2014 by Pen and Sword Aviation.

3 Group Bomber Command. An Operational History
by Chris Ward and Steve Smith, published 2008 by Pen and Sword Aviation.

4 Group Bomber Command. An Operational History
by Chris Ward, published 2012 by Pen and Sword Aviation.

5 Group Bomber Command. An Operational History
by Chris Ward, published 2007 by Pen and Sword Aviation.

6 Group Bomber Command. An Operational History
by Chris Ward, published 2009 by Pen and Sword Aviation.

Contents

Introduction

RAF Bomber Command Squadron Profiles first appeared in the late nineties, and proved to be very popular with enthusiasts of RAF Bomber Command during the Second World War. They became a useful research tool, particularly for those whose family members had served and were no longer around. The original purpose was to provide a point of reference for all of the gallant men and women who had fought the war, either in the air, or on the ground in a support capacity, and for whom no written history of their unit or station existed. I wanted to provide them with something they could hold up, point to and say, "this was my unit, this is what I did in the war". Many veterans were reticent to talk about their time on bombers, partly because of modesty, but perhaps mostly because the majority of those with whom they came into contact had no notion of what it was to be a "Bomber Boy", to face the prospect of death every time they took to the air, whether during training or on operations. Only those who shared the experience really understood what it was to go to war in bombers, which is why reunions were so important. As they approached the end of their lives, many veterans began to speak openly for the first time about their life in wartime Bomber Command, and most were hurt by the callous treatment they received at the hands of successive governments with regard to the lack of recognition of their contribution to victory. It is sad that this recognition in the form of a national memorial and the granting of a campaign medal came too late for the majority. Now this inspirational, noble generation, the like of which will probably never grace this earth again, has all but departed from us, and the world will be a poorer place as a result.

RAF Bomber Command Squadron Profiles are back. The basic format remains, but, where needed, additional information has been provided. Squadron Profiles do not claim to be comprehensive histories, but rather detailed overviews of the activities of the squadron. There is insufficient space to mention as many names as one would like, but all aircraft losses are accompanied by the name of the pilot. Fundamentally, the narrative section is an account of Bomber Command's war from the perspective of the bomber group under which the individual squadron served, and the deeds of the squadron are interwoven into this story. Information has been drawn from official records, such as group, squadron and station ORBs, and from the many, like myself, amateur enthusiasts, who dedicate much of their time to researching individual units, and become unrivalled authorities on them. I am grateful for their generous contributions, and their names will appear in the appropriate Profiles. The statistics quoted in this series are taken from The Bomber Command War Diaries, that indispensable tome written by Martin Middlebrook and Chris Everitt, and I am indebted to Martin for his kind permission to use them.

Finally, let me apologise in advance for the inevitable errors, for no matter how hard I and other authors try to write "nothing but the truth", there is no such thing as a definitive account of history, and there will always be room for disagreement and debate. Official records are notoriously unreliable tools, and yet we have little choice but to put our faith in them. It is not my intention to misrepresent any person or RAF unit, and I ask my readers to understand the enormity of the task I have undertaken. It is relatively easy to become an authority on single units or even a bomber group, but I chose to write about them all, idiot that I am, which means 128 squadrons serving operationally in Bomber Command at some time between the 3rd of September 1939 and the 8th of May 1945. I am dealing with eight bomber groups, in which some

120,000 airmen served, and I am juggling around 28,000 aircraft serial numbers, code letters and details of provenance and fate. I ask not for your sympathy, it was, after all, my choice, but rather your understanding if you should find something with which you disagree. My thanks to you, my readers, for making the original series of RAF Bomber Command Squadron Profiles so popular, and I hope you receive this new incarnation equally enthusiastically. My thanks also to Simon Hepworth of Mention The War Publications for seeing the potential of bringing them back, and for investing so much effort and time in the project.

When I first wrote this 106 Squadron Profile in the late nineties, I was afforded much assistance by the late and much-missed Des Richards, the acknowledged expert on 106 Squadron. He generously gave of his time to answer my questions, proof read my original manuscript, and purge it of errors. He also provided additional information to enable me to complete the work, and ensure that the deeds of the gallant air and ground crews of this magnificent squadron are accurately represented. This time around I am equally indebted to my friend, Herman Bijlard, from the Netherlands, who knows more about 106 Squadron than anyone else on the planet. He kindly shared his research information with me, sending me copious amounts of data and some photos, all of which has been put to good use. It is thanks to the dedication of archivists like Des and Herman that we can read today of the gallantry of the amazing generation that contested and saw this country through the Second World War. My thanks also to the Friends of Metheringham Association at Westmoor Farm, Martin Moor, Metheringham, for granting me access to their photo archive, and special thanks to curator and archivist Rod Sanders, who assisted in selecting the pictures and then processed them for me.

Chris Ward. Lutterworth. June 2016.

Section One: Narrative WWII History

106 SQUADRON

MOTTO **PRO LIBERTATE** (For freedom) Code **ZN**

106 Squadron at Abingdon in 1938.

A Fairey Battle in 1938, bearing the pre-war markings of 106 Sqn.

1939/40

First formed on the 30th of September 1917, 106 Squadron fulfilled a corps reconnaissance role, moving to Ireland in May 1918, before becoming one of a vast number of squadrons to be disbanded in late 1919. It remained on the shelf until being resurrected at Abingdon on the 1st of June 1938. W/C Montgommerie had been appointed to command the squadron on the 8th of October, and during his periods of absence S/L Sheen stepped up. The squadron was initially equipped with Hawker Hinds, which were replaced by Fairey Battles, and a number of Ansons and Oxfords were also taken on charge. In May 1939 Hampdens arrived, and this type would remain with the squadron until well into 1942. The outbreak of war on the 3rd of September 1939 found 106 Squadron at Cottesmore in the county of Rutland, where it had resided for just two days. Each of Bomber Command's operational groups had been ordered to designate one squadron for group pool training duties, to feed new crews into the front line. This important role was handed to 106 Squadron, and it would be thus occupied for the entire first year of war.

The squadron consisted of two flights, with F/O Johnson in command of A Flight and S/L Parker in command of B Flight. The training role took its toll of Hampdens during 1939 and 1940, and the accidents began on the 24th of October, when L4175 undershot a night landing and hit trees and a hut. No one was killed but the pilot, P/O Dier, did sustain injuries. S/L Sheen took over command of A Flight at the start of November for what would be a short-lived tenure. On the 11th of November L4186 stalled and crashed in Lincolnshire during a low level bombing exercise in the hands of P/O Loew, and one member of the crew was injured. On the 2nd of December S/L Sheen was posted from his role as A Flight commander, and moved to Scampton to replace W/C Johnnie Chick as the commanding officer of 49 Squadron. The vacancy as A Flight commander at 106 Squadron was filled by S/L Weir.

1940

The winter of 1939/40 was particularly harsh, and seemed to deepen as the year progressed. As a consequence, flying was extremely restricted, and in the context of what the Americans dubbed "the "Phoney War", there was very little to occupy the Command's front-line squadrons. It was the end of February before conditions had improved sufficiently for limited operations to be conducted, and these amounted predominantly to reconnaissance and leafleting (nickelling) sorties. The first experience of a bombing operation for the front line squadrons of 5 Group came on the night of the 19/20th of March, when twenty Hampdens followed a force of Whitleys in an attack on the German seaplane base at Hörnum on the island of Sylt. This was in response to the inadvertent slaying by a stray bomb of a British civilian on the island of Hoy, during a Luftwaffe raid on elements of the Royal Navy at Scapa Flow two nights earlier. Despite enthusiastic claims of success by the returning crews, photographic reconnaissance on the 6th of April failed to detect any signs of damage, and the over-optimistic assessments of results would eventually return in eighteen months' time to haunt the Command. Not until the German landings in southern Norway, and the simultaneous unopposed march into Denmark by German troops on the 9th of April, did the Command gird its loins for a major battle. However, restricted by the range from directly supporting the British response at Narvik in the north, its forays against the airfields at Oslo and Stavanger in the south, and the shipping in coastal waters, were both heroic and largely futile. It was an ill-fated campaign, which was lost before it began, but during its course, on the night of the 13/14th, Hampdens of 5 Group carried out the first mining (gardening) operation of the war, when sowing mines (vegetables) in the sea lanes between Germany and Norway. It was a task to which the Hampden was to prove itself eminently suited, and one that would also turn out to be highly profitable.

Events in Scandinavia were superseded by others closer to home in the early hours of the 10th of May. The German advance into the Low Countries ended the pretence and shadow boxing of the Phoney War, and pitched the Battle and Blenheim squadrons of the French based Advanced Air Striking Force (AASF) into a ferocious and unequal fight against impossible odds. This conflict also dragged in the Blenheim squadrons of Bomber Command's home-based 2 Group, and, within days, both had suffered grievous casualties. A number of the Battle squadrons were effectively knocked out of the battle altogether, while the others would struggle on for a further month. The heavy groups played their part by attacking communications and industrial targets behind enemy lines, principally in the Ruhr, and this resulted in the first bombs falling on mainland Germany. They were also employed in support of the desperate efforts to stem the tide of enemy troops and armour advancing across the Low Countries into France, and this would go on until Dunkerque.

It had been a relatively uneventful year thus far for 106 Squadron, which continued in its training role throughout the ill-fated campaign across the Channel. P1336 was lost on the night of the 24th of May, when it struck a barrage balloon cable over Coventry during a training flight, and crashed into the city killing P/O Irvine and the others on board. On the 31st L4174 came down near Finningley without injury to the crew of Sgt Wilkes, and P/O Potts and the occupants of L4181 likewise escaped damage when it crashed through tented accommodation on the airfield during night training on the 6th of July, but sadly, three men inside were killed. By this time W/C Montgommerie had concluded his tenure as commanding officer, and had been temporarily succeeded on the 16th of June by S/L Stubbs. As events were to prove, he would still be at the helm at the time of the transition from training to operations a few months hence.

The fall of France brought with it invasion fever, and the next four months would see the Command directing its efforts against German industry, airfields in the occupied countries, and ports, while a proportion of the Hampden forced continued to ply its mining trade in the major sea-lanes. August brought just one casualty to 106 Squadron, L4187 crashing in Lincolnshire during night flying training on the night of the 7/8th, killing Sgt Dalgress and the other three men on board. As the Battle of Britain began to gain momentum overhead, a campaign began to destroy the barges and other marine craft, which were being gathered in the occupied ports to ferry the enemy invasion across to Britain. The Hampden crews were among those thrust into the cauldron of flak protecting these concentrations, and many heroic actions took place, resulting in numerous Hampdens failing to return. The first Victoria Cross of the war to be awarded to a Bomber Command airmen was gained by S/L Learoyd of 49 Squadron for an attack in a Hampden on the Dortmund-Ems Canal at Ladbergen on the night of the 12/13th, and this was a target which, by war's end, would have developed a particular, almost personal association with 5 Group. *(At the time of the posthumous awards of the VC to F/O Garland and Sgt Gray of 12 Squadron in May, the AASF was not technically part of Bomber Command.)*

September was the month in which 106 Squadron acceded to the front-line and began conducting mining operations, while retaining its training function. It started inauspiciously with the loss while on a night training exercise of L4188, which exploded over Buckinghamshire on the 1st and crashed, and there were no survivors from the crew of Sgt Duncan. S/L Cooper was posted in from 14 O.T.U at Cottesmore on the 4th, and he would succeed S/L Weir as A Flight commander. Sgt Mills was carrying out night circuits and landings in P1254 on the 5th, when attacked by an enemy aircraft. The Hampden sustained damage, but, happily, there were no crew casualties. On the 7th London was heavily bombed over a period of more than nine hours, and the squadron received Invasion Alert Warning No1, which required its aircraft to be bombed up.

The main focus of the Command's attention at this point continued to be the build-up of invasion craft in the occupied ports. As the Battle of Britain reached its climax towards mid-month, invasion fever gripped the nation, and plans were put in place to repel landings by sea. 106 Squadron would not be involved in this campaign, but undertook its first offensive action on the night of the 8/9th, when S/Ls Weir and Parker and P/O Altmann were dispatched in fine weather conditions to lay mines in the waters of the Gironde Estuary. They took off between 20.00 and 20.20, and all returned safely around eight hours later. The operation was repeated on the night of the 11/12th, when S/L Stubbs was first away from Finningley at 19.45, to be followed at 20.00 by S/L Cooper and at 20.10 by F/L Eustace. The weather was again fine, and they landed back home between 03.30 and 03.50 after an uneventful trip.

On the 18th X2960 was crash-landed near Finningley by P/O Grant during training, happily without injury to those on board, but that night, the inevitable first operational casualty came as the result of a mining sortie. P1259 departed Finningley at 19.40 as one of three Hampdens involved, and it was brought down by flak, the chief enemy of low-level mine-layers, while sowing its vegetables in the Elbe Estuary. There were no survivors, and P/O Watkin and his crew thus became the first from the squadron to be killed as a result of enemy action. P/Os Howell and Hall and their crews were the others taking part in this operation, and they returned safely. The next operation for the squadron came on the night of the 26/27th, when P/Os Howell and Hall and Sgt Huggins took off between 19.10 and 19.30 to lay mines in French coastal waters off la Rochelle. Returning during the early hours of the 27th, X2914 ran out of fuel and was abandoned by its pilot, Sgt Huggins, over Weston Zoyland airfield in Somerset, but his crew failed to leave the aircraft and perished in the ensuing crash. Later that day P1256 crashed near Finningley while on a training flight, and P/O Lowe of 44 Squadron and his passenger died. It was another training crash that killed Sgt Gow and two of his crew on the last day of the month, when L4189 crashed into high ground near Buxton in Derbyshire during a navigation exercise. That night P/Os Howell and Hall took off at 18.30 to join others to lay mines in the mouth of the Elbe, and good weather conditions helped them to complete a successful operation.

1940 Final Quarter

October was a kinder month for the squadron, perhaps largely because operations were curtailed somewhat by unfavourable weather conditions. The first operation involved three aircraft taking off in the early evening to lay mines in the Elbe Estuary on the night of the 11/12th. P/Os Hall and Howells and Sgt Stevenson took off either side of 18.00 in doubtful weather conditions, which prevented accurate identification of the target area, and only one vegetable was successfully delivered in the face of intense anti-aircraft fire from shore batteries and a flak ship. The only incident of note thus far in the month was an undercarriage collapse suffered by L4184 during training on the 13th, but Sgt Grainger and the other occupants were unharmed. P/O Howell and Sgt Stevenson took off at 18.00 and 18.10 respectively to lay mines off Kiel on the night of the 15/16th, but encountered low cloud in the garden area and intense anti-aircraft fire. One mine was successfully planted, but the other was brought home. P/O Street and Sgt Stevenson took off at 01.50 and 02.00 respectively on the 25th for a gardening operation off Brest, enjoying favourable weather conditions throughout with no opposition of any kind, and they returned safely at 08.00.

On the 28th the squadron's stand-in commanding officer, S/L Stubbs, was posted to 144 Squadron at Hemswell. On the 18th of February 1941 he would be posted to Waddington to take over as B Flight commander at 207 Squadron, the first Manchester unit, before moving on again with the rest of his flight on the 27th of February to form the nucleus of the newly-reforming 97 Squadron, which was to be the second Manchester unit. After a successful tour, S/L Stubbs would be promoted to the rank of wing commander, and eventually be given command of 49 Squadron at Scampton on the 17th of July. Also posted out on the 28th were P/O Hall to 61 Squadron at Hemswell and P/O Howell to 49 Squadron at Scampton. S/L Norris succeeded S/L Stubbs as B Flight commander at 106 Squadron.

While the other 5 Group squadrons were assigned to bombing operations over Germany, 106 Squadron continued to focus exclusively on mining, and provided three of five Hampden to be dispatched to the Baltic to lay mines off Copenhagen on the night of the 29/30th. F/O Hill led them away at 23.40, to be followed by P/O Price at 23.45 and Sgt Stammers at 23.59. P1220 developed engine trouble, forcing P/O Price to turn back, and he landed safely at 01.30. The weather was very bad, and included severe icing conditions, as a result of which neither of the remaining Hampdens reached the target area. L4180 was fixed at 05.50, and crashed into the North Sea twenty miles off Spurn Head at around 07.00 without survivors from the crew of F/O Hill. Three aircraft were sent on a sea search later in the morning, and another on the 31st, but no trace of the aircraft or crew was found.

November would bring a similar pattern of activity for the squadron, but the first event of note in 5 Group took place on the 1st with the reformation of 207 Squadron to introduce the new twin-engine Avro Manchester into operational service. The new month's operations began for 106 Squadron on the night of the 1/2nd with three sorties to lay mines in the Jellyfish sea area, which was code for the waters off Brest. P/O Streat, Sgt Stammers and S/L Norris took off either side of 02.00, and all reached the garden area, where two mines were successfully planted. Technical problems prevented the third from being released, and it was brought back to store after an otherwise uneventful trip. W/C Lindlay was posted in from 16 O.T.U at Upper Heyford later on the 2nd, and installed as the new commanding officer.

There were three further mining sorties on the night of the 7/8th, one of them to Lorient, which was successfully undertaken by S/L Norris after departing Finningley at 18.30. The other two, by P/O Wilson and Sgt Stammers, were directed at the waters off the port of Brest, one of them being completed as briefed, while the other was thwarted by an electrical failure. F/L French DFC was posted to 207 Squadron on the 10th, where he would be joined shortly by F/O Eustace. There are contradictory entries in the squadron and group ORBs for the period of the 15th to the 17th. Three crews took part in gardening operations, those of P/O Wilson, and Sgts Stammers and Galloway, and the Squadron records them as taking off in the early hours of the 16th to lay mines in the sea lanes off Brest and Lorient, while the group record states the target area was the mouth of the Elbe. The squadron ORB states that two of the sorties were successful, but that the third crew was unable to locate the garden area and brought its mine home. It then claims that three further sorties were carried out on the 17th, on a night when 5 Group operations were cancelled because of unfavourable weather conditions. It seems clear that there were not two nights of operations, but just one.

On the night of the 16/17th the main operation was against Hamburg, for which 130 aircraft were made ready. The three 106 Squadron Hampdens were to follow up this attack by laying mines in the Elbe Estuary, and P/O Wilson took off first at 02.00 in X2970 in rain and poor visibility. While outbound he encountered icing conditions, which forced him to turn back, and he crashed on landing at 03.40, although without injury to himself or his crew. Meanwhile, Sgts Stammers and Galloway had taken off at 02.30 and 02.35 respectively, and one of them delivered a mine successfully in the face of heavy anti-aircraft fire from a shore battery and a flak ship, while the other was unable to locate the garden area and brought the mine home. S/L Weir was posted to 61 Squadron on the 21st, to fulfil the role of flight commander, and he was succeeded as commander of the Operational Flight at 106 Squadron by S/L Threapleton, who arrived from 14 O.T.U at Cottesmore.

Another mining operation in the coastal waters around Lorient involved three of the squadron's Hampdens on the night of the 22/23rd. Sgts Galloway, Osborne and Ward took off between 17.00 and 17.25, and the first two-mentioned successfully carried out their brief, one also attacking a railway junction at St Brieve with 250lb wing-mounted bombs, both of which were seen to explode on the target. L4194 failed to make it home, and is believed to have fallen victim to the heavy anti-aircraft fire reported by the other crews on their return. It crashed into the sea in the target area, killing Sgt Ward and his crew. On the 25th P1320 spiralled into the ground just north of Stamford in Lincolnshire, after Sgt Bagnall lost control while engaged in night training, and, although he and one other survived with injuries, two of his crew were killed. The summary section of the squadron ORB mentions two crews being dispatched to lay mines off the Brittany coast on the night of the 27/28th, but the detailed section carries no such entry, and the 5 Group ORB makes no mention of Finningley operating on this night. Sgts Galloway and Osborne went mining off Brest on the evening of the 29th, departing Finningley between 16.35 and 16.45. Perhaps the erroneous entry for the 27/28th, which describes one crew finding its target area under ten-tenths cloud with a base as low as 1,200 feet, applied to this occasion, and was the reason one of them attacked an aerodrome, before returning safely to report observing bomb bursts on the edge of it.

Fog curtailed all flying at the start of December, and it was the early hours of the 5th before operations from Finningley could be resumed. Sgts Topping and Osborne took off shortly after 04.00 bound for Brest, where they successfully delivered a mine each before returning safely home. An unfortunate training incident on the 7th of December cost the life of Sgt Shilling and crew, who were on detachment from 50 Squadron, after L4103 lost a propeller to a lightning strike, and crashed close to the airfield. The squadron began sending fresher crews out on daylight North Sea sweeps at this time, and one on the 11th had a more serious intention, to search for a missing crew from 50 Squadron at Lindholme, which, it was falsely believed, may have come down in the sea. Sgts Osborne, Topping and Howard took off in a fifteen minute slot from 03.00 on the 16th to lay mines off Lorient and Brest, and, although one failed to locate the garden area, the two others successfully carried out their briefs. Sgt Howard then attacked with wing bombs a merchant ship estimated to be of two-to-three thousand tons, and the rear gunner reported a direct hit on the starboard aft deck.

Sgts Osborne, Galloway and Howard departed Finningley in the late afternoon of the 19th and headed for the waters off Brest. All successfully planted their vegetables, before Sgt Galloway attacked the airfield at Plouescat, near the Brittany coast, and saw both wing bombs explode close to the flare path. Two further training accidents had vastly different outcomes on the 21st. P1304 hit trees in Yorkshire, and crashed without injury to the crew of Sgt Wells, but when X3154 struck high ground near Chapel-en-le-Frith in Derbyshire, the entire crew of P/O Hubbard perished. Four Hampdens took off from Finningley either side of 03.00 on the 23rd carrying the crews of Sgts Osborne, Galloway, Howard and Sidebotham. They were bound for the Elbe Estuary to lay mines, but Sgt Sidebotham was back within an hour with engine problems. The remaining aircraft pressed on to the target area, where one was unable to pin-point the dropping zone because of poor visibility, and returned with mine and wing bombs. Sgt Howard met with no such difficulties, and planted his vegetables accurately, while Sgt Galloway was still outbound when he encountered a convoy off Wangeroog, and claimed two near misses with his wing bombs. Neither he nor his navigator were certain of their precise position, however, and, while searching for the dropping zone, they stumbled into fierce defensive fire from the ground. They ultimately planted the mine in an incorrect, but probably useful spot, before returning safely home. At 19.30 that same day P2071 apparently crashed three miles from Market Drayton in Shropshire while training, but Sgt Sowden and the other occupant walked away unscathed. The 106 Squadron ORB makes no mention of this incident in the general summary of events.

Just one further crew was lost during the year, and that was as the result of a mining sortie. 106 Squadron provided four of thirteen Hampdens sent to mine the waters off St Nazaire on the night of the 27/28th. Sgts Sidebotham, Howard, Galloway and F/O Burr-Thomas took off between 02.35 and 02.50, and one attacked a flak ship with bombs on the way out, although without observing the result. Otherwise, the three returning crews reported an uneventful trip with only slight opposition. P2098 did not arrive back with the others, however, and disappeared without trace with the crew of Sgt Sidebotham.

Since beginning its offensive career in early September, 106 Squadron had launched fifty-four Hampdens on exclusively mining operations, and five had failed to make it home, a loss rate of almost 11%. It had been a strange year for the Command, characterised by relative inactivity at either end and a period of unbelievable ferocity in the middle. It had been a backs-to-the-wall struggle until the Battle of Britain was won and the threat of invasion had been banished, but then had come the realisation that the road ahead was long and rock-strewn, and for the time being at least, the best that the Command could hope to do was to present a defiant and belligerent face to the, as yet, all-conquering enemy.

January 1941

Another harsh winter heralded the arrival of the New Year, which began for the squadron with a continuation of the training function, interspersed with gardening operations. There would be no operational losses during January, and just one training accident. This involved P4314, which force-landed near the airfield in the hands of Sgt Mapp of 61 Squadron on the 3rd, happily without casualties. That night training included sweeps over the North Sea, which passed without incident. It was at this time that the new bomber station at Coningsby opened on a care-and-maintenance basis, and it would soon be home to 106 Squadron. The Command's attention during the period was focused on German and French ports, particularly Bremen at the start, and Wilhelmshaven at the end. The first operational activity for 106 Squadron came on the evening of the 4th, when four Hampdens took off to lay mines off Lorient. Sgts Galloway, Topping, Osborne and West were airborne between 17.00 and 17.40, and three of them successfully delivered their stores, while the fourth was unable to locate the dropping zone and brought the mine back. Four 106 Squadron Hampdens were sent to lay mines in Kiel Bay on the night of the 9/10, Sgts Howard, Topping, West and P/O Wareing all getting away safely either side of 17.00. Again, three were successful, and one planted his vegetable in the Elbe Estuary as an alternative, after failing to locate the briefed dropping zone. Sgt Howard also attacked Flensburg aerodrome with his wing bombs, but was unable to determine the result.

The same four crews were on duty again on the evening of the 12th to lay mines off Lorient, and they got away safely at 17.00 and soon after to successfully carry out their brief. P/O Wareing also attacked an aerodrome near the Brittany coast, and saw his bombs burst in the centre of the landing field. All four from the squadron were diverted to St Eval on return, and landed safely either side of 23.00. On the 15th a new Air Ministry directive reaffirmed oil as the priority objective, and a list of seventeen sites was drawn up accordingly. The destruction of the nine most important refineries would, it was suggested, reduce Germany's production capacity by 80%, a wholly unrealistic assessment in view of the all-out assault by giant armadas of four engine bombers during the second half of 1944. Sgts Howard and Topping carried out mining sorties off Brest on the evening of the 16th, and returned without incident. It was at this point that the weather closed in, and no operations were possible for twelve straight nights. 106 Squadron concluded the month with a tally of fourteen sorties without loss from four operations.

February 1941

February's operational account opened for the squadron with a record number of sorties on the evening of the 4th. The 5 Group ORB mentions six of seven Finningley mining sorties being carried out successfully off St Nazaire. The 106 Squadron ORB cites six crews, including those of the usual suspects, Sgts Galloway, Topping, Osborne and West, and they all got away safely from 17.00. One of the other crews was that of F/O Burr-Thomas, who failed to return after AD750 crashed near Nantes. Four mines were delivered successfully, and two crews then turned their attention upon a nearby airfield at Chateau Rougnon, which they attacked with their wing bombs. Bomb bursts were observed on hangars, and also on a factory north-east of the aerodrome. It seems that some aircraft landed at St Eval, and returned to Finningley on the 6th. During the course of this transit, AD736 force-landed near the airfield through fuel shortage, but Sgt Osborne and his crew walked away unscathed. Some quite sizeable operations took place

The Officer Commanding 106 Squadron, Wing Commander Patrick Polglase, is believed to have been the first pilot to land an aircraft, Hampden P2083, at RAF Coningsby. His time as OC 106 Sqn was cut tragically short when, on 4th April 1941, he was killed attacking Brest.

against German cities during the month, the first of which was against Hanover on the night of the 10/11th, for which over two hundred aircraft were dispatched.

Finningley was transferred from 5 to 7 Group on the 20th, and over the 22nd and 23rd 106 Squadron moved into Coningsby, the new station situated about three miles to the south-east of Woodhall Spa. The crews spent the remainder of the month familiarizing themselves with their new home, and identifying important land marks like the nearby Tattershall Castle. The squadron would not be the sole resident for long, as a new squadron, 97, was about to be reformed as an offshoot of 207 Squadron to be the second Manchester unit, and would shortly also take up residence at Coningsby. 106 Squadron's operational record for the month was a single operation involving six sorties and one missing crew. News came through from the International Red Cross on the 28th, that the Burr-Thomas crew had all been killed.

March 1941

March was to bring an increase in activity and a shift in accent from mining to bombing operations. The account opened on the night of the 1/2nd, when 106 Squadron provided five Hampdens to an overall force of 131 aircraft bound for Cologne. This would be the first time that the squadron's bomb bays had contained bombs rather than mines. F/O Price and P/O Altmann were the senior pilots on duty, and they joined the three NCO crews in taking off between 20.00 and 20.30. They arrived over the target to find good weather conditions, and four crews reported observing their bombs bursting within sight of the briefed aiming point. The fifth Hampden was unsuccessful through its bombs failing to release. Photo-reconnaissance revealed some useful damage in the docks area in return for the loss of six aircraft, but fourteen others were abandoned over England after fog made landing impossible. Later on the 2nd S/L Nelms arrived from 14 O.T.U at Cottesmore, and was installed as the new A Flight commander.

A follow-up operation two nights later by seventy aircraft included a new record of nine from 106 Squadron. W/C Polglase had been appointed by this time to command the squadron, and the first mention of his name in the squadron ORB appears in the Order of Battle for this night, when he took the opportunity to lead the squadron for the first time, supported by S/L Parker. They departed Coningsby either side of 20.00, and arrived in the target area to find large amounts of cloud with gaps, but generally fair conditions, which allowed them to gain glimpses of the city. Bombing took place from between 10,000 and 12,000 feet in the face of considerable searchlight activity, but little flak, and returning crews reported a positive outcome, when, in fact, only a few locations in the western fringes of the city had been hit. Sgt Howard was thwarted by ten-tenths cloud and bombed Eindhoven aerodrome as an alternative on the way home, while Sgt Galloway experienced W/T failure soon after take-off and was unable to complete the operation. X3002 failed to return to Coningsby having crashed near Antwerp in Belgium, and Sgt Good and his crew were killed, thus becoming the first to be posted missing from 106 Squadron as the result of a bombing operation.

A new Air Ministry directive issued on the 9th presented the Command with a different priority, in response to mounting losses to U-Boots in the Atlantic. From now on, this menace and its partner in crime, the Focke-Wulf Kondor long range maritime reconnaissance bomber, were to be attacked where-ever they could be found, at sea, in their bases, on the slipways and in the assembly and component factories. 106 Squadron welcomed new neighbours at Coningsby on the 10th, when 97 Squadron moved in from Waddington with its Manchesters. The new maritime campaign began at Hamburg on the night of the 12/13th, when a force of eighty-eight aircraft included seven Hampdens from 106 Squadron, which took off from Lindholme. F/Ls Altmann and Boylan were the senior pilots on duty as they took to the air either side of midnight, but F/O Price was forced to return early with engine trouble. The remainder pressed on to find good visibility in the target area, and bombing took place from between 10,000 and 15,000 feet in the face of considerable opposition from the ground. The Blohm & Voss shipyards were hit and two slipways containing U-Boots were damaged. Other yards also sustained damage and eighteen large fires were started. Also, on this night of major activity, over eighty aircraft were sent to Bremen, home to a Focke-Wulf factory, while more than seventy others produced a scattered attack on Berlin.

A 5 Group element joined forces with others to return to Hamburg on the night of the 13/14th, but 106 Squadron sat this one out. On the following night, however, the squadron contributed four Hampdens to a force of a hundred aircraft, whose crews were briefed to attack the oil town of Gelsenkirchen in the Ruhr. S/L Nelms took the lead for the first time, and led the way at 19.15, with F/L Boylan bringing up the rear forty-five minutes later. Crews reported that haze made it difficult to identify ground detail, but this was an ever present problem over the Ruhr, and a solution would not be found for a further two years. The defences were highly active, but all from Coningsby reported bombing as briefed and observing explosions and large fires. The Hydriewerk refinery in the Scholven district sustained quite serious damage, and production was temporarily halted. S/L Tudor was posted in on the 16th to assume command of B Flight as successor to S/L Parker, who departed for a post at the Air Ministry. S/L Tudor, who possessed a high-pitched voice, would bear the nickname "Mary" throughout his career.

Bremen and Wilhelmshaven were the main targets on the night of the 17/18th, 106 Squadron supporting the former operation with seven Hampdens led by W/C Polglase and S/L Nelms. They took off after midnight, with the commanding officer last away at 01.00, and five reached the target to find excellent weather conditions. They had been briefed to aim for the ship yards, and bombing took place from between 10,000 and 11,000 feet, after which, many explosions were observed. S/L Nelms was attacked by a ME110 and Junkers 88 over the Dutch coast on the way home. The former was seen to burst into flames after being hit by the Hampden's return fire, while the latter broke off the attack. P/O Wareing returned to discover that he had attacked Oldenburg in error, and Sgt Osborne had been forced to return early with W/T failure.

A relatively large mining effort by 5 Group on the night of the 20/21st involved forty-two Hampdens, seven of them belonging to 106 Squadron. The garden areas were off the ports of Brest, Lorient and St Nazaire, and 106 Squadron was assigned to the first-mentioned. S/Ls Nelms and Tudor were the senior pilots on duty, the latter undertaking his first operation with the squadron. They began taking off at 18.30, and all reached the target area, but S/L Nelms was unable to locate his dropping zone and brought his mine back to base. S/L Tudor planted his mine successfully, before dropping his wing bombs among vessels moored close to a jetty on the west coast of the island of Ushant off the Brittany coast. The night of the 23/24th was moonless and attended by marginal weather conditions. On such nights the policy was to send small forces to a number of targets to cause as much damage and disruption as possible, but in truth, such operations were generally ineffective, and could be costly in aircraft and crews. Over sixty aircraft were sent to Berlin on this night, while thirty 5 Group Hampdens targeted Kiel with little effect. 106 Squadron supported the operation with seven aircraft, led by S/L Nelms, and they took off either side of 18.00. Sgt Topping experienced severe icing early on during the outward flight, compelling him to turn back, and he landed P2099 safely at Coningsby at 19.35. The remainder reached the target area to find intense searchlight activity and anti-aircraft fire that prevented an accurate assessment of their efforts. S/L Nelms bombed from 12,000 feet, aiming at marshalling yards to the west of the inner docks basin, and, although F/L Boylan could not make out his bomb bursts, he estimated that they fell also upon railway lines.

On the 29th W/C Lindlay was posted to HQ 4 Group, but it seems that he had already left 106 Squadron by this time. Also on the 29th, the German cruisers Scharnhorst and Gneisenau were reported to be off Brest, and by the following day they had taken up residence, thus beginning a long-running saga which would occupy the Command's attention for the next ten-and-a-half months. It was to become almost an obsession, and the first major operation against the raiders was mounted on the night of the 30/31st, when over a hundred aircraft were despatched, but scored no hits. 106 Squadron did not take part in the main attack, but contributed seven of ten Hampdens laying mines off the port. It was a late take-off, either side of 01.00, with S/L Nelms again taking the lead. P/O Wareing had to return early after experiencing W/T failure even before reaching the south coast, but the remainder pressed on in ten-tenths cloud and sleet showers to reach the target area. It was an intensely dark night, and this contributed to S/L Nelms' inability to locate the dropping zone and bring his mine home. F/O Price DFC was posted to 97 Squadron during the final week of the month, a move which kept him at Coningsby. During the month the squadron participated in six bombing and two mining operations, and launched fifty-three sorties for the loss of a single aircraft and crew.

April 1941

A line up of Hampdens at Coningsby.

The first few nights of the new month passed uneventfully with mostly night flying exercises. Crews were called to briefing on the 4th, and the relevance of the coming operation was written into the squadron records. The entry speaks of the importance of winning the Battle of the Atlantic, and mentions the heavy toll of merchant ships being lost to U-Boots, "even before surface raider are let loose upon our convoys". It recalls the recent mining operation off Brest to prevent Scharnhorst and Gneisenau from escaping into open sea, and stresses the importance of destroying or crippling these enemy assets. On this night fifty-four aircraft were to attack the ships in their berths, and eight of the Hampdens were to be provided by 106 Squadron. The plan called for four of them to carry out standard high-level attacks, and for four other volunteer crews to sneak in at low level, while the attention of the defences was concentrated on the main force above. In the finest traditions of leadership, W/C Polglase put himself at the head of the low-level element, with Sgts Topping and Osborne and P/O Wareing.

They got away from Coningsby between 19.00 and 19.20, and on reaching the target area P/O Wareing glided down to 1,000 feet. Unfortunately he misjudged his approach, and bravely decided to go round again, this time delivering an accurate attack. Sgt Topping dived down to just 50 feet, where his aircraft was hit by tracer, wounding the navigator, and he was forced to drop his bombs too early. Sgt Osborne arrived late on target, and chose not to go in at low level, and W/C Polglase and his crew all died when AD738 was hit by flak and crashed at Saint-Renan, north-west of the target, presumably after carrying out an attack. Returning crews claimed to have witnessed a direct hit on one of the enemy vessels, which was not confirmed, but one bomb did fall into the dry dock in which the Gneisenau was berthed, and failed to explode after settling in the water trapped at the bottom of the dock alongside the ship. The captain decided to move his vessel out into the harbour on the following day while the bomb was dealt with, and it was while she was there that a lone Coastal Command Beaufort arrived on the scene. It carried out a suicidal torpedo attack in the face of the most ferocious flak defence, and scored a direct hit, which inflicted damage serious enough to warrant six months of repair work. The Beaufort was shot down with the loss of all on board, and the pilot, F/O Campbell, was awarded a posthumous VC. A Flight commander S/L Nelms stepped up to the helm, and remained temporarily in charge of 106 Squadron until the appointment of a new commanding officer.

Sixty-one Hampdens were among over two hundred aircraft sent to Kiel on the night of the 7/8th, and ten of them were contributed by 106 Squadron. F/Ls Boylan and Altmann were the senior pilots on duty, and they took off with the others either side of 20.00. P/O Paramore experienced W/T failure shortly after crossing the coast and turned back, and Sgt Wotherspoon was north of Heligoland when oxygen-supply failure curtailed his sortie. The remainder pressed on to reach the target, which was bathed in brilliant moonlight, and all delivered their bombs in the face of a spirited flak defence, before returning home safely. It should be borne in mind that this period preceded the advent of the bomber stream and strict timings, and attacks could be spread over many hours. On this occasions bombs were falling for five hours, and resulted in many fires and widespread damage. Two U-Boot yards suffered damage and loss of production, the eastern docks area was badly effected, and naval, industrial and civilian housing also suffered destruction.

Twenty-nine Hampdens were included in a force of 160 aircraft sent back there on the following night, of which ten were from 106 Squadron, led by S/L Tudor. Sgt Topping returned early after a photo-flash device exploded on the wing, and he believed the problem to be more serious that it was later found to be. The remainder found the target in good visibility and well-defended, and some made glide attacks to aid accuracy, while others bombed from as high as 15,000 feet. S/L Tudor was at 10,000 feet when his aircraft was hit by shrapnel from an exploding flak shell. The wireless operator was wounded in the leg, but he was able to carry on, and a safe return was made. Night fighters were seen, but no engagements were reported by the squadron's crews. The town area bore the brunt of the attack on this night, and a long list was produced by local authorities of damaged buildings and disruption to utilities. The casualty figure of 125 dead and three hundred injured was probably the largest from a Bomber Command attack thus far in the war.

The squadron contributed seven Hampdens to a 4 and 5 Group attack on Düsseldorf on the night of the 10/11th, led by S/L Nelms. They took off either side of 20.00, but P/O Lakin was back in the circuit a little more than an hour later after experiencing W/T failure. S/L Nelms described intense searchlight activity, but little flak, and he was one of four from the squadron to bomb the target. Five Hampdens failed to return, and two of them, both with experienced crews, were from 106 Squadron, the first time that two of its crews had been posted missing from a single operation. Both had the misfortune to be intercepted over Holland by Hpt Werner Streib of 1./NJG1 based at Venlo. The first to fall to his guns was X3153, which crashed at 22.49 about eight miles north of Roermond. Sgt Osborne and one of his crew survived to be taken into captivity, but two others died in the wreckage. Twelve minutes later X3148 came down near Weert some miles to the west of the first crash site, and Sgt West alone of his crew survived to become a PoW. By the end of the year Streib would have twenty-two kills to his credit, one more than the famed Helmut Lent, who operated from Leeuwarden, known as the Wespennest or wasp's nest.

Despite his Germanic name, Flight Lieutenant Reginald Otto Altmann (second from right) became one of the squadron's senior pilots. He went on to become a Wing Commander, receiving the DSO and sustaining wounds whilst flying a Dakota glider tug at Arnhem (Simon Sanders).

The squadron returned to gardening operations on the night of the 13/14th, when sending seven aircraft to plant vegetables in the waters off la Rochelle. The weather at home was fine and clear as they took off shortly before 23.00 led by S/L Nelms, who was back on the ground half an hour later after an engine failed. Cloud en-route hampered identification of the dropping zone, and Sgt Topping failed to locate it, eventually jettisoning his mine into the sea. The force encountered accurate flak from shore batteries and flak ships, and P/O Paramore's AD758 was hit. The lower rear gunner was wounded, but continued to offer return fire to help the aircraft escape, and his actions were later said to be instrumental in its safe return. Sadly, despite receiving first-aid from the wireless operator, he died before Coningsby was reached. Later on the 14th the awards of a DFC to P/O Wareing and a DFM to Sgt Furnell were announced, and these represented the first decorations to be bestowed upon active members of the squadron.

Shortly after midnight on the 16th F/Ls Boylan and Altmann, along with Sgts Howard and Galloway, took off to plant mines in the "Jellyfish" (Brest) garden area. Conditions were described as excellent, and all carried out their assigned tasks before returning safely home. The night of the 17/18th was momentous for the squadron, as it was to participate in an attack on Berlin for the first time. Seven crews were briefed, including those of S/Ls Nelms and Tudor, and they were instructed to aim at railway targets as part of an overall force of 118 aircraft. They took off either side of 20.30 and soon began to encounter unfavourable conditions, which included poor visibility in the target area. S/L Nelms decided to drop his bombs on Cuxhaven as an alternative, while F/L Altmann was defeated by the intense darkness and attacked Hanover, but the remaining five crews returned to report bombing in the briefed target area. While this operation was in progress, P/O Paramore carried out a mining sortie off the Frisians, and dropped his wing bombs on the seaplane base on the island of Norderney. A total of eleven aircraft failed to return from the night's various operations, and this represented the highest loss to date in a single night. On the 19th a number of crews carried out formation flying over Woodhall Spa and Hornchurch in support of War Weapons Week.

Sixty-one aircraft set off for Cologne on the night of the 20/21st, this number including only eleven Hampdens, seven of which were provided by 106 Squadron. S/Ls Boylan and Altmann were the senior 106 Squadron pilots for this operation, and they led the take-off procedure, which spanned midnight.

Neither was able to complete the operation, however, as first F/L Altmann was forced to turn back with technical difficulties, and thick cloud prevented F/L Boylan from identifying the target, causing him to abandon his sortie. P/O Wareing was one of three crews from Coningsby to bomb the target, which he identified through gaps in the cloud from 10,000 feet. Sgt Galloway and P/O Paramore also bombed as briefed, and the former strafed an aerodrome near Aachen on the way home. Sgt Tilbury also failed to locate the target through the thick cloud, and he dropped his bombs on an unidentified aerodrome on the way home. X2986 crashed near Cologne, and there were no survivors from the crew of P/O Lakin.

Another assault by more than sixty aircraft on Brest and its lodgers took place on the night of the 23/24th, while 106 Squadron sent seven Hampdens to mine the sea lanes off Lorient. F/L Altmann led them off at 19.45, but he was unable to locate the target in conditions of cloud and intense darkness. The others enjoyed greater success, and after planting their vegetables, five of them delivered their wing bombs onto buildings on the Quiberon Peninsular, south of the port. A scattered attack on Kiel on the 24/25th did not involve 106 Squadron, but a follow-up attack twenty-four hours later saw a contingent of six aircraft depart Coningsby after 22.00, led by S/L Nelms. They encountered poor visibility and strong winds during the outward flight, and Sgt Tilbury was forced to return early with an engine problem. S/L Nelms failed to reach the target after the oxygen system failed on AD799, and he bombed Emden as an alternative. F/L Boylan became lost while searching for the target, and eventually abandoned the attempt and turned for home. Sgt Topping was beaten by the visibility, and bombed an unidentified airfield on the Frisians on his way home, and only P/O Oliver and Sgt Galloway reached the primary target to deliver their bombs.

A force of fifty Hampdens and Wellingtons took off for Hamburg on the evening of the 26th, among them three from 106 Squadron, bearing the crews of Sgts Howard and Wotherspoon along with that of P/O Wareing. They departed Coningsby between 20.20 and 20.30, and soon encountered unfavourable weather conditions, characterized by strong winds and low cloud. Hamburg lay under a blanket of cloud, rendering any chance of precision impossible, and Sgt Howard opted for a glide attack, releasing his bombs on estimated position from 12,000 feet. P/O Wareing found the target area illuminated by a flare, which he presumed came from another aircraft, and bombed from 14,000 feet. Sgt Wotherspoon commented on heavy flak from the Frisians on the way out, and unable to see the target, bombed a flak concentration in its vicinity. The final operation of the month for 106 Squadron took place on the night of the 29/30th, when seven of its Hampdens joined over sixty other aircraft bound for Mannheim. They took off either side of 21.00, with S/L Nelms the senior pilot on duty. Sgt Tilbury again had to return early with a faulty engine, but the others managed to reach the target, where low ten-tenths cloud made identification difficult. Bombing took place from between 7,000 and 12,000 feet in the face of intense searchlight activity, but little flak, and it was possible to report only that bombs had been seen to burst in the vicinity of the target. The squadron operated twelve times during the month, and dispatched eighty-four sorties for the loss of four aircraft.

May 1941

Hamburg was to feature prominently during the first two weeks of May, and the first of five attacks on Germany's second city took place on the night of the 2/3rd. 106 Squadron was not involved, and remained at home also on the following night when Cologne was targeted to little effect by a force approaching a hundred aircraft. 106 Squadron put up nine Hampdens for yet another attack on Brest, this time by a force of over ninety aircraft on the night of the 4/5th. S/L Tudor was the senior pilot on duty as the squadron contingent got away from Coningsby shortly after 21.00, and he and Sgt Galloway claimed very near misses on the Scharnhorst and starting large fires alongside her. A number of direct hits were claimed on the enemy ships by crews from other squadrons, but they were not confirmed. The squadron sat out a large-scale operation to Mannheim on the night of the 5/6th, which involved 140 aircraft, but produced disappointing results. An operation to Hamburg on the following night by more than a hundred aircraft was ruined by poor weather conditions, including low cloud. Seven 106 Squadron Hampdens took off either side of 23.00 led by S/L Nelms, who was undertaking his final operation as the stand-in squadron commander. Five 106 Squadron crews were among eighty-one claiming to have bombed in the target area in the face of intense opposition, and F/L Boylan reported starting large fires, while Sgt Galloway saw his bombs burst between the docks and the Binnen-Alster Lake, a little to the north-west of the city centre and Altstadt districts.

Wing Commander Bob Allen's youthful looks belied his experience. He laid firm foundations for the squadron in his ten-month spell as squadron CO (Simon Sanders).

On the 7th W/C Bob Allen was posted in from his flight commander duties at 49 Squadron at Scampton as the new commanding officer. He was to lay the foundations for later commanders to mould 106 Squadron into one of the finest units in the Command. S/L Nelms, meanwhile, reverted to his former role as A Flight commander. Hamburg hosted its next raid on the night of the 8/9th, when 188 aircraft took off, including a record eighty-seven from 5 Group, of which nine represented 106 Squadron. They departed Coningsby either side of 23.00, led by S/Ls Nelms and Tudor, and were among 119 crews briefed to attack shipyard targets, while the remainder went for the city. S/L Nelms was back on the ground thirty-five minutes after take-off, after his wireless operator became ill, and Sgt Wotherspoon likewise reported being indisposed and dropped his bombs on the northern end of Sylt on the way home. The others pressed on to bomb in the target area, and Sgt Howard claimed a direct hit on his aiming point with a 1,000 pounder, before being attacked by a night fighter, which he ultimately evaded. Many large fires were started within the city, and the death toll of 185 people was the largest to date at a German target.

146 aircraft set off for the twin cities of Mannheim and Ludwigshafen in southern Germany on the night of the 9/10th, and among them were five Hampdens of 106 Squadron. P/Os Oliver and Paramore were the senior officers on duty, and they took off either side of 22.30 with three Sgt pilots captaining the other crews. Bombing took place from between 8,000 and 10,000 feet, and two crews claimed direct hits on their aiming points. While this operation was in progress, Sgt Lockyer carried out a mining sortie off the Frisians, and machine-gunned an enemy vessel off the island of Juist. The assault on Hamburg continued on the night of the 11/12th at the hands of a force of ninety aircraft, while Bremen was also targeted by eighty, and it was for the latter that seven 106 Squadron Hampdens took off between 22.10 and 22.30, led

for the first time by W/C Allen. They met heavy opposition from the ground as they arrived in the target area, and W/C Allen was coned by searchlights and subjected to a flak barrage. He made a straight and level run across the aiming point, and released his bombs from 10,000 feet without observing the results. In contrast, Sgt Galloway released his bombs from 7,000 feet after a glide approach, and he reported the position of a convoy spotted by his crew on the way home. Eagle-eyed P/O Paramore saw his incendiaries burst in the target area, and his high explosives on a foundry and engine shop, creating large fires. Sgt Lockyer was unable to identify the target, and dropped his bombs on riverside buildings south of the target. Both operations produced good results, particularly at Bremen, where the harbour took some hits and a floating dock was sunk.

News came through from the International Red Cross on the 14th concerning the fate of some of the crews failing to return during April, and it confirmed the deaths of P/O Lakin and crew, and the survival in captivity of Sgts West and Osborne and one of Osborne's gunners. A hundred aircraft set off for Hanover on the night of the 15/16th, among them eight 106 Squadron Hampdens. A new record of twelve had been detailed for this night, but doubts about the weather saw four sorties scrubbed. S/Ls Boylan and Altmann were the senior pilots on duty as the squadron contingent got away from Coningsby either side of 22.30. Two crews returned early, those of Sgt Wotherspoon with oxygen system failure, and P/O Wareing with engine trouble, and F/L Boylan missed his navigation point on the Dutch coast, and went on to bomb Emden as an alternative. The others pressed on eastwards into northern Germany, where they were able to locate the target area, but were prevented by cloud from identifying the briefed aiming point. The crews had been instructed, somewhat optimistically, to use the main post office and telephone exchange as their aiming points, but bombs were dropped blind and no results were observed. With this operation Sgt Galloway completed two hundred hours of operational flying to finish his first tour, and was the first to achieve this milestone entirely in the service of 106 Squadron. S/L Tudor and F/O Price spent much of the afternoon of the 16th engaged in a search for a 97 Squadron Manchester, which was believed to have come down in the North Sea. Nothing was found, but two bodies washed ashore on the Danish coast some time later, thus confirming its fate.

Forces of ninety-three and ninety-five aircraft set off for Cologne on the nights of the 16/17th and 17/18th respectively, and produced scattered bombing in the absence of a 106 Squadron involvement. Earlier on the 17th P2099 had crashed in Rutland during training, and P/O Harvey and two of his crew died in the wreckage, while the wireless operator sustained serious injuries. The squadron put up a record dozen Hampdens for Kiel on the night of the 18/19th, when unfavourable weather conditions prevailed. They took off either side of 22.30, with F/L Altmann the senior pilot on duty, and ten made it to the target area, where bombs were delivered blindly through cloud and haze in the face of a spirited opposition. P/O Paramore was unable to identify his position, and ultimately dropped his bombs on the Blohm & Voss shipyards at Hamburg, while Sgt Tilbury delivered his onto a searchlight concentration on the island of Terschelling after his oxygen system failed.

Fifty aircraft set off for Cologne on the night of the 23/24th, and among them were a dozen 106 Squadron Hampdens led off by S/L Nelms at 23.15. Ten of them arrived to find the city almost completely obscured by cloud, and they delivered their bombs on estimated positions without being able to observe the results. Sgt Hadland couldn't positively identify his position, and dropped his bombs on Düsseldorf as an alternative, while Sgt Clark attacked Gilze-Rijen aerodrome in Holland. The squadron operated for the final time in the month on the night of the 26/27th, when contributing a new record of thirteen Hampdens for a 5 Group mining effort off Brest. The squadron ORB describes this operation as being indirectly part

P/O (later F/L) J Henderson at the control of a Hampden. The later 'heavies' appear to be very spacious in comparison with the Handley-Page medium bomber (Simon Sanders).

of the plan to destroy the battleship Bismarck, which, to the disbelief of the entire nation, had sunk the Hood, the pride of the Royal Navy, in a brief engagement in the Denmark Straits on the 24th. Cyphers decoded at Bletchley Park suggested that Bismarck was making for Brest, but on the 26th she was crippled by a torpedo attack launched from the carrier HMS Victorious, and by the morning of the 27th she would be at the mercy of the Royal Navy. This was not yet apparent as the 106 Squadron contingent began setting out from Coningsby at 22.30 led by F/L Boylan, to mine the approaches to the port. Weather conditions were poor, but ten crews successfully planted their vegetables, while three others failed to locate the dropping zone. Returning low on fuel P2083 crashed during an emergency landing at Wellesbourne Mountford in Warwickshire, and the pilot, Sgt Forty, was killed. This was his maiden operation since joining the squadron. The squadron operated on nine nights during the month, and dispatched eighty-three sorties. Both losses occurred at home, and neither was the result of enemy action.

June 1941

The pattern of operations would remain largely the same during June, generally with small to medium sized forces attacking three or more different targets simultaneously. Düsseldorf provided the objective for 150 aircraft for the first major operation of the month on the night of the 2/3rd, for which 106 Squadron contributed a dozen Hampdens. They took off from Coningsby either side of 23.00 on a night of very poor weather conditions, which persisted throughout the operation. Sgt Lyon lost his starboard engine while flying through a snow storm, and he was forced to abandon his sortie, jettison his bombs and return home. P/O Harwood failed to identify the target, and he dropped his bombs on Duisburg instead. The remaining ten pressed on to deliver their bombs through low cloud in the general target area, Sgt Tilbury having spotted the Rhine through a gap to provide some sense of his location. It was impossible to observe any results in the conditions, but at least all returned home without major incident, but also without any confidence that their efforts had borne fruit. In that regard they were correct, but what they were ignorant of, was the fact that the results of attacks during this month and July were being scrutinized, and the findings were to be published in a report.

Minor operations held sway for the next eight nights, and during this period 106 Squadron expanded, with the addition of a third flight commanded by the newly promoted S/L Tommy Boylan. This would mean the squadron having an increased presence on operations, and the first evidence of this came on the night of the 11/12th, when Düsseldorf was targeted again, this time by a force of ninety-two aircraft, while a simultaneous operation by eighty aircraft went ahead at Duisburg. 106 Squadron supported the latter with a new squadron record of eighteen Hampdens, while two others went mining off the Frisians. S/L Nelms was the senior pilot on duty as they took off either side of 23.00, and among other pilots making their operational debut was one of particular note. P/O David Maltby would soon be on his way across the tarmac to 97 Squadron, from which unit, in March 1943, he would be posted to become a founder member of 617 Squadron. He would take part in Operation Chastise, the epic attack on the Ruhr dams on the night of the 16/17th May, when his bomb would seal the fate of the Möhne Dam. Now he was just setting out on his operational career, with thoughts on this night of doing the job to the best of his ability and returning his aircraft and crew safely home. The 106 Squadron contingent made their way eastwards in unfavourable weather conditions, where sixteen of them arrived to find the target partially obscured by cloud. They met a spirited response from the defences, with heavy flak and searchlights, and with accuracy out of the question, they could only deliver their bombs in the general vicinity of the city. Maltby reported bombing from 15,000 feet, higher than the others, who were mostly at 11,000 and a little above. P/O Henderson failed to identify the target, and dropped his bombs on the little town of Wipperfürth, situated on the southern fringe of the Ruhr south-east of Remscheid, and another attacked Essen as an alternative. While this operation was in progress P/O Baker and Sgt Brownhill went mining off the Frisians, and returned safely having fulfilled their brief.

All twenty returned safely, and were made ready for the next night, when four main targets were scheduled along with a number of small-scale operations. A total of 339 aircraft took off for the various targets, of which eighteen represented 106 Squadron, whose crews had been briefed to attack the small town of Soest, situated a few miles to the north of the soon-to-be-famous Möhne Dam. W/C Allen was the senior pilot on duty, and S/Ls Boylan and Tudor were also on the Order of Battle as they departed Coningsby either side of 23.30. Weather conditions were very poor as they made their way to the target, and S/L Tudor and P/O Baker were forced to return early with technical failures. Only six crews were able to locate the general area of the briefed target to deliver their bombs, and among them was S/L Boylan, who dropped his from 13,000 feet. Sgt Hadland was at 8,000 feet, and observed his bombs bursting across the target, while P/O Robinson released his on the marshalling yards from 6,000 feet, and felt, as well as saw, the resulting explosion. W/C Allen made four runs across the target at 5,000 feet, and watched two bombs burst on the tracks. P/O Paramore also hit the marshalling yards, in his case from 1,000 feet, and P/O Henderson went lowest of all, down to 850 feet, and observed his bombs bursting along the tracks and his incendiaries starting a fire. Of the other crews, four joined in the Wellington attack on nearby Hamm, where they experienced intense flak and searchlight activity, two bombed a railway junction at Wesel, and one each attacked Essen, Recklinghausen and Gilze-Rijen aerodrome.

An all-5 Group attack on Cologne was conducted through complete cloud cover on the night of the 14/15th, for which 106 Squadron put up ten Hampdens in an overall force of twenty-nine. F/L Altmann was the senior pilot on duty as they departed Coningsby in the minutes up to 23.30, but P/Os Oliver and Paramore and Sgt Haggar all returned early with technical difficulties. The remaining seven bombed on estimated positions from heights ranging from 11,000 to 20,000 feet, (P/O Henderson), guided to some extent by flak, and all returned safely. Düsseldorf and Cologne were targeted on the night of the 15/16th, the first of seven occasions during the second half of the month on which the two cities would be attacked simultaneously. Ninety Wellingtons and Hampdens took off for Cologne, among them sixteen from 106 Squadron, which departed Coningsby either side of 23.00 with S/L Nelms the senior pilot on duty. Sgt Lyon was forced to turn back early with an overheating engine, but the remainder pressed on in conditions of ten-tenths cloud, which persisted all the way to the target. Bombing took place from between 5,000 and 15,000 feet on estimated positions helped by the glow of searchlights and flak bursts, but most of it fell outside of the city. The only loss was the squadron's AD863, which disappeared without trace into the North Sea, taking with it the crew of P/O Dickie. While this operation was in progress P/O Walker headed for the Frisians to lay a mine in company with three Hampdens from other units, but finding the cloud base to be at only 300 feet, he brought his store home. In the late morning of the 16th, F/O Price and P/O Robinson took off to conduct a search for the missing Hampden and crew, and the latter spent eight hours over the North Sea, for a time within sight of the Dutch coast, sadly to no avail.

It was Cologne and Düsseldorf again on the night of the 16/17th, when 106 Squadron stayed at home. At 11.55 on the 17th, W/C Allen took off in P2129 to carry out a bomb-load test. He was carrying two 2,000 pounders with a full crew and petrol tanks, and attained an altitude of 14,200 feet in one hour, forty minutes. He returned to declare that such a bomb load was practicable. That night a force of seventy-six Hampdens and Whitleys took off for Cologne to continue the campaign against the Rhineland capital, while more than fifty Wellingtons targeted Düsseldorf. 106 Squadron dispatched nineteen aircraft either side of 23.00, led by S/L Tudor, but he was one of three to return early with technical problems. Weather conditions generally were good, but thick ground haze was present, and although this did not hamper identification of the target area, it did prevent accurate bombing. Fifteen crews returned to report bombing, some remarking on intense searchlight activity but little flak. Sgt Bannister was unable to reach Cologne in time, so attacked Eindhoven aerodrome as an alternative.

The night of the 21/22nd was one of those that would demonstrate the problems facing the Command, and would feature prominently in the forthcoming report on its performance. Sixty-eight aircraft set out for Cologne, while fifty-six Hampdens and Whitleys turned their attention upon the marshalling yards at Düsseldorf, 106 Squadron supporting the latter with twenty aircraft led by S/L Nelms. The ORB records triumphantly all twenty aircraft getting away in a group-record time of fourteen and a half minutes, although the individual take-off times recorded in the log entries suggests at least twenty minutes. Sgt Clark was forced to return early, but the others carried on, some identifying the marshalling yards, while others were unable to pick out ground detail. S/L Nelms encountered fierce flak over the target, and was forced down to 2,500 feet to escape, before delivering his bombs at 3,000 feet and observing them burst in the target area. Returning crews claimed that many fires had been started, but the local authorities recorded just two bomb loads falling within the city. It was a similar story at Cologne, where none of the five hundred high explosives or five thousand incendiaries found the mark. P/O Herd suffered engine problems, and attempted to bomb the docks at Dunkerque, but his load fell short.

On the 22nd the squadron was informed that it might be required to carry out daylight operations, and a training programme was immediately put into effect that included formation flying. After a brief period off the Order of Battle, the night of the 24/25th brought an operation by forty-eight Hampdens and Wellingtons against Kiel, where the naval dockyards generally were the objectives, and the Deutsche Werke ship yards in particular, while other elements of the Command continued their attempts to cause serious damage at Cologne and Düsseldorf. 106 Squadron committed fourteen Hampdens to the Kiel operation, which, in view of the likelihood of encountering enemy night fighters in the good conditions, were to proceed much of the way to the target in formation. They took off in their boxes, two of four aircraft each and two of three, and all were airborne within eight-and-a-half minutes either side of 22.30, with S/L Boylan the senior pilot on duty. The plan was to fly to a predetermined map reference, before breaking up for the final approach to the target, and eleven crews achieved this to bomb from between 7,000 and 14,000 feet in the face of intense light and heavy flak up to 13,000 feet. P/O Maltby, who was operating with the squadron for the final time, suffered engine problems, and jettisoned his load into the sea before returning home. Sgt Lyon was unable to locate the target, and, as an alternative, he bombed the town of Kappeln, situated on the Schleswig-Holstein peninsular south-east of Flensburg. Sgt Tilbury, likewise, was unable to find his aiming point, and dropped his bombs on a flak concentration. Sgt Wotherspoon ran into a heavy flak barrage over Sylt, and was forced down to 1,000 feet to escape. He eventually reached the target to bomb from 4,000 feet.

Continuing the maritime theme, the night of the 27/28th was devoted to Bremen and its northern district of Vegesack, where major ship-building yards were located. The Vegesack force consisted of twenty-eight Hampdens, of which a dozen were provided by 106 Squadron. They began taking off shortly after 23.00, and made their way to the target area in very unpleasant weather conditions, which included storms and icing. Nine aircraft delivered their bombs in the target area, some clearly identifying the shipyards in cloudy conditions, and others not. There were reports of large explosions and fires, and two claims of direct hits, in addition to which a 2,000 pounder was seen to burst on or very close to the aiming point. P/O Walker and Sgt Purnell bombed the main city of Bremen after failing to locate their briefed targets, and F/L Sharp, the senior pilot on duty, bombed a nearby aerodrome as a last resort. Crews returning from Bremen reported intense night fighter activity, the first time that special mention had been made of this kind of defence. Fourteen aircraft failed to return home, a new record loss in a single night, and eleven of the casualties were Whitleys. While all this was going on, Sgt Mooney went mining off the Frisians. It was his first sortie as crew captain, and he brought his aircraft and crew safely home to report some opposition from a flak ship, but a successful maiden operation.

Bremen was again selected to host an operation on the night of the 29/30th, when 106 aircraft set out, among them nine Hampdens representing 106 Squadron. The number was somewhat depleted because of the need to train crews for the forthcoming daylight operations mentioned earlier. They began taking off shortly after 23.00 on a night of fine weather conditions and excellent visibility. Sgt Hadland was attacked by an enemy night fighter over Groningen in Holland while outbound, and AD925 sustained damage but no crew casualties, and made a safe return to Coningsby. Sgt Purnell was also forced to return early with an engine problem in AD929. Sgt Mooney was unable to identify his aiming point, and dropped his bombs on warehouses on the west bank of the Weser, starting three large fires. Four crews positively identified and bombed the target, and whether or not F/O Baker and crew did also is uncertain, as AD895 was despatched by a night fighter north-west of Hamburg, and there were no survivors. The squadron operated ten times during the month, dispatching 152 sorties for the loss of two aircraft and crews.

July 1941

Pilot Officer Brian Oliver, who was eventually to attain the rank of Squadron Leader (Simon Sanders).

Having been prominent during the final few days of June, it fell to Bremen to open the Command's July account on the night of the 2/3rd, while smaller forces targeted Cologne and Duisburg. The last-mentioned was an all-Hampden affair, for which 106 Squadron provided thirteen aircraft in an overall force of thirty-nine. They were briefed to aim for the marshalling yards, but were given Cologne and Düsseldorf as alternatives, and they departed Coningsby shortly after 23.00 with S/L Boylan the senior pilot on duty. Sgt Brownbill was forced to turn back with engine problems shortly after crossing the Dutch coast, but the others pressed on in fine weather with some cloud, and eighteen crews would later claim to have bombed in the target area. Six of these were from 106 Squadron, including P/O Oliver, who bombed from 13,000 feet, and reported starting a large fire that was visible up to twenty minutes into the return flight. Sgt Bowering delivered his bombs in a stick from west to east but saw no results, while Sgt Hadland bombed from 12,500 feet and was prevented by searchlight glare from identifying their burst. He also described heavy and accurate flak over the target, which was echoed by Sgt Mooney, who released his load from 10,000 feet. S/L Boylan found the town centre with his stick of bombs and commented on the searchlight activity, and F/L Stenner also attacked Duisburg, but delivered his bombs across the northern district of Hamborn. F/O Harwood and P/O Herd went for the alternative of Cologne, while P/O Greenhalgh and Sgt Lockyer selected Düsseldorf. Two of the 106 Squadron contingent failed to return, AD862 falling victim to a night fighter over Belgium. It was flown by Lt Reinhold Knacke of II/NJG1 based at Leeuwarden, the Wespennest. P/O Walker and two of his crew survived as PoWs, but one of the gunners, Sgt Diggory, lost his life. AD873 crashed near Frechen on the western approaches to Cologne, and there were no survivors from the crew of F/L Sharp.

Two nights later it was the turn of French ports to host a visit from elements of the Command. Brest was targeted by more than eighty Wellingtons and Whitleys in an attempt to hit the resident enemy cruisers, while forty-seven Hampdens and Wellingtons went for the U-Boot base at Lorient. Five 106 Squadron crews were briefed for the latter, and they took off either side of 22.30, to be followed shortly afterwards by six aircraft bound for nuisance attacks over the Ruhr. Visibility over Lorient was excellent, and F/L

Stenner watched his bombs miss the U-Boots but burst across the docks. F/O Harwood saw three bomb bursts, which started fires, and commented on the lack of interference from the defences. P/O Oliver circled the target for twenty-five minutes before making his attack, and P/O Herd claimed to have started two fires, one of them close to the power station. Sgt Hadland mentioned only dropping his "bombs in the target area, visibility perfect, no opposition". The six crews on a roving commission over the Ruhr fared less well, and only three of them returned home. Sgts Daniels and Mooney attacked Cologne, while Sgt Lockyer went for Hamborn, (Duisburg) and made three attacks in all, one on a railway junction north-east of Wesel, docks on the east side of the river north of Hamborn, and the southern end of a steel works in the town itself. These three crews made it back safely to Coningsby, but the arrival of three others was awaited in vain. Dortmund and Düsseldorf had been the objectives for them, and a message was received from P/O Greenhalgh calling for assistance after his engines had failed on the way home. Nothing more was heard, and news eventually came through that L4185 had come down in the Thames Estuary with fatal consequences for the occupants. AD914 crashed in Holland without survivors from the crew of F/S Bowering, and news also eventually came through that AD986 had come down in Germany to the east of Hamm, and Sgt Brownbill and his crew had also all perished. These three losses represented the squadron's heaviest casualties thus far in a single night, and, perhaps, also demonstrated the futility of such operations.

On the night of the 6/7th over a hundred aircraft took off for Brest for another shot at the German capital ships. Thirteen 106 Squadron Hampdens were among them, but not all contained 106 Squadron crews. The persistent problems with the Manchester had caused the type's grounding while modifications were carried out, and some frustrated 97 Squadron crews, among them a number formerly belonging to 106, took the opportunity to "get some ops in" in a 106 Squadron Hampden. Most of the aircraft were airborne by 22.30, but Sgts Haggar and Wotherspoon had to return early with engine trouble. The others pressed on to find the warships concealed beneath an effective smoke screen. and the bombing was aimed at the general area of the docks. F/L Stenner and P/Os Harwood and Oliver were carrying two 2,000 pounders each, and they saw them burst in the target area, before Harwood was caught in twenty-to-thirty searchlights. P/O Herd also stumbled into searchlights, and had to dive to 3,000 feet to evade them, all the time machine-gunning them. AD861 had been borrowed by Sgt Field and his crew from 97 Squadron, and ended up in Plymouth Sound after colliding with a balloon cable over the town on the way back. The pilot and observer survived, but both gunners lost their lives.

On the following night forces of Wellingtons went to Cologne and Münster, while Whitleys and Wellingtons attacked Osnabrück and 5 Group sent forty Hampdens to attend to the main railway station at Mönchengladbach. This last-mentioned operation was supported by a dozen 106 Squadron aircraft, some again containing crews from 97 Squadron. P/Os Oliver and Herd were the only officer pilots on duty as they departed Coningsby either side of 22.45, and only five crews would locate and attack the briefed target. Sgt Purnell returned early with an engine problem, but Sgts Daniels, Mooney, Tilbury and Clark and P/O Oliver all identified the primary target and carried out an attack. Two crews selected Düsseldorf as an alternative, and two others Krefeld, while P/O Herd failed to find Mönchengladbach, was driven off by flak at Düsseldorf, and finally achieved a near-miss on a steel works at Essen AD735 was shot down over Holland by a night fighter flown by Oblt Heinrich Griese of I/NJG/1, and Sgt Wotherspoon, who had recently been posted from 106 to 97 Squadron, survived to fall into enemy hands, while the other three crew members were killed. The attrition rate among the squadron's Hampdens was becoming alarming, with seven lost in the space of six nights and four operations, and that represented almost an entire flight.

A new Air Ministry directive issued on the 9th pointed to the German transportation system and the morale of the civilian population as the enemy's chief weaknesses, and a list of targets was drawn up accordingly, which took in the major railway centres ringing the Ruhr. These were to be attacked on moonlit nights, while the Rhine cities of Cologne, Düsseldorf and Duisburg would be easier to locate on dark nights. On dark nights in unfavourable weather conditions, the C-in-C, Sir Richard Peirse, was to send his forces to more distant objectives in northern, eastern and southern Germany. Thirty-nine Hampdens joined forces with Whitleys and Wellingtons for the first major raid of the war on Aachen on the night of the 9/10th, for which 106 Squadron put up seventeen aircraft. The crews had been briefed to use the Nazi Party HQ in the town centre as the aiming point, and they began taking off in good weather conditions shortly after 23.00 hours. F/L Stenner was the senior pilot on duty, and he arrived over the target to find excellent visibility, which enabled him to make his attack from 14,000 feet, and observe his bombs bursting just east of the aiming point. Others carried out their attacks from much lower, and P/O Robinson was one of those, releasing his bombs from 5,000 feet before descending to 1,500 feet to strafe the town. Sgt Hadland was intercepted by a BF110, which he evaded, but it threw his navigation off, and he ultimately bombed the Dutch town of Maastricht in error. P/O Hardy was also attacked by a BF110, in his case north-east of Brussels, but return fire was seen to hit the enemy, and it was considered possibly destroyed. Testimony from other crews during debriefing seemed to confirm its destruction. It was a successful operation, in which many commercial properties and houses were hit, and almost 3,500 people were rendered homeless.

While elements of 5 Group went to Cologne on the following night, 106 Squadron remained at home, but provided a third of the thirty-six-strong 5 Group force bound for Wilhelmshaven on the night of the 11/12th. The crews had been briefed to aim for the main railway station, and the omens were good as they took off between 23.10 and 23.30 in fine weather conditions with good visibility. S/L Nelms was undertaking his first operation for some time, and he bombed from 9,000 feet, observing four bursts, before gliding down to 800 feet to escape from the heavy flak. His experiences were typical for the night, although some crews did not experience the same level of flak activity. All returned safely, four crews to claim direct hits on the aiming point, and the others to report bombing in the target area. Not unusually for the period, the crew claims did not tally with local reports, which suggested that most of the ordnance had fallen onto open ground and in the harbour.

Bremen and Hanover were the principal targets for the night of the 14/15th, and it was to the latter that forty-four Hampdens took off, as part of an overall force of eighty-five aircraft. Among them were thirteen crews representing 106 Squadron, who had been briefed to use the main railway station as their aiming point. They departed Coningsby between 23.00 and 23.30 with S/L Boylan the senior pilot on duty. The role of observer in a Hampden was usually performed by a pilot gaining experience, as there was no room for a second pilot in the single-seat fighter-style configuration of the cockpit. Flying with S/L Boylan on this night was Sgt Mycock, who would eventually be posted to 97 Squadron and be selected to take part, with fatal consequences, in the audacious daylight attack on the M.A.N diesel engine works at Augsburg, deep in southern Germany in April 1942. P/Os Herd, McGruer and Sgt Hadland flew out in formation as a continuation of the training that had been taking place in preparation for the imminent daylight operations, and their decision to do this was prompted by good weather conditions and clear visibility. Sgts Davies and Daniels returned early with technical problems, leaving the others to locate Hanover without difficulty, but unable to pinpoint the station. S/L Boylan and crew found themselves held in searchlights for a short period and persistently fired upon, and their bombs were delivered into the city area. The same scenario was experienced by the remaining crews, although two did claim near misses on the aiming point.

An ineffective operation against Hamburg took place on the night of the 16/17th, while 106 Squadron remained at home, and an equally disappointing effort was mounted against Cologne on the following night. This time 106 Squadron provided twelve of the seventy-five-strong Wellington and Hampden force, and they departed Coningsby either side of 23.00, briefed to aim for the marshalling yards. Sgt Ratcliffe's intercom failed, and he bombed Vlissingen aerodrome on the island of Walcheren in the Scheldt Estuary on the way home, while Sgt Daniels was also forced to return early with an overheating starboard engine. The remaining crews found Cologne, but not the briefed aiming point in the thick haze, and they dropped their bombs in the main town area. Many fires were reported, but the evidence suggests that few bomb loads hit the city, and that damage was slight.

106 Squadron sat out the next failure at Cologne on the 20/21st, but was ready with thirteen Hampdens to support an overall force of seventy aircraft for the first of a number of raids against Frankfurt on the night of the 21/22nd. F/O Harwood was the senior pilot on duty as twelve of them departed Coningsby in an eighteen minute slot to 22.58, and P/O Hardy brought up the rear some seventeen minutes later. P/O Haywood was forced to return early with engine problems, but the others pressed on across France to find the target area bathed in thick haze. They had been briefed to aim for the main post office, which would guarantee damage in the city centre, but few were able to identify such a precise aiming point in the conditions, and most delivered their bombs in a stick across the main built-up area. Sgt Curties did, however, claim a very near miss on the aiming point. There were maiden operations for Sgts Dashwood and Richardson, and both found the target area with their bombs. Sgt Lockyer was unable to locate the city, but found an aerodrome nearby and saw three of his bombs burst on it. Despite the confident claims by returning crews, it seems that most of the bombs missed the target on this night, some falling on Darmstadt some fifteen miles away, but at least no aircraft were lost.

Twenty-four hours later the squadron put up ten Hampdens as part of a mixed force of sixty-three aircraft for another crack at this southern city. S/L Nelms and 97 Squadron's S/L "Flap" Sherwood were the senior pilots on duty as they began departing Coningsby at 22.40, but S/L Nelms couldn't coax sufficient altitude out of AE151, and, two hours into the outward flight decided to jettison his bomb load and turn for home. The others pressed on in very unfavourable weather conditions of thick cloud, rain and violent electrical storms, but one by one three others turned back. P/O Hayward was one of four to reach and bomb the target area, and he came home on one engine after his starboard power plant failed an hour out from Coningsby. F/L Stenner, P/O Rodwell and Sgt Bannister were the others to reach Frankfurt to bomb blindly through ten-tenths cloud, while P/O Oliver attacked Mannheim as an alternative, and S/L Sherwood dropped his bombs on what he believed to be Bonn.

The most complex operation for July was planned for the 24th, when a concerted effort, under the codename Sunrise, was mounted in daylight against the Scharnhorst and Gneisenau at Brest. The bombing was to be carried out by Halifaxes and Wellingtons, while other elements of the Command attempted to divert the attention of the defences. The meticulous preparations had to be changed at the last minute, however, after it was discovered that Scharnhorst had slipped away and was now at berth at la Pallice, some two hundred miles further south. It was decided to send the Halifax element to attend to her, while the original plan went ahead at Brest. The operation began with three Fortress 1s of 2 Group's 90 Squadron going in at 30,000 feet to draw up the enemy fighters, while eighteen Hampdens acted as further bait at a less rarefied altitude under the umbrella of a Spitfire escort. This activity was intended to leave the way clear for the seventy-nine Wellingtons of 1 and 3 Groups to sneak in in waves and attack the objectives unescorted.

If successful, this would clearly be a prestigious operation to be involved in, even though highly dangerous, and one wonders if that played a part in the selection of exclusively officer pilots at a time when NCO pilots were the most numerous on other operations. It is noticeable that the six crews chosen had been absent from recent operations while formation training took place, so the selection process must have taken place when the operation was first devised back in June. The crews at final briefing for this first ever daylight operation for the squadron were those of W/C Allen, F/L Altmann and P/Os Wareing, Robinson, Paramore and Henderson, and they took off in two vics of three at 10.40 and 10.45 before joining up to form a box of six, which was to remain together throughout the attack. They met up with the two other Hampden formations from Waddington and North Luffenham, and took the lead, before picking up the fighter escort at Predannack on the Cornish coast. In the event, the flak and fighter opposition proved more fierce than anticipated, and ten of the Wellingtons were brought down along with two Hampdens. The Hampden element delivered fifty-nine 500lb bombs onto the target from 14,500 feet, but no hits were claimed, and, to its credit, the 106 Squadron box held firm despite the opposition, and all returned safely to Coningsby after six hours in the air. A number of hits on Gneisenau were claimed by the Wellington element, although not confirmed, but Scharnhorst did suffer significant damage, while inflicting heavy casualties on the attacking Halifaxes. Ultimately, she was forced to return to Brest to take advantage of the superior repair facilities on offer there.

Later on the evening of the 24th the squadron contributed nine Hampdens with NCO crews, as part of a force of sixty aircraft targeting the Germania Werft shipbuilding yards at Kiel. They took off between 22.10 and 22.25, and arrived in the target area to find good weather conditions and a spirited flak defence. Sgt Lyon bombed the target from 10,000 feet, and was then attacked by a BF110 during the return flight, which inflicted severe damage on AE123. The ORB credits the skill of the pilot as the main factor in the crew's safe return home. Sgt Haggar bombed oil tanks south of the Kiel Canal, and was fired upon by a British convoy as he crossed the North Sea homebound. Sgt Curties claimed hits on the main station, and other returning crews were also enthusiastic about the bomb bursts they had observed and the resulting fires, but in keeping with the performances of the times, very little damage actually resulted.

The squadron operated for the final time during the month on the night of the 27/28th, when providing sixteen Hampdens for a 5 Group mining effort in the "Beeches" and "Artichokes" areas off Lorient and St Nazaire. Seventeen 106 Squadron crews had been briefed for the latter, but one had a slight incident on take-off and was scrubbed. Most were airborne by 22.00 in good weather conditions, and all but one experienced no difficulty in locating the garden area in excellent visibility. P/O McGruer failed to find his drop zone, and laid his mine instead off la Pallice. Following the spate of losses during the first week of the month, the squadron had come through the remainder unscathed. Sadly, the Reaper returned to the squadron on the 30th to claim the life of one of Sgt Lockyer's crew, Sgt Thurston, after AD970 stalled at low level and crashed into the sea half a mile off Skegness pier during a training flight. During the course of July the squadron carried out thirteen operations, twelve of them by night, and dispatched 159 sorties for the loss of seven aircraft and five crews.

August 1941

Multiple targets opened the August account on the night of the 2/3rd, when the Hampdens winged their way back to Kiel to attack the Deutsche Werke shipbuilding yards, while Hamburg and Berlin played host to other types. 106 Squadron contributed eighteen of the fifty Hampdens for Kiel, and they departed Coningsby in a fifteen minute slot to 22.30, with F/Ls Altmann and Stenner the senior pilots on duty. They

Roger Purnell and crew (Simon Sanders).

found cloud and haze in the target area, and many crews were unable to positively identify the briefed aiming point. Seven claimed direct hits, while nine others reported bombing in the target area and observing bomb bursts and many fires. The local report shows just one house hit within the town, but makes no mention of the outcome for the target itself. A busy night on the 5/6th saw three separate forces set off for southern Germany, ninety-eight of them bound for Mannheim/Ludwigshafen, the twin cities facing each other on the east and west banks respectively of the Rhine. A further ninety-seven aircraft were to hit Karlsruhe and sixty-eight others Frankfurt. 106 Squadron supported the first-mentioned operation with eleven Hampdens, whose crews had been briefed to attack the main railway station at Ludwigshafen, led by S/L Nelms. Five other crews, those of P/Os Henderson, Paramore and Herd and Sgts Mooney and Hadland were to attack the railway workshops at Karlsruhe, and all were airborne from Coningsby by 22.30. Sgt Ratcliffe responded to a recall signal meant for another aircraft, and he was back on the ground at Coningsby three hours later, and Sgt Daniels was another to abort his sortie after his intercom failed. Only three of the Ludwigshafen element, Sgts Richardson, Curties and Purnell, identified the aiming point and delivered their bombs, while five others, including S/L Nelms, went for Mannheim as an alternative. In contrast all five of the Karlsruhe contingent reported bombing within the target area. Local reports revealed significant damage in Mannheim and the northern part of Ludwigshafen, and in the Rhine harbour and western districts of Karlsruhe. The sole Hampden loss from Mannheim was 106 Squadron's AE120, which suffered engine failure after being shot up by a night fighter over Holland, and crashed onto a house, killing Sgt Knowles RNZAF and his crew, along with two people in the house. It was just their second operation.

Hampdens made up more than half of the hundred-strong force targeting the Krupp works at Essen on the night of the 7/8th, for which 106 Squadron put up fourteen aircraft. S/Ls Boylan and Tudor were the senior pilots on duty, supported by F/Ls Stenner and Altmann, and they got away from Coningsby in fine weather conditions with excellent visibility, which persisted all the way to the target. S/L Tudor claimed a direct hit on the centre of the complex, F/L Altmann found the aiming point obscured by haze, while P/O Wareing recorded it as being clearly seen. S/L Boylan concurred with the latter assessment, releasing his bombs from 13,000 feet and observing them to bursts in the target area. P/O Herd dropped his bombs, and then descended to ground level to machine gun the searchlights. F/L Stenner failed to locate the objective, and delivered his bombs on Düsseldorf instead. Despite the claims of returning crews, only a few bomb loads fell in the city, and the destruction of a bakery was the most serious incident. Twenty-four hours later fifty Hampdens, a dozen of them from 106 Squadron, were sent to Kiel with a handful of Whitleys for another crack at the Deutsche Werke yards. They departed Coningsby either side of 22.00, and found themselves flying over ten-tenths cloud almost all the way to the target, where, as if by royal command, it dissipated to provide excellent visibility. Nine crews returned with confident claims of direct hits or near misses, and reported observing explosions and a number of large fires. Two other crews reported bombing the town, while Sgt Jeffers failed to locate the target at all, and he bombed the town of Rendsburg on the Schleswig-Holstein peninsular as an alternative. The 5 Group ORB describes this as a very successful operation, but, in truth, it once more failed to produce damage worthy of the effort expended.

Awards were announced on the 9th to a number of those who had taken part in Operation Sunrise at Brest on the 24th of July. W/C Allen DFC received the DSO, and his observer, P/O Erly, the DFC. There was a DFC also for P/O Henderson, and a DFM for Sgt Overall, who was P/O Wareing's observer.

Another special daylight operation was mounted on the 12th against power stations in the Cologne area. The intention, apparently, was to assist the Russians, by drawing Luftwaffe fighters away from the Eastern Front. The main attacks on the plants at Knapsack and Quadrath were to be carried out by fifty-four Blenheims of 2 Group, while supporting and diversionary operations went ahead elsewhere. Six Hampdens each from Waddington and Coningsby were involved in the latter, the Waddington contingent briefed to attack an airfield, while the 106 Squadron element attended to a power station at Gosnay in France, both under the umbrella of a fighter escort. This would be 106 Squadron's second daylight operation, and was likely to be extremely hazardous in view of its intention to attract enemy fighters. It was, in effect, a typical 2 Group "circus" operation, which involved the blatant use of RAF bombers as bait to bring enemy fighters into the gunsights of Spitfires and Hurricanes in a battle of attrition. As one might expect from a commanding officer of W/C Allen's calibre, he placed himself at the forefront, and led the 106 Squadron element away from Coningsby at 09.55. The other five crews were those of F/L Altmann and P/Os Oliver, Wareing, Paramore and Henderson, and again there was a noticeable absence of NCO pilots. The target area was free of cloud, allowing the power station to be easily identified and bombed, and twenty-four 500 pounders and two 250 pounders went down to explode close to the aiming point. Although no enemy fighters appeared on the scene, anti-aircraft fire was accurate, and most of the Hampdens sustained shrapnel damage, but no crew casualties.

That night a further fourteen 106 Squadron crews were briefed for operations against railway communications in Magdeburg and Hanover, while a force containing the new generation of heavy bombers headed for Berlin. At the last minute eight 106 Squadron sorties were scrubbed, and the six remaining crews took off between 21.10 and 21.55, two bound for Magdeburg and four for Hanover. Sgt Mooney and P/O Watts misinterpreted a recall signal and abandoned their sorties, while F/L Stenner failed to locate Magdeburg and bombed another town, believed to be Osnabrück. F/O Harwood failed to find Hanover, so continued on eastwards to Magdeburg, where he dropped his bombs just east of the target, and caused a terrific explosion. P/O Hayward encountered ground haze, which made identification difficult, but he dropped his bombs in the target area, and also witnessed a large explosion. Sgt Roberts reported ten-tenths cloud throughout the trip, but he was able to identify Hanover and bombed the town from 10,000 feet. Nothing of value was achieved at either target, but at least no Hampdens were lost. The policy of attacks on multiple targets would continue, as would their lack of effectiveness in terms of damage inflicted, but the propaganda value to the morale of the civilian population was priceless at a time of gloomy news from all fronts. In fact, the impression that Bomber Command was laying waste to German industry was about to be shattered.

Briefings took place for three main targets on the night of the 16/17th, including Düsseldorf, which was assigned to 5 Group and involved fifty Hampdens and six Manchesters. 106 Squadron equalled its record of dispatching twenty Hampdens on this night, led by S/L Nelms and F/L Stenner. P/O Watts was the first to take off, at 22.05, and Sgt Daniels brought up the rear at 22.40. The crews had been briefed to aim for railway installations, and, on arrival in the target area, they found generally fine conditions with medium cloud and the expected ground haze. S/L Nelms delivered his bombs from 14,000 feet, and saw them burst in what he believed to be the town centre, and he was one of fourteen to report attacking the primary target. Returning crews reported seeing many fires, some of them large. A number of others bombed Essen as an alternative and Leeuwarden aerodrome as a last resort, and two crews failed to return. As events were to prove, these represented the first of a flurry of casualties to afflict the squadron in the second half of the month. AD756 was intercepted by Oblt Redlich of 1.NJG/1 over Belgium, and P/O Watts died with one of his usual crew in the crash near Gembloux. A P/O Grant had been given permission to join the crew to gain operational experience, and he also lost his life, while the two survivors became PoWs. AE134 crashed in Holland after an encounter with Oblt Wolfgang Thimmig, also of 1.NJG/1, although not before P/O Robinson and his crew had managed to extricate themselves, and float down into the waiting arms of their captors. Sadly, P/O Robinson died later in the year while a prisoner. (Bomber Command Losses Vol 2 W R Chorley).

The 18th was the day on which civil servant, Mr D M Butt, presented his infamous report to the Air Ministry, and its disclosures sent shock waves reverberating around the halls of power. Having studied four thousand photographs taken during a hundred night raids in June and July, he concluded that only a fraction of the bombs delivered had fallen within miles of their intended targets, and this was particularly evident in operations against the Ruhr, the very heartland of Germany's war production. This swept away at a stroke any notion that the Command was having a materiel effect on the enemy's war effort, and demonstrated that its claims of success were without foundation. It also provided the detractors with a bountiful supply of ammunition to back up their calls for the dissolution of an independent bomber force, and for the redistribution of its aircraft to the U-Boot campaign and to redress reversals in the Middle East. Peirse had done his best to fulfil the often unrealistic demands of his superiors, but the damning Butt Report was a major blow to morale, and would forever unfairly blight his period of tenure as commander-in-chief.

That night 4 and 5 Groups sent sixty-two aircraft to Cologne to aim for the main post office and the west station. 106 Squadron dispatched fourteen Hampdens, led off by P/Os Oliver and Herd and Sgt Curties at 23.00. Sgt Field left Coningsby at 23.10, and force-landed in a field ten miles north-west of Boston five minutes later after engine failure, and all on board sustained injuries. Conditions in the target area were good, with no cloud and good visibility, but ground haze blurred the detail of what lay below. Sgt Lyon bombed from 9,000 feet, and observed bomb bursts west of the river, and his report was typical of those from the eleven crews who reached and attacked the primary target. Local reports suggest that the operation was a total failure, and that the fires were decoys.

After a few nights off, during which the squadron sat out an operation by over a hundred aircraft to Kiel, nineteen Hampdens were detailed as part of an overall force of ninety-seven aircraft for an operation to Mannheim on the night of the 22/23rd. It seems that formation take-offs had become the order of the day, as six aircraft are recorded as departing Coningsby at 21.00, three at 21.05 and five at 21.40, but it still took more than an hour to get them all away, with Sgt McGinley last off at 22.05. F/L Altmann was the senior pilot on duty, and, like his squadron colleagues, he had been briefed to aim for the main railway station and marshalling yards. Weather conditions over the target were good, with only small amounts of medium cloud, but haze and darkness made identification of a precise aiming point difficult. He bombed the town from 11,000 feet, and on return reported being unable to observe his bombs bursting because of intense searchlight activity. This was typical of the experiences of the other sixteen crews claiming to have attacked the primary target, but all seemed adamant that their bombs had found the mark, and were fairly precise in their assessment of where their bombs had fallen. P/O Herd was unable to locate Mannheim, and dropped his bombs on Karlsruhe instead. AE246 suffered a port undercarriage collapse on landing, but Sgt Curties and crew emerged unscathed. AE220 became the only loss of the night's activity, when it was shot down by flak over southern Germany with no survivors from the crew of P/O McGruer RNZAF. Also on board as observer was P/O Early DFC of the RCAF. Despite the confidence of crews that this had been a successful operation causing many fires, Mannheim authorities recorded just six high explosive bombs falling, and six houses sustaining damage.

Sgt. ERH Lyon and his crew fell into enemy hands when they ditched their Hampden in the North Sea returning from Duisburg.

A return to Cologne by over ninety aircraft on the night of the 26/27th was supported by thirteen Hampdens from 106 Squadron, which got away from Coningsby either side of 23.00. There were no senior officers on duty as they made their way towards the Rhineland capital to bomb a railway junction, and on arrival they found broken cloud that allowed them sight of the ground. Bombing took place from a variety of altitudes between 7,000 and 17,000 feet, and most observed their bombs to fall onto the eastern bank of the river. Opposition was described as heavy and accurate, and P/O Hadland's AE151 was hit by flak, although not seriously damaged. Local reports confirm that the main weight of the attack was on the eastern side of the city, but most of it fell outside of the city limits. AE302 failed to return from this disappointing operation, and no trace was ever found of Sgt Wilkinson and his crew. While this operation was in progress, five other crews from the squadron were engaged in gardening duties in the Baltic. They had actually taken off before the Cologne contingent, and made their way to northern waters in fair conditions. P/O Oliver was assigned to the Quince garden area, which was the Great Belt Denmark Strait, where he delivered his mine accurately from 600 feet. During the course of the operation he reached two hundred hours operational flying, and had, therefore, completed his first tour, although starboard engine failure on the way home probably had his heart racing. P/O Henderson was also successful in delivering his mine from 750 feet into the Hollyhocks garden area of Travemünde, while Sgt Tilbury planted his from 800 feet in Ringkoping Fjord as an alternative. F/L Stenner was the senior pilot on duty, and he was at 12,000 feet on approach to his garden, when he opened his bomb doors and the mine fell out. AE301 was brought down by flak while gardening in the western Baltic off Aalborg, and just one of F/O Harwood's crew survived to be taken prisoner.

The target for the night of the 28/29th was Duisburg, for which a force of 118 aircraft was made ready. 106 Squadron briefed fourteen crews, some to attack the town or marshalling yards, while a number of others were assigned to searchlight suppression duties. They took off either side of 23.30, and made their way to the target in fine weather conditions with excellent visibility. F/L Stenner was the senior pilot on duty, and he could only report bombing on the estimated position of the target from 16,000 feet. Others were more certain of their position, P/O Henderson specifying the west end of the marshalling yards as his aiming point from 9,800 feet, although he did not observe his bombs bursting. On the way home he shot up a searchlight battery at Wesel from 1,000 feet. Sgt Dashwood was one of those briefed to attack the town centre, and he delivered his bombs on or near the aiming point from 12,000 feet, but was prevented by flak from observing his bombs burst. P/O Hadland carried out intruder duties between 01.40 and 02.15, during which he attacked searchlight batteries with bombs, incendiaries and guns from between 1,500 and 2,000 feet. P/O Herd flew up and down the searchlight belt at altitudes ranging from 2,000 feet down to 100 feet, and observed all of his bombs bursting, one definitely hitting a blue (master) searchlight. AE193 had also been assigned to intruder duties, and ultimately ditched off the Frisian island of Texel. The experienced crew of Sgt Lyon was picked up by a Dutch trawler after four days adrift, but such was their state of exhaustion, that they felt unable to try to evade capture, and decided to surrender rather than put their rescuers at risk. Despite the claims of accurate bombing, only a few loads fell within the city of Duisburg, and it is unlikely that significant damage resulted.

The largest single operation of the month involved 143 aircraft, half of them Hampdens, whose crews were briefed to attack the inland docks at Frankfurt on the night of the 29/30th. 106 Squadron's contribution was just three aircraft, captained by F/L Altmann, P/O Hayward and Sgt Purnell. They took off either side of 22.00, and arrived in the target area to find large amounts of cloud obscuring most of the ground detail. Sgt Purnell identified Frankfurt, and believed his bombs to have slightly overshot his aiming point from 12,000 feet, while F/L Altmann also positively identified the city, but lost sight of the docks on the run in to bomb at 9,000 feet, and believed they fell short. P/O Hayward was unable to positively identify anything, and delivered his bombs on estimated position from 13,500 feet. This was the experience of most crews taking part, and local reports confirm the ineffectiveness of the attack.

The night of the 31st brought an operation by a hundred aircraft on Cologne, for which 106 Squadron contributed ten Hampdens. P/O Hadland was the only officer pilot on duty for this operation, and he got away at 20.10, to encounter very unfavourable weather conditions in the target area. He was unable to locate the target in the dense cloud, and bombed on estimated position without observing any bursts. This was typical of the reports at debriefing, although some crews did see the glow of bursts beneath the cloud, and even the suggestion of a large fire. The reality was, that damage in the city was slight, and the operation, like so many before it, was a failure. While the activity over Cologne was in progress, five other 106 Squadron crews were involved in gardening duties in Kiel Bay. Sgt Roberts delivered his mine accurately from 700 feet into Kiel Fjord, and observed the parachute deploy and the store strike the water. Sgt Purnell dropped his in the briefed location in the Little Belt Denmark Strait from 600 feet, while P/Os Henderson, Herd and Hayward were all successful also in Lübeck Bay, Great Belt South and Kiel Harbour respectively. On return from the night's activities, many crews landed at North Luffenham and Waddington because of unfavourable conditions at Coningsby. During the course of August the squadron operated on thirteen occasions by night and once by day, dispatching a total of 175 sorties for the loss of eight aircraft.

September 1941

September would prove to be a less active month generally, and began with a relatively small-scale attack on Cologne on the night of the 1/2nd, which did not involve 106 Squadron. The squadron also sat out operations to Frankfurt and Berlin on the following night, before thirteen crews were called to briefing on the 3rd, to be told they were to attack the enemy warships holed up at Brest. P/Os Hadland and Loftus were the only commissioned pilots on duty as the squadron took off between 19.00 and 19.40, and they were around ninety minutes into the outward flight when a recall signal was sent, to which all responded. There was a fear that fog might provide lethal conditions for landing, and 1 and 4 Groups were also brought home. For whatever reason, landing times at Coningsby ranged from the first back at 21.55 to 01.00 in the case of Sgt Lockwood.

It was not until the night of the 6/7th that the squadron had its chance to get at the enemy again, when a mixed force of eighty-six Wellingtons, Whitleys and Hampdens was sent to bomb the Chemische Werke synthetic rubber factory at Hüls, a town in the Ruhr just north of Krefeld and south-west of Duisburg. 106 Squadron provided all eighteen of the participating Hampdens, and they took off from Coningsby in what the summary section of the ORB claims as a record six minutes, although the take-off times as recorded in the daily log range from 19.30 to 1945. On arrival in the target area the crews encountered good weather conditions and visibility, but also heavy flak and searchlights. Despite this, fourteen of them delivered their bombs from between 9,000 and 13,000 feet, mostly reporting to have done so on estimated position over the centre of the target. Some bomb bursts were observed, but searchlight dazzle became a problem and prevented an accurate assessment of results. Sgt Mooney spent an hour searching for the target, before bombing from 12,000 feet and observing three bursts. During the course of his sortie he notched up two hundred hours operational flying and thereby completed his first tour. P/O Hadland found himself in a spiral dive in AE151, which he managed to correct, and he delivered his bombs from 8,000 feet on the centre of Hamborn. P/O Loftus was one of three others to fail to locate the primary target, and he bombed the town of Dorsten from 8,000 feet. Returning crews were adamant in their claims of a successful operation, and were dumbfounded when photographic reconnaissance revealed the factory to be almost completely unscathed.

What would prove to be the month's largest operation took place twenty-four hours later, when Berlin was the target for 197 aircraft, of which sixteen were Hampdens from 106 Squadron. P/Os Herd, Hayward and Hardy were the only commissioned pilots involved as they departed Coningsby between 21.20 and 22.05, and headed eastwards into excellent weather conditions and clear visibility. Not all from the original numbers would reach Berlin, but there were eight 106 Squadron crews among the 137 who would claim on return to have reached and bombed the Capital, where a significant amount of damage was inflicted upon industrial and residential property. AD760's heating system failed three-quarters of an hour after take-off, but Sgt Roberts and crew pressed on until the cold became too intense to continue. They bombed Kiel Canal locks from 11,000 feet before returning home to land at 04.35 and get themselves thawed out. Sgt Dashwood failed to locate the primary target, and he selected Neuruppin, a town north-west of Berlin as the destination for his bombs, and he observed six bursts in the town centre. Sgt Tilbury was diverted from Berlin by heavy flak, and he eventually bombed the coastal city of Lübeck from 8,000 feet. Sgt Jefferies experienced excessive fuel consumption after his mixture control switch became inoperative, and this forced him to curtail his sortie and drop his bombs on Cuxhaven from 15,000 feet on the way home. P/Os Herd and Hardy bombed Kiel, the former delivering his load from 11,000 feet across a line of eight or more ships anchored in the harbour. Sgt Richardson and crew had an eventful time after being caught in searchlights and flak at 12,000 feet. They dived for the ground and lost the flak at 5,000 feet, but continued descending and were attacked by a BF109, which they also shook off at 1,500 feet. They pulled out at 100 feet, and evaded further attention by flying for ten to fifteen miles at 50 feet. Most of the other crews reported bombing on or near the aiming point, which was the main post office, and observing bursts, and many also reported a large fire in the city centre. Fifteen aircraft failed to return, and the squadron was represented among them by AE299, which crashed near the north German coast with just the pilot, Sgt Curties, surviving as a PoW.

Kassel was raided for the first time in numbers on the night of the 8/9th, when railway installations were the aiming points, and no aircraft were lost. 106 Squadron sat this one out, but dispatched fifteen Hampdens on the 11/12th to the Baltic port of Rostock, where the Neptun shipyards and port installations were their aiming point, while other elements of the fifty-six-strong force went for a Heinkel aircraft factory. There were no senior officers among those taking-off from Coningsby either side of 21.30, on a night of unfavourable weather conditions characterized by heavy cloud. It proved difficult to locate an aiming point at the target, and most crews bombed the town area from between 8,000 and 15,000 feet, some observing bursts and others not. Sgt Clarke observed a large fire, which he estimated to be at or near the location of the Heinkel works, while Sgt Dashwood was the only participant to specify aiming for the Neptun yards. Sgt Daniels mistook Warnemünde for the primary target, and he dropped his bombs there to add to those from the Whitley force for which it was the primary target. P/O Hardy also bombed at Warnemünde, and observed three bursts through gaps in the cloud. An S.O.S. message was received from AE300 at 02.23, stating that an engine had cut, and placing the Hampden fifty miles from Sylt. The signal faded away within three minutes, and Sgt Bannister and crew failed to return home. They had actually abandoned their stricken Hampden to its fate over Denmark, and arrived safely on the ground, where they found themselves in enemy hands within forty-eight hours. This was the second experienced crew to go missing in successive operations, and they would be missed.

Frankfurt was the main target for the night of the 12/13th, but the 5 Group contribution came from Waddington, Swinderby and Scampton, allowing the 106 Squadron crews to spend the evening in the local hostelries. Fifteen crews were called to briefing on the 13th, to learn that they were to take part in the next round in the eternal battle of Brest. Whether it was the status of the Scharnhorst and Gneisenau that brought the Squadron's "big guns" out is uncertain, but the Order of Battle was headed by S/Ls Nelms and Boylan, along with the recently promoted F/L Henderson and P/Os Hardy, Hadland, Hayward and Loftus. They began taking off at 01.05 on the 14th, as part of an overall force of 147 aircraft, and arrived in the target area to find low cloud and the usual effective smoke screen. Bombing took place from between 10,000 and 17,000 feet on estimated positions, and the glow of bursts could be seen beneath the clouds.

Ten crews were back in the briefing room on the 15th, eight of them to learn that they were to participate in a heavy raid on Hamburg that night, while the other two were to carry out freshman sorties at le Havre. The Hamburg contingent had the Blohm & Voss shipyards as their aiming point, and F/L Henderson was the senior pilot on duty as they departed Coningsby either side of 16.30 as part of an overall force of 169 aircraft. Sgt Lockwood's AD768 soon developed engine trouble, and he was forced to return after just thirty minutes in the air. Whatever the problem, it was put right quickly, and he set out again in the hope of reaching the target in time. In the event he delivered his bombs from 10,000 feet on Wilhelmshaven, and returned safely home for the second time that night. Sgt Purnell had his helmet microphone become unserviceable, and this delayed their time on target to the extent that he decided to bomb Cuxhaven instead. Sgt Tilbury also ran out of time, and he bombed Kiel as an alternative, observing two bursts within the town and his incendiaries starting a fire. The four successful 106 Squadron crews bombed from between 9,000 and 15,000 feet, but the clear skies over Hamburg allowed searchlight glare to compromise visibility, and it proved difficult to assess the outcome. In fact, the attack was unusually effective, and caused a number of large fires and property damage, which led to a thousand people being rendered homeless. Among the eight missing bombers from this raid were two Hampdens, one of which was AE232 from 106 Squadron. It fell victim to a night fighter flown by Oblt Walter Barte of 1.NJG/1, and crashed just south of Hamburg at 22.51. Sgt Richardson and both gunners survived to fall into enemy hands, but the Canadian observer lost his life. P4413 was flying on fumes as it approached Pocklington in Yorkshire after almost nine hours aloft, and the port engine cut out over the threshold, causing P/O Loftus to pull off a crash-landing, which he accomplished with only minor injuries to the occupants. The two freshmen crews completed their sorties successfully and returned safely home.

The weather closed in at this point, and there would be no further operations for 106 Squadron for thirteen nights, and, in fact, for an entire week from the 21st to the 27th the poor weather conditions would prevent the Command from mounting any night operations. It was during the evening of the 28th that small forces took off for Frankfurt, Genoa and Emden, with 106 Squadron supporting the first-mentioned with eleven Hampdens. Eighteen crews had been briefed to attack the main railway station, but the weather at take-off and anticipated landing times was considered to be too challenging for the less experienced pilots, and their participation was scrubbed. The newly-promoted F/L Hayward was the senior pilot on duty as they began taking off at 22.30, and headed across France to find fog, rain and intense darkness in the target area. All reached the objective, where they bombed on estimated positions based on flak and searchlight activity, and all made it safely home, although landing at a variety of stations from Manston in the south to Linton-on-Ouse in the north.

Hampdens accounted for more than half of the eighty-two-strong force sent to Hamburg on the last night of the month, to follow up a raid there twenty-four hours earlier. Seven 106 Squadron crews took part, briefed to aim for the Blohm & Voss aircraft factory, where seaplanes were under construction. P/O Hadland was the senior pilot on duty, and he was supported by two recent additions to the squadron, P/Os Firth and Wood, and the remaining four crews were captained by stalwart NCO pilots. They took off either side of 18.00, and soon found themselves in icing conditions, which Sgt Newby assumed was responsible for their Hampden's inability to maintain height. He turned back to land at 21.25, and was joined on the ground an hour and twenty minutes later by Sgt Jefferies, who was seventy-five miles from the Danish coast when severe icing forced him to turn back. Conditions over Hamburg for the others were fair, but cloud and haze prevented accurate bombing. Attacks were carried out from between 13,000 and 20,000 feet, but there was no assessment, and the local authorities later recorded ten fires. While this operation was in progress eight other crews from the squadron carried out a low-level practice raid on a target in Yorkshire. During the course of the month the squadron operated on eight nights, dispatching 105 sorties, including those recalled from Brest, and losing four aircraft, including the crash at home.

October 1941

The new month began for 106 Squadron with a call to arms for five crews, who were briefed on the 1st for an attack on marshalling yards at Karlsruhe that night. The numbers were small because eight other crews had been held in reserve for an unspecified special task. A total of forty-five aircraft took off, all but one of them Hampdens, the 106 Squadron element departing Coningsby between 18.20 and 18.30 led by S/Ls Nelms and Stenner, the latter now promoted to become B Flight commander. At 21.00 a recall signal was sent to the force because of the fear of fog developing at landing time, and the 106 Squadron crews were told to divert to North Luffenham. S/L Stenner was so close to the target by this time, that he decided to press on, and he bombed the west side of the town from 10,000 feet before returning safely. S/L Nelms turned back as ordered, and he bombed the harbour at Calais before landing at Manston. P/O Wood bombed an unidentified aerodrome twenty miles south of Lille, and landed at Wittering. P/O Hardy had intended to drop his bombs on a Channel port, but found them all cloud-covered, and he returned to West Malling with his bombs still on board. There was no sign of Sgt Newby and crew in AD768, and it turned out that they had travelled a mite further than necessary. They completely overflew England with dwindling fuel supplies, and they were forced to abandon their mount as the tanks ran dry. Fortunately they were over Ireland at the time, and the always hospitable Irish authorities transferred them to an internment camp for a period of rest and recuperation.

The weather curtailed operations from that point until the night of the 10/11th, when Essen and Cologne were the main targets. 106 Squadron put up sixteen Hampdens for the former, where the Krupp works was the aiming point, and they departed Coningsby either side of midnight as part of an overall force of seventy-eight aircraft, with F/Ls Henderson and Hayward the senior pilots on duty. It seems that in 106 Squadron it helped if your name began with the letter H, Hayward, Harwood, Herd, Henderson, Hardy to name but a few. Thirteen crews from the squadron reached Essen, and they were the only ones to do so. They encountered cloud, haze and a fierce searchlight and flak defence, and many would return with shrapnel damage. P/O Loftus bombed through haze from 10,000 feet on estimated position, and saw some bursts, but stumbled into the searchlight belt on the way home, and was forced down to 800 feet. He decided to attack the searchlight batteries as he fought his way out over a thirty-minute period, and extinguished a number of the six he hit. Sgt Dashwood bombed in the general area from 11,000 feet, before also being caught in searchlights and hit by flak near the Zuider Zee. He escaped by flying across Holland and Belgium at 600 feet. Most crews bombed from between 9,000 and 13,000 feet, but Sgt Tilbury came down to 6,000 feet, where he was able to observe two bursts and several fires. AE144 failed to return to Coningsby, and eventually news came through that it had crashed on the northern rim of the Ruhr, killing the recently-arrived P/O Gordon and his crew.

The night of the 12/13th brought the first major raid of the war on Nuremberg, the birthplace of Nazism, for which a force of 152 aircraft was prepared. 5 Group did not take part, but contributed twenty Hampdens to an attack on Bremen, while sending the bulk of its strength back to the Chemische Werke synthetic rubber factory at Hüls. This was an all-5 Group show involving seventy-nine Hampdens and eleven Manchesters, of which a dozen Hampdens were provided by 106 Squadron led by S/L Boylan. The plan called for eight selected crews to go in slightly ahead of the main body, to light up the target with their all-incendiary loads. The Coningsby contingent began taking off thirty minutes after midnight, and arrived in the target area to find ten-tenths cloud with a base at only 5,000 feet, and very few gaps. Only three of the lead crews were able to identify the factory, and only a handful of others claimed to have bombed it. S/L Boylan was one of five from 106 Squadron to bomb in the target area, without observing results, and the remainder bombed other Ruhr locations before returning safely home.

Düsseldorf and Cologne occupied elements of the Command on the night of the 13/14th, the latter assigned to thirty Hampdens and nine Manchesters from 5 Group, whose crews were briefed to aim for the main railway station. 106 Squadron dispatched five Hampdens, which departed Coningsby between 00.45 and 01.00 led by S/L Stenner. He bombed from 13,000 feet, and watched his bombs burst across the centre of the town in the face of very strong opposition from the ground. Sgt Scatchard, in contrast, reported little opposition and excellent visibility as he delivered his bombs into the city centre. Sgts McGinley and Cooke also reported bombing the centre of the target, both from 14,000 feet, but Sgt Jefferis was attacked by a BF110 while outbound in the Ostende area, and jettisoned his bombs in order to evade his pursuer. Local reports described only a few bombs finding the city, and many returning crews blamed searchlight glare for making identification difficult. While this operation was in progress, five others from the squadron were gardening in the Kiel Bay region. F/L Henderson was the senior pilot among these, and he made a number of attempts to sow his vegetables in the briefed location, but flak ships prevented him from doing so. He finally released his load over the Little Belt in the Denmark Straits before returning safely. P/O Loftus and Sgt Tilbury carried out successful sorties, Sgt Lockyer was unable to locate his garden and dropped his mines in an alternative location, and Sgt Roberts returned early with wireless failure.

The month's largest effort was by 153 aircraft against Bremen on the night of the 20/21st, for which two aiming points were selected. The 5 Group element of eighty-two Hampdens and eight Manchesters included eighteen from 106 Squadron, whose crews had been briefed to bomb a railway junction. They began taking off at 18.25 led by F/L Henderson, but those reaching the target area found intense darkness and ground haze preventing them from clearly identifying the aiming point. Sgt Purnell was confident that his bombs had fallen close to the briefed aiming point, but the majority of the thirteen crews claiming to have reached Bremen, could only report bombing in the general area, while the remainder attacked alternatives, including Cuxhaven and Bremerhaven. Despite enthusiastic claims of fires by returning crews, the local authorities described the attack as small. One of the two missing Hampdens was AD984 from 106 Squadron, which crashed in northern Germany, taking the crew of Sgt Lockwood RCAF to their deaths. Their squadron colleagues, Sgt Cooke and crew, made it back to Coningsby in AD746, after machine-gunning an aerodrome from 1,000 feet on the way home, but engine failure caused a stall and a landing crash, from which they walked away apparently unscathed.

Sgt. Edward Smith is borne by colleagues into church at his funeral. He and his crew were killed when they crashed in North Yorkshire returning from Hamburg (Simon Sanders).

The squadron sat out operations to Bremen and Mannheim on the nights of the 21/22nd and 22/23rd, neither of which produced results commensurate with the effort expended. 114 aircraft set out for Kiel on the night of the 23/24th, among them eighteen provided by 106 Squadron. F/L Henderson was the senior pilot on duty as they began taking off at 23.30, and sixteen of them managed to reach the target area to aim for the Germania Werft shipyards. In the overall context of the operation, this was a magnificent effort, as only sixty-nine in total of the original force managed to reach the target area to deliver their bombs. The force seemed to split into two distinct waves, and the second one produced some useful damage in the naval base and the shipyard. F/L Henderson positively identified the Deutsche Werke yards and dropped his bombs and incendiaries on them from 9,000 feet, while the remainder delivered theirs in the general target area or on the town. Sgt Cooke ran into searchlights, and was forced down to 2,000 feet before he escaped, but then climbed back up to 7,000 feet to drop his bombs.

A flurry of losses was to afflict the squadron at the end of the month, beginning on the night of a modestly successful operation to Hamburg on the 26/27th. Eighteen Hampdens departed Coningsby either side of 18.00, bound for the Blohm & Voss shipyards. S/L Boylan and F/L Henderson were the senior pilots on duty, but the former was one of three forced to return early, in his case after problems developed with his instrument panel. Those reaching the target area found the city bathed in moonlight, but this was countered by searchlight glare, which made identification of ground detail difficult. F/L Henderson bombed from 12,000 feet, but was unable to assess the result, while F/O Webber believed that he saw his bombs burst in the yards from 7,000 feet. In all thirteen of the squadron's crews reported bombing in the docks or town area, and P/O Loftus delivered his on the town of Rendsburg after failing to locate Hamburg. AE136 failed to return home after crashing midway between Hamburg and Bremen, and only the pilot, P/O Wood, survived, to be taken into captivity. AD785 crashed on the Whitby to Scarborough road at 02.15 following a mid-air explosion, and this resulted in the deaths of Sgt Smith and his crew.

Harry Stoffer after he was commissioned as a Pilot Officer.

Aerial reconnaissance had discovered a large fleet of enemy bombers assembled on the airfield at Schiphol near Amsterdam, and it was assumed that they were being prepared for a major attack on England. 5 Group was handed the task of preventing this, and dispatched forty Hampdens and five Manchesters to carry out an attack. 106 Squadron provided eight aircraft, led by S/Ls Nelms and Boylan, who took off at 21.45 in unfavourable weather conditions. Cloud tops over the target were at 4,000 feet with a base as low as 1,000 feet, and this made identification of the target almost impossible. S/L Nelms made a long and careful search, but was unable to locate it, but P/O Firth was more successful and delivered his bombs in a stick. P/O Hardy also managed to find it and dropped his bombs from 700 feet. Sgt Jefferis was the only other successful pilot, and he had to descend to 600 feet before bombing. X3021 failed to return after crashing into the sea off the Lincolnshire coast, and only the body of the pilot, Sgt Panting, was recovered.

Over 120 aircraft were sent against Hamburg again on the last night of the month, for another crack at the Blohm & Voss shipyards. Fifteen 106 Squadron Hampdens set out from Coningsby between 17.30 and 17.55, with F/L Hayward the senior pilot on duty. He reported his bombs falling in the target area and starting a fire, and eleven other crews from the squadron claimed to have bombed in the area of the yards or the town. Three crews were unable to locate the target, and two of these bombed Kiel and one Eckernförde on the east side of the Schleswig-Holstein peninsular. Only fifty-six crews, less than half of the original force, claimed to have reached the target to bomb, and local authorities reported that seven large fires were started. 106 Squadron operated on nine occasions during the month, and launched 119 sorties, one of which was the 1,000th. Seven aircraft were lost and six crews, one of which was safe in internment.

November 1941

The autumn weather had done nothing to ease the path for the beleaguered Commander-in-Chief, who badly needed some successes following the Butt Report. It did not arrive with the first operation of the month, which was directed at a cloud-covered Kiel. Around half of the 130-strong force reached the target area, and people on the ground heard the sound of aircraft in the vicinity, but no bombs fell in the town. November was to be a month of very little operational activity for 106 Squadron, which remained at home until the night of the 4/5th, when six of its Hampdens, described in the ORB as "pirates", were sent on anti-shipping patrols off the Frisians in search of enemy convoys. The newly-promoted F/L Herd spotted two or perhaps three small vessels off Texel, (the 106 and 5 Group ORBs differ), which he proceeded to attack from 500 feet, but his bombs overshot. The other five made no contact with the enemy, and all returned to Coningsby. Meanwhile, the squadron had sent a further nine aircraft to lay mines in Kiel Bay, and also to attack targets of opportunity with their wing bombs. Sgt Roberts successfully planted his mine in the correct position, before going for a ship with his bombs and missing. Undaunted, he went round again and machine-gunned the vessel. Sgt Dashwood dropped his bombs on the island of Nordstrand, but not on any specific structure, while P/O Hardy swooped down to 800 feet to deliver his on Sylt. Sgt Healey was unable to locate his briefed dropping zone, so sowed his vegetable off the Frisians on the way home, and then attacked and failed to hit a motor vessel with his bombs. In all, seven of the squadron's crews were successful in their primary task, on a night when cloud made for unhelpful conditions.

On the 6th sixteen crews departed Coningsby for Skitten airfield at Wick in northern Scotland, which they were to use as a forward base for mining operations off Norway. This meant that they would play only a small part in a major night of operations planned for the 7/8th. The main operation on this night was intended to be by more than two hundred aircraft against Berlin. A weather report predicted thick cloud, storms and icing conditions, but Peirse remained resolute in his decision to launch the attack. However, the doubts about the weather were sufficient to prompt the 5 Group A-O-C, AVM Slessor, to object to the plan, and he was allowed to withdraw his contribution, and send it instead to Cologne. The Berlin contingent ultimately amounted to 169 aircraft of 1, 3 and 4 Groups, while sixty-one Hampdens, including two freshmen from 106 Squadron, and fourteen Manchesters made up the Cologne force, and fifty-three Wellingtons and two Stirlings from 1 and 3 Groups were prepared for Mannheim. In all 392 aircraft were to be active in the night's various operations, and this was a new record for a single night. It would turn out to be a record-breaking night for other reasons also for both the Command and 106 Squadron.

Seventy-three of the Berlin force reached the general area of the city, and bombs were scattered over a wide area. Some damage was caused, but only fourteen houses were classed as destroyed. In return for this meagre haul twenty-one aircraft were lost, more than 12% of those dispatched, and the Mannheim force, which failed to find their target with a single bomb, lost seven Wellingtons. The 5 Group force did, at least, come away from Cologne unscathed, but had managed to destroy only two houses and damage fourteen others. Sgt Moore of 106 Squadron reported identifying the target and bombing from only 4,000 feet, a very creditable performance for a freshman crew, but Sgt Power returned early with an engine problem.

The minor operations also fared badly, with six aircraft missing from "rover" patrols over the Ruhr, and three from the 106 Squadron mining effort. F/Ls Henderson, Hayward and Herd were the senior pilots on duty as they took off for their respective gardens between 00.35 and 02.00, and six crews returned to report sowing their vegetable in or very near the correct location. One delivered his in Stavangar Fjord as an alternative, two were unable to find a suitable garden and brought their stores home, and one jettisoned his in the sea because of an overheating engine. This left three crews unaccounted for, those of F/L Henderson DFC, F/L Herd DFC and P/O Firth. P1290 and AD760 were both picked off by flak in the target area, and P/O Firth and one of his crew died in the former, and two of F/L Henderson's crew were also killed in the latter, the survivors all falling into enemy hands. The crew of AD932 was heard calling for assistance seven hours and forty minutes after take-off, and a fix put them at forty-eight miles from Wick, but nothing more was heard from them. The body of a gunner, Sgt Jones, eventually came ashore, but of the others, which included P/O McIver DFC of the RCAF, there was no trace. It was a disastrous night for the Command, which registered a new record loss of thirty-seven aircraft, more than twice the previous highest at night. This night of disaster was the final straw for the Air Ministry, and on the 13th Peirse was ordered to restrict further operations while the future of the Command was considered at the highest level. In the meantime Peirse was summoned to a personal meeting with Churchill to explain himself, but his time at the helm of Bomber Command was effectively over, and he would leave his post in January.

On the night following the Berlin debacle over fifty aircraft were sent to bomb the Krupp works at Essen. Six Hampdens were detailed to attack the Bocholt searchlight belt in the Ruhr in support, and S/L Stenner and Sgt Roberts were the 106 Squadron representatives. S/L Stenner spent his time at between 4,000 and 10,000 feet, dropping his bombs at intervals, while Sgt Roberts chose 500 to 2,000 feet, bombing and machine-gunning as he went. Also on this night, Sgt Power joined in on a freshman attack on Dunkerque, and watched his bombs fall from 7,000 feet to burst among the docks and produce a great shower of sparks. Hamburg hosted a raid by seventy-one aircraft on the 9/10th, and a few fires were started. 106 Squadron was not involved, and a period of bad weather kept most of the Command on the ground from then until mid-month. Relatively small-scale operations against German and French ports occupied much of the remainder of the month, the first against Emden on the night of the 15/16th, which 106 Squadron supported with a single freshman crew. Sgt Hartgroves and crew arrived over the target to find it hidden by cloud, and he dropped his bombs on a flak and searchlight concentration, and thought he saw a red glow beneath the clouds. Sixteen crews had actually been briefed to take part in a raid on Kiel on this night, but the 5 Group effort was withdrawn less than an hour before take-off because of doubts about the weather.

There were no operations for 5 Group at all between the 16/17th and 22/23rd, but offensive matters resumed with a raid on Lorient docks on the night of the 23/24th, which 106 Squadron sat out. Three nights later Emden was the objective for a hundred Wellingtons and Hampdens, for which 106 Squadron contributed six freshman crews. The all-NCO-captained Hampdens took off between 17.00 and 17.15 on an evening of poor weather conditions, but at least five were among the fifty-five crews who reported bombing in the target area. They all cited ten-tenths cloud as the cause of their problems, and bombing was carried out on estimated positions. Sgt Moss and crew were missing from debriefing, and it would be a long time before news came through of their fate. AE317 had crashed into the sea off the Frisians, and only the body of a gunner eventually washed ashore for burial.

5 Group participated in an operation to Düsseldorf on the night of the 27/28th, but only after cutting sixteen Hampdens and two Manchesters from its original plan because of doubts about the weather. As a result, 106 Squadron did not take part, and the local authorities reported only light damage. On the last night of the month 180 aircraft were sent to Hamburg to attack the Blohm & Voss shipyards and a number of other aiming points within the city. Fourteen 106 Squadron Hampdens took off either side of 16.30, with F/L

Hayward and the newly-promoted F/L Webber the senior pilots on duty. The weather, for a change, was excellent as they climbed away from Coningsby, but Sgt Dashwood became unwell two hours into his sortie and turned back. By that time Sgt Power had already landed after aborting his sortie through a defective boost gauge. F/L Webber dropped his bombs from 7,500 feet into the docks area, two miles east of the briefed aiming point, and saw no bursts. Sgt Scatchard was at 16,000 feet when he released his bombs on what he believed to be the target, but also saw no results. Sgt Picken bombed from 14,000 feet and thought he had scored a "near-miss", while Sgt Stoffer reckoned his was a direct hit from 6,500 feet, but again was unable to observe anything to back up his claim. As the final hour of November ticked away, a dozen 106 Squadron Hampdens were well into their return journey to Coningsby, Sgt Roberts no doubt buoyed up be the knowledge that he had now completed two hundred hours of operational flying, and could look forward to a rest. A number of fires were raised in Hamburg for the loss of thirteen aircraft, and this figure included 106 Squadron's P1228 and AT115 with the crews of Sgts Moore and Rolfe respectively. Both were lost without trace, and were presumably further victims of the cold North Sea. During the course of the month the squadron operated on seven nights and dispatched fifty-four sorties for the loss of six aircraft and crews.

December 1941

The first week of December passed by without operational activity as the weather closed in again and snow lay on the airfields. The first offensive action took place on the night of the 7/8th, when the Nazi Party HQ in the centre of Aachen provided the target for a force of 130 aircraft, of which six Hampdens were provided by 106 Squadron. The night was characterized by wintry showers and low cloud as the Coningsby contingent began taking off from 02.30, led by P/Os Loftus and Hardy. Sgts Brown and Healey and P/O Hardy all failed to identify the primary target, but each delivered their bombs onto the town without being able to observe anything below the cloud. P/O Loftus abandoned his search and bombed Ostend from 5,000 feet on the way home. Sgt Dashwood bombed railway lines and saw bursts across them, and Sgt Cooke also attacked railway lines and lock gates. In all only sixty-four crews returned to claim having reached and bombed the general area, and local authorities reported a raid by an estimated sixteen aircraft with little damage. Meanwhile, numerous minor operations were taking place, including one by a small force of Wellingtons and Stirlings against the enemy ships still sheltering in the port of Brest. This would be the first of fifteen attacks of varying sizes sent against the port during the month, as the Command sought a conclusion to this annoying distraction.

Although daylight operations had largely become the preserve of the outstandingly courageous crews of 2 Group, occasional daylight forays were attempted by small numbers of aircraft, when there was sufficient cloud to cloak them. These operations, known as "moling", were rarely, if ever effective, and were frequently aborted over enemy territory, if the cloud cover were deemed insufficient. Such operations involved small numbers of 5 Group aircraft on successive days from the 10th to the 13th, with targets in Germany and Holland including shipping, airfields and anything else that presented itself, along with mining. On the morning of the 12th four 106 Squadron Hampdens stood ready for take-off in conditions which promised sufficient cloud to provide the necessary cover, and F/L Webber was first away at 10.40, with unquestionably the toughest brief of the quartet. His target was an oil refinery at Gelsenkirchen, at the eastern end of the Ruhr, and one has to question the sanity of senior officers in sending a single experienced and valuable crew deep into enemy territory by daylight to attack a heavily defended target. Even if successful, the bombs from a single medium bomber could not create more than a nuisance, and certainly were not worth sacrificing the lives of four experienced and valuable young men.

S/L Nelms took off five minutes after F/L Webber, and headed towards Oldenburg, a town to the west of Bremen, where he was to attack the marshalling yards. He was followed immediately by F/L Hayward, whose target was an oil refinery at Emmerich on the German side of the Rhine on the border with Holland. Five minutes later Sgt Cooke departed for a smelting works at Nordenham, a town across the bay from Wilhelmshaven. S/L Nelms turned back when his cloud cover deserted him, and he landed at 13.05. F/L Hayward attacked his objective with bombs and machine-gun fire from 300 feet, and claimed four direct hits followed by clouds of black smoke. Sgt Cooke carried out two runs at 50 feet against a factory south of the one he was supposed to attack, scoring direct hits and causing terrific explosions. During his low-level dash for home across Germany he strafed a ship in the Elbe, a train and a railway station, before arriving back at Coningsby at 15.50. The return of F/L Webber and his crew was awaited in vain, and news would be received at the end of the month,that AE391 had crashed at Osterfeld, a suburb of Oberhausen, well to the west of Gelsenkirchen, and all on board had been killed. It is not known whether they were outbound or homebound at the time.

106 Squadron remained at home thereafter until the night of the 15/16th, when providing two freshman crews for a small-scale operation to Ostend. Both P/Os Selfe and Horner were carrying out their first operations as crew captain, and good weather conditions and clear visibility helped them to complete their briefs successfully and return safely home. On the following night, after eleven crews had been briefed for an attack on Wilhelmshaven, the squadron's involvement was scrubbed at the last minute, and eight crews were sent instead to mine the waters off Brest, while two freshman crews bombed the docks at Dunkerque. The latter, in the shape of Sgt Bishop and P/O Hodgson and their crews took off first before 18.00, but P/O Hodgson was forced to turn back when his intercom failed. Sgt Bishop pressed on, but was unable to locate the target in the conditions, and brought his bombs home. S/L Boylan led the gardening contingent away at 18.15, and the others took off over the following seventy-five minutes. Five were able to deposit their vegetables in precisely the correct position, but S/L Boylan, F/S Jefferis and Sgt Power planted theirs within a quarter of a mile and two miles of the briefed locations.

Another unusual type of role for Hampdens was "intruding", which fortunately was not frequently undertaken. This differed from moling in being a roving commission to attack targets of opportunity rather than a specific objective. Shortly after noon on the 21st six Hampdens each from 106 and 49 Squadrons took off for north-west Germany to find individual targets. Sgt Scatchard was soon back on the ground with technical problems, and a reserve crew was sent up to replace him. S/L Stenner was the senior 106 Squadron pilot on duty, and he was one of five to abandon his sortie when the cloud disappeared. A recall signal was sent to Sgt Hartgroves, but it was not acknowledged, and AE151 failed to return. A German broadcast that evening announced that a British bomber had been shot down during the afternoon, and news eventually came through that it had crashed in Holland, and that the pilot and his two gunners had survived and were now in enemy hands.

The main target for the night of the 23/24th was Cologne, for which a force of almost seventy Wellingtons, Hampdens and Whitleys took off. They were unable to locate the target in conditions of complete cloud cover, and no bombs found the mark. 106 Squadron did not take part in this operation, but sent two aircraft to join others from the group mining off Kiel. There was heavy rain and low cloud as Sgt Young and P/O Hodgson arrived in the target area, but the former was able to deliver his mine in the correct position, while his colleague was beaten by the conditions and brought his back. A major raid on Düsseldorf was mounted on the night of the 27/28th, to which 5 Group contributed thirty-seven aircraft to an overall force of 132. The only departure from Coningsby was a single 97 Squadron Manchester as 106 Squadron remained at home.

The final operation of the year for the squadron took place on the night of the 28/29th, when two main targets were briefed, Wilhelmshaven for a force of eighty-six Wellingtons, and the Chemische Werke synthetic rubber factory at Hüls for eighty-one Hampdens. This would be the third attempt to destroy the factory since September, but it should be remembered that it represented a precision target at a time when precision at night was beyond the capabilities of the available equipment. Fifteen Hampdens departed Coningsby from 18.00 onwards led by S/Ls Nelms and Stenner, and headed to what would be a moonlit target made even clearer by snow on the ground. F/L Hayward and P/O Horner both experienced engine failure, and landed back at Coningsby around three hours after taking off. Sgt Dashwood had been assigned to fire-raising duties, but he did not arrive at the target in time, and in accordance with instructions brought his bombs home. Sgt Power could not locate the target, and he also returned his bombs to the store. This left eleven crews, all of whom reported a successful attack. Sgt Brown scored a direct hit from 12,000 feet, and claimed his bombs started a large fire, while Sgt Bishop attacked from 4,500 feet and hit the south-west corner of the complex. S/L Stenner reported one of his bombs exploding on the target and causing a vivid green flash followed by a fire. He was then attacked and damaged by a BF110, which was hit by return fire and possibly destroyed. Sgt Scatchard claimed the fires were visible from fifty miles into the return journey. Once all had returned and undergone debriefing, the consensus was that the raid had been highly successful. The sad news came through on the 31st confirming that F/L Webber and his crew had lost their lives. During the course of the month the squadron operated on five nights and two days, launching forty-five sorties for the loss of two aircraft and crews.

1941 had been the squadron's first full year as an operational unit, and its experiences were similar to those of any other squadron in the group. However, the coming year would see changes in equipment and leadership, which would see it go from strength to strength. As far as the Command as a whole was concerned, it had been a disappointing year, with few improvements on 1940. The new aircraft types had failed to deliver the performance and reliability required of them, and had spent long periods on the ground undergoing modifications. The Manchester in particular had been a disaster, but had at least prompted the development of the Lancaster, which was now undergoing proving trials in the hands of 44 Squadron. Its introduction to operational service in the spring under a new and inspirational leader would begin the slow evolution of the Command towards becoming a war-winning weapon.

January 1942

The new year began for 106 Squadron with the dispatch of four NCO-captained Hampdens for daylight "sneaker" operations over north-western Germany on the 2nd. They took off in the late morning, but there were early signs of thinning cloud, and after an hour's eastward progress, Sgts Scatchard, Lipton and Power turned back. Sgt Dashwood pressed on until reaching the Frisian island of Schiermonikoog, where he was fired upon by a convoy and decided also to abandon what was clearly a futile sortie. 5 Group sent thirty-six Hampdens mining on the night of the 2/3rd, while 106 Squadron stayed at home, and then repeated the exercise twenty-four hours later with smaller numbers. This time 106 Squadron contributed five of ten Hampdens, whose crews were briefed to mine the waters around the Frisians. Sgt Dashwood was first away at 16.20, and the others followed during the ensuing thirty minutes. They encountered heavy rain and low cloud in the target area, despite which, three crews managed to identify their garden location and plant their mines. By this time F/S Jefferis had returned home with an engine problem, and P/O Howard and crew were in trouble. A message was received, "S.O.S landing in sea", and a fix located them at around 130 miles off the English coast, but, despite a sea search by two crews on the 4th, no trace of AT123 or its crew was ever found. This was the first in a series of losses for the squadron during a month in which the preoccupation with the German cruisers at Brest would grind on inexorably towards its conclusion.

Another moling operation was mounted on the 4th, which 106 Squadron supported with three Hampdens, captained by Sgts Power and Cooke and P/O Loftus. Sgts Power and Loftus ran out of cloud and turned back at 3° east, although there was sufficient of the white stuff for Sgt Power to dive into to evade a single engine enemy fighter. Sgt Cooke, however, seemed to have a particular taste for this kind of operation, as demonstrated in his exploits in December, and he reached the town of Leer, on Germany's northern-most border with Holland. He delivered his 250lb bombs across the railway station and a junction from 300 feet, and tried but failed to bomb a train. During a further pass he machine-gunned trains, and installations, and encountered some return fire for his cheek.

The campaign against Brest continued on the night of the 5/6th, when 5 Group contributed twenty-seven Hampdens and twelve Manchesters to an overall force of 154 aircraft, some briefed to aim for the Scharnhorst and Gneisenau, while the remainder concentrated on the naval docks. The 106 Squadron contingent of nine took off either side of 03.30, and like the other participants, the seven NCO and two officer-captained crews were thwarted by an effective smoke screen and eight to ten-tenths cloud. They bombed on estimated positions from between 10,000 and 14,000 feet in the face of heavy flak, and despite claims of large fires by some returning crews, no accurate assessment of results could be made. Roving patrols over north-western Germany on the night of the 6/7th did not involve 106 Squadron, and it stayed at home on the following two nights, before contributing a dozen Hampdens to an overall force of eighty-two aircraft committed to a further attack on Brest on the 9/10th. W/C Allen took the lead on this night, departing Coningsby at a minute after midnight to be followed over the next twenty-nine minutes by the others. Sgt Dashwood was back shortly before 04.00 with engine trouble, and he landed at Boscombe Down. The weather in the target area continued to be unhelpful, but W/C Allen described the visibility as good as he delivered his bombs onto the docks from 12,000 feet at around 02.40. The others reported nine to ten-tenths cloud obscuring the target area, and all bombed on approximate positions without observing any results. Returning crews mentioned quite heavy but inaccurate flak, but none of them was hit.

There were no further operations for 106 Squadron over the ensuing few nights, despite the group contributing forty-six Hampdens and ten Manchesters to attacks on Wilhelmshaven and Emden and a mining effort on the 10/11th. While on a training flight on the morning of the 14th, AE292 span in and crashed four miles north-east of Boston, killing Sgt Lawton and the other occupant. That night came the first of two raids on consecutive nights on Hamburg. Ninety-five aircraft took off to attack the shipyards and an airframe factory, among them a 5 Group contingent, but 106 Squadron remained on the ground. Only half of the force reached the target area, and they managed to start seven large fires. The following night's effort by a force of ninety-six aircraft included nine Hampdens from 106 Squadron, but little went according to plan. They began taking off at 16.35, but X3131 crashed without injury to Sgt Power and his crew, and this slightly delayed the other departures. Most got away shortly after 17.00, but P/O Loftus and Sgt Lipton were soon back in the circuit with engine problems. The others pressed on led by S/L Stenner, now the only commissioned pilot on duty, but only four reached the target area to bomb, and this was representative of the force as a whole. Sgt Picken dropped two 500lb bombs onto searchlights, but brought his incendiaries home. Sgt Bishop delivered two 500 pounders from 12,000 feet, and believed they had fallen in the town area, and similar reports were given by Sgt Young and S/L Stenner. A total of fifty-two crews claimed to have reached Hamburg, and they created thirty-six fires, three of them large, but otherwise no damage of significance. Four aircraft failed to return, among them P1341 of 106 Squadron, which crashed at the well-defended port of Esbjerg in south-western Denmark after being hit by flak. Happily, New Zealander, Sgt Dashwood, and his crew all survived, and were soon in enemy hands. While this operation was in progress, F/O Bareham successfully carried out a freshman mining sortie off the Frisians. Two nights later over eighty aircraft returned to northern Germany, this time to attack Bremen, but only eight crews reported reaching the city, and some of the others bombed at Hamburg instead.

106 Squadron was enjoying another six-night stand-down at the time, and did not participate. It was during this period, on the 20th, that the squadron accepted its first Manchesters in preparation for the forthcoming conversion to the type. 106 Squadron became the fifth unit in the group to receive Manchesters, doing so at a time when its operational career was approaching its conclusion. The Achilles Heel of the Manchester was its Rolls Royce Vulture engines, which had not achieved expected performance levels, and frequently failed. There was no guarantee that the aircraft could remain aloft on one engine, and more of them fell victim to non-operational accidents than were lost to enemy action. L7390, L7398 and L7463 were shunted across the tarmac from 97 Squadron, and they would be joined on the 26th by L7474.

When Bremen was next raided on the night of the 21/22nd, 106 Squadron put up six Hampdens as part of an overall force of fifty-four aircraft. P/O Selfe was the senior pilot on duty on an intensely cold night, which would severely curtail the squadron's efforts. They took off either side of 17.00, and Sgt Scatchard was one of only two from the squadron to reach the target, which he found to be free of cloud. The visibility was excellent, and he was preparing to bomb when he was snared in a cone of thirty searchlights. He evaded them by diving down to 3,000 feet, from which altitude he delivered his bombs into the town. Sgt Stoffer also described it as cloudless over the target, and he dropped his bombs from 12,000 feet before returning home in temperatures of minus forty-one degrees at 17,000 feet. Three other crews abandoned their sorties after the heating system in their aircraft broke down, exposing them to temperatures of around minus fifteen degrees Celcius at 7,500 feet. The general pattern of failure continued as only half of the crews involved reported reaching the target area, and the operation cost the squadron the crew of Sgt Deere. His body was found in the wreckage of AE123 near Zwolle in Holland, but his three crew mates survived as PoWs. While this operation was in progress, Sgt Sporny, of the Polish Air Force, carried out his first sortie by bombing the port of Emden. The weather was good, but the target was obscured by mist,

106 Sqn aircrew pose in front of an Avro Manchester. Second from left is Ronny Churcher.

making it difficult to pinpoint ground detail. Never the less, he delivered his bomb load, and observed bursts in the target area.

The first foray into inland Germany for a month took place on the night of the 22/23rd, when Münster was the destination for forty-seven aircraft. 106 Squadron, meanwhile sent two Hampdens with freshman NCO crews to mine the waters around the Frisians. Sgt Kent took off at 17.30, and returned at 21.20 to report finding fair weather and no cloud in the garden area, and that he had located his drop zone without difficulty and planted his mine in the correct position. Sgt Ellis and crew had taken off at 17.35, never to be seen again, and it has to be assumed that AT146 went into the North Sea. Overnight it began to snow heavily, and this continued for a number of days, rendering Coningsby unserviceable, and incapable of launching any aircraft. This situation persisted until the 27th, although the other 5 Group stations were able to continue operating, and contributed to raids on Brest on the 25/26th and Hanover on the 26/27th. 5 Group dispatched over forty Hampdens and Manchesters to attack the cruisers at Brest on the night of the 27/28th, when most of the force reached the target and bombed, although no crews were able to identify the ships, and haze prevented any assessment of results.

Over eighty aircraft returned to Münster on the night of the 28/29th, and this time 106 Squadron supported the operation with ten Hampdens. F/L Bareham, who was probably a flying officer acting as a flight lieutenant, was the senior pilot on duty, as the squadron contingent took off either side of 18.00. The night was intensely cold, with snow storms and severe icing conditions, and this undoubtedly contributed to the unfolding tragedy. They arrived in the target area to find ten-tenths cloud, which led to just four aircraft bombing on estimated positions, and not a single bomb found the mark. One Wellington and four Hampdens failed to return, and it was a disastrous night for 106 Squadron, to which all four belonged. Sgt Sporny and his crew were killed when P4398 crashed near Düsseldorf, and there were no survivors also among the crew of P/O Selfe. They had successfully crash-landed AT122 in a forest about seven miles north-west of Winterswijk in Holland, and, possibly badly injured, had remained with the aircraft only to freeze to death during the night. An S.O.S signal was received from AT121 at 21.22 reporting "one engine failed", and a fix located it in the general area of the Zuider Zee. Nothing more was heard, until news eventually filtered through that the Hampden had been homebound when it crashed into a house in Den Helder, at the tip of the peninsular pointing towards Texel. F/L Bareham and his observer survived, and they were taken into captivity. Gunner, Sgt Snelling, had baled out over the sea, and in such weather conditions he would have succumbed to the cold within minutes. His body eventually came ashore nine months later on the island of Amrum off the western side of the Schleswig-Holstein peninsular. Finally, X3058 was successfully ditched off East Anglia on the homeward flight by Sgt Brown, and all four members of the crew managed to get into the dinghy. Rescue by lifeboat did not occur until sixteen hours later, by which time three had frozen to death, and only Sgt Brown was still alive.

While the operation was in progress P/O Paget undertook his first freshman operation to Boulogne in company with forty-seven other aircraft. He found the target easily in fair but hazy conditions, and from 12,000 feet observed his bombs bursting across the docks. This night had brought the squadron's worst reversal of the war to date, and raised the month's losses to eight aircraft from seven night and two daylight operations, during which sixty-five sorties were launched. February was about to bring major changes, both for the squadron and the Command as a whole, although one wonders how the crews at 106 Squadron greeted the prospect of going to war in the Manchester, the reputation of which had preceded it.

February 1942

As it turned out, the squadron's brief association with the type would produce a record of serviceability second to none, but that still lay in the future, and during the working up period, operations continued with the trusty, but now obsolete Hampden. Snow kept 106 Squadron on the ground for the first five nights of the new month, and the first operation to which it contributed took place in daylight on the 6th, when 5 Group sent forty-six Hampdens and Manchesters to mine the waters around the Frisians. 106 Squadron supported the effort with five aircraft, which took off between 10.55 and 11.20 led by F/L Hayward. Low cloud was helpful in concealing their approach to the garden area, and weather conditions were described as ideal with good visibility under a complete cloud cover. Sgts Scatchard, Picken, and Stoffer and P/O Loftus all successfully delivered their mines into the correct positions, but F/L Hayward's attempt to release his from 1,500 feet failed because of a fault in the bomb release mechanism.

Forty-nine aircraft were dispatched to Mannheim on the night of the 11/12th, six of them provided by 106 Squadron. They began departing Coningsby shortly after 18.00 with P/O Horner the senior pilot on duty. They had been briefed to aim for the main railway station, and were given a new route over Belgium in an attempt to avoid the searchlight belt. AE425 lost its port engine at forty feet as it took off, and it struggled the couple of miles to Woodhall Spa before crashing at Kirkstead, fortunately without injury to the crew of P/O Horner. *(The account in the squadron ORB is entirely different, and reports P/O Horner reaching and bombing the target, while Sgt Scatchard returned early with engine trouble and landed three-and-three-quarter hours after take-off.)* The remainder found the target blanketed in snow, but under clear, starlit skies, and bombed from between 11,000 and 14,000 feet before returning safely home, although not to Coningsby. This was the night on which the final sorties were mounted in the long-running saga involving Brest and its lodgers. Eighteen Wellingtons took part, and as they turned back towards the English coast, the weather conditions were fairly benign, a situation which would alter to the enemy's advantage before long.

Scharnhorst and Prinz Eugen, along with Gneisenau, broke the British sea blockade in what was known as the 'Channel Dash'. The three German capital ships successfully survived a marine and air onslaught by British forces; air casualties exceeded those on board the ships.

Vice Admiral Otto Cilliax, the Brest Group commander, whose flag was on Scharnhorst, put Operation Cerberus into action shortly after the latest Bomber Command attack. The Scharnhorst, Gneisenau and Prinz Eugen slipped anchor at 21.14, and headed into the English Channel under an escort of destroyers and E-Boats. It was an audacious bid for freedom, covered by widespread jamming and meticulously planned support by the Kriegsmarine and the Luftwaffe, all of which had been practiced extensively during January. The planning and a little good fortune allowed the fleet to make undetected progress until spotted off le Touquet by two Spitfires piloted by G/C Victor Beamish, the commanding officer of Kenley, and W/C Finlay Boyd, who maintained radio silence and did not report their find until landing at 10.42 on the morning of the 12th. 5 Group was standing by at four hours readiness when Operation Fuller, which had been planned well in advance for precisely this eventuality, ground slowly into action. The problem seemed to be, that few people in the areas that mattered had been fully appraised of the operation's requirements, and some, it seems, were totally ignorant of it. The first of a record number of 242 daylight sorties were despatched at 13.30, but the squally conditions and low cloud prevented all but a few crews from catching sight of their quarry, and those attacks that did take place failed to find the mark. 106 Squadron contributed four Hampdens to the operation, S/Ls Stenner and Nelms and Sgt Cooke, taking off between 14.45 and 15.00, and P/O Paget at 16.35. The last-mentioned returned with engine and intercom problems, while S/L Nelms ran out of cloud cover and decided to abandon his sortie. Sgt Cooke found cloud at 700 feet and visibility at a thousand yards, and he, too returned home after searching in vain for forty-five minutes. S/L Stenner found the enemy after breaking cloud, and was fired upon by a destroyer. He carried out an attack on Scharnhorst in a shallow dive from 4,000 down to 1,300 feet, but his bombs overshot. Despite the best efforts of Bomber and Coastal Commands, which were committed too late to the chase, the ships passed through the Straits of Dover and into open sea, making good their escape. The only consolation was that Scharnhorst struck two mines, no doubt planted by 5 Group Hampdens, and, although her progress was slowed as a result, she was able to make port in Wilhelmshaven by the following morning, where she would require three months to repair. This debacle known as "The Channel Dash" was a huge embarrassment to the government and the nation, and cost the Command another fifteen gallant crews, on top of all those sacrificed during the long-running campaign.

On a positive note, however, this annoying itch had been scratched for the last time, and there was nothing now to distract the Command from its main purpose.

On the 14th a new Air Ministry directive paved the way for the area bombing of German towns and cities without the pretence of aiming at industrial and military objectives. The morale of the enemy civilian population was to be the target, particularly that of the workers, and this was a reaffirmation of the directive of July 1941. Waiting in the wings, in fact, at that very moment, on his way across the Atlantic from America in the armed merchantman Alcantara, was a new leader, who would pursue this policy with a will, and have the character and strength of personality to fight his corner against the critics. 5 Group sent a force of Hampdens and Manchesters to carry out mining duties in the Frisians on the night of the 16/17th, for which 106 Squadron provided two freshman crews, those of Sgt O'Hare and P/O Aytoun, who took off forty-five minutes apart in the early evening. They encountered ten-tenths cloud with a base below 1,000 feet, poor visibility and icing conditions, and neither was able to complete their brief.

The first mention of the squadron training in Manchesters appears in the ORB on the 17th, and that night the Command carried out a roving commission operation over Germany, which did not involve 106 Squadron. The night of the 21/22nd brought more of the same, and this time six 106 Squadron Hampdens were among the twenty detailed for targets of opportunity between Cologne and Koblenz to the south-east. The plan had been to raid Mannheim, but this was changed at the last minute. The newly-commissioned P/Os Picken and Stoffer were the senior pilots on duty as they got away from Coningsby at 18.30, and headed towards enemy territory in decent weather conditions. Sgt Cooke found Cologne in good visibility and free of cloud, and released his bombs from 9,000 feet, observing them to burst in the northern part of the town. P/O Stoffer also described excellent visibility and no cloud, and he reported dropping a thousand pounder on Neuweid, a little to the north of Koblenz, and another at a second location, which is undecipherable in the ORB entry. Both were direct hits, for which he was fired upon and hit, but not seriously. Sgt Kent bombed Siegen, east of Cologne, from 10,000 feet, and also a flak concentration in the searchlight belt near Maastricht, and he also was hit by flak for his pains. P/O Picken returned early with wireless failure, and Sgt Power's heating system broke down. He pushed on for a time, but was ultimately beaten by the intense cold and turned back. P4414 failed to return with the crew of Sgt Bishop, and no trace of the aircraft and crew was ever found, leading to the conclusion that it found a final resting place in the North Sea.

Air Chief Marshal Sir Arthur Harris took his place at the helm of Bomber Command on the 22nd. He had commanded 5 Group for the first year of war, before going to the USA to help Churchill to bring that country into the conflict. Harris was the man who would direct the bomber war right to the end, and he arrived at a time when the existence of an independent bomber force was still being questioned in high places, particularly at the Admiralty. He took up his appointment with firm ideas already in place on how to win the war by bombing alone. He recognized, that in order to destroy an urban target, it was necessary to concentrate his forces in time and space to overwhelm the defences. This was the birth of the bomber stream, and it brought an end to the former practice, whereby crews and squadron commanders determined for themselves the details of their sorties. He also knew that built-up areas are most efficiently destroyed by fire rather than blast, and that by concentrating the effort, fires would have a chance to gain a hold before the emergency services could reach them through rubble-strewn streets. It would not be long before the bomb loads carried in Harris's aircraft reflected this thinking. It was a policy of the bludgeon over the scalpel, but the war to date had demonstrated that precision bombing was a dream still awaiting the scientific means to realise it.

On the night of the 23/24th 106 Squadron contributed six Hampdens to a mining operation off Wilhelmshaven. The usual suspects were involved, Sgts Scatchard, Cooke, Power and Kent, along with P/Os Picken and Stoffer, and they took off either side of 02.00. Sgt Scatchard found no cloud but poor visibility, and he pinpointed on Westerhever on the west side of the Schleswig-Holstein peninsular, before making a run from there to the Rosemary garden, and dropping his mine on dead-reckoning in the approximate briefed position. P/O Stoffer did exactly the same, and believed his mine was accurately placed. Sgt Kent and crew were also assigned to this garden, but P4323 was shot down by naval flak in the target area, and crashed on Sylt killing all on board. As events were to prove, this was the final crew to be posted missing by the squadron in a Hampden. The other three crews were assigned to the Yams garden, and Sgts Cooke and Power pinpointed on the Danish coast before dropping their mines on e.t.a. P/O Picken was unable to locate his drop zone, and returned by way of the Dutch Frisians. He observed flak and searchlights off Terschelling, and planted his mine there. At 18.10 that evening Sgt Hurd and P/O Gallacher took off to carry out freshman mining sorties off the Frisians. The former pinpointed on Schiermonikoog before planting his mine in the correct location in good visibility, and the latter likewise reported a successful and uneventful trip.

For his first week at the helm, Harris continued to send relatively small forces to the German ports of Wilhelmshaven and Kiel, the latter, where the Gneisenau had been sheltering since the Channel Dash episode, providing the objective on three consecutive nights from the 25th. During the second operation on the night of the 26/27th a high explosive bomb struck the bows of the Gneisenau, causing severe damage and killing more than a hundred of her crew. This ended her sea-going career for good, and her main armament was removed for use as a coastal battery. It was somewhat ironic that she should come to grief in a supposedly safe home port after surviving almost a year of constant bombardment at Brest. 106 Squadron was not involved in this success, but sent a single freshman crew, that of P/O Cockbain, to mine the waters off the Frisians. Unfortunately, he experienced engine problems while outbound, and decided to abandon the sortie.

Having dealt with Gneisenau, an attempt was made on Scharnhorst, at berth and under repair at Wilhelmshaven. While a simultaneous operation went ahead at Kiel on the night of the 27/28th, S/L Nelms led six 106 Squadron Hampdens away from Coningsby between 18.10 and 18.45. Sgt Power turned back with wireless failure, and P/O Gallacher was persistently harried by night fighters, which persuaded him to jettison his bombs and turn for home. The remainder arrived over Wilhelmshaven in entirely the wrong weather conditions for any realistic chance of success. There was complete cloud cover with tops at 12,000 feet, and although there was bright moonlight above the cloud, that was of benefit only to night fighters. S/L Nelms bombed on e.t.a., aiming at a flak concentration from 10,000 feet, and Sgt Young dropped his load onto the town and observed four bursts. Sgt Hurd bombed a flak concentration from 17,000 feet and saw six bursts, and there was a similar report from Sgt O'Hara. This was the squadron's final operation of the month, during the course of which it had undertaken operations on seven nights and two days, and dispatched thirty-eight sorties for the loss of three aircraft.

March 1942

By the end of the 2nd 106 Squadron had become the sole resident of Coningsby, after 97 Squadron completed its move to Woodhall Spa, a new station about three miles away to the north-west. The weather had prevented operations from taking place on the first two nights, but the unmistakeable sign of a new hand on the tiller came on the night of the 3/4th, when a force of 235 aircraft, a new record for a single target, was made ready for an attack on the Renault lorry factory at Billancourt in Paris. The meticulously prepared plan called for the operation to be conducted in three waves, led by experienced crews, and with extensive use of flares to assist target identification. In the face of what was expected to be scant opposition, the bombing was to be carried out from as low a level as practicable in order to aid accuracy, and to avoid as far as possible collateral damage to adjacent residential districts.

106 Squadron briefed seven crews, who would be led by F/L Hayward as the senior pilot on duty. They took off from Coningsby at 18.15 on an evening of fine weather, which would persist throughout the operation, and arrived in the target area a little under three hours later to find bright moonlight, and the factory easily identifiable in the light from flares and already burgeoning fires. The newly promoted F/S Scatchard delivered his bombs from 2,000 feet at 21.10, and watched them burst across the target and cause a large explosion. P/O Picken reached Paris at 21.00, but hung around until 21.28 before dropping his bombs from 3,000 feet at 21.28. He also released bundles of nickels (leaflets) over the city, as did F/L Hayward, who observed his bombs falling onto the diesel engine repair shops. All from Coningsby returned safely from this outstandingly successful operation, which cost just a single aircraft. The success was marred only by the deaths of 367 French civilians, and this question of collateral damage, when attacking targets in urban areas in the occupied countries, would prove to be one without a solution. It was, however, a sign of things to come, and it was something of a paradox that Harris, as a champion of the area bombing policy, should gain his first victory through one reliant on precision.

The squadron stayed at home for the next three nights before supporting a small-scale attack on the U-Boot base at St Nazaire with two Hampdens. It was the graveyard shift for F/S Duff and P/O Cockbain, as they took off at 01.30 and 01.45 respectively, and both were back in time for a late breakfast after successfully bombing the docks in excellent weather conditions. It would soon be clear to all, that Harris's attention was firmly focussed on Essen, the great city in the centre of the industrial Ruhr region that was home to the giant armaments producing Krupp organisation. On the night of the 8/9th he began a campaign against it, which would last until mid April and involve eight major attacks. 211 aircraft were committed to this first operation, which was led by Gee-equipped aircraft to assist with navigation. 5 Group contributed fifty-nine Hampdens and Manchesters, among them three of the former from 106 Squadron. P/Os Churcher and Aytoun and Sgt O'Hara got away shortly after 01.00 on another night of good weather, and they benefited from Gee, which helped to get the force to the general area of the target. Once there, however, the ever-present industrial haze that hung over the Ruhr like a blanket, prevented the crews from picking out ground detail, although P/O Churcher was confident that he had identified the aiming point when he released his bombs from 15,000 feet. The city authorities reported a light raid with little damage, and Bomber Command recorded eight failures to return.

187 aircraft took off twenty-four hours later to return to Essen, for which 106 Squadron put up just two Hampdens, captained by F/S Duff and Sgt Young. The former reported the target to be easily identifiable from 11,000 feet in excellent visibility, and he watched his bombs burst across the target and cause fires. Again damage was light, and bombs were deposited in many other locations in the region at a cost this time of three aircraft. For the third night running Harris tried again, although this time with a force of a little over 120 aircraft, of which four represented 106 Squadron. Surprisingly, this was the first time that the squadron had operated on four consecutive nights. P/Os Cockbain, Churcher and Aytoun and Sgt O'Hara took off between 19.20 and 19.30, but P/O Aytoun suffered engine failure, and P/O Churcher lost his heating and oxygen systems, and both were compelled to return. This 50% failure rate was reflected in the force as a whole, and only half reached the target, where bombing was again scattered and

ineffective at a cost of four aircraft. Neither 106 Squadron crew was able to positively identify the aiming point, and delivered their bombs from around 12,000 feet onto the general area of the city. Both returned safely, and when Sgt O'Hara touched down at 00.30 in AT160, he brought an end to the 106 Squadron Hampden era.

The squadron adjutant took great pains to record the statistics of the Hampden operational era in the ORB, and according to his calculations the squadron had operated on 136 nights and eight days, launching 1,230 sorties, and accumulating 7,018 hours of operational flying time. Over eight hundred tons of bombs and incendiaries had been delivered, along with 180 mines, in return for the loss of fifty-five aircraft, a loss rate of 4.4% of those dispatched.

The squadron would not be required to operate now for nine nights as it prepared to go to war in Manchesters. During this period just two major operations were carried out by the Command, the first of them against Kiel on the night of the 12/13th. This was a relatively successful attack, which caused damage to two U-Boot yards and the naval dockyard. While this operation was in progress the squadron suffered its first Manchester incident. An undercarriage problem persuaded Sgt Carter and passengers to abandon an attempt to land at Coningsby, and instead to take to their parachutes over rural Lincolnshire, leaving L7474 to its inevitable fate. The crew survived their coming to earth without injury, but the Manchester was destroyed in the crash at Winceby, a few miles to the north-east of Coningsby. On the following night 135 aircraft set off for Cologne, and delivered an attack that was many times more effective than any previous raid on the Rhineland Capital. Over fifteen hundred houses were destroyed or damaged, and a number of war industry factories suffered a serious loss of production. Thereafter only very minor operational activity took place until the last third of the month, and it was during this time that 106 Squadron changed commanding officer and went to war in Manchesters for the first time.

On the 20th W/C Bob Allen departed the squadron at the end of a very successful tour as commanding officer, and he left behind him a spirit of efficiency and confidence, that future commanders would build on. His replacement was acting W/C Guy Gibson, whose finest hour lay more than twelve months hence, but who would use his time at 106 Squadron to enhance not only his own reputation, but also that of the squadron. Having completed a tour of operations with 83 Squadron during the first year of war, Gibson had managed to obtain a posting to 29 Squadron as a Beaufighter night fighter pilot, rather than be screened from operations altogether. While at 83 Squadron he had developed a reputation for "line-shooting", but he had impressed Harris, his A-O-C at 5 Group, with his desire to get at the enemy at every opportunity. His time on night fighters had been largely a period of frustration for him, as he failed to match the success of those who would become legendary in the role, like Cunningham and Braham. However, before leaving Bomber Command he had extracted from Harris the promise of a return to bombers in the future. Harris had recommended to AVM Slessor, the A-O-C of 5 Group, that 207 Squadron would be a suitable first command for Gibson, but allowed him to make his own decision, and it was through the main gate at Coningsby that Gibson swept on the day of Allen's departure.

Having redeemed that promise from Harris, Gibson immediately set about improving standards of efficiency in all areas of 106 Squadron, and he would managed to drag out of the troubled Manchester an operational serviceability, that other squadrons had been unable to achieve. It has to be said, of course, that by this time many of the serviceability problems had been ironed out, but the type was entering its final three months as a front-line bomber. By no means would Gibson be universally popular, and he admitted to an inability to relate to "other ranks", or to those whose jobs did not require them to put their lives at risk. Having spent his earliest years in India with authority over the native servants, he had a rigid view of class, and exercised it constantly during his service life. To those aircrew officers who managed to find a place in his inner circle, he was an inspirational leader, and he collected around him pilots with potential, who, under his tutelage, would achieve reputations in their own right.

As events turned out, Gibson's arrival coincided with the squadron's first operational foray in Manchesters. Seven crews had been briefed on the 19th for a daylight mining operation off the Frisians, but it was scrubbed and rescheduled for the following day. During the period of stand-down many new faces had arrived at Coningsby to fill the vacancies created by the seven-man crew required by the Manchester. Among the new arrivals were a number of pilots who would become mainstays of the squadron, like P/O Whamond, who came in from 97 Squadron and found himself on the Order of Battle for this maiden operation. Beside him in R5839, and flying as second pilot, was P/O John Hopgood, who would become a member of Gibson's inner circle and follow him to greater things a year hence. They took off between 14.35 and 15.00, and headed into very unfavourable weather conditions and a low cloud base. P/O Whamond's Manchester suffered a hydraulics system failure, and was forced to return early, and the problem led to a crash on landing, from which the crew walked away unhurt. P/O Worswick abandoned his sortie after encountering cloud at 200 feet and deciding that it would be impossible to locate the garden, and W/O Young did likewise after carrying out a long search. F/S Appleyard encountered identical conditions, but located his drop zone and delivered his mines in the correct position, and W/O Merralls was also successful. F/S Brown and P/O Loftus found cloud at sea level, and released their four mines on e.t.a after failing to find a pinpoint to work off.

In his classic book, Enemy Coast Ahead, Gibson recounts an event, which he claimed took place on the day of his arrival, but was actually on the 24th. It involved the former 106 Squadron C Flight commander, S/L "Tommy" Boylan, who was now with 97 Squadron, and had landed his Lancaster at Coningsby during the morning. Gibson must have looked with envy at the grace and power of the new bomber, born out of the failure of the Manchester. He knew it was only a matter of time before he and his crews got their hands on them, but it must have been hugely frustrating to have to wait. Gibson was watching that afternoon as Boylan began his take-off run for the short hop to Woodhall Spa, and knew instinctively that something was wrong. This was confirmed when the Lancaster failed to become unstuck, and careered out of control to collide with a crane near the bomb dump. Some time later Boylan appeared in the officers mess, where he ordered a pint, and downed it with the steadiest of hands, or so the story goes. Later that evening 106 Squadron dispatched two Manchesters, captained by P/O Picken, who had P/O Churcher alongside him, and P/O Whamond, for whom Hopgood again acted as second pilot, to join a 3 and 5 Group mining operation off Lorient, from which a 44 Squadron Lancaster became the first of the type to go missing. Both 106 Squadron crews easily identified their garden area in excellent visibility, and delivered four mines each into the correct position before returning safely.

Harris turned his attention back upon Essen on the following night, and sent a new record force to a single target. 254 aircraft answered the call, including four Manchesters from Coningsby, led by F/L Dunlop-Mackenzie. They got away from Coningsby between 19.55 and 20.10, and, despite encountering fine weather conditions, were thwarted by the ground haze. P/O Worswick dropped his bombs from 11,500 feet, but was unable to observe the results, while W/O Merralls was aided by the light of flares, and saw his bombs burst in the town. He reported heavy flak, and returned with slight damage to his aircraft. W/O Young bombed from 15,000 feet and observed a large burst in the town, and he also described the flak as heavy, but inaccurate. A total of 181 crews reported bombing in the target area, some even claiming hits on the Krupp complex. In fact, only a handful of bombs had fallen within the city, the majority having been drawn away by a decoy fire site at Rheinberg. The inevitable loss of its first Manchester occurred for 106 Squadron during this operation and involved L7390 and the crew of F/L Dunlop-Mackenzie. It was shot down into the ice-covered Ijsselmeer at 22.28 by a night fighter flown by the ace, Oblt Ludwig Becker of 6.NJG/2, and all on board were killed. The squadron had sent another aircraft on this night to lay mines in Kiel Bay, but F/S Cooke was forced to turn back after hydraulics leaks developed in the front and rear turrets.

106 Sqn officers with John Hopgood (third from right), Gray Healy (third from left) and Brian Ollivers.

Harris tried again at Essen on the night of the 26/27th, this time with a more modest force of 115 Wellingtons and Stirlings, but another failure ensued at a cost of almost 10% of those dispatched, and Harris was left wondering how he might overcome the problem of target identification over a blacked-out, often cloud-covered, hostile city nestling under a blanket of industrial haze. While this operation was in progress 106 Squadron sent five Manchesters for mining duties in the Gironde Estuary and Heligoland Bay in the Deodars and Yams gardens respectively. P/Os Loftus and Whamond and F/S Appleyard took off for the former, while F/S Cooke and P/O Stoffer were assigned to the latter, and all got away safely between 18.55 and 19.05. P/O Loftus described the weather as good at first but deteriorating, and he jettisoned his mines after failing to locate his target area. While trying to land at Exeter he overshot the runway, but no casualties were incurred. P/O Whamond's L7391 was damaged by light flak on the way out, and he deposited his mines in an alternative location. F/S Appleyard described an uneventful trip, during which he successfully delivered his mines into the briefed location. F/S Blake and P/O Stoffer had no problems in northern waters, and each planted four mines in the required location before returning safely.

Despite Harris's frustrations with the failures at Essen, he was certain of one thing. If he could provide his crews with easily identifiable pinpoints on the ground, they would be able put their bombs where intended, as had been the case at the Renault factory at Billancourt at the start of the month. The immediate answer to the problem was to target a city close to a coastline, to provide clear and unmistakeable pinpoints. Accordingly, on the night of the 28/29th, Harris dispatched a force of 234 aircraft to Lübeck, an historic Hanseatic (free trade) city at the western end of Germany's Baltic coast. The operation was to be conducted along the same lines as that against the Renault factory, which meant three waves, led by experienced crews in Gee-equipped aircraft. The target was actually beyond the range of Gee, but it would provide a useful navigation tool for as long as reception lasted. The defences were expected to be light, and this would enable crews to bomb from as low as 2,000 feet in conditions of bright moonlight. The layout of the city with narrow streets and half-timbered buildings in the Altstadt would be ideal for a fire-raising attack, and the predominantly incendiary bomb loads carried by the force reflected this intention. 106 Squadron detailed five crews, captained by F/Ss Appleyard and Cooke, W/Os Young and Merralls and P/O Worswick, and they took off between 21.40 and 22.00. On arrival at the target they found the town already burning furiously, and this hampered to a degree their ability to pick out the briefed aiming point. They dropped their 1,000 pounders from between 4,000 and 12,000 feet in perfect conditions of bright moonlight, and as F/S Appleyard was already at low level after bombing, he shot up searchlights on his way out of the target area. The outcome for Lübeck was precisely as Harris had intended, and an estimated 30% of the city's built-up area lay in ruins. This was the first major success for the area bombing policy.

On the following night, the squadron dispatched three Manchesters to lay mines off the Frisians, and P/O Stoffer and Sgt Carter experienced no difficulty in identifying the garden area in good conditions, and planting their vegetables as required. F/S Dimond and his crew failed to return in L7394, which was lost without trace, presumably in the North Sea. During the course of the month the squadron operated ten times by night and once by day, launching a total of eighteen Hampden sorties and twenty-seven by Manchesters for the loss of two of the latter.

April 1942

April would prove to be the busiest month of the war yet for 106 Squadron, and Operations began on the night of the 1/2nd with mining sorties by four Manchesters in the Gironde Estuary. S/L Stenner took off at 18.50 for the long round trip, but lost his starboard engine while over France, and had little choice but to return. According to the ORB he brought his mines home, which was a very courageous act considering the perils of flying a Manchester on one engine. F/S Cooke and W/Os Merralls and Young found the garden area with ease in fine weather and excellent visibility, although a strong wind was found to be troublesome. All delivered their four mines each into the correct location, and returned safely home. Minor operations occupied the Command as a whole for the first four nights, until Harris selected Cologne as the objective for a new record force of 263 aircraft on the night of the 5/6th. 106 Squadron supported the operation with four Manchesters, whose crews, like the majority of those involved, were briefed to aim for the Klöckner-Humboldt-Deutz works, which was manufacturing artillery. There was a late take-off for the Coningsby crews, either side of 01.00, and S/L Stenner was once more the senior pilot on duty. They flew to the target in ten-tenths cloud, but gaps appeared as they closed on the city, and this helped with identification. Visibility was moderate, and all four from the squadron bombed from between 10,000 and 12,000 feet in the face of heavy and accurate flak. Over two hundred crews claimed to have bombed as briefed, but bombing photographs revealed a different story, and it was clear that the attack had been scattered and largely ineffective.

On the following night Harris returned to Essen with a force of 157 aircraft, of which just two represented 106 Squadron. W/O Young and F/S Cooke took off at 00.30 and 00.40 respectively, and flew towards the Ruhr in complete cloud cover on a night of bad weather. Both bombed the approximate location of the target on e.t.a from 16,000 and 11,000 feet, again in the face of a hostile defence, and W/O Young's R5840 was damaged by flak. Only a third of the overall force battled the stormy conditions to reach the cloud-covered target, and thus another disappointing operation ensued at a cost of five aircraft. After a night's rest a new record force of 272 aircraft set off for Hamburg, among them five Manchesters from Coningsby. They took off between 22.10 and 22.30 on another night of storms and icing conditions, and P/O Loftus found his Manchester struggling to make height. He pressed on for a time, but ultimately jettisoned his bombs and returned home. F/S Brown was an estimated twenty minutes from Heligoland when his aircraft iced-up severely and began losing height rapidly. He also jettisoned his bomb load and turned back, leaving P/Os Picken, Whamond and W/O Young to press on towards the target. None was able to positively identify Hamburg, and bombs were delivered on estimated positions from between 11,000 and

Ready for battle. Aircrew at Coningsby await the arrival of transport to dispersal.

14,000 feet. Despite claims of attacking the target by 188 crews, very few bomb loads fell within the city, and damage was not significant.

There were four 106 Squadron crews among the 254 taking off for Essen late on the 10th. P/O Loftus was last away at 22.45, and returned seventy-six minutes later with W/T failure. F/S Brown and P/Os Picken and Whamond had taken off a few minutes before Loftus, and had been briefed to expect clear conditions over the Ruhr. What they actually encountered was five to eight-tenths cloud, which prevented identification of the target, and bombs were delivered on dead reckoning. Flak was described as heavy and accurate, and P/O Picken came home with a Manchester displaying the scars of battle, while P/O Whamond was held in searchlights for forty-five minutes during the return journey, but escaped damage. It was F/S Brown and crew who experience the most torrid time, after taking a serious flak hit, which appeared to be terminal for L7461. The pilot lost control and ordered his crew to bale out, while he fought to give them time to do so. During the course of this he regained control, and cancelled the bale-out order, by which time the navigator and wireless operator had already jumped. F/S Brown coaxed the Manchester back to English air space, and pulled off a crash-landing at Martlesham Heath, near Ipswich, without casualty to the occupants. It had been yet another scattered and ineffective attack, which, according to local authority reports, had destroyed a dozen houses.

Two nights later Harris tried for the final time in the current series to deliver a decisive blow against Essen. 251 aircraft were made ready, among them five Manchesters representing 106 Squadron, and they took off between 22.10 and 22.40. P/O Whamond experienced excessive fuel consumption and an inability to maintain height, and turned back a little over an hour into the outward flight. It was a starlit night, and clear of cloud over the Ruhr, but ground haze hampered identification, and only P/O Picken was able to bomb in the general target area in the face of intense flak and searchlight activity. W/O Merralls failed to locate the aiming point, and dropped his bombs on a flak concentration south-east of the target. P/Os Loftus and Worswick chose Koblenz as an alternative target, and were, therefore, not among the 173 crews claiming to have bombed the primary. A number of bombs did hit the Krupp works, but generally the level of destruction fell woefully short of what might be expected from such a large force. Eight operations had now been directed at Essen since the first one in early March, and 1,555 sorties had been launched for the loss of sixty-four aircraft, one more than the number of civilians killed. While this operation was in progress, S/L Nelms carried out his first Manchester freshman sortie, delivering leaflets over Lille.

The night of the 13/14th was one of minor operations, during which 106 Squadron committed five Manchesters to mining sorties in Heligoland Bay, four of them with pilots undertaking their first Manchester operations as crew captain. F/L Robertson was a Rhodesian, like Whamond, and had arrived at 106 Squadron on the same day as Gibson. He led them off at 20.35 along with P/O Hopgood in L7317 and L7319 respectively, and they were followed five minutes later by F/S Appleyard and Sgt Hurd in R5796 and R5840. Finally, at 21.00, Sgt Young lifted off in L7463. The weather was good, and the visibility excellent, but despite this, Sgt Hurd was unable to locate his garden after a long search, and he brought his four mines home. The others all located their respective gardens without difficulty, and planted their vegetables in the correct positions.

On the following night Harris returned to the Ruhr, this time to Dortmund, upon which he unleashed a force of 208 aircraft, including just two Manchesters from 106 Squadron, containing the crews of P/Os Worswick and Whamond. They departed Coningsby at 22.40 and 22.45 respectively, and headed into clear skies over the Ruhr. The usual thick blanket of ground haze prevented an accurate identification of the target, but P/O Worswick found the general area and saw his bombs burst in the southern part of the town. P/O Whamond, meanwhile, had not been able pinpoint the target, and dropped his bombs onto a built-up area before returning safely home. L7317 had strayed well off track during its homebound journey, and was critically short of fuel as it approached the south coast with the intention of landing at Lee-on-Solent naval air station. The tanks ran dry a mile short, and P/O Worswick carried out a successful ditching in the Solent, from which he and his crew emerged unscathed. Sadly, it would be a temporary reprieve for this crew. This operation had been the largest effort yet against Dortmund, but it went the way of the others directed at targets in this region, and bombs were sprayed over a forty-mile stretch.

Harris tried again twenty-four hours later, with a force of 152 aircraft, which included five 106 Squadron Manchesters led by S/L Nelms. They took off either side of midnight, and flew into ten-tenths cloud, heavy rain and severe icing conditions, which inevitably took their toll. S/L Nelms was unable to locate the target, or even maintain height, and he jettisoned his load and turned for home. F/S Brown searched long and hard for a pinpoint, but ultimately gave up and also dumped his bombs "safe". F/S Appleyard reported cloud from 14,000 feet down to 2,500 feet, and he, too, abandoned his sortie, but he brought his bombs back. Sgt Young dropped his bombs on a flak concentration, which he thought was at Cologne, and only W/O Merralls was able to convince himself that he was in the correct general area when he released his bombs through the clouds from 9,000 feet, and believed that they fell to the west of the target. A little over half of the crews from the original force reported reaching the target area, and damage was minimal.

Just two 106 Squadron Manchesters were involved in operations on the night of the 16/17th, and their task was to plant vegetables in the Gironde Estuary. The crews of P/O Picken and the newly commissioned P/O Scatchard took off at 20.50 in R5796 and L7485 respectively, and headed for the south coast. The weather was fine with good visibility, and, apart from a little inaccurate flak at the French coast, P/O Picken enjoyed an uneventful trip, during which he located the garden and delivered his four mines accurately. L7485 did not return to Coningsby, and it was learned later that it had gone down in the English Channel. The bodies of P/O Scatchard and four of his crew eventually washed ashore in France, but two were never recovered. This was an experienced crew, and its presence in the squadron would be missed.

If the Germans had not yet had a close-up view of a Lancaster, they now had seven smouldering wrecks to pick over following the epic and audacious daylight raid by elements of 44 and 97 Squadrons on the M.A.N diesel engine factory at Augsburg during the afternoon of the 17th. That night, and for a record sixth night in a row, 106 Squadron found itself called into action, when contributing two Manchesters to an attack on Hamburg. P/Os Hopgood and Stoffer took off at 23.00, each carrying what the ORB describes as fourteen 250lb oil bombs. The Luftwaffe had used similar weapons as incendiary devices during the Blitz. Both aircraft arrived over the city at 12,000 feet in a cloudless sky with good visibility, and watched their bombs burst in the town area. Over a hundred other crews claimed to have bombed the city, and it was, in view of the recent run of total failures, a modestly successful raid, which started thirty-three large fires if nothing else. After a rare night off the squadron contributed three Manchesters to a largish mining effort in the Nectarines garden around the Frisians on the night of the 19/20th. S/L Nelms, F/S Appleyard and Sgt Hurd were airborne by 21.00, but Sgt Hurd found visibility to be very poor, and he was unable to locate his garden. S/L Nelms described the night as very dark, and made a timed run from Terschelling to deliver his four mines into the correct position. F/S Appleyard used similar tactics, and his rear gunner shot out searchlights on Terschelling.

It was a month into his tour before Gibson felt himself to be fully converted to the Manchester, but wasted no time once he was ready. His first Manchester operation was carried out in L7418 on the night of the 22/23rd, when the squadron put up six Manchesters to lay mines in northern waters, Gibson and S/L Stenner in Radishes, which was the Fehmarn Belt, and F/L Robertson, P/O Worswick and the newly commissioned P/O Cooke and Sgt Young in Quinces, the Kiel Bay area of the Great Belt. They took off from Coningsby between 20.20 and 20.25 in good weather with a half moon and clear visibility. Gibson used Fehmarn island as a pinpoint for his run to the garden, and delivered his four mines into the correct position. S/L Stenner experienced a mechanical failure, and decided to shorten the trip by dropping his mines in the Hawthorn garden off Esbjerg as an alternative. Sgt Young's port engine began to give cause for concern, and he also chose the Hawthorn garden as a suitable recipient of his vegetables, as did P/O Worswick, who failed to locate his briefed drop zone. F/L Robertson found a pinpoint on the Danish coast, and made a successful run from there, and P/O Cooke also experienced no difficulty in fulfilling his brief.

In an attempt to repeat the success of Lübeck, Harris launched a series of four raids on consecutive nights against Rostock, another Baltic port, beginning on the 23/24th. An added incentive was the presence on the southern outskirts of the town of the Heinkel aircraft factory, to which eighteen aircraft were sent, while 143 others targeted the town. 106 Squadron dispatched six Manchesters to hit the aircraft factory, and they departed Coningsby between 21.50 and 22.00 with S/L Nelms the senior pilot on duty. They flew out at what, for the time, was low-level for a night raid, and approached the target at between 4,000 and 5,000 feet in moonlit, cloudless conditions which afforded excellent visibility. S/L Nelms was able to identify the runway and factory buildings, and watched his bombs burst across the target. P/O Hopgood

106 Sqn started to re-equip with the iconic Lancaster in April 1942. ZN-E, R5676, is seen shortly after arriving at Coningsby.

delivered his six 1,000 pounders from 4,500 feet, and also saw them explode across the target. F/S Appleyard did not observe the results of his efforts as he was taking evasive action to avoid the light flak, which damaged his aircraft slightly. W/O Young and Sgt Hurd reported similar experiences, and these five crews returned home confident that they had inflicted massive damage on the factory. L7463 had an overheating engine, which eventually erupted into flames over Denmark. P/O Stoffer ordered his crew to take to their parachutes, and they reached the ground safely to be taken prisoner. He was probably attempting a forced landing when the Manchester broke up at low level and crashed, and he failed to survive. In Enemy Coast Ahead, Gibson relates being in the ops room that night, watching a pretty WAAF climbing the step ladder to write landing times on the large wall-mounted operations board. She turned out to be Mary Stoffer, and Gibson ended up driving the distraught young woman home at the end of her shift.

The ORB described the enormous damage inflicted upon the factory, and when the reconnaissance photos were eventually posted, the participating crews would be incredulous to discover that it had escaped damage. It seems that the photos were not immediately available for scrutiny at squadron level, as the ORB would report the second attack, that night, as producing as much damage as the first one. In fact, it was accurate, in that neither landed a bomb on the factory buildings. The attack on the town had also been disappointing, and had fallen between two and six miles from the Altstadt aiming point. Five 106 Squadron Manchesters were detailed to accompany 120 other aircraft in a return to Rostock on the night of the 24/25th, but the ORB lists only three as taking off, and states in the summary that two experienced engine problems. One must assume that this occurred before departure, and that their participation was scrubbed. F/L Robertson was the senior pilot on duty as they took off at 22.00 on another night of excellent weather conditions and visibility. They experienced no problems in identifying the target, and all three delivered their bombs from between 5,000 and 6,000 feet, observing them to burst among the factory buildings. Again, it seems, they were mistaken, as the factory escaped damage, but the town did not, and its centre suffered a great deal of destruction.

F/O Cockbain completed his first tour with 106 Sqn before going on to complete a second with 44 Sqn, where he achieved the rank of Squadron Leader. Posted to Ferry Command, S/Ldr. Cockbain was flying a Short Stirling MK III EH 988 on a flight from RAF Syerston on 14th January 1945. After take-off the aircraft suffered an engine fire. S/Ldr. Cockbain attempted to land at Hucknall, Nottinghamshire, but he was killed when the aircraft crashed (Simon Sanders).

On the following night Gibson carried out his second operation with the squadron, when leading a contingent of five 106 Squadron Manchesters back to the Heinkel factory in R5770. They departed Coningsby either side of 22.00 on yet another night of clear conditions and bright moonlight, but F/S Young was forced to turn back when L7276 refused to run on the weak mixture necessary to make the fuel last. Gibson made a level run at 4,500 feet at an indicated air speed of 220 mph, and dropped his bombs onto the target. He was unable to accurately assess his work because of smoke, but there was no doubt in his mind that the factory had been hit. P/O Cockbain, who had Whamond alongside him as second pilot, found the target obscured by smoke as he attacked from 5,000 feet, and he was uncertain as to where his bombs had fallen, but believed them to be on the primary target. Sgt Herd and F/S Heddon were too busy taking evasive action to observe the fall of their bombs, but they believed them to be accurate. This time they were correct, and the remainder of the force had also produced further extensive damage in the town. The fourth raid by 109 aircraft included another five Manchesters from 106 Squadron, and P/Os Cooke, Worswick and Picken were the senior pilots on duty. They got away shortly after 22.00, but L7457 developed intercom problems, and F/S Browne turned back. The force of a little over a hundred aircraft was divided roughly in two to attack the town and the factory. P/O Picken was caught in searchlights and subjected to intense flak, forcing him to take violent evasive action, following which he was unable to locate the target and jettisoned his bombs. P/O Worswick was attacked by a JU88 after bombing, but he successfully evaded it without sustaining damage. Both sections of the attack achieved accuracy, and by the end of the four-raid series 1,765 buildings had been destroyed, and more than five hundred seriously damaged. This amounted to an estimated 60% of the town's built-up area being reduced to ruins. It was also the first time that the word Terrorangriff, or terror raid, appeared in German reports.

The first Lancaster to be taken on charge by the squadron was L7569, which arrived from 44 Squadron on the 28th, and this made the squadron the fifth in the Command to receive the type. In the meantime, operations would continue with Manchesters, and the final operation of the month for 106 Squadron was mounted that night, when five crews were sent mining in northern waters off Kiel harbour, Kiel Bay and the Fehmarn belt. Four took off shortly after 22.30, but the recently promoted F/O Cockbain suffered W/T failure, and he was back home within three hours. The remaining three found their respective gardens without difficulty in favourable weather conditions, and all returned safely. It was after midnight before P/O Loftus took off, but he also fell foul of W/T failure, and was forced to abandon his sortie. Other elements of 5 Group took part in bombing operations against Kiel that night, and on the Gnome & Rhone aero engine factory at Gennevilliers in Paris on the following night. During the course of the month the squadron had operated on eighteen nights, and dispatched forty-four sorties for the loss of three aircraft and two crews.

May 1942

The new month began with a major mining effort by 3 and 5 Groups on the night of the 2/3rd, when 106 Squadron contributed eight Manchesters to an overall force of ninety-six aircraft. Getting eight Manchesters off the ground for a single operation was a new record for the squadron, and something of a feat. The type's serviceability record generally precluded any possibility of achieving a maximum effort, and this night's performance was very much to the credit of Gibson. Various garden areas were involved from the Baltic to the Brittany coast, and the 106 Squadron contingent plied its trade in the Forget-me-not and Wallflower gardens off Kiel. They took off in a ten-minute slot to 22.30, and reached their respective target areas to find clear skies and good visibility. Four crews planted their four mines each in the required location, while two others, one with engine problems, selected Hawthorn as an alternative. Just two aircraft were lost from the night's activities, and both were from Coningsby. L7399 crashed in Denmark, killing F/S Young and all but a gunner and the wireless operator, and they fell into enemy hands. They were soon joined in captivity by F/S Hurd and his crew, who had survived the coming-to-earth of R5840 on the German island of Pelworm after it had been damaged by flak.

On the following night a forecast of unfavourable weather persuaded Harris to send a modest force of eighty aircraft to Hamburg. Fifty-four of them reached the target area to bomb through cloud, and despite the odds stacked against them produced a remarkably effective raid that started over fifty large fires and bombed out more than sixteen hundred people. 5 Group supported the operation with a token force of five Hampdens, and 106 Squadron did not take part. A series of operations against Stuttgart and its resident Bosch factory on consecutive nights began on the 4/5th, at the hands of a force of 120 aircraft, but 106 Squadron would not be involved. Instead, on this night, it sent five crews to lay mines in the Rosemary region off Sylt, and Gibson led them away at 21.15 in L7378, with the recently promoted F/Os Whamond and Hopgood and P/Os Aytoun and Cockbain in his wake. They arrived in the target area to find some cloud but good visibility, and all were able to deliver their four mines each into the briefed locations. In addition to these sorties, P/O Duff had departed Coningsby at 21.55 to drop leaflets (nickels) on Amiens, but a faulty compass forced him to give up and return home.

The nickelling of Amiens was rescheduled for the night of the 6/7th, and this time P/Os Duff and Churcher were able to deliver between them 320 bundles of what Harris referred to as toilet paper. The first Stuttgart operation, which had taken place on a cloud-covered target, had failed, partly because of a decoy fire site, and had scattered bombs across the city. The second raid took place on the following night in clear conditions, but this time ground haze and the decoy site caused the bombing to fall outside of the city. The third attack, on this night, was a carbon copy of the second one, but at least the loss of ten aircraft from 295 sorties over the three operations could be seen as modest. Mining in northern waters off Denmark and Kiel occupied the night of the 7/8th, and 106 Squadron supported it with four Manchesters assigned to the Rosemary garden off Sylt. They departed Coningsby either side of midnight, but P/O Aytoun was forced to turn back twenty minutes after crossing the coast when his starboard engine failed. The others reached their respective target areas in clear conditions and good visibility, and used the islands of Sylt and Pellworm as pinpoints from which to make their runs.

Having been successful at Lübeck and Rostock on the Baltic coast in recent weeks, the Baltic port of Warnemünde was selected for attention on the night of the 8/9th, partly because of the presence nearby of another Heinkel aircraft factory. The 5 Group element among the 193-strong force was assigned to the factory, which was considered suitable for a low-level attack. The 106 Squadron contingent of six Manchesters took off either side of 22.00 led by Gibson in R5770, with the newly promoted F/L Whamond, F/L Robertson, F/O Hopgood, P/O Cockbain and W/O Merralls close behind. P/O Cockbain turned back with an electrical fault, and F/L Whamond had to nurse his port engine to get as far as the Danish coast, where he finally gave up and also abandoned his sortie. The others arrived in the target area to find clear skies and excellent visibility, but also an intense searchlight and flak response. A huge concentration of searchlights had been laid horizontally to dazzle approaching aircraft, but Gibson was able to carry out a straight and level run, and believed his bombs had fallen across the target. Robertson and Hopgood went in at 2,000 feet, and also thought they were on the mark, although they were unable to make an accurate assessment because of the need to take evasive action. W/O Merralls adopted a glide approach, delivering his bombs from 4,500 feet and observing them burst across the buildings of the factory. The operation was actually something of a disaster, which cost nineteen aircraft, including four Lancasters from 44 Squadron, one of which contained its newly appointed commanding officer. There was not even any confirmation of a successful outcome in compensation.

Thereafter, 106 Squadron stayed at home for a week, during which time the crews continued with the ground-based part of their conversion training on Lancasters. The Command, too, remained largely dormant, and most of the small-scale operations that did take place were devoted to mining. Hopgood's rapid rise through the ranks continued, as he now became a flight lieutenant, and this was a sure sign of his popularity with Gibson and his acceptance into the inner circle. Hopgood, W/O Young and F/S Appleyard were sent mining off Sylt on the night of the 16/17th, and all returned safely after successfully planting four mines each in the briefed locations. On the 19th Sgt McHardy and crew took off in L7418 to carry out a navigation exercise over the route Base-Aberystwyth-Lands End-Hurn-Base, and were last seen off the Pembrokeshire coast. They failed to arrive back, and it is assumed that the Manchester crashed somewhere in the Irish Sea. Also on this day the first flight took place of a 106 Squadron Lancaster. That night almost two hundred aircraft took off for the first major operation since the Warnemünde debacle. The target was Mannheim, for which 106 Squadron contributed a single Manchester containing the crew of P/O Cockbain. They took off at 22.45, and had reached the Belgian coast when the oxygen system failed and the mid-upper gunner passed out. The cause of the problem could not be located, and the sortie had to be abandoned. In keeping with the performances of the period, most of the bombs fell into open

Guy Gibson with a colleague (Simon Sanders).

Gibson in typical pose with colleagues from 106 Sqn (Simon Sanders).

Guy Gibson and his crew. From left: unnamed; Hutch' Hutchinson; Gibson; Frank Russell; Brian Oliver and Johnny Wickins . Gibson carried a stick because of gout (Simon Sanders).

From left: Johnny Wickins, Guy Gibson and CO McGregor (Simon Sanders).

From left: S/Ldr John Searby, W/C Guy Gibson and S/Ldr Peter Ward Hunt (Simon Sanders).

country, and the operation was a failure. Meanwhile, the crews of P/Os Duff and Churcher, who were still considered to be freshmen, joined an attack on the port of St Nazaire. The latter found the target under clear skies but shrouded in mist and well-defended, and he delivered his bombs from 7,000 feet, observing them to burst in the target area. P/O Duff was unable to locate the aiming point despite searching, but selected a pinpoint and dropped his bombs on e.t.a on a flak concentration. Back home it was discovered that he had produced an outstanding photograph of his twelve 500 pounders bursting in a stick across the inland docks at Nantes, some miles to the east of the intended target.

Sea mines ready for loading onto Lancaster W4118, ZN-Y. Note the Avro Manchester in the background.

There was little activity during the final third of May as Harris prepared for his masterstroke, Operation Millennium, which, whatever the outcome, would probably decide the fate of his Command one way or the other. As an advocate of the area bombing policy, Harris understood the need to overwhelm the enemy's defences and emergency services by concentrating the maximum possible number of aircraft over the target in the shortest possible time frame. He also needed a success or two, and perhaps a dose of symbolism, to provide him with ammunition to throw back at the detractors. Most important, however, was the need to safeguard his supply of new aircraft in the face of calls for them to be diverted to other theatres. When taking up his appointment he had stated the case for being given four thousand heavy bombers with which to win the war. There was never the slightest chance of getting them, but he needed to demonstrate that Bomber Command was the only worthwhile recipient, and thereby ensure that those earmarked for him, were not spirited away to Coastal Command or the Middle East. Out of this was born the Thousand Plan, Operation Millennium, the commitment of a thousand aircraft in one night to a single target, for which Hamburg was pencilled in.

One small fly in the ointment was the fact that Harris didn't have a thousand frontline aircraft to call upon, and to attain the magic figure he would need the goodwill and support of other Commands, principally Coastal and Flying Training, and this was forthcoming initially, and confirmed in letters dated the 22nd and 23rd of May respectively. However, after objections by the Admiralty, Coastal Command withdrew its contribution of over a hundred aircraft, but sent along a handful of navigators to help out. Undaunted, Harris, or more probably his affable and very able deputy, AM Sir Robert Saundby, scraped together every airframe capable of something resembling controlled flight, and assembled them on airfields in the North, the Midlands and East Anglia, and pulled in the screened crews from their instructional duties.

106 Squadron began high-level training in Lancasters on the 25th, the day on which orders were received to stand by for a "special effort", and to restrict flying so as not to impair serviceability. In accordance, all crews were recalled from leave. On the 26th Gibson undertook his first flight in a Lancaster, with B Flight commander, S/L Stenner, alongside him to assist in his conversion. Within days, however, Gibson had

Squadron Leader John 'Dim' Wooldridge (Simon Sanders).

fallen ill, although the precise nature of his indisposition has never been established. He would spend a frustrating two weeks in Rauceby Hospital and three more convalescing, and would miss the impending series of massive operations under the Thousand Plan. Gibson hated to miss out on any innovation, and the forthcoming Operation Millennium would be the largest employment to date of the bomber stream, the tactic that would be standard practice for the remainder of the war.

As the build-up of the giant armada took place, it gave rise to much speculation, and with the days ticking by inexorably towards the end of May, and the weather seemingly not entering into the spirit of the occasion, a genuine risk arose that it might draw attention to itself, and thereby compromise security. "Morning prayers" took place in an atmosphere of high tension at Harris's High Wycombe HQ on the 30th, and the planning room awaited the pronouncement from Harris's chief meteorological adviser, Magnus Spence. His initial forecast was of swathes of cloud blanketing Germany's north-west, but he went on to predict a break in the cloud over the Rhineland, and a chance of moonlight after midnight. Thus did the fickle finger of fate turn away from Hamburg and point instead at Cologne, and in so doing decree that the Rhineland capital would have the dubious honour of hosting the first one thousand bomber raid in history.

The lull in operations had allowed 106 Squadron sufficient time to work up on its Lancasters, and this epic occasion would provide a fitting operational baptism. The operation was to conform to the now established pattern of three waves, with the genuine heavy bombers bringing up the rear. The first away of an eventual 1047 assorted aircraft either side of 23.00 would be the Wellingtons, Hampdens and Whitleys of the training units along with the front line Wellingtons equipped with Gee. Some of the older training hacks were long past their best, and would take somewhat reluctantly into the air, lifted more, perhaps, by the enthusiasm of their crews than by the power of their engines. A number of these, unable to climb to a respectable height, would fall easy prey to the defences, or just drop out of the sky through mechanical breakdown. 106 Squadron prepared nine Lancasters on their maiden operation, plus two borrowed from 97 Squadron, along with five Manchesters, while two of the spare Manchesters would be borrowed by 50 Squadron, one of them, as events turned out, being involved in the award of a posthumous Victoria Cross.

Never one to be camera-shy, Wing Commander Guy Gibson poses happily with crews who have just returned from the first 'Thousand Bomber' raid, on Cologne. In the background can be seen two Avro Manchesters, five of which had taken part in Operation Millennium, along with nine Lancasters.

At briefings on bomber stations from north to south, crews were coming to terms with the prospect of being one of many competing for the same airspace at the same time as they funnelled towards the aiming point. They were assured that statisticians had predicted that just two aircraft would be involved in a collision, and the story goes that the cry went up from a "wag" at the back of every room asking, "Do they know which two?" Among the new arrivals at Coningsby during the month was S/L John "Dim" Wooldridge, one of the great characters to grace Bomber Command. He had been posted in from 207 Squadron at Bottesford, shortly to succeed S/L Stenner as B Flight commander, and Millennium was to be his maiden operation with 106 Squadron. He took off at 23.59 in L7579, six minutes ahead of S/L Robertson in R5573, and these, along with S/L Stenner in R5844, were the senior pilots on duty on this momentous occasion. The other participating crews were those of F/Ls Hopgood and Whamond, P/Os Picken, Cooke, Worswick and Healey, and W/Os Young and Merralls in Lancasters, which all got away either side of midnight, while the Manchester crews of P/Os Aytoun, Cockbain, Duff and Churcher and F/S Appleyard had actually taken off earlier, between 23.10 and 23.20. It was to be a disappointing night for Hopgood, whose intercom failed shortly after take-off, and despite desperate attempts to rectify the problem, was defeated and forced to return home. The remainder pressed on in good weather conditions, and found the target precisely as predicted by Magnus Spence, clear of cloud and under bright moonlight. S/L Wooldridge bombed at 01.45 from 12,000 feet, and watched his bombs fall among already-burning buildings, and it was a similar story as far as the other squadron crews were concerned. Bombing took place from 15,000 feet by F/L Whamond, down to 7,500 by F/S Appleyard, and all returned safely home, W/O Merralls the last to land at 05.50.

By any standards at any time, Operation Millennium was a major success, which destroyed over 3,300 buildings and damaged thousands more. It was a bold move at this stage of the war to attempt to funnel a thousand aircraft across an aiming point in ninety minutes, and it worked to perfection. True, it was achieved at a cost of a new record of forty-one aircraft, but in conditions that were favourable to attackers and defenders alike, and in view of the scale of the success, it was an acceptable, and, indeed, a sustainable figure. Two of the Manchesters borrowed by 50 Squadron, L7301 and L7456, were among the casualties. The former crashed in Belgium after sustaining severe flak damage over Cologne, and the pilot, F/O Manser, sacrificed his life in allowing his six crew colleagues to parachute to safety. All but one evaded capture, and their testimony led to the award to Manser of a posthumous VC. An interesting postscript to this incident involved P/O Horsley, the wireless operator/gunner in Manser's crew. He eventually re-mustered as a pilot, and joined 617 Squadron with a crew of his own in November 1944. During the course of the month the squadron had operated on seven nights, and dispatched forty-nine sorties, thirty-seven by Manchester and eleven by Lancaster, for the operational loss of two Manchesters and one during training.

June 1942

While his giant force was still assembled, Harris wanted to use it again as soon as possible, and selected Essen as the appropriate target for what he hoped would be another successful night on the 1/2nd. As a result of the losses from Cologne and the unavailability of aircraft undergoing repair 956 aircraft presented themselves for take-off late on the 1st. The operation would be conducted in similar fashion to that on Cologne, with experienced crews in 3 Group Wellingtons leading the way with an abundance of flares for illumination. 106 Squadron made ready nine Lancasters and six Manchesters, and the latter took off first between 23.05 and 23.55, to be followed by the Lancasters immediately afterwards in a fifty minute slot. S/L Robertson had now been installed as the successor to S/L Nelms as commander of A Flight, and he and S/L Wooldridge were the senior pilots on duty. They arrived in the target area to find a layer of low cloud concealing the ground, and it proved impossible to positively identify Essen. S/L Robertson aimed his bombs at a large fire believed to be in the city, and he observed bursts which could not be plotted. F/L Whamond climbed above the cloud to bomb from 16,000 feet on what was estimated to be Essen. S/L Wooldridge bombed on a Gee-fix from 13,000 feet, and claimed to see bomb bursts in the western part of the target. Others delivered their loads on e.t.a, and all but one returned to report having little clue as to what went on beneath the clouds.

Absent from debriefing was the crew of P/O Worswick, who had been called back from leave to take part in the Thousand raids. R5844, which actually belonged to the Conversion Flight, came down in a suburb of Essen after being hit by flak. There were no survivors from this experienced crew, and this was the first of many Lancasters of 106 Squadron to be lost in the remaining three years of war. P/O Worswick held a DFC, and his navigator and bomb-aimer, W/O Robson and P/O Bake respectively, were holders of the DFM. It will be recalled that this crew had survived the ditching in the Solent in mid April, and their loss would be felt at Coningsby. Two nights earlier, Worswick's wireless operator had been P/O Bob Hutchison, who would find himself a respected member of Gibson's "Chastise" crew a year hence. Sadly, the scale of the failure of this operation was equal to the scale of success at Cologne, as the usual problems of target location prevented the majority of the force from finding the city. Bombs were scattered all over the Ruhr, with only eleven houses classified as destroyed in Essen, and all this was in return for the loss of thirty-one aircraft.

A follow-up raid by 195 aircraft twenty-four hours later was just as disappointing and cost fourteen aircraft. 5 Group put up thirty-nine Lancasters and Hampdens, but left 106 Squadron at home. The night of the 3/4th was devoted to Bremen, which had remained largely unmolested for seven months. 106 Squadron sent two freshman crews in Manchesters as part of an overall force of 170 aircraft, and they were to act as fire-raisers, each carrying 1,260 4lb incendiaries. Sgts Brinkhurst and Jones were both flying as crew captains for the first time, and they took off at 23.10, and returned safely at 04.00 to report bombing the target from 10,000 and 9,000 feet respectively, and observing their incendiaries to ignite in the target area. Most of the other returning crews were less than enthusiastic about the probable outcome, but in fact, this was the most destructive raid to date on this target. Damage was visited upon residential and industrial buildings, and there were hits on U-Boot construction yards, an aircraft factory and the harbour. The freshman crew of Sgt Crowfoot had been detailed to take part in this operation, but their Manchester became unserviceable at the last minute. Their chance came twenty-four hours later, when they were sent to deliver nickels on Amiens, a task which they completed successfully.

On the 5th the squadron was ordered to stand down from operations in order to devote all of its energy to the conversion programme. During this period further attempts were made on Essen, on the nights of the 5/6th, 8/9th and 16/17th, and each failed to produce anything other than scattered and ineffective bombing. The five operations mounted against Essen during these first sixteen nights of June had produced no industrial damage, but cost the Command eighty-four aircraft. Emden was the month's other principal target, and suffered extensive damage on the night of the 6/7th, but escaped relatively lightly during the follow-up raids on the 19/20th, 20/21st and 22/23rd. Throughout this period 106 Squadron remained off the Order of Battle, and on the 10th, S/L John Wooldridge was appointed to command B Flight. Wooldridge was an enigmatic character with great creative abilities as an author and composer, and he preferred to spend his nights off indulging in these pastimes, rather than carouse in the mess bar or local watering holes. As such, he was the kind of person that Gibson found difficult to fathom and of which he was faintly suspicious. Wooldridge was a good organiser, was popular with the crews, and sported a luxuriant "wizard prang" moustache in the finest traditions of the heroic aviator. Perhaps most important was the fact that he was a seasoned campaigner, having served with 44 and 61 Squadrons during 1940, and had completed forty-one operations by that autumn. Within a year he was back on operations at 61 Squadron, before the brief spell with 207 Squadron preceded his arrival at 106. He would never be invited into Gibson's inner circle, and would certainly have declined the opportunity, had it been offered. There would always be a degree of strain between the two men, and one suspects that Wooldridge employed his superior intellect to unsettle Gibson. On the 15th, perhaps, as a break from the intensity of conversion training, but mostly to provide a morale-boost for the workforce, a party of twenty-eight pilots from Coningsby visited the Rolls Royce factory at Derby, where the Merlin engine was being built.

On the 25th the ground crews were hard at work preparing the squadron for the third and final thousand bomber raid, which was to be launched against Bremen that night. The Command was able to put together a force of 960 aircraft of ten types, including Blenheims, Bostons and Mosquitos from 2 Group, and 106

Oxygen is loaded aboard a Lancaster before a raid in Summer 1942.

Squadron's contribution amounted to seventeen Lancasters and two Manchesters. It would have been a record-equalling twenty aircraft had one Manchester not become unserviceable at the last minute. This would prove to be the final operation of the war for the Manchester, and all remaining examples with operational squadrons would find their way to a new life in training units. Churchill played his part on this night by ordering Coastal Command to participate, and a contingent of 102 Hudsons and Wellingtons duly took off in what was classed as a separate operation. Whatever the official classification of the attacking force, the numbers converging on Bremen on this night amounted to 1,067, including five contributed by Army Co-operation Command, and thus exceeded those dispatched to Cologne three and a half weeks earlier.

The 106 Squadron contingent took off either side of midnight, with S/Ls Robertson and Wooldridge once more the senior pilots on duty. Flying as second pilot to S/L Robertson was P/O Cooper, another who would join 617 Squadron, although after Operation Chastise. Sadly, he was destined to lose his life in April 1944 during a Cheshire-led operation to Munich. It turned into another disappointing night for Hopgood, who lost both starboard engines shortly after crossing the Dutch coast, and had to turn back. For the others funnelling in a crowded sky towards the city of Bremen, there was brilliant moonlight, but a layer of low cloud almost completely obscured the ground and made identification of aiming points impossible. S/L Robertson bombed on e.t.a, which happened to be over a flak concentration, but he was not able to determine the outcome. Bill Whamond came down to 8,000 feet to bomb on dead reckoning, and observed bursts beneath the clouds and the start of a fire. In contrast, P/O Churcher let his bombs go from 15,000 feet, aimed at the glow of a large fire, and P/O "Wimpy" Wellington, who was undertaking his first operation as a Lancaster captain, dropped his from 12,000 feet, and was certain they fell in Bremen. Sgt Jones recorded the lowest bombing height of 7,000 feet, where his Manchester must have been in danger from the hardware falling from above. Happily, he dodged the lot, and was one of three crews last back with a landing time of 05.50. His wireless operator on this night was the previously-mentioned Bob Hutchison, who was one of those dogged characters that suffered from air-sickness. He would "throw up" into his RAF-issue "spewbag", and then get on with his job without fuss or complaint.

While not equalling the success at Cologne, the attack on Bremen far surpassed the performance at Essen, with 572 houses destroyed and more than six thousand damaged to some extent. A modest amount of industrial damage was also achieved, but the night brought a new record loss of forty-eight aircraft, although 106 Squadron came through unscathed. The fifty-four tons of bombs delivered by 106 Squadron on this night represented a new 5 Group record. The 26th brought a well-deserved DSO for S/L Stenner, to add to his DFC. It was reward for his great courage, skill and devotion to duty during his second tour of operations, and for his leadership while serving as a flight commander with 106 Squadron. The month ended with two follow-up raids on Bremen by smaller numbers of aircraft, the first taking place on the night of 27/28th in the absence of a 106 Squadron contribution. On the following night the squadron sent seven Lancasters with freshman crews to mine the Gironde Estuary. They departed Coningsby in a fifteen minute slot to 23.00, and all reached the target area under cloudless skies and in bright moonlight. They experienced no difficulty in establishing their positions, and each delivered five mines into their briefed locations before returning safely home.

The second Bremen follow-up took place on the night of the 29/30th, when weather conditions were less favourable, and the seven participating 106 Squadron crews were ordered to bomb on a Gee-fix. They took off either side of midnight as part of a force of 253 aircraft, and this was the first time that four-engine aircraft had represented more than 50% of the overall numbers on a major operation. S/L Wooldridge was the senior 106 Squadron pilot on duty, and he had beside him as second pilot P/O David Shannon, a twenty-year-old Australian, who had a glittering operational career ahead of him. The target was covered by nine to ten-tenths cloud, but the burst of the 4,000lb "cookies" could be seen. Wooldridge bombed from 10,000 feet, and was chased out of the target area by two enemy night fighters, but they were shaken off. Even from 15,000 feet F/S Appleyard was able to observe the flash of his bombs detonating, and he believed himself to be over the city at the time. Each of the Bremen raids added to the recent damage, and on this night there was a particular emphasis on industrial premises. The Focke-Wulf factory and the A.G Weser U-Boot yards were the most high-profile war production concerns to sustain extensive damage, while residential districts escaped relatively lightly. The squadron operated on six nights during the month, and dispatched forty-five Lancaster sorties and nine by Manchesters for the loss of a single Lancaster and crew.

July 1942

The campaign against Bremen would span the turn of the month, but 106 Squadron's first task in July was to send a single Lancasters to northern waters on the night of the 1/2nd, to lay mines in the northern end of The Sound, off the eastern coast of Denmark. Sgt Crowfoot took off at 21.55, with P/O Cooper flying as second pilot, and they carried out their brief in excellent weather conditions before returning safely home. On the following night the Command was aloft with over three hundred aircraft to conclude the current campaign against Bremen, an operation supported by five 106 Squadron Lancasters, all with captains of pilot officer rank. The previous night's good weather conditions had held firm, and they got away safely from Coningsby either side of midnight to find the target clear of cloud and easily identifiable. It was also well-defended, and they had to run the gauntlet of flak as they neared the aiming point, each carrying a cookie and eight small bomb canisters (SBCs). The 106 Squadron element bombed from between 13,500 and 17,000 feet, and much of it found the southern fringes of the city, where a thousand houses sustained damage, as did the docks, dock installations and seven ships in the port.

Gibson had now returned from his sick leave, and reacquainted himself with the Lancaster in a familiarization flight with Hopgood on the 4th. A five night respite for most squadrons ended on the night of the 8/9th, when 285 aircraft set off to return to northern Germany, only this time to the port of Wilhelmshaven, where the U-Boot construction yards were the main targets. This operation gave Gibson the opportunity to go to war in a Lancaster for the first time, and having assisted in Gibson's conversion, the young Australian David Shannon accompanied him as second pilot. Unlike many, Shannon was not fazed by Gibson's martinet tendencies, and, once a member of the inner circle, a bond of genuine friendship would develop between the two, and Shannon's allegiance to his leader would remain throughout his life. On this night they were on board R5681, one of ten 106 Squadron Lancasters involved, which took off either side of midnight and headed for the coast. The squadron's usual high level of serviceability was missing on this night, and Sgt Cassels turned back after just forty miles with wireless failure. Sgt Crowfoot and P/O Churcher both suffered engine failure early on, and were forced to also abandon their sorties. The others pressed on to find the target in good weather conditions, although the darkness was intense. S/L Robertson bombed from 12,500 feet, but was too busy taking evasive action to observe the result. Gibson saw his bombs fall into the docks area from 12,000 feet, but could not confirm that they hit the U-Boot yards. Hopgood bombed on a Gee-fix, but did not observe the results, and like the others, he commented on the fairly heavy response thrown up by the defenders. In fact, they had contributed to a disappointing attack that largely missed the target on its western side. This operation brought to an end a five-week loss-free period for 106 Squadron, after a night fighter sent R5861 crashing into the sea about twenty-five miles off the North Frisian island of Ameland, killing P/O Brodrick and his crew.

A special operation was mounted by 5 Group on the 11th involving forty-four Lancasters, of which nine were provided by 106 Squadron, led again by Gibson in R5681. The plan called for a low-level crossing of the North Sea in formation until approaching Denmark, at which point the force was to split up and each aircraft climb independently into the forecast cloud. They were then to follow the Baltic coast to the target of Danzig, arriving at dusk to attack the U-Boot yards from normal bombing height. The return leg of the 1,700 mile round trip would be completed under cover of darkness. This was the longest range operation yet attempted by the Command, and, unfortunately, the day selected was beset by the most unfavourable weather conditions. The 106 Squadron contingent departed Coningsby at 17.00 in three sections of three, with Gibson and S/L Robertson the senior pilots on duty, and Shannon once again acting as Gibson's second pilot. The plan worked well at first, but too much cloud, much of it down to 500 feet near the Danish coast, forced the formations to split up to search individually for their navigation pinpoints. Hopgood's run of bad luck continued with a fuel-flow problem, which had become so bad by the time he crossed the Danish coast, that he was forced to turn back. P/O Cockbain's Lancaster developed generator problems while he was outbound over the sea, and he also turned back. P/O Aytoun broke formation and remained at low level, to ultimately locate the target, and bomb it from 3,500 feet at 22.07, claiming a direct hit with his four 1,000lb RDX load. Some crews found it difficult to identify Danzig, and it became dark before they could pinpoint the yards. Gibson was among these, and he attacked an eight-hundred ton ship at Gdynia, but watched the nearest bomb fall twenty yards away. P/O Churcher reached the target at 22.20, and released his bombs from 5,000 feet, F/S Appleyard turned up three minutes later to bomb from 4,000 feet, and S/L Robertson was the last to arrive, locating the target at 22.45, and bombing from 3,500 feet. The others all searched long and hard, but were defeated by diminishing fuel reserves and the weather, and were forced to give up and return home. In all, twenty-four crews reported bombing, and two Lancasters were lost to flak in the target area.

Harris turned his attention back upon the Ruhr on the night of the 13/14th, and sent a force of almost two hundred aircraft to attack Duisburg. This was to be the first of a series of attacks on this heavily industrialized city on the north-western edge of the Ruhr, for which 106 Squadron contributed seven Lancasters, led by F/L Hopgood. They took off either side of 00.30 on a night of unhelpful weather conditions, and each carrying an unusual bomb load of five 2,000 pounders. For once, Hopgood's Lancaster held together to allow him to reach the target, which he found under seven-tenths cloud and bombed on a TR-fix (Gee) from 14,000 feet. R5638 was hit by flak and seriously damaged over the well-defended target, but W/O Merralls completed the bombing run, and brought his aircraft and crew home on three engines and with a wounded flight engineer. No one returned with a positive identification of the target, after all had bombed on e.t.a or TR fix, and the scattered attack achieved only a very modest amount of housing damage. The following night was devoted to mining and nickelling operations, and 106 Squadron sent the lone freshman crew of Sgt Jones to dispense 216 bundles of leaflets over the Amiens region of France.

The 17th brought the award of a DFM to F/S Appleyard and his navigator, F/S Darvill, for their excellent work during the Danzig operation. Gibson's next operation was supposed to be a small-scale "moling" attack on Essen on the 18th, for which he and three other 106 Squadron crews took off from Coningsby between 13.00 and 13.30 to join up with six more from 83 and 44 Squadrons. It is described in the 5 Group ORB as a "Porpoise" operation, with the objective as "Stoat C". After messages were received from the 44 Squadron aircraft of lack of cloud, and also a signal from an 83 Squadron crew stating they had a badly injured mid-upper gunner, a recall signal was sent to the 106 Squadron element. Gibson turned R5678 back near Flushing, at the mouth of the Scheldt, and it was on this occasion that he spotted a Lancaster a mile ahead, which he caught up for mutual protection. It was then that he noticed his favourite Lancaster, R5681, O-Orange, being piloted by S/L Wooldridge, who had led Gibson to believe that it was unserviceable, and, therefore, unavailable to him. Wooldridge was five miles north of Walcheren when he picked up the recall signal, and it was just rank bad luck that Gibson happened to see him. He landed at Mildenhall, and one wonders if that was, in part, to delay the inevitable confrontation with Gibson. W/O Merralls was outbound over Holland when called back, and he aimed his bombs at a ship in the Oosterschelde, but overshot it. He was then attacked simultaneously by a BF109 and an FW190, which inflicted slight damage on his Lancaster. His gunners, in turn, shot down the 109 and damaged the 190, and he brought his aircraft and crew safely home to make their claim. Gibson sought out his B Flight commander afterwards, and one can imagine an explosive encounter taking place behind closed doors. To his credit, Gibson speaks of "Dim" Wooldridge in glowing terms in Enemy Coast Ahead, extolling his skill and courage as a bomber pilot, his popularity and standing in the squadron, and his organisational ability, particularly with regard to crew training. However, he also referred to Wooldridge's underhand tactics to get what he wanted, like borrowing Gibson's car without permission, and arranging postings-in of people he wanted around him.

An all-four engine force of ninety-nine aircraft took off late on the 19th to bomb the Vulcan U-Boot yards at Vegesack, in Bremen. 106 Squadron sent four Lancasters, which took off either side of midnight, led by Bill Whamond, and each carrying fourteen SBCs of 4lb incendiaries. Just like the rest of the force, they were unable to identify the target visually because of cloud cover, and the back-up plan, to use Gee, resulted in the attack missing the town altogether. Taffy Williams picked up a pinpoint on the River Weser, and that enabled him to make a timed-run, but he was too busy evading the heavy flak to notice any results. P/O Picken was also having difficulty with the flak barrage, and he picked up serious damage at 12,000 feet, but delivered his load and made it safely back. A particularly tragic incident occurred on the 21st, when R5576 was taking off for bombing practice. An engine on the port side cut as the Lancaster climbed away, and it stalled at two hundred feet before crashing near the airfield, killing P/O Carlyle and the nine others on board, some of whom were ground crew. At 00.50 on the 22nd, F/S Church set out for a nickelling trip to Lille, but both generators failed during the outward flight, and the sortie was abandoned.

Duisburg was targeted again on the night of the 21/22nd by a force of 290 aircraft, although none from 106 Squadron. Those crews reaching the target returned with enthusiastic claims of many fires, but photographic evidence contradicted the reports, and showed the bombing to have fallen west of the Rhine and short of the city. Another attempt was mounted two nights later by over two hundred aircraft, and this

F/O AG Williams who became a squadron leader in 617 squadron in late 1944, participating in attacks on the Tirpitz.

time 106 Squadron was represented by five Lancasters. They took off between 01.00 and 01.40, with Hopgood the senior pilot on duty, and he found sufficient breaks in the seven to ten-tenths cloud to pick up a number of pinpoints to keep him on track. It was necessary to use a TR fix to put himself over the target, and he delivered his cookie and mix of 500 and 250 pounders from 12,000 feet. Taffy Williams and Ginger Crowfoot used TR fixes confirmed by the glow of fires, the former flying in Gibson's R5681, which he brought home full of holes from shrapnel. It was another scattered attack, which caused some housing damage, but nothing commensurate with the effort expended.

The night of the 25/26th brought a return to Duisburg by more than three hundred aircraft, among them three Lancasters from 106 Squadron. F/S Appleyard DFM was first to take off, at 00.10 in R5683, and shortly afterwards it blew up and crashed onto a mud bank in the Wash, four miles north-east of Boston. The entire crew was killed, and only two bodies were identified. F/S Jones and Sgt Cassels pressed on to reach the target in good visibility and six to eight-tenths cloud, and delivered their all-incendiary loads into the target area. Opposition was described as not heavy, but there was a night fighter presence, and Sgt Cassels was chased out of the target area, but escaped undamaged. While this unsuccessful operation was in progress, Sgt Church, whose maiden sortie as crew captain on the 22nd had been thwarted by technical malfunctions, took off for a long freshman trip to lay mines in the Gironde Estuary. He didn't return, and news eventually came through that R5608 had crashed somewhere near St Nazaire, and that only the pilot and one gunner had survived to fall into enemy hands.

Hamburg received two visits in quick succession, the first by a force approaching four hundred aircraft on the night of the 26/27th, for which 106 Squadron put up nine Lancasters led by Gibson in his beloved, and now repaired, R5681. P/O "Wimpy" Wellington was the first to take off, at 22.55, and the others followed over the ensuing forty-five minutes. The weather conditions were perfect for a successful attack, and for once, the attacking force did not disappoint. Gibson, who had Shannon with him as second pilot, bombed in bright moonlight from 14,000 feet, and watched his bombs explode south-west of the aiming point, and cause further fires in the already-burning shipyards. Hopgood dropped his cookie and mix of 500 and 250 pounders from 11,000 feet into the old city, where they started new fires. Taffy Williams and Johnny Coates each carried fourteen SBCs of 4lb incendiaries, while Bill Whamond, Ginger Crowfoot, Wimpy Wellington and P/O Crowe all had high-explosive loads, which all but Wellington used to good effect. His R5749 was caught in a heavy flak barrage during the bombing run, and sustained extensive damage as a result. This difficulty was exacerbated by the fact that the electrical circuits of the bomb-release gear had been severed, preventing the bombs from being jettisoned to save weight. Added to this, three members of the crew had been wounded. On the way home, still carrying the full bomb load, they were attacked by a night fighter, which the gunners drove off. P/O Wellington brought the Lancaster home on three engines, and praised his crew for their outstanding work. The outcome of the operation was a rare major success for the period, which caused widespread damage in residential districts and started eight hundred fires, over five hundred of them large. It was not a one-sided affair, however, and twenty-nine aircraft failed to return, among them 106 Squadron's R5748, which fell to the guns of a night fighter flown by Lt Lothar Linke of II.NJG/1. It crashed near Drachten in northern Holland at 02.05, killing S/L Robertson and three of his crew, while the navigator and both gunners survived in enemy hands.

Two nights later the command dispatched 250 aircraft to Hamburg, but worsening weather conditions caused a recall of part of the force, and others turned back to leave just sixty-eight to press home their attack and inflict some useful damage. 106 Squadron was not involved on that night, but made ready three Lancasters for an attack on Saarbrücken on the night of the 29/30th. The town had been targeted before, but never by 106 Squadron or by a force as large as the 290-strong one assembling in the late evening. Sgts Crowfoot and Cassels took off at 23.50, to be followed fifteen minutes later by P/O Crowe. Weather conditions were not particularly favourable, and the crews met with a low cloud base in the target area. In order to see the ground they were required to descend to 5,000 feet, and P/O Crowe made three runs across the target to confirm that he was over the correct town. He delivered his bombs from 4,000 feet, and saw them burst across the target. The defenders responded with intense light flak, and R5780 collected a number of holes. Ginger Crowfoot's report was almost a carbon copy, but Sgt Cassels and crew experienced a much more action-packed operation. They bombed the target from 4,400 feet, and on return reported being attacked by night fighters on five separate occasions. Two were shaken off by evasive action, two were driven off by the gunners, and one was shot down in flames and seen to impact the ground. All of this was accomplished without sustaining any damage. The operation was highly successful, and caused the destruction of almost four hundred buildings, mostly in central and north-western districts.

A major raid on Düsseldorf was mounted on the last night of July, when elements from the training units helped to swell the numbers to over six hundred. 106 Squadron had been dispatching single figures of late, but managed a new record of twenty-one Lancasters on this night, led by Gibson in R5681. "Dim" Wooldridge was first to take off at 00.15, and "Bunny" Grein brought up the rear an hour later. All were carrying a cookie, some with small calibre HE bombs and others with incendiaries, but W/O Merralls was carrying the first 8,000 pounder to be delivered by the squadron. Sgt Cassels began to experience engine trouble shortly after taking off, but pushed on until seventy miles from the target, where he gave up and brought his bombs home. P/O Aytoun was five minutes from the target when his starboard-outer engine cut, and sent the heavily-laden Lancaster temporarily out of control. Once back on an even keel, it was discovered that the front and rear turrets were out of action, and it was decided to head for home and bomb Mönchengladbach on the way. Gibson arrived over the target to find it already well alight, and he added to the destruction in the city centre by dropping into it his cookie and twelve 500 and 250 pounder GP bombs. He recorded his speed while over enemy territory as 230 mph. Weather conditions were excellent, with clear skies and good visibility, and bombing by the 106 Squadron participants took place between 9,000 and 16,000 feet. Sgt Lace was leaving the target when an engine failed, and then another before the Dutch coast was reached. The entire North Sea crossing was carried out on two engines, but these failed over England, and the crew, who had been prepared for the bale-out order for some time, took to their parachutes, leaving the pilot, and second pilot, Sgt Brinkhurst, to bring the crippled Lancaster to a safe landing at Docking in Norfolk.

Although some of the bombing was wasted in open country, a considerable amount of damage was caused in Düsseldorf and nearby Neuss to the tune of 450 buildings destroyed and fifteen thousand damaged to some extent. Many large fires had also been created, but the operation was expensive, and again cost twenty-nine aircraft, including another one from 106 Squadron. R5604 crashed north-west of Cologne, and there were no survivors from the crew of the experienced W/O Merralls DFM. The wisdom of employing aircraft from the training units must have been called into question after this operation, as sixteen of them were among the missing. This was on top of more than sixty lost through participation in the three Thousand Bomber raids. During the course of the month the squadron carried out fourteen operations on twelve nights, and dispatched eighty-four sorties for the loss of five aircraft. The 239.7 tons of bombs delivered represented a new record for the squadron, and surpassed the efforts of all other 5 Group squadrons.

August 1942

Sgt Geoff Lace and crew (Simon Sanders).

August was to be a busy month for the Command, and by the time operations began for 106 Squadron it would average better than one operation every two nights. There was a soggy start, however, as rain washed out flying at Coningsby until the 3rd. The first operational activity for the squadron took place on the night of the 4/5th, when two Lancasters were supposed to join others mining off the Frisians. In the event, one was scrubbed after becoming unserviceable at the last minute, and Sgt Smith, flying as crew captain for the first time, took off at 01.50 as the sole squadron representative. He found his garden without difficulty and delivered his five mines into the correct location. It was the same fare on the following night for two more gardeners from the squadron, P/O Cooper and Sgt Lace, who also took off in the early hours to carry out their brief successfully.

The spate of post-midnight take-offs continued on the night of the 6/7th, when the fifth and final raid was mounted in the current series against Duisburg. Over two hundred aircraft took part, eight of them Lancasters from 106 Squadron, which departed Coningsby between 01.00 and 01.20. Dim Wooldridge was the senior pilot on duty, but he lost both starboard engines while outbound, and had to jettison the bombs in order to maintain control and get back home. Taffy Williams had a fuel system and TR failure, and also had to turn back early. W4102 became uncontrollable shortly after take-off through an aileron malfunction, but P/O Butterworth pressed on and completed the entire operation on "George" (automatic pilot). The crews encountered almost complete cloud cover over the target, and all bombed on e.t.a or TR, without being able to plot the fall of their bombs. It was another unsatisfactory operation, and the statistics of the past three weeks made discouraging reading for Harris. He had committed 1,229 sorties over the five Duisburg operations, of which forty-three had failed to return in exchange for the destruction of 212 houses and some industrial damage.

Crews debrief after a raid in August 1942.

On the night of the 8/9th the squadron returned to mining duties in the Great Belt and Silverthorn areas off the eastern coast of the Schleswig-Holstein peninsular. Four crews were assigned to each garden, and the ORB made the point that this must be a very important operation, otherwise the appalling weather conditions would have caused a scrub. Gibson took off in R5637 at 23.00, and for once he had a flight engineer rather than Dave Shannon beside him in the cockpit. P/Os Butterworth and Coates were unable to locate their target areas despite searching long and hard, and both abandoned their sorties. Despite the rain, mist and low cloud the others all found pinpoints from which to make a timed run, and the four assigned to the Great Belt each delivered five mines, as did two in the Kiel Harbour area. Just three of the squadron's Lancasters were involved in an attack on Osnabrück on the following night, Sgts Lace, Smith and the recently promoted F/O Aytoun all getting away safely after midnight. The skies over the target were clear, but it was very dark, and the use of flares enabled the crews to identify ground detail and carry out a moderately successful raid, that destroyed over two hundred houses and caused widespread damage in the docks. The 106 Squadron participants bombed from between 9,000 and 13,000 feet, and returned to report many fires, numerous searchlights but little flak opposition. The squadron also sent Sgt Hamilton and crew on a freshman sortie to lay mines off the Frisians, and they successfully delivered six at eight-second intervals into the correct location. There was further mining in the Baltic for three Coningsby Lancasters on the night of the 10/11th, including R5901 with Gibson at the controls. He, Dim Wooldridge and Johnny Coates all got away at 21.15, and proceeded to the Great Belt, where Gibson made a timed run from Helskov Point and accurately delivered his five mines. Wooldridge was also successful, but Coates was unable to locate his garden, and jettisoned his mines "safe".

Two strikes on consecutive nights against Mainz began on the 11/12th, when 154 aircraft were detailed, among them eight 106 Squadron Lancasters. This was a new target for the squadron to add to its already impressive list, and the honour of being the senior pilots on duty fell to F/Os Aytoun and Churcher. After successive sorties as second pilot to Dim Wooldridge, P/O Cooper returned to the pilot's seat for this operation. They took off either side of 23.00 on a night of good weather conditions, and the three to five-tenths cloud during the outward flight had largely cleared by the time the target was reached. F/O Churcher bombed from 7,000 feet by the light of flares, and saw his bombs burst on a large building, possibly a factory, and start a fire. Apart from Coates, who attacked from 8,000 feet, the others bombed from between 13,000 and 15,000 feet, and all but one returned to report a successful outcome. Absent from debriefing were Bunny Grein and crew, whose W4109 had crashed about six miles south-south west of Koblenz without survivors.

P/O Tony Burcher RAAF, DFM, rear gunner for 'Hoppy' Hopgood, was one of three airmen to survive as a POW after being shot down on the Dams Raid.

The operation had, indeed, been effective, with much damage in central districts, but a second one was sent against it twenty-four hours later, which the squadron supported this time with seven Lancasters led by Gibson. A number of names that would become familiar as future "Dambusters" were appearing in the ORB at this time. Tony Burcher has already been mentioned, and George Chalmers had recently flown with Sgt Smith as mid-upper gunner. On this night Charles Brennan was beside Dim Wooldridge in the cockpit of W4118, and, like Burcher, he would go to the dams in Hopgood's crew, in his case as flight engineer. Gibson found the target under ten-tenths cloud with a base at 6,000 feet, and dropped beneath it, where he found a pinpoint on an island in the Rhine. He delivered his load of four 2,000 pounders with the target in his sights, but intense light flak had him diving for the ground, and he was unable to plot their fall. Wimpy Wellington caught sight of the target through one of the few gaps in the cloud, and he bombed from 16,000 feet, a full 10,000 feet higher than Gibson. S/L Wooldridge searched for forty-five minutes, by which time the cloud base had ascended to 7,000 feet, and he bombed from there, as did a number of others. F/O Aytoun was unable to identify the target, and dropped his bombs on e.t.a from 17,000 feet before returning safely along with the others. This was another successful operation, and caused further damage in central districts, where, according to Bomber Command estimates, 135 acres had been destroyed over the two nights.

A force of 130 aircraft was dispatched to Düsseldorf on the night of the 15/16th, and among them were nine Lancasters representing 106 Squadron. F/L Hopgood was the senior pilot on duty, and Sgt Brennan was on board as his flight engineer. They took off either side of 00.30, and arrived in the target area to find varying amounts of cloud from five to ten-tenths. It was a very dark night, with ground haze adding to the difficulties, and only P/O Wellington identified the target through a chink in the cloud coinciding with a TR fix. All attacked on e.t.a or TR from between 9,000 and 16,000 feet, but had no idea where their bombs had fallen. It was, in fact, a scattered and largely ineffective raid in the face of heavy and accurate flak. Hopgood was coned by searchlights and targeted by flak, but managed to avoid damage. Ginger Crowfoot's W4118 was badly damaged by flak, and P/O Butterworth's R5673 gained a hole in the fuselage, but they at least came home. R5678 failed to do so after crashing into the target city, and there were no survivors from the crew of P/O Johnny Coates RAAF.

It was on the 15th that the Command took another step towards becoming a war-winning weapon, with the formation of the Pathfinder Force. The four founder-member heavy squadrons, 7, 35, 83 and 156, arrived at their new stations on this day, each representing a Group from which they would draw their future crews. The HQ was initially at Wyton in Cambridgeshire, and this was the new home of 83 Squadron, formerly of 5 Group, and the squadron of which Gibson was a member for the first year of war. Also posted to the new organisation was 109 Squadron, which would spend the remainder of the year marrying the Oboe blind bombing system to the Mosquito under the watchful eye of W/C Hal Bufton. The magnificent pioneering work carried out by this squadron would bear fruit in the coming year, and would change the face of bombing. At this stage the new force came under the direct control of 3 Group, upon whose stations it resided, and would not gain group status in its own right until the start of 1943. At its head Harris had controversially placed the relatively junior G/C Don Bennett, who could claim recent operational experience as the commanding officer first of 77 Squadron and then 10 Squadron, both in 4 Group. He had recently returned to duty after crashing in Norway and evading capture during an attack on the Tirpitz. He possessed, perhaps, the most brilliant mind in the service, but absolutely no sense of humour. He was acknowledged as a master airman, and his knowledge of navigation was unsurpassed. His appointment ruffled a few feathers amongst more senior officers, particularly the group commanders, who, with the exception of 4 Group's AVM Roddy Carr, were opposed in principal, as was Harris, to an elite target finding and marking force. In fact, Bennett proved to be an inspired choice.

The night of the 16/17th was devoted to mining operations, for which 106 Squadron detailed six Lancasters, three each for Willow, which was off the island of Sassnitz in the Baltic, and Spinach, which required a 1,700 mile round trip to the waters off the port of Danzig in Germany's north-eastern corner. Hopgood, Williams and Crowfoot were assigned to the latter, and took off between 20.30 and 20.45 for the four-and-a-half hour outward flight. It was around two hours later before P/Os Wellington and Butterworth and Sgt Cassels departed Coningsby for their shorter-duration trip, but the intense darkness was the same for both elements. The weather conditions, however, were very different, with clear skies and haze to the east, and electrical storms and ten-tenths cloud down to 600 feet further west. Visibility was good enough for the Danzig trio to pick up pinpoints on the coast, and each successfully laid their mines as briefed. Of the others, P/O Wellington failed to locate his drop zone and abandoned the attempt. P/O Butterworth was grateful to the enemy for throwing up sufficient numbers of flares to light up the coastline and give him a pinpoint from where he made a DR run. Sgt Cassels dropped a flare float, which enabled him, likewise, to complete a successful operation.

Harris had hoped to employ the fledgling Pathfinder Force immediately at Osnabrück on the night of the 17/18th, but the squadron commanders felt they were unready, and the operation went ahead in standard fashion in the absence of a 106 Squadron contribution. It was, therefore, on the following night, that an ultimately illustrious career in target locating and marking began in an inauspicious manner. Thirty-one Pathfinders took off at the head of an overall force of 118 aircraft, of which nine Lancasters belonged to 106 Squadron. Their destination was the port of Flensburg, situated on the eastern side of the Schleswig-Holstein peninsular, a little to the north of Kiel. It was chosen as an easy-to-locate maiden target, in a region frequently visited in recent times for mining operations. Hopgood was the senior pilot on duty as the 106 Squadron element began to depart Coningsby between 21.10 and 21.30. It was another very dark night, and haze in the target area made identification of ground detail all but impossible. Hopgood circled the target area for thirty minutes, but was unable to pick up a definite pinpoint, and dropped his five 1,900 pounders from 9,000 feet on estimated position. Six crews pinpointed on Flensburger Fjord, and delivered their hardware from between 5,000 and 10,000 feet. In the event, no bombs found the mark, but a number of Danish towns reported being hit.

It would be almost a week before the next Pathfinder-led operation took place, and in the meantime 106 Squadron committed six Lancasters to gardening in the eastern Baltic off Danzig and Gdynia on the night of the 20/21st. They set off from Coningsby for what would be a nine-hour round trip, with Bill Whamond as the senior pilot on duty. He enjoyed an uneventful sortie on a dark night with good visibility, and delivered his four mines after finding a strong coastal pinpoint. He spotted a convoy, and reported its position by W/T, and returned safely to land at 05.20. P/O Crowe experienced navigational difficulties, and delivered a number of mines further west than intended, off Sassnitz and Bornholm. Sgt Lace reached his target area only to find that his bomb doors would not open, and he was forced to abandon his sortie. The others fulfilled their briefs, and returned without incident.

Frankfurt was selected to host the second Pathfinder-led operation on the night of the 24/25th, when 226 aircraft were made ready, among them fifteen Lancasters of 106 Squadron. Doubts about the weather reduced the 106 Squadron contribution to seven aircraft, and they departed Coningsby either side of 21.30 led by Whamond and Hopgood. Seven-tenths cloud in the target area made it difficult to establish an aiming point, but a number of crews managed to pick up a pinpoint on the Rhine, while Hopgood glimpsed Koblenz through the cloud and plotted his navigation accordingly. He bombed the target from 10,000 feet, and as he turned away was approached by a night fighter, which was evaded. Shortly afterwards an FW190 attacked, and was shot down by the rear gunner, Sgt Hobson, whose claim was later confirmed. Although some damage was caused within the city, most of the bombing fell into open country to the north and west. 106 Squadron's R5684 crashed into the sea off the Belgian coast, and only the mid-upper gunner survived from the crew of W/O Young DFM, who had earned his decoration while serving on Hampdens with 144 Squadron in 1941.

The squadron took part in two operations on the night of the 27/28th, the first of which involved three Lancasters captained by Gibson, Whamond and Hopgood, who were to join up with six from 97 Squadron for a special operation against the new German aircraft carrier, Graf Zeppelin, which was believed to be ready for sea-going trials out of Gdynia. This would explain the focus on the region, which had led to the recent mining sorties. Built in the Deutsche Werke yards at Kiel, the carrier had been launched in December 1938, but her fitting-out was delayed by other priorities, and she would never leave the Baltic or see completion. This was, of course, not known as the trio departed Coningsby either side of 20.00 for the long trip out. Each of the Lancasters was carrying a single 5,500lb Capital Ship Bomb, designed for use against large warships, and it was believed that a single direct hit would be enough to do the job. Also freshly installed was the new Stabilized Automatic Bomb Sight (SABS), which had been undergoing trials at Coningsby, and was the closest thing yet to a computerised sighting system. Two specialist bomb-aimers conversant with SABS had been drafted in for the operation, S/L Richardson and W/O Naylor from the Armament School at Manby, and they would fly with Gibson and Hopgood respectively, while the squadron's own Sgt McNair would be with Whamond. Richardson would become almost a fixture during extensive work with 617 Squadron at Woodhall Spa in 1944, and his enthusiasm for the topic of bombing would see him christened "Talking Bomb". They arrived in the target area to find nine-tenths cloud that made it impossible to locate the warships, and despite making a dozen runs across the docks, Gibson was forced to bomb from 8,000 feet on the estimated whereabouts of the Gneisenau. Whamond occasionally caught a glimpse of the docks through gaps in the cloud, but after thirty minutes of searching he, too, bombed the docks from 8,500 feet. Hopgood, in contrast, identified the docks easily, but saw no ships, and bombed from 10,000 feet on a hunch as to where the Graf Zeppelin might be. He witnessed a large explosion, and returned home safely with the others without a clue as to the outcome of his ten-hour sortie.

While this operation was in progress, a force of 306 aircraft had set out for Kassel to carry out the third Pathfinder-led operation. 106 Squadron provided thirteen Lancasters, which departed Coningsby between 20.50 and 21.30. For the first time the Pathfinder element positively identified the target, and illuminated it for the main force following behind. Dim Wooldridge was the senior 106 Squadron pilot on duty, and he spotted a Wellington under attack from a JU88, which his rear gunner drove off. The target was located easily in bright moonlight, and Wooldridge delivered his cookie and 30lb incendiaries from 10,000 feet. Sgt Lace and crew delivered their load of five 2,000 pounders from 10,500 feet, and were then attacked by a JU88 at the Dutch coast on the way home. After a brief engagement, during which the Lancaster sustained slight damage, the enemy fighter was claimed as probably destroyed. Perhaps this was the same JU88 that had tried to attack P/O Butterworth also off the Dutch coast, but had lost the Lancaster after it took evasive action. Ginger Crowfoot brought R5680 back on three engines after it had been badly damaged by flak, and F/S Jones and crew also experienced a torrid time. They were driven off course by an intense flak barrage near Münster, and held in searchlights for more than forty-five minutes. By this time thoroughly lost, they dropped their bombs on an unidentified built-up area and came home. The operation was partially successful, and caused widespread damage in south-western districts, but the intervention by a strong night fighter force led to the loss of thirty-one bombers, a massive 10% of those dispatched.

The following night brought an operation to Nuremberg in southern Germany, for which a force of 159 aircraft took off. 106 Squadron had detailed ten Lancasters, but some of those damaged twenty-four hours earlier could not be made ready in time, and only six presented themselves for departure from Coningsby between 21.10 and 21.25. F/O Aytoun was the senior pilot for this operation, and like the other participants, he had been ordered to bomb from as low as possible. They found good conditions in the target area, which they identified easily, possibly assisted by the efforts of the Pathfinders, who were employing rudimentary target indicators in 250lb bomb casings for the first time. The squadron crews bombed from 12,000 to 13,000 feet, and watched their bombs burst in the target area before returning home to report a successful outcome. Sgt Lace and crew had a different story to tell, after L5574 was badly damaged by a night fighter while outbound. The rear turret was knocked out and its occupant wounded, and then a fire in the fuselage was extinguished by the mid-upper gunner, who sustained burns as a result. By this time they were over southern Germany, and dropped their bombs on Darmstadt before turning back. Photo-reconnaissance revealed that many bomb loads had missed the mark by some distance. Some damage did occur within the Altstadt, but at a cost of twenty-three aircraft, of which more than half were Wellingtons. During the course of the month the squadron took part in fifteen operations, dispatching one hundred sorties for the loss of three aircraft and crews.

September 1942

The new month began with the posting of a "black" by the Pathfinders on the night of the 1/2nd, when they mistook the non-industrial town of Saarlouis in error for its neighbour Saarbrücken, a dozen miles to the south-east. An overall force of 230 aircraft took off on a clear night, and headed for the target area close to the borders with Luxembourg and France. 106 Squadron contributed eleven Lancasters, most of which took off from Coningsby in the minutes leading to midnight. Bringing up the rear was Gibson in R5551, and he lifted off at 00.10 with a single 8,000 pounder in the bomb bay, while the others were carrying a cookie and SBCs. Bill Whamond delivered his bombs from 7,000 feet, and the others from varying heights up to 14,500, and all described hits in the town centre and many large fires. Gibson's bomb caused an enormous explosion, and, like the others, he was forced to admit that he had hit the wrong target, having been misled by the Pathfinders. Hopgood was the only one to claim to have bombed Saarbrücken, which he found on e.t.a and by the light of flares, but local reports suggest that no hardware at all fell in the intended target city.

Gradually, however, the Pathfinder crews were beginning to get to grips with the difficult task of target finding and marking, and on the following night, 106 Squadron contributed eight Lancasters to a force of two hundred aircraft bound for Karlsruhe. F/O Aytoun was the senior pilot as the Coningsby contingent departed either side of 23.30 to penetrate a little deeper into the same region of Germany as visited on the previous night. Weather conditions were again ideal, and this time there was no doubt about the identity of the urban area marked by the Pathfinder element. P/O Cooper and Sgt Crowfoot were carrying four 2,000 pounders each, while the others were loaded with the standard cargo of a 4,000lb cookie and SBCs. Bombing took place from between 10,000 and 13,000 feet, although in the face of little opposition, Sgt Lace came down to 7,000 feet. All returned safely to describe the town as being well-alight, and most brought back photographs of their bomb bursts within two miles of the aiming point.

This was, in fact, the start of an unprecedented run of successful operations during the first half of the month, which continued at Bremen on the night of the 4/5th, when the evolving tactics of the Pathfinders introduced a three-phase system. Illuminator crews lit up the target area with white flares, so that visual marker crews could identify and mark the aiming point, while backers-up, spread through the force, kept the aiming point marked for the duration of the raid. A force of 250 aircraft was employed on this night, of which thirteen Lancasters were provided by 106 Squadron. They took off in an impressive eighteen minute slot either side of 00.30, led by Dim Wooldridge, who had beside him the recently-arrived S/L Howell, who had been posted in to replace the missing A Flight commander, S/L Robertson. On his first operation as crew captain was P/O David Shannon, but his wireless failed during the outward flight, and he was forced to return early. On arrival in the target area the crews encountered good weather conditions and a heavy and accurate response from the defenders. According to the 5 Group ORB ten of the crews had been briefed to attack the city, while three others were among a contingent of twenty-four assigned to the Focke-Wulf factory. The 106 Squadron ORB suggests that all had been briefed to attack the factory, however, and although the city was identified with ease, haze, smoke and fires prevented the factory from standing out, and bombing photographs would show that most missed the mark. Hopgood eventually bombed the docks from 15,000 feet, a little higher than his squadron colleagues, who chose altitudes of 11,000 to 13,000 feet from which to deliver their loads of a cookie and SBCs or five 1,900 pounders. Bill Whamond's bomb bursts were plotted to be more than three miles from the aiming point, and this was about average. He had an engine fail, and came home on three. All in all, the operation met with considerable success, and destroyed 450 houses, with more than a thousand others seriously damaged, and there was even some useful industrial destruction to celebrate. For the second operation running, 106 Squadron brought back more target area photos than any other squadron in the Command.

Operations on the night of the 6/7th began for 106 Squadron with the departure shortly before 01.00 of P/Os Shannon and Downer on freshman mining sorties in the Rosemary garden area, off the western coast of Schleswig-Holstein. Shannon found the target area without difficulty, and delivered six mines into the correct location after pinpointing on the island of Pellworm and making a timed run. P/O Downer's intercom failed shortly after take-off, but, to his credit, he pressed on to reach the target area, and delivered his mines into what he hoped was the correct position, but which was plotted later to be just north of Pellworm. Meanwhile, back at Coningsby, seven Lancasters had taken off from 01.10 as part of a force of more than two hundred bound for the notoriously difficult-to-hit Ruhr city of Duisburg. Bill Whamond lost an engine early on, and was back on the ground at 03.40, but the others reached the target area to find clear skies but thick ground haze. Ginger Crowfoot picked out the River Rhine and a railway bridge, and these pinpoints coincided with a TR fix. He dropped his cookie from 12,500 feet, and saw it burst in a built-up area, before bringing back a splendid photograph of the docks. Most returning crews described a successful outcome, and commented on the intensity of the flak, and a number of Lancasters displayed shrapnel damage. The destruction of 114 buildings, while not large, did represent something of a victory at this target, and was reported by the local authorities to be the heaviest raid to date.

The only failure during this period came at Frankfurt on the night of the 8/9th, when 249 aircraft were dispatched to this similarly difficult-to-identify target. They took off either side of 21.00, and Sgt Hamilton was two hours into the flight out when his oxygen system failed, and he turned back. The predicted fine weather did not materialize, and cloud and ground haze made it difficult to pick up navigational pinpoints. Most identified the target area by rivers and other ground features illuminated by Pathfinder flares, and F/S Jones made three runs across the target to be sure, before releasing his cookie from 10,000 feet on an estimated position. Sgt Lace had the target in his bomb sight as he dropped his load from 11,500 feet, but his bombing photo was plotted at Laubenheim, many miles to the south-west. This was Shannon's first bombing operation as crew captain, and he identified the target by flares, bridges over the river and e.t.a, commenting on the abundance of searchlights but little flak. Most of the bombing on this night fell south-west of the city, but some of it found useful industrial property in nearby Rüsselsheim.

The squadron had just four Lancasters operating on the following night, as part of a thirty-four-strong force of minelayers operating off Denmark's east coast. Sgts Phair, Brinkhurst and Tucker and P/O White took off at 23.30, and all found their respective gardens, in the Kraut and Silverthorn areas, before planting four vegetables each as briefed. The training units were drafted in on the night of the 10/11th to swell the numbers available for Düsseldorf to 479, of which thirteen Lancasters represented 106 Squadron. S/L Wooldridge was the senior pilot on duty as most took off in the minutes leading to 21.00, and S/L Howell hitched a lift on this occasion with Bill Whamond to act as his second pilot. Sgt Tucker was the last to lift off, at 21.05, but R5559 clipped the boundary fence with an undercarriage leg, and returned two-and-a-half hours later after jettisoning the bombs into the sea and burning off some fuel. P/Os Downer and Wellington also came back early with technical problems, but those reaching the target area were treated to a new Pathfinder technique, the "pink pansy" target indicator (TI), in a converted 4,000lb bomb casing. Bill Whamond described clear conditions over the target with slight ground haze, and reported dropping his cookie from 15,000 feet. The city was already burning by this time, and he was unable to distinguish the blast of his bomb, but his bombing photo plotted it as a mile-and-a-half from the aiming point. Dim Wooldridge bombed from 14,000 feet on a straight run across the target, and believed he was just short of the aiming point. The bombing photo revealed it be about two miles short, but the US Army Air Corps major, who was on board to "see for himself", was apparently impressed. The operation was highly successful, creating widespread damage throughout the city, and destroying nine hundred houses, although at a cost of thirty-three aircraft, over 7% of the force. Sixteen of these were from the training units. Among the missing was 106 Squadron's R5638, which crashed into the target with no survivors from the experienced crew of Sgt Smith RAAF.

Bremen was selected as the target for the night of the 13/14th, for which a force of 446 aircraft took off, including another batch from the training units. 106 Squadron put up fourteen Lancasters, led by Gibson in W4127, which he had borrowed from the Conversion Flight, and S/L Howell was undertaking his first sortie as captain since joining the squadron. They took off either side of 23.30, but P/O Butterworth lost both starboard engines and was back within two hours, to be followed by Sgt Cassels with a rigging problem some time afterwards. Those reaching the target were unanimous in their descriptions of the conditions, clear with thick ground haze, and Gibson, Whamond and Wellington commented on the intensity and accuracy of the flak. Whamond had just cause. As R5573 was on its bombing run at 12,000 feet carrying the squadron's only 8,000 pounder, a flak shell exploded nearby, wounding the bomb-aimer, Sgt Humphreys. The bomb was jettisoned "live", but its burst was not observed. The Lancaster came home safely, and Whamond praised the performance of his crew in difficult circumstances. The bombing photo plotted his bomb some two miles short of the aiming point. S/L Howell picked up the river as his pinpoint, and bombed from 13,000 feet, without being able to observe a burst. His bombing photo showed it to have fallen a little over two miles from the aiming point in a semi-built-up area. Overall, the operation was a major success, which inflicted damage considerably in excess of that caused by the Thousand raid in June. Over eight hundred houses were destroyed, and substantial damage was caused to war-industry factories. Twenty-one aircraft failed to return, and the training units took another beating, with eleven missing and four others crashing at home.

Wilhelmshaven was targeted on the following night, when 106 Squadron contributed nine Lancaster to an overall force of 202. Among those taking off were four Hampdens from 408 Squadron RCAF, and their participation would bring down the curtain on the operational career of this stalwart. Hopgood led the 106 Squadron contingent away at 20.15, but S/L Howell was the senior pilot on duty, and he found clear skies and ground haze as he approached the target. The coastline and docks were visible, and he bombed from 12,000 feet on the approximate position of the aiming point. The others bombed from between 8,000 and 14,000 feet, mostly after picking out ground detail by the light of the Pathfinder flares, and four crews had their impressions confirmed by bombing photographs. The success of the operation was confirmed by local reports, which showed this to be the most destructive raid on the town thus far, with much damage in the town centre and residential districts.

At this stage of the war Essen was always the ultimate test of the Command's ability to locate and mark a target, and thus far, much to Harris's frustration, it had failed. Could the recent run of successes continue even at Essen, when Harris launched his latest assault on the city on the night of the 16/17th? Over 360 aircraft were made ready, including eleven Lancasters from 106 Squadron, along with another contingent from the training units. S/L Howell was the senior pilot on duty as they departed Coningsby either side of 20.30 and headed for the south coast. They arrived in the target area to find varying amounts of cloud between five and eight tenths, and the usual heavy haze, which blotted out all ground detail. Not one crew was able to positively identify Essen, let alone the Krupp works aiming point, despite the presence of Pathfinder flares, and all bombed on e.t.a. They were unanimous in their descriptions of heavy and accurate flak, and P/O Crowe commented that it was particularly active over the French coast. He bombed on e.t.a, and his bomb burst was plotted later to be almost eight miles from the aiming point. Sgt Hamilton saw a built-up area on e.t.a, which he bombed from 15,000 feet, and observed a number of aircraft going down. Hopgood pinpointed on a canal to the north of the town, and bombed ninety seconds after e.t.a. His bombing photo showed only cloud with numerous fire tracks. Sgt Stamp returned on three engines having watched many aircraft go down over the target, but he did, at least, get back, while thirty-nine others failed to do so, a loss rate in excess of 10%.

Tail gunner PO Robert Chase, in the crew of P/O Downer, was one of the twenty one members of the squadron who failed to return from Essen on 16th / 17th September 1942. All lost their lives.

Photo reconnaissance revealed, that despite scattered bombing, the city had received its most destructive attack to date, which created over a hundred large and medium fires. The Krupp works had been hit by fifteen high explosive bombs and a crashing bomber with incendiaries on board, and housing had suffered heavily, whilst the towns of Bochum and Wuppertal also sustained substantial damage. On the debit side the Command paid a massive price, nineteen of the aircraft lost had been from the training units. This was the final time that they would be asked to support major operations. Three empty dispersals at Coningsby on the morning of the 17th told of a particularly bad night for 106 Squadron. R5681 crashed over twenty miles to the east of Essen, between Datteln and Oer-Erkenschwick, W4178 found the sea off the Dutch coast near Egmond, and W4179 crashed in a monastery garden in a north-eastern suburb of Aachen, and there was not a single survivor from the crews of P/O "Taffy" Williams, P/O Downer and A Flight commander S/L Howell respectively. Despite the tragedies, if any period in Bomber Command's struggle to effectiveness could be identified as the turning point, then perhaps these two weeks in September 1942 were it, and it can be no coincidence that it came just as the fledgling Pathfinder Force was coming to terms with the complexities of its demanding role.

Two nights later more than a hundred aircraft took part in mining operations in the Baltic, for which 106 Squadron put up six Lancasters. F/L Whamond was the senior pilot on duty as they took off from Coningsby in a ten-minute slot from 19.10, each carrying three 1,570lb mines. The target garden, coded Privet, lay off the coast of Poland, east of Sweden, and the crews used the mouth of the River Vistula as a pinpoint from which to make a timed run. In clear conditions and good visibility, five crews planted their vegetables in the required location, before returning home to report some flak activity from coastal batteries, but more particularly from flak ships. R5899 fell victim to the defences when at around eight hundred feet, and following a successful ditching off the Danzig coast, broke in two. Sgt Stamp and four of his crew were rescued and became PoWs, but both gunners failed to survive.

The main targets for the night of the 19/20th were Saarbrücken and Munich, and 106 Squadron supported the latter with six Lancasters. Surprisingly, this would be a new destination on the squadron's target list. Hopgood was the senior pilot on duty as they took off shortly after 20.00, and climbed into clear skies with good visibility. The target was located with ease, and was already burning as they began their bombing runs from surprisingly low altitudes of between 7,500 and 9,000 feet. Hopgood described the opposition as intense at times, and reported an encounter with a JU88, which his gunners drove off and claimed as damaged. The others mostly found the flak defences to be slight, and all returned safely after round-trips lasting between seven hours fifty minutes and nine hours thirty. Less than half of the eighty-nine participating Lancaster and Stirling crews reported bombing within three miles of the target, and only the suburbs are believed to have sustained some damage.

The squadron operated for the final time during the month on the night of the 23/24th, when a 5 Group operation involving eighty-three Lancasters was mounted against the Baltic coastal town and Hansastadt (free trade city) of Wismar and its nearby Dornier aircraft factory. Gibson was in W4102 as he led the 106 Squadron contingent of thirteen Lancasters away at 22.30, with Dim Wooldridge, Bill Whamond and Hopgood also on the Order of Battle. They had been briefed to attack the factory, for which clear conditions were required, and, indeed, forecast, but as they made their way out over the North Sea, low cloud rolled in bringing rain and icing. Despite that, Gibson and Sgt Phair described the visibility as good, and both had the factory in their bomb sights as they released their loads. Gibson let his fourteen SBCs of 30lb incendiaries go at 2,000 feet, and Phair delivered his six 1,000 pounders from a little higher, and saw them burst in a built-up area. Light flak was intense, and Phair would return on three engines. Whamond picked up a number of pinpoints during the final leg to the target, which enabled him to make his run on the factory at 1,000 feet, and he was certain that his 1,000lb RDX bombs had scored direct hits or near misses. S/L Wooldridge had arrived early, and while circling the target waiting for the attack to begin, his starboard-outer engine burst into flames. The Lancaster, W4118, became temporarily uncontrollable, and his all-incendiary load had to be dumped. Hopgood bombed from 2,000 feet, and descended to 500 feet to clear the target area, allowing his rear gunner to shoot out a searchlight. P/O Cooper couldn't find the target, but made a timed run at 1,500 feet, and delivered his 1,000 pounders without seeing any results. P/O White found ten-tenths cloud at 1,000 feet, so he delivered his SBCs into the town from 800 feet, and picked up considerable light flak damage for his pains. Numerous fires were claimed, including a large one in or near the factory, and local reports confirmed that some housing and eight industrial buildings had sustained severe damage.

During the course of the month the squadron operated on thirteen nights, and launched 128 sorties for the loss of five aircraft. A major programme of airfield development was under way at this time to lay concrete runways to support the increasing weight of heavy bombers and their loads. All grass fields had to be upgraded, and it was now the turn of Coningsby. The final three days of September were occupied by 106 Squadron's move to Syerston, an airfield nestling alongside the A46 in Nottinghamshire, midway between Leicester and Lincoln. The station had opened on the 1st of December 1940, and had originally belonged to 1 Group. It had been home to two Polish Wellington squadrons, and on their departure in the summer of 1941, the station was transferred to 5 Group and was occupied by 408 Squadron RCAF. The Canadians moved out in December to allow concrete runways to be laid, and the station was reopened in the first week of May 1942 with 61 Squadron as its first and still current residents. S/L Hill was posted in towards

Lancaster ZN-S in very dirty conditions at Coningsby

the end of the month to fulfil the role of A Flight commander following the loss of S/L Howell. Sadly, his tenure would be brief.

October 1942

Despite the move, 106 Squadron was on the order of battle for the night of the 1/2nd, and supported a return to Wismar with thirteen Lancasters in an overall 5 Group force of seventy-eight. Hopgood was the senior pilot on duty, and he was first away at 18.05, to be followed by the others in a forty-minute slot. P/O Butterworth misinterpreted a recall signal and came home early, by which time P/O Cooper had landed with engine trouble. The others pressed on in unfavourable weather conditions, which including varying amounts of cloud with a base at 5,000 feet, and ground haze blotting out pinpoints. Hopgood couldn't get a fix on the target, and ultimately dropped his all-incendiary load on what he believed to be Warnemünde. P/O Healey actually caught a glimpse of the town on e.t.a, and dropped his mixed HE and incendiary load from 5,000 feet. P/O Cassels was immediately coned by searchlights and forced down to 2,500 feet, at which point he jettisoned his bombs "live" into the town. Shannon dropped his load on estimated position, and caught sight of an aerodrome and runways. His bombing photo revealed him to have been near the Heinkel works at Warnemünde. Wimpy Wellington had all four engines cut out during the return flight, but they restarted before any of the crew had time to respond to the bale-out order. Post-raid analyses suggested that bombing was scattered, and it was unlikely that any telling damage had been inflicted.

The Ruhr town of Krefeld was the target on the following night, for which 106 Squadron contributed five Lancasters to an overall force of 188 aircraft. F/L Whamond was the senior pilot on duty as they departed Syerston at 18.50, but he returned early after apparently receiving a recall signal. Probably not yet accustomed to the lie of the land after the move from Coningsby, Whamond inadvertently joined the circuit at nearby Newton, a former 1 Group station on the A46 a few miles south-west of Syerston, which was no longer in use as an operational bomber airfield. Whamond made his approach in the belief that he was about to land at Syerston, and was caught out by the shorter runway, which he overshot. W4238 crashed into a defence post at 21.25, and caught fire after the crew had scrambled away to safety. The Lancaster was burnt-out, but happily, no injuries were reported. The other crews were not able to positively identify the target, which was hidden beneath haze and mist, and they bombed on e.t.a and TR fix without causing significant damage. W4768 failed to return after being brought down by flak near

Bochum, killing P/O Butterworth and his navigator, P/O Osmond. The wireless operator, Sgt Pitchford, was found with a fractured skull, and he succumbed to his injuries on the 7th of October.

Over 250 aircraft took off for Aachen in the early evening of the 5th, among them ten Lancasters from 106 Squadron led by Hopgood, who was first away at 18.50. An hour after its departure W4102 was back over Nottinghamshire with a failed engine, and a bomb load of one cookie and a dozen SBCs. Had the Lancaster reached the coast, the ordnance would have been jettisoned, but a crash-landing was successfully accomplished at Langar, another neighbouring station on the Leicestershire/Nottinghamshire boundary. The Lancaster caught fire, but Sgt Lace and his crew escaped unhurt, and were well away from the scene before the cookie exploded and ripped the aircraft apart. The others mostly claimed to have found the target without difficulty, and bombed from 11,000 to 12,000 feet, either visually or on e.t.a and TR fix. Local reports admitted to some housing damage in a southern suburb, where a surprisingly large number of industrial premises were hit, but the Dutch town of Lutterade, seventeen miles away, was heavily bombed after being illuminated by the Pathfinders, and eight hundred houses were seriously damaged. This was not known at the time, and would have consequences when the town's power station was selected as a test target for the new Oboe blind-bombing device in the coming December.

Osnabrück provided the target for over 230 aircraft on the night of the 6/7th, for which 106 Squadron put up five Lancasters, their crews briefed to aim for the town's marshalling yards. No senior pilots were called into action as P/Os Wellington, Curtin, Crowfoot and Cassels and Sgt Phair departed Syerston either side of 19.30 and headed for the region of Germany immediately north of the Ruhr. The Pathfinders illuminated the Dummer Lake as a pinpoint north-east of the target, and the crews made timed runs from there. There was patchy seven-tenths cloud, but the target area was easily identified, although the yards could not be singled out. Most of the bombing fell within the town, where central and southern districts sustained significant damage. The squadron remained at home for the next few nights, and on the 9th began a series of formation flying exercises, the first one involving six aircraft. On the 10th twelve aircraft took part in a low-level formation practice lasting five hours, and this was repeated on the 11th, when the route was Base-Sea-southern Scotland-Northern Ireland-North Wales-Upper Heyford-Base. Clearly something was afoot at 5 Group, which the crews would not be told about until the last minute!

The night of the 12/13th, brought the third attempt to destroy the Dornier aircraft factory at Wismar. A 5 Group force of fifty-nine Lancasters included ten from 106 Squadron, led by Bill Whamond. Most got away in a twenty-five minute slot to 18.00, and Sgt Phair was last off at 18.05. P/O Healey was back an hour later with a port-outer engine streaming oil, and P/O Cassels was almost at the Danish coast when his starboard-outer failed, and he was forced to turn back also. It proved to be an ill-chosen night to attack a precision target, with ten-tenths cloud blotting out ground detail and forcing the crews to bomb on e.t.a. F/S Jones tried a square search that lasted forty-five minutes, but saw nothing, and eventually dropped his fourteen SBCs of 30lb incendiaries from 6,200 feet on the approximate position of Wismar. Ginger Crowfoot caught a glimpse of the estuary and timed his run from there, bombing from 6,000 feet on what he hoped was the town. David Shannon searched long and hard, and even came down to 500 feet, but found nothing and abandoned his sortie. Sgt Phair spotted aerodrome runways, which he bombed from 6,000 feet, and was the only one from the squadron to get close to the aiming point. Even so, some returning crews from other squadrons claimed to have started a large fire within the target.

On the following night Kiel was the objective for more than 280 aircraft, of which eight Lancasters represented 106 Squadron. S/L Hill was the senior pilot on duty for the first time since his recent arrival, and he was backed up by F/L Hopgood. They took off either side of 19.00, and arrived in the target area to find clear skies and no haze, but an effective smoke screen and a heavy and accurate response from the flak batteries. Hopgood pinpointed on the Selenter Lake and carried out a DR run from there to bomb visually from 12,000 feet by the light of Pathfinder flares. Others did likewise, and believed they watched their loads burst in the town. S/L Hill's bombing photo was plotted at seven miles from the aiming point, while a number of others were a little closer at three miles. It is known that a decoy fire site lured away half of the bomb loads, while the remainder fell into the town and its surrounds causing a significant degree of damage.

A night's rest was followed by an operation against Cologne, for which 288 aircraft took off. 106 Squadron's contribution amounted to eleven Lancasters, led by Gibson in W4118, with S/L Hill also on the Order of Battle. S/L Hill was first away at 19.00 for the relatively short trip to the Rhineland capital, and although the conditions were favourable with varying amounts of broken cloud and good visibility, the winds were not as forecast, and this made it difficult for the Pathfinders to establish their position. A large decoy fire site proved more alluring than the sparse marking, and most of the bomb loads were wasted. Many crews pinpointed on the river, and made timed runs, and believed their bombs had fallen into the city, and some did return with photos showing built-up areas. Gibson identified bridges over the Rhine, and dropped his bombs from 10,000 feet, watching them burst on the eastern bank. He described the opposition as heavy, and his aircraft picked up some damage. Hopgood was attacked three times by a JU88 on the way home, but his gunners beat it off and claimed it as damaged. Not all of the squadron participants were destined to return, and for the second time in the space of a month, daylight revealed three empty 106 Squadron dispersals. W4195 was on its way home over Holland when it was intercepted by a night fighter, and it crashed at 22.45 about eight miles south-west of Arnhem. P/O White RCAF and three of his crew, including two other Canadians, managed to bale out and they fell into enemy hands. W4771 was also on the way home, and was at 17,000 feet between the target and Mönchengladbach, when hit by flak, which killed the wireless operator and rear gunner. Four others managed to escape from the Lancaster, probably because Ginger Crowfoot DFC remained at the controls to give them time. His body was found in the wreckage with those of his wireless operator and rear gunner, and the survivors all became PoWs. S/L Hill DFC and his crew all died when W4302 crashed in Germany. F/L Whamond became the temporary successor to S/L Hill as A Flight commander, until a permanent appointment could be arranged.

The purpose behind the recent formation flying exercises was revealed to 5 Group crews early on the 17th, as they were briefed on Operation Robinson, a daylight attack on the Schneider armaments works at le Creusot, deep in eastern France, and the nearby Montchanin transformer station which provided its power. Often referred to as the French "Krupp", the company belonged to the Schneider family, which had donated the famous trophy bearing its name. The Schneider Trophy was initially a prize to encourage technical advances in civil aviation, but eventually became a speed contest for float and seaplanes competed for biannually by Britain, France, Italy and the USA. It was a massively prestigious and popular spectator event that drew crowds of 200,000 people. Britain claimed it outright after three consecutive wins culminating in 1931, when the revolutionary Supermarine S6B triumphed. Ninety-four Lancasters were to take part in the operation, which required an outward flight at low level by daylight, the attack at dusk, and a return under the cover of darkness. It was a bold plan to send such a large force, which would be difficult to conceal, and it was only six months since six 44 Squadron Lancasters had been caught by German fighters over France while on their way to Augsburg, and four had been shot down in a matter of minutes.

Lancasters en route to Le Creusot at very low level over the sea.

The plan called for eighty-eight aircraft to bomb the factory complex from as low as practicable, led by W/C Len Slee of 49 Squadron, while six others, two each from 106, 61 and 97 Squadrons, led by Gibson, went for the power station in a line-astern attack. The full 106 Squadron contribution amounted to ten crews, flying out in two formations of three and one of four. They would join up with the rest of the force over Upper Heyford, and head for a point just south of the Ile d'Yeu, before crossing the French coast midway between St Nazaire and la Rochelle. From there it was a low-level dash across France to a predetermined point, where the main force would break up and climb to a bombing height of between 5,000 and 7,000 feet. The 106 Squadron element took off either side of noon, and arrived safely in the target area some five hours later in good weather conditions. They chose varying altitudes from which to deliver their five 1,000 pounders, P/O Crowe from 3,400 feet, Sgt Lace and P/O Shannon from 7,000 feet, and others from between 5,500 and 7,500 feet, but all claimed to have watched them burst among the factory buildings. A few miles to the south-east, Gibson went in at 500 feet to attack the power station, while Hopgood chose 150 feet, and picked up some damage from the blast of his own bombs. A 61 Squadron Lancaster in Gibson's formation was so low that it crashed into a building, and was the operation's only casualty. The return across France under cover of darkness was accomplished without incident, and the returnees landed at Syerston between 21.40 and 22.40 after a very long round-trip. Without exception the crews reported both targets to have been severely damaged, but photographic reconnaissance revealed that much of the bombing had fallen short onto the workers' housing estate, and that damage to the factory was not as extensive as believed.

A low-level Lancaster raid launched in daylight was not generally recommended as a bombing tactic at this stage of the war. However only one aircraft on the Le Creusot raid was lost, when it flew into a building.

A well-publicised and iconic photo shows crews returning to Syerston after the Genoa raid on 22nd / 23rd October 1942.

A new campaign against Italy opened at Genoa on the night of the 22/23rd at the hands of a Pathfinder and 5 Group force of 112 aircraft. It was in support of the Eighth Army's impending offensive that would ultimately lead to victory over Rommel at El Alamein. 106 Squadron provided a dozen Lancasters for its first operation to Italy, and they were led away from Syerston by W/C Gibson in W4118 at 17.30. P/O Crowe experienced engine trouble, and Sgt Brinkhurst's oxygen system failed, precluding any chance of either being able to cross the Alps, and they were forced to turn back. The remainder pushed on in perfect moonlight conditions, and Gibson identified the target visually, before releasing his two 1,000 pounders and seven SBCs of 4lb incendiaries from 10,000 feet. His bombing photo would plot the bomb bursts to a mile-and-a-half from the aiming point. The others bombed from between 9,000 and 12,300 feet, and all returned safely to report a highly successful operation. The effectiveness of the attack was confirmed by photo-reconnaissance, which revealed substantial damage in central and eastern districts.

An audacious return to Italy was carried out by eighty-eight Lancasters from the Group in daylight on the 24th, for which 106 Squadron put up eleven aircraft, again lead by Gibson in W4118. Gibson had a regular all-officer crew, other than the flight engineer, and his wireless operator was P/O Bob Hutchison, who would be the only one to remain as one of Gibson's Dams crew. The flight engineer on this occasion was Sgt Guy Pegler, who would also go to the Dams, and would not return. Gibson led them off at 12.20, and headed for the Channel to join up with the others and pick up a fighter escort for the sea crossing. Once over France they used cloud cover, but this was higher than expected, forcing Gibson to fly at 6,000 feet. They rendezvoused with the main force over Lake Annecy, and arrived at the target of Milan to find complete cloud cover. Gibson came down to 4,000 feet to obtain his bearings, and identified the railway station, before climbing back to 6,000 feet to bomb through a break in the cloud. It is astonishing how different experiences were from crew to crew. P/O Wellington flew in formation to the French coast, where he found a complete absence of cloud cover, and after flying inland for a short time, decided to turn back. Bill Whamond found plenty of cloud cover at first, and when this dissipated he dropped down to 50 feet, before climbing back up to 15,000 feet on approach to the target. He reduced height to 7,000 feet, and saw the city through a break in the cloud, whereupon he delivered his fourteen SBCs of 30lb incendiaries, and watched them burst among large buildings. Before returning home he circled for a time taking photographs. Sgt Brinkhurst formated on four other Lancasters over the Alps, and arrived over the target at 8,000 feet, before diving to 4,500 feet to make his attack. He brought back a sequence of nineteen excellent photographs of the city. The operation achieved complete surprise. and produced significant damage to residential, industrial and administrative buildings.

This proved to be the final operation of the month for 106 Squadron as minor operations held sway for the final week. During the course of the month the squadron had operated on eight nights and two days, dispatching a total of ninety-five sorties for the loss of four crews and five Lancasters. S/L Wooldridge was posted from the squadron at the end of the month following the completion of his tour. His tally of operational sorties now stood at seventy-three, fourteen of which had been undertaken with 106 Squadron. He was posted to the tri-Service Petroleum Warfare Department in London, where his academic skills could be put to good use in various scientific projects. In March 1943 he would return to operations as the commanding officer of 105 Squadron, a 2 Group Mosquito unit engaged in daring low-level daylight operations over Germany. He would undertake a further twenty-four operations before returning to desk duties, and would survive the war. In 1948 he married the actress Margaretta Scott, best known for her role as Mrs Pomfrey in television's All Creatures Great and Small, and continued to write and compose. He wrote the screenplay and score for the 1953 film, Appointment in London, which depicted a Lancaster squadron at war and starred Dirk Bogarde as W/C Mason, the squadron commander. He wrote a number of plays, which were staged in London theatres, but he tragically died as the result of a motoring accident in 1958.

November 1942

Once 83 Squadron had departed 5 Group to take up its duties with the Pathfinders, 106 Squadron found itself at the top of the group bombing ladder. As a result its growing reputation invited the kind of attention that would see it selected for any special tasks that presented themselves. One of these had been to deliver the first Capital Ship Bomb at Gdynia at the end of August. With the continuing offensive against Italian targets, which would remain the main focus of attention for the rest of the year, the squadron would also drop the first 8,000lb HC bomb in anger on Italy. Gibson always led from the front, particularly when there was a difficult operation, or when it was in some way innovative, and he was also ever ready to experiment. As an example, he was the first to have photo-flash cameras fitted to every squadron aircraft to enable him to assess and improve bombing accuracy, at a time when such matters were only in the discussion stage at HQ.

Most of the first week of November passed with no main force activity, and the first operation of any consequence took place on the night of the 6/7th, when 5 Group dispatched a force of seventy-two Lancasters to Genoa. 106 Squadron sent a contingent of six aircraft, led for the first time by the twenty-nine-year-old S/L John Searby, who had been posted in on the 1st of the month to succeed S/L Wooldridge as B Flight commander. His previous post had been as Group Navigation Officer at 2 Group, but he had joined the RAF in 1929 as a "Halton Brat" engineering apprentice, before becoming a sergeant pilot in the mid-thirties. As he took off in W4771 at 21.40, he was embarking on his first ever operational sortie. Sgt McDonald returned early with hydraulics failure, but the others pressed on to arrive in the target area in clear skies and excellent visibility. Searby was able to pick out ground detail with ease, and he delivered his load of ten SBCs of 4lb incendiaries from 10,000 feet, observing them to ignite just west of the aiming point. The others described similar experiences, and all made it safely home to land between 06.30 and 07.50.

Arriving as a Squadron Leader, John Searby was to command 106 Sqn for two months in 1943.

The Italian campaign was a welcome break from the nightly grind to Germany, with its hostile and well organised defences. In comparison, and in the context of the period, Italy was considered to be a soft touch, illustrated by the painting of an ice cream cone rather than a bomb symbol on the side of the fuselage to signify an operation. Other groups joined in when a return to Genoa was made on the 7/8th, for which 106 Squadron put up eight Lancasters as part of an overall force of 175. They took off either side of 17.30 with Gibson the senior pilot on duty in W4118. There was a maiden operation on this night for F/S Lewis 'John' Burpee RCAF, who would follow Gibson to Scampton as a founder member of 617 Squadron. Two members of his Dams crew, flight engineer, Guy Pegler, and rear gunner, Joe Brady, were with him for their 106 Squadron baptism. Sadly, on this occasion, R5677 was not performing at its best, and lost an engine soon after crossing the French coast, and then had TR failure. The final straw came with the incapacitation by illness of the navigator, and the sortie was abandoned. Gibson found the target under clear skies in good visibility, and he was able to pick out the detail of the town and docks area. He dropped his two 1,000 pounders and six SBCs from 9,500 feet, and saw them burst slightly to the east of the aiming point. Sgt Hamilton was on his bombing run at 9,500 feet, when an explosion occurred. Thinking they had been hit by flak, he ordered the bombs to be jettisoned, only to discover that the noise had been caused by the TR set blowing up. Returning crews reported a successful attack, which was confirmed later by photographic reconnaissance.

Shannon had now been promoted to flying officer rank, and he was the senior pilot among the nine from 106 Squadron detailed to join a force of more than two hundred aircraft to attack Hamburg on the night of the 9/10th. They were all away from Syerston by 18.00, and initially encountered reasonable weather, which deteriorated over the North Sea. Sgt Hamilton returned early with engine trouble, while the others pressed on in increasingly difficult conditions of heavy cloud and icing, and a stronger-than-forecast head wind. None of the crews managed to positively identify the target, and all were forced to bomb on estimated positions. The result was that much of the bombing fell short, and that which found the city caused three large fires and a score of smaller ones. Local reports suggested also, that a proportion of the effort had been wasted by falling into the Elbe and into open country. Later on the 10th awards were announced to a number of 106 Squadron personnel as a result of the recent daylight operations to France and Italy. Gibson received a DSO, P/O Healey DFM was awarded a DFC, as was P/O Pennington, the navigator in F/O Aytoun's crew, and F/S Crosier, Sgt Smith's bomb-aimer, earned a DFM.

Genoa was not to be left long to lick its wounds, and the third raid within a week took place on the night of the 13/14th at the hands of a modest force numbering seventy Lancasters and Stirlings from 5 Group and the Pathfinders. 106 Squadron put up ten aircraft, whose crews had been briefed to aim for the Ansaldo works. This was probably the aircraft factory of the multi-faceted engineering company, which also had a major shipbuilding yard in the city. S/L Searby was the senior pilot on duty as they departed Syerston either side of 18.00, and, for once, there were no early returns. Conditions throughout the flight were good, and clear skies with just a little ground haze at the target enabled the bomb-aimers to pick out the aiming point with ease. Each Lancaster was carrying five 1,000 pounders, and these rained down from between 8,500 and 11,000 feet to fall across and around the aiming point. Many excellent bombing photographs were brought back, three of which showed the aiming point, while others were plotted within a few hundred yards. Sgt Phair was one with an aiming point photo, which he secured while on three engines, and he flew part of the return journey on just two after everything moveable had been jettisoned to save weight.

The squadron sent two Lancasters to join others for mining operations in the Kattegat Channel between Denmark and Sweden on the night of the 16/17th, and this gave F/S Burpee the opportunity to complete his first sortie as crew captain, having had to abort an earlier attempt. He and Sgt McDonald took off at 17.00 on a clear but hazy night, and Burpee made a timed run from Anholt Island to deliver his four mines into the correct location. Sgt McDonald searched long and hard, but failed to find his garden, and brought his mines back. On the following night P/Os Cassels and Curtin and F/S Hamilton set off either side of 18.00 for the long trek to the waters off Danzig, where weather conditions allowed them to locate the target area without difficulty, and deliver their three mines each. The Italian campaign continued on the night of the 18/19th, when a force of seventy-seven aircraft included eight Lancasters from 106 Squadron. They took off either side of 18.00, with Gibson leading and S/L Searby and F/L Hopgood in support as the other senior pilots. The aiming point was the Fiat aircraft works at Turin, which they found under clear skies in excellent visibility, and bombed from between 8,500 and 10,000 feet. After making his attack, Searby circled in the target area to watch others bomb, and confirmed that the factory was hit a number of times. All returned safely with reports of a highly successful attack, and Searby, Shannon and Sgt Lace brought back aiming point photos, while the others were plotted within two miles. Photo-reconnaissance confirmed that the city centre and Fiat works had sustained significant damage.

The largest force yet sent against an Italian target returned to Turin on the night of the 20/21st, with ten 106 Squadron Lancasters among them. They took off between 18.10 and 18.45, led by S/L Searby, but Sgts Freeman and Price were forced back early with technical malfunctions, while P/O Cooper lost an engine before reaching the Alps, but hauled R5750 over the snow-covered peaks and carried on. Conditions over the target were less favourable than for the previous raid, with thick haze and then smoke from the burgeoning fires blotting out ground detail. Most crews picked up a pinpoint south of the city, and made timed runs, but Sgt Brinkhurst caught a glimpse of the target through a break in the smoke, and it was definitely in the bomb sight as his load fell away from 10,000 feet. P/O Curtin also picked out the factory, and saw his bombs fall on the edge of it. F/S Hamilton thought his bombs burst about half a mile short of the factory, but probably hit the adjacent aerodrome. P/O Cooper re-crossed the Alps on thee engines on the way home, and all arrived safely to report a successful trip, but heavier than usual defences.

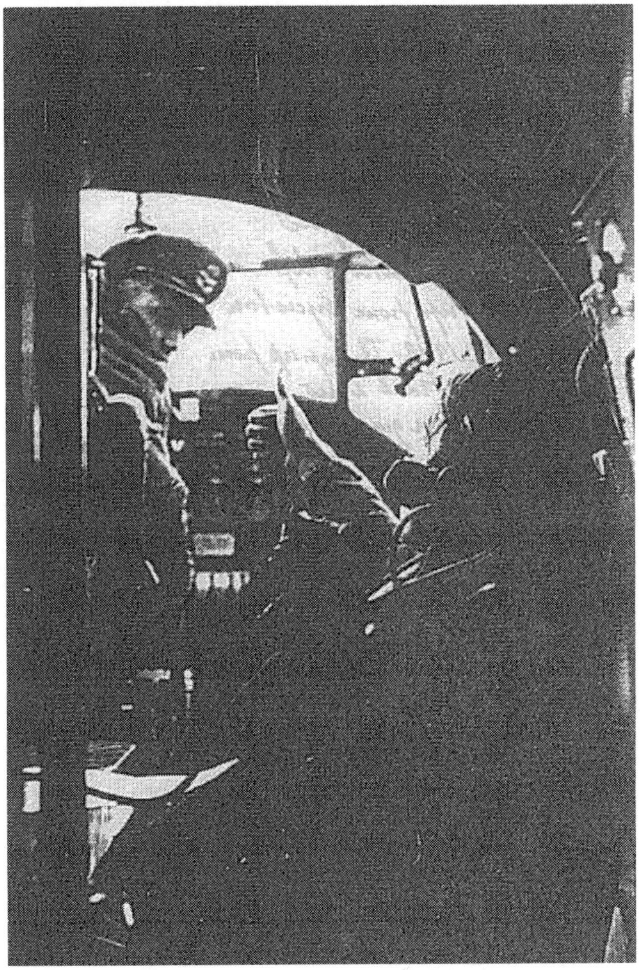

Pilot Officer Cooper receives the thumbs up from his navigator whilst at the controls of his Lancaster. His exploits included flying over the Alps with an engine out. Cooper later moved on to 617 Sqn, along with several others from 106 Sqn.

More than two hundred aircraft set off for Stuttgart on the night of the 22/23rd, for an operation that involved just four 106 Squadron Lancasters, captained by Searby, Shannon, Burpee and Lace. Despite having been attacked many times before, this was a new target to add to 106 Squadron's impressive list. They were off the ground by 18.30, and crossed France uneventfully, before encountering a thin layer of cloud that obscured the target. The Pathfinders were not able to identify the city centre, and the 106 Squadron crews relied on their navigators' timings. Searby did find a gap in the clouds, but was still not able to positively identify ground detail, and dropped his bombs on green marker flares from 10,000 feet, believing them to have burst near the railway station. Sgt Lace's bomb-aimer claimed to have seen marshalling yards, which he bombed from 11,000 feet, but didn't observe the results. Lace and Searby raced back across France at 100 feet, and the former was damaged by light flak. Reconnaissance revealed that much of the bombing had fallen onto residential districts on the fringes of the city, some five miles from the centre, and eighty-eight houses were destroyed, while more than three hundred sustained serious damage.

The final major operation of the month was directed at Turin on the night of the 28/29th, for which 106 Squadron contributed thirteen Lancasters to a force of more than two hundred aircraft from all groups. Gibson led the squadron contingent in R5551, and had on board Major Mulloch, the 5 Group Flak Liaison Officer, as an observer. Gibson, Whamond and P/O Healey were also each carrying an 8,000lb blast bomb, which were to be the first to be delivered on an Italian target. They took off either side of 19.00, but Healey was unable to retract his undercarriage, and sadly, had to dump his 8,000 pounder in the sea before returning home. Sgt Hayward lost an engine over the Alps, and, unable to maintain height, turned back. Over France he was attacked first by four enemy fighters, and then fifteen, which he evaded, and later by a FW190, which was seen to burst into flames after a long burst of fire from the rear turret. The others pushed on to the target, where they found clear skies, and good visibility. Gibson bombed from 8,000 feet, watching his blockbuster explode in the centre of the city, and then circled for thirty minutes taking cine-film of the attack. Whamond's 8,000 pounder fell just north of the city centre, leaving a large red mushroom with black smoke rising from it. Sgt McDonald's bombing photo showed the Fiat works, and most others were plotted within two miles of the aiming point. All from Syerston returned safely, thus sealing a loss-free month for 106 Squadron, during which ten operations had been carried out, involving seventy-three sorties.

December 1942

Frankfurt hosted the first operation of the new month on the night of the 2/3rd, which involved a little over a hundred aircraft from all groups. 106 Squadron was not required to take part, and enjoyed a relatively restful first five nights away from the operational scene. Briefings took place on the 6th for an operation that night to Mannheim, for which 272 aircraft were prepared. 106 Squadron's contribution to the main fare was eight Lancasters, while three freshman crews were to join a handful of others for mining duties off the Frisians. Take-offs were accomplished safely, firstly by the gardening brigade of Sgts Markland, Page and Irvine by 17.00, and then by the bombers between 17.20 and 17.40, with S/L Searby last away. Sgt Phair had an engine burst into flames shortly after take-off, and the failure of the propeller to feather forced him to turn back. The others pressed on in increasingly unfavourable weather conditions, and the target was found to be completely covered by cloud. The Pathfinders were unable to establish their position, and only a few flares were released. S/L Searby dropped his fourteen SBCs on e.t.a on flak concentrations from 8,500 feet, and the other crews described similar experiences on return. Bombing took place from between 6,000 and 10,000 feet, without any chance of assessing the results, and local reports confirmed the ineffectiveness of the attack. The gardeners fared much better, and all three located their drop zones and delivered four mines into the required locations.

The Pathfinders led a 5 Group main Force to Turin on the night of the 8/9th, for an operation supported by eleven 106 Squadron Lancasters. This was the occasion on which Gibson and station commander G/C "Gus" Walker were watching proceedings from the control tower, and saw some incendiaries fall from the bomb bay of a 61 Squadron Lancasters, which was in danger of catching fire. Walker jumped into his car and raced across the airfield to warn everyone to get clear, and then ran towards the aircraft, hoping to be able to rake the burning incendiaries from underneath and prevent the detonation of the cookie. Sadly, it went off when he was yards away, and a piece of shrapnel took off his right arm below the elbow. *(He would return to duty with a prosthetic arm two months to the day later.)* Sgts Page and Irvine were taking part in their first bombing operation, and, according to the ORB, took off well in advance of the others, shortly before 17.00, and perhaps this was to enable them to carry out a fully loaded air-test before setting out for the target. The others followed over the ensuing hour, with S/L Searby the senior pilot on duty. Sgt McDonald's rear gunner became ill, causing the sortie to be abandoned, and F/O Curtin lost his starboard-outer engine. The remainder pushed on in excellent weather conditions to find the target under clear skies and well-illuminated by the Pathfinders. P/O Cooper bombed from 6,000 feet, and watched his cookie and SBCs burst near a bridge a thousand yards from the aiming point. Rather than heading straight for home to celebrate the completion of his first tour of operations, he hung around for eighteen minutes to watch the show unfolding beneath him. Sgt Irvine bombed from 7,000 feet, and brought back a photo covering the aiming point, while Peter Page's photo showed an area 2,000 yards away. The attack caused extensive damage in both industrial and residential districts, and the fires were still visible a hundred miles into the return flight.

Over two hundred aircraft returned to Turin on the following night, and among them were eight 106 Squadron Lancasters. Sgts Page and Irvine were first off again, shortly before 17.00, and the others followed within thirty-five minutes. Matters began to go awry for the 106 Squadron aircraft soon after take-off, when Burpee's generators became unserviceable. He pressed on for a couple of hours until crossing the French coast, at which point he turned back. Peter Page was well into the outward flight when both port engines cut, and he struggled back on two. Sgt Freeman became ill, and turned back, while Sgt Irvine was concerned about not reaching the target in time, and also abandoned his sortie. Conditions at the target were not ideal, as fires were still burning from the previous night, causing smoke to drift across the aiming point and upwards. The Pathfinder illumination was not as effective, but the four 106 Squadron crews dropped their bombs from between 5,550 and 8,000 feet, and watched them burst in built-up areas of the city, before returning safely home.

The majority of the squadron would now enjoy ten nights off, and, therefore, miss the third raid on Turin on the 11/12th, which turned out to be a complete failure. This was, in fact, the final operation in the current campaign against Italy, and despite participating in ten of the operations since the 22nd of October, the squadron had lost no crews. Two crews were called to briefing on the 14th for mining duties off the Frisians that night, and Sgt Anderson and F/L E.L. Hayward (not to be confused with Sgt V.G.Hayward), who, it is believed, had just returned for a second tour, took off shortly after 17.00. In the event, all 5 Group aircraft were recalled because of doubts about weather conditions at base. This would have been Anderson's first sortie as crew captain, but he would now have to wait a further six nights. The squadron was fortunate not to be involved in the ill-conceived venture on the night of the 17/18th, when 5 Group sent twenty-seven Lancasters on moling sorties to a number of towns in Germany. Weather conditions were unhelpful, and nine Lancasters failed to return for little or no gain.

Group Captain 'Gus' Walker, Station Commander at Syerston, who lost an arm in heroic circumstances whilst trying to stop the cookie on a Lancaster blowing up. With his prosthetic arm he became known as 'One Armed Bandit' and later rose to the rank of Air Chief Marshal.

The night of the 20/21st was one of great significance for Bomber Command in its evolution to becoming an effective and, potentially, war-winning weapon. The main operation was against Duisburg, for which 232 aircraft took off in the early evening, among them a dozen Lancasters representing 106 Squadron. They took off between 17.40 and 18.05, with F/Os Cooke, Shannon, Healey and Curtin the senior pilots on duty. F/O Cooke DFC, DFM had just returned for his second tour, and although the ORB shows his rank as flying officer, it is believed that he was an acting flight lieutenant, which would have been entirely consistent with his decorations and experience. Sgt Anderson was also on the Order of Battle, hoping to complete his first sortie as crew captain. Sgt Hayward turned back with engine trouble, but the remainder pushed on to the Ruhr, and arrived over the target, where the sky below the 16,000 foot cloud base was clear. Bright moonlight helped to beat the haze and this allowed the crews to pick up ground features like the Rhine, bridges and the docks. Bombing took place from between 9,500 and 15,000 feet, but most crews were not able to distinguish their bomb bursts. One aiming point photo was brought back, along with others up to two miles away, and all returning crews were confident of a successful outcome. Twelve aircraft failed to make it home, and among them was 106 Squadron's R5697, which crashed about nine miles north-east of Amsterdam on the way home at 20.42, killing Sgt Anderson and his crew.

Almost unnoticed while this operation was in progress, six Mosquitos of 109 Squadron delivered the first Oboe-aimed bombs on a coking plant at Lutterade in Holland in a calibration exercise to determine the device's margin of error. The target had been selected to provide a crater-free environment to accurately plot the fall of bombs. Unfortunately, post-raid reconnaissance revealed the presence of many craters from misplaced bombs during the October attack on Aachen, and it proved impossible to identify the Oboe deliveries. Further calibration tests would take place in the coming weeks, however, and the device would be ready for employment by the time Harris launched his first major campaign in the spring of 1943.

Dave Shannon (left) and Don Curtin (Simon Sanders).

On the following night 5 Group contributed eighty-two Lancasters to an overall 1, 5 and 8 Group force of 137 aircraft, whose crews had been briefed to attack Munich. S/L Searby was the senior pilot as Bill Whamond led them off from Syerston at 16.45, but Sgt Page turned back very early with an engine problem. The others enjoyed excellent weather conditions as they pushed on into Germany, where, according to the 8 Group ORB, the Pathfinders illuminated the Wiensee as a pinpoint from which to make a timed run[1]. By the time the target was reached, however, it was found to be hidden beneath a layer of cloud, and without sight of the ground, the bombing was blind, and no crew was able to positively identify the fall of their bombs. A decoy fire site was also in operation, and its glow was probably responsible for luring some of the bombing away to fall into open country. A number of crews made mention of accurate flak and the presence of numerous night fighters, and twelve aircraft failed to return. It was a bad night for 106 Squadron, which posted missing two crews. R5574 went down over France, killing F/L Cooke and all but his navigator, P/O Moore, who became a PoW. It was just the

[1] It has not been possible to find this location on a map, but the Wiessee lies south of Munich, and may be the body of water referred to.

Crew of PO David Shannon, standing first right (Simon Sanders).

second operation of their second tour. His wireless operator, F/S Louch, and mid-upper gunner, P/O Goodwin, were also holders of the coveted DFM[2]. R5914 was shot down at 23.55 by a night fighter, while homebound over Belgium, and four men escaped by parachute to be taken prisoner. Their survival was largely due to the gallantry of the pilot, Sgt Brinkhurst, who freed the jammed forward hatch before returning to the controls to hold the aircraft steady. Testimony from the survivors after the war led to the award to their gallant pilot of a posthumous DFM. This was the final operation of a month severely hampered by bad weather. Planned operations were cancelled on sixteen occasions, and another had been subject to a recall. During the course of the month the squadron took part in six bombing and one mining operation, and launched fifty-four sorties for the loss of three aircraft and crews.

In comparison with 1941, it had been a successful year for the Command, characterized by improving serviceability, the accession to operational status of the Lancaster, and the coming together of new tactics and technology. Failures still outnumbered successes, but as 1943 beckoned, the writing was on the wall for Germany's industrial heartland, and although it would be a testing time for the front-line squadrons of Bomber Command, the days of treading water were over.

[2] F/L Cooke's twin brother, Sgt Harold Cooke, had also lost his life in a 10 O.T.U Whitley during the final Thousand Bomber operation against Bremen in June.

January 1943

New Year's Day brought the official formation of 6 Group, which was made up of squadrons from the Royal Canadian Air Force, and financed by the Canadian government. Up to this point the units had existed mostly in 4 Group, and their home stations in the Yorkshire and County Durham areas were transferred to 6 Group ownership. Further south in Lincolnshire and Nottinghamshire the new year began with a series of "Oboe" trials, which involved the Mosquitos of 109 Squadron marking for small forces of 1 and 5 Group Lancasters. Essen was the principal target, against which seven such raids would be directed during the first two weeks of January, along with a single attack on Duisburg. The programme got under way on the night of the 3/4th, when three Oboe Mosquitos led nineteen Lancasters, of which five were provided by 106 Squadron. Wimpy Wellington was the senior pilot on duty as they got away from Syerston at 17.20, but F/S Phair was forced to return early with communications problems. The others arrived over the target two hours twenty-five minutes later, in conditions of little cloud and good visibility. They watched the Mosquito-delivered parachute marker flares igniting over the target as they fell, and aimed their bombs at these from around 20,000 feet. There were plenty of searchlights and some flak, and P/O Lace picked up some damage, but got home safely with the others. The centre of the city sustained some damage, which had not happened too frequently in the past, and this suggested that Oboe might perhaps, indeed, provide the answer to hitting Ruhr targets.

106 Squadron sat out the next attack twenty-four hours later, and sent just one Lancaster on the third raid on the night of the 7/8th. Five crews plus a reserve had been briefed, but serviceability problems kept all but one on the ground, and only the newly promoted F/L Don Curtin and crew managed to take-off at 03.15. He encountered ten-tenths cloud with tops at 12,000 feet, but identified the target by Pathfinder flares. He delivered his cookie and ten SBCs from 20,000 feet at 06.08 in the face of heavy opposition, but was unable to determine the results. The 8th was a momentous day for the Pathfinder Force, which was awarded group status as 8 Group. It was unusual for 106 Squadron to suffer serviceability difficulties, but for the second night running, its contribution was reduced significantly by the return of four aircraft from the single attack of the Oboe trials series on Duisburg on the night of the 8/9th. Six Lancasters took off between 16.30 and 17.05 to join up with thirty-two others from the group, but, between 19.30 and 19.55, F/S Burpee, Sgt McDonald and Sgt Hayward returned to Syerston with engine failures. P/O Lace was last back of the early-returnees after his TR1335 equipment failed, and this left just F/S Phair and F/O Wellington to represent the squadron. They found good visibility above the eight to ten-tenths cloud tops at 14,000 feet, and identified the target by the Pathfinder flares. F/S Phair bombed from 20,500 feet at 19.23, a minute after P/O Wellington, who was at 18,000 feet, and neither was able to assess the results of their efforts. This was, in a way, what Oboe was all about, the ability to bomb blind, secure in the knowledge that the genius of electronic warfare had guided you to within a few hundred yards of an aiming point.

While this operation was in progress, six other crews from the squadron were undertaking mining duties off Rostock in the Baltic and the Frisians. Sgts Page, Price and Markland and F/L Hayward had the longer trip to make to the Baltic, where visibility was described by Sgt Markland as very poor. He searched long and hard, but failed to locate his garden, and ultimately abandoned the attempt. The others all found Moen Island from which to make a timed run, and each delivered four 1,570lb mines in the correct location. Sgts Marsh and Thompson, meanwhile, pinpointed on Baltrum Island in the Ostfrisian chain, and also successfully completed their sorties.

The size of the main force element for the Oboe trials series gradually increased raid by raid, and fifty Lancasters were dispatched to Essen on the night of the 9/10th, of which five represented 106 Squadron. They were all airborne by 17.00, but Sgt McDonald had a starboard-outer engine issue that prevented R5665 from maintaining height, and he turned back. The others all reached the target to find it clear of cloud, but blanketed by considerable haze. Some ground detail was identified, but three of the 106 Squadron crews relied on the accuracy of the Pathfinder flares, and delivered their loads from 18,000 to 20,000 feet between 19.22 and 19.30. P/O Wellington saw the flares late, and bombed visually onto a built-up area that he believed to be Essen. He described the flak defences as heavy, and returned with a number of holes in his Lancaster as proof. Sgt Thompson bombed on the release-point marker flares, and brought back a photo revealing roads, a railway and open country, which was plotted to be thirteen miles from the Krupp works. There was still much work to do to perfect the system.

On the 10th the squadron welcomed to its bosom Major Richard Dimbleby, the acclaimed BBC war correspondent, who was to stay for a number of days and fulfil a "special" assignment. Seventy-two Lancasters of 1 and 5 Groups took off for Essen on the night of the 11/12th, and among them were nine from 106 Squadron led by Gibson in LM303. This would prove to be the largest raid of the series. Gibson was first away from Syerston at 16.30, and they were all safely airborne within forty minutes. F/L Wellington turned back with engine failure, and he was followed by Burpee, whose rear turret became unserviceable. Finally, F/L Hayward was forced to abandon his sortie after W4265 proved unable to climb satisfactorily, and this left six aircraft to represent the squadron at the target. The Pathfinders employed skymarker flares, which tended to drift across the target at the behest of the wind, and on this night there were red and green warning flares and white flares as aiming point indicators. Gibson bombed from 20,000 feet at 19.35 in the face of heavy flak, and came away with a feeling that it had not been a successful attack. P/O Lace did not see the white flares, but bombed at 19.34 from 21,500 feet on release of the second warning flares. This was the final operation of his first tour, during which he had earned a DFM and Bar, and he returned safely with his crew to celebrate. Sgt Phair echoed Gibson's doubts about the effectiveness of the operation, and this was the general feeling at debriefing.

The operation on the night of the 12/13th involved fifty-five Lancasters of 1 and 5 Groups, of which seven were provided by 106 Squadron. F/S Burpee was the first to take off at 02.30, and for the second operation in a row he returned early, after his bomb-aimer inadvertently jettisoned the entire bomb load while testing the bomb doors off the English coast. The others reached the target area to find ten-tenths cloud with tops at 15,000 feet. F/L Wellington saw the release point marker flares, and bombed from 20,000 feet at 06.22, and his colleagues reported similar experiences, making particular mention of the heavy flak, and their inability to assess the results of their efforts. The operation failed largely because the Oboe equipment in the lead Mosquito became unserviceable, and the three other Mosquitos arrived late, resulting in sparse and inadequate marking. The final operation of the series was mounted on the night of the 13/14th, when the squadron put up ten Lancasters as part of a main force of sixty-six. They took off either side of 16.30 with S/L Searby the senior pilot on duty and Dave Shannon, now a flight lieutenant, back on the Order of Battle. F/L Curtin returned early after his mid-upper turret failed, but the remainder pressed on to the target, where S/L Searby reported eight-tenths cloud at 10,000 feet. He saw the release point marker flares, and dropped his cookie and twelve SBCs of 4lb incendiaries from 20,000 feet at 19.31. He was unable to comment on the outcome, but did describe heavy flak and searchlight activity, and returned with some damage to W4118. The others also saw the marker flares, with the exception of Shannon, who ended up bombing on estimated position. Sgt Reed carried out a three-minute timed run after seeing the warning flares, and believed his attack to be successful. On leaving the target he was attacked by a FW190, which raked R5700 from tail to nose, and then made a second attack raking it from nose to tail. The mid-upper gunner, Sgt Hood, was killed, the rear gunner, Sgt Twinn wounded, and the Lancaster was severely damaged. Sgt Reed coaxed it back to England, where a forced landing was made at Hardwicke in Norfolk without further casualties. Problems had again afflicted the Oboe element, with two Mosquitos returning early and the flares from a third failing to ignite above the clouds, but despite this, many bombs did fall within the city, where fifty-two buildings were destroyed. This operation brought to an end a loss-free period for the squadron, which had lasted since just before Christmas. R5680 was shot down by a night fighter on the way out over Holland, and crashed near Apeldoorn, killing the crew of F/L Healey DFC, DFM. This was a highly experienced and popular crew, which included navigator F/O Pennington DFC and bomb-aimer P/O Crosier DFM RCAF, and their presence would be missed. W4261 crashed near Düsseldorf, almost certainly after bombing, and there were no survivors either from the crew of F/S Phair RCAF, another experienced and valued crew.

A new Air Ministry directive was issued on the 14th, which authorized the area bombing of the French ports that contained U-Boot bases. A list of four targets was drawn up accordingly headed by Lorient, and the first of nine operations against it over the succeeding month took place that night. 5 Group was not called upon to participate, but its aircraft were prepared for a major operation two nights hence against Germany's capital city. Berlin had not been attacked for fourteen months, and on this night it was intended it would face two hundred aircraft, the majority of them Lancasters, which took off in the early evening of the 16th. This was the kind of operation that Gibson liked to be involved in, and he led the thirteen-strong 106 Squadron contingent in R5611, with an 8,000 pounder on board, along with the BBC journalist, Richard Dimbleby, who was to record his impressions for a broadcast to the nation. This was the first operation for S/L McDougall, who had been posted in as the new A Flight commander following the loss of S/L Hill back in October. S/L Searby was also on the Order of Battle, and was first to take off at 16.00. Sgts Irvine and Reed and F/L Hayward returned early with a variety of technical issues, but the remainder reached Berlin, which was beyond the range of any electronic navigation and blind bombing device. Gibson made three runs across the target before dropping his 8,000 pounder from 18,000 feet, and, on return, commented on the haze that made pinpointing difficult. Some crews caught sight of red marker flares, while others bombed on estimated positions, and all were left feeling disappointed with their efforts. Bombs were scattered around the southern districts, and the only notable success was the total destruction of the ten-thousand-seat Deutschlandhalle, the largest covered venue in Europe. Remarkably, only one aircraft failed to return, but as half of the personnel from the flak crews were away on a course, this may be viewed as a lucky escape.

The operation was repeated on the following night, when 170 Lancasters and seventeen Halifaxes took off and made their way eastwards in better weather conditions than twenty-four hours earlier. Burpee was first off of the nine 106 Squadron participants, on a night when the senior officers stayed at home. F/Ls Wellington, Curtin and Hayward were the commissioned captains operating, the first-two-mentioned carrying an 8,000 pounder each, as was Sgt Markland. The force was routed-in from the north, and visibility on the way out was good with little cloud. Sgt Irvine showed commendable fortitude after his port-outer engine failed shortly after crossing the English coast, but he decided to continue on. Later his starboard-inner also cut, and still he attempted to reach the target, until finally giving up and dumping his bombs in the Baltic. Wimpy Wellington found eight-tenths cloud over Berlin, but saw the ground through a gap, and witnessed the flash as his blockbuster detonated. His bombing photo showed an area containing important war production factories, Daimler-Benz, Fritz Wernher and Siemens, but these were six miles from the intended aiming point. Sgt Glaholme found no gaps in the cloud, but managed to find the

Müggelsee in the city's south-eastern suburbs, and made a timed run from there. Remarkably, the other crews found little or no cloud, and F/L Hayward pinpointed on two lakes north of the city, before circling for thirty minutes to confirm his whereabouts. F/L Curtin found the target by the light of the Pathfinder flares, and his 8,000 pounder caused a mighty explosion, which was caught by the camera and illuminated suburbs. Sgt Markland bombed from 22,000 feet, and observed the flash of his 8,000 pounder bursting, but little else. He was hit by flak over Kiel, probably on the way out, and later on was attacked twice by a JU88, probably on the way home. It was driven off by the gunners during the first attack, and shot down in flames during the second, after which the gunners shot up a searchlight battery at Flensburg. Sgt Reed was becoming accustomed to eventful sorties, and on this night R5900, "Admiral Air Goosk", was hit by flak, which damaged the hydraulics. It was necessary to "pull the bottle" to get the wheels down for landing, but they collapsed on touch-down, and the Lancaster was written-off, happily without crew casualties. Post raid analysis revealed that the Pathfinders had again missed the city centre aiming point, and bombing was scattered over the southern districts, causing no serious damage. In contrast to the previous night, twenty-two aircraft failed to return, 11% of the force.

The Command returned to Essen on the night of the 21/22nd with a force of seventy-nine Lancasters led by three Oboe Mosquitos. Five of the former were provided by 106 Squadron, all captained by NCOs, and they departed Syerston either side of 17.00. On the way out F/S Hayward was attacked by a FW190 and later by a BF110, both of which were thrown off by skilful flying and crew co-operation. During the violent manoeuvres, however, the dinghy came loose from its stowage, and fouled the elevator, making control difficult. As a result the bombs were jettisoned and the sortie abandoned. He arrived back in the Syerston circuit at the same time as Burpee, who had been hit by flak at 18,000 feet during the bombing run. W4842 was damaged in many places, and a fire broke out in the bomb bay, at which point Burpee ordered the load to be jettisoned. The remaining three crews bombed in the target area, but were unable to assess the results.

Two nights later eight 106 Squadron Lancasters joined forces with seventy-two others and three Oboe Mosquitos to target Düsseldorf. They were again all captained by NCOs, and Burpee was the first to take off at 16.15. He often seemed to leave well ahead of the others, perhaps to carry out a fully-loaded air-test before setting out, and for this operation he got away a full thirty-five minutes before the next departure. Sgt Markland had just crossed the enemy coast when he was attacked by a night fighter, which he was unable to shake off. During the evasive action he shed a lot of height, and ultimately decided there was insufficient time to complete the operation. F/S Hayward's W4256 lost the use of its rear turret through hydraulics failure, and he also returned without completing his brief. The others arrived over the target to find complete cloud cover, with tops ranging from 14,000 up to 20,000 feet, and Sgts Irvine and Price circled to await the release-point flares. Irvine dropped his cookie and SBCs from 20,000 feet at 19.52, and saw the flash of the impact through the clouds. Price released his load eight minutes later, but observed nothing. Burpee, McGregor and Glaholme bombed on the warning flares between 19.52 and 19.54, and they also were unable to comment on the outcome.

The 26th brought further decorations for squadron members, a Bar to his DFC for F/L Curtin, a DFC for Gibson's wireless operator, P/O Bob Hutchison, and a DFM each to Sgts Greep and Parry, mid-upper and rear gunners respectively in Sgt Markland's crew. On the night of the 27/28th Düsseldorf was selected as the target for the first use of Oboe ground markers, which were designed to burst and cascade at low level, and would become the standard method of marking when the target could be identified visually. These were much more accurate than the parachute flares in use thus far, which, as already mentioned, tended to drift with the wind. In conditions of heavy cloud, however, skymarking (parachute flares) would still offer the best option, while sometimes a combination of sky and ground marking would provide the crews with a choice. 106 Squadron contributed a dozen Lancasters to this operation, which began with the departure of Sgts Marsh and McDonald at 17.30, and not a single one would return early. The senior pilot on duty was S/L Searby, who reported ten-tenths cloud throughout the trip. Over the target the cloud tops were at between 10,000 and 15,000 feet, but the layer was thin enough to allow sight of the ground markers detonating, and Searby saw two reds and one green. He bombed the second red at 20.00 from 20,000 feet, without being able to observe any bursts, but he did bring back an excellent photograph of the clouds. The other crews reported similar experiences, and F/L Hayward picked up some damage from heavy flak. Just as Searby was releasing his bomb load, R5637 was crashing about four miles south-west of Roermond in Holland, killing Sgt Marsh RNZAF and his crew. A monument has since been erected on the crash site. The new marking technique on this night led to an accurate and concentrated raid on the southern half of Düsseldorf, which left in its wake quite considerable damage to industrial, municipal and residential property.

The month closed with the first H2S attack of the war on the night of the 30/31st, with Hamburg as the target. H2S was a radar device carried in a blister beneath the aircraft, which sent images of the terrain below to a cathode ray tube in the navigator's compartment. It took great skill to interpret what was being seen, and the early version was not able to provide the hoped-for clarity. In time it would become a useful aid to bombing through cloud, but its baptism on this night in the hands of Pathfinder Stirlings and Halifaxes of 7 and 35 Squadrons respectively, would not be outstandingly successful. 106 Squadron dispatched fifteen Lancasters as part of an overall force of 148, but, as if to compensate for the lack of early returns from the previous operation, there were five on this night. Take-off was late, either side of midnight, with S/L McDougall the senior pilot on duty, but his rear turret became unserviceable almost immediately, and he was forced to abort his sortie. Sgt McGregor turned back with the same problem, and Sgt Reed's engines behaved erratically, preventing him from maintaining height. Sgt McDonald's oxygen system failed, as did Sgt Burton's TR1335 equipment, and they too came home early. Over the target there was a thin layer of five to eight-tenths cloud, and F/L Curtin had the green marker bomb in his sights as he let his cookie and SBCs go from 17,000 feet at 03.06. F/L Hayward bombed two minutes later from a thousand feet higher, and commented that the only incident in an otherwise uneventful trip was excessive static, which temporarily blinded the whole crew and slightly burned the wireless operator. The attack was scattered around the city, with no point of concentration, but there were seventy large fires, and the destruction of a railway bridge shut down the city's rail network for two days. W4826 failed to return to Syerston with the crew of Sgt Johnson, who were all killed when it crashed at 03.20 into the railway station at Imsum, a northern suburb of Bremerhaven. During the course of the month the squadron notched up its 2,000th sortie. It operated on thirteen occasions, dispatching 109 sorties for the loss of five aircraft and four crews.

February 1943

The new month began with an attack on Cologne by over 150 aircraft on the night of the 2/3rd, when both Oboe and H2S marking were employed over a cloud-covered target. 106 Squadron contributed eight Lancasters, which departed Syerston in a fifteen minute slot to 18.05. There were no senior pilots on duty, but a F/L Burnside was the highest-ranking officer, flying as second pilot to Sgt Renshaw. Sgt Reed and crew were in ED409, which suddenly went out of control, leading the pilot to think they had been hit by flak. In the confusion he ordered the bombs to be jettisoned, and the sortie was abandoned. The others reached the target, which they were able to see in conditions of three to seven-tenths cloud, and they bombed either visually or on the markers from between 13,000 and 19,000 feet shortly after 21.00. Only F/O Edmonds and Sgt McGregor saw the burst of their cookies, and they returned safely with the others to report a seemingly successful attack. In fact, the bombing was scattered across the city with no point of concentration, and, therefore, no significant damage.

When Hamburg was next targeted on the following night, the weather proved to be its ally, producing ten-tenths cloud and severe icing conditions. Over 250 aircraft took part, including six Lancasters from 106 Squadron, which took off from Syerston either side of 18.00 with F/L Hayward the senior pilot on duty. Sgt Renshaw had been entrusted with W4118, Admiral Prune I, a Lancaster frequently used by Gibson and Searby, but he abandoned his sortie in the belief that he would not arrive at the target in time. The others were settling onto their final approach by 21.00, and had the warning and release point flares in their sights as they bombed from between 17,500 and 19,000 feet in a slot from 21.03 to 21.11. Sgt Irvine reported a brilliant red colour beneath the clouds that lasted for ten seconds, and all were aware of fires, but none could assess their own work. Sgt Reed and crew, who had crashed on landing after the Berlin raid two weeks earlier, and had rarely experienced an uneventful sortie, failed to return from this operation. Clearly, they had used up their ration of luck, and all died when W4770 crashed in northern Germany, possibly after colliding with another aircraft.

A drawing, possibly commemorating the trip by Sgt McGregor and crew to Turin on 4th / 5th February 1943 (Simon Sanders).

The city of Turin and its Fiat motor works were the objective for a mixed force of 150 aircraft on the following night. 106 Squadron waved off six Lancasters between 18.05 and 18.20, led by F/Ls Hayward, Curtin and Shannon, with W4118 on this night in the hands of Sgt Thompson and crew. Sgt Hayward's rear turret became unserviceable on the way out, and he jettisoned his 8,000 pounder and turned back. Shannon was on his bombing run when W4156 was hit in the bomb bay by flak, which set the all-incendiary bomb load on fire. He jettisoned it immediately, and had the satisfaction of watching the individual incendiaries fall into a wooded area just short of the city, which was subsequently engulfed by a raging fire that swept towards the suburbs. F/Ls Curtin and Hayward found the target easily, the former delivering his 8,000 pounder from 11,000 feet, and the latter his fourteen SBCs from 12,500 feet. Bombing photos showed their fall to be 1¾ and 3,000 yards respectively from the aiming point. Sgt McGregor bombed from 15,000 feet at 21.51, and his bomb would later be plotted at 5,000 yards from the aiming point. A message was received from W4118 at 22.30 stating that an engine had failed and height was rapidly being lost. A fix placed the Lancaster near Dijon in France, and although the timing suggests that it was homebound at the time, it seems, according to survivor testimony, that it was, in fact, still outbound. It emerged later that both port engines had failed, and Sgt Thompson RCAF was forced to crash-land on a hill at Valsonne, a little over twenty miles north-west of Lyons. Four of the eight men on board lost their lives, but Thompson and three others joined the growing roll call of Bomber Command airmen on extended leave in Germany. The operation was highly successful, and left widespread destruction behind it for a loss of three Lancasters.

Over three hundred aircraft took part in the continuing assault on Lorient on the night of the 7/8th, four of them Lancasters from 106 Squadron. F/O Edmonds led off three NCO pilots at 18.55, and they all arrived at the target to find it ablaze, and ground detail obliterated by smoke. The Pathfinders did their job well, and the main force element followed up with accurate and highly destructive bombing. F/O Edmonds spent five minutes looking for a place to bomb, and eventually let his cookie and SBCs go at 21.35, watching them burst within a ring of fires, before bringing back an aiming-point photo. After a busy first week of the month the majority of the Command enjoyed a few nights at home courtesy of unfavourable weather conditions. Over 170 crews returned to the briefing rooms on the 11th for an attack that night on Wilhelmshaven. 106 Squadron put up eight Lancasters, which took off between 17.15 and 17.35 and headed into heavy cloud. The senior pilot on duty was F/O Picken, who had returned to the squadron to begin a second tour. Burpee and crew were in W4156, the Lancaster Shannon had brought back in a damaged state from Turin on the 5th, and this time its rear turret became unserviceable, forcing them to turn back. Sgt Markland was still in the climbing-out phase when aileron problems struck, and although he set course for the target, the malfunction became more acute, and he too abandoned his sortie. The others arrived to find the target to be completely hidden by cloud, as expected after they were told at briefing that this was to be a blind-bombing attack. The Pathfinders resorted to skymarking by H2S, the least reliable method of target marking, but on this night it proved to be highly effective. F/O Picken had the markers in his bomb sight as the cookie and twelve SBCs went down from 16,000 feet at 20.07, and he saw the flash of their impact about twenty seconds later. Sgt McDonald didn't see the burst of his bombs from 19,500 feet at 20.08, but two minutes later he, and most of the other crews, witnessed a giant explosion, that lit up the sky like day for many seconds. What they had seen was the destruction of the Mariensiel naval ammunition dump, which devastated 120 acres of the naval dockyard and town. Only three Lancasters failed to return, and among them was 106 Squadron's LM303, which was shot down by a night fighter off Borkum on the way home, killing F/S Hayward RCAF and his crew. This was the first successful operation for blind-bombing by H2S skymarking.

A return to Lorient was made by over 460 aircraft in a two-wave attack on the night of the 13/14th. Eleven Lancasters from 106 Squadron took off between 18.40 and 18.55 led by S/L Searby, and, for once, there were no early returns. They were part of the first wave, which found the target in good visibility under clear skies, and accurately marked by the Pathfinders. The town was already well alight when F/O Picken bombed from 12,000 feet, but smoke obscured the impact, and the other crews were similarly unable to plot the fall of their bombs. F/O Picken and S/L Searby brought back aiming point photos from what was a highly effective attack, which delivered more than a thousand tons of bombs onto the already rubble-strewn port. Twenty-four hours later it was the turn of Milan to face the bombers, and eleven Lancasters from 106 Squadron set off towards the Alps in company with 131 others from 1, 5 and 8 Groups. At the same time 240 aircraft from the other groups were sent to attack Cologne. Gibson led off the 106 Squadron contingent between 18.20 and 18.45, and he had F/L Morrison beside his as second pilot, and Sgt Cartwright as the movie camera operator. Sgt Glaholme lost the use of his compass, and he was forced to turn back. S/L Searby was also on the Order of Battle, and he found the target easy to identify in excellent weather conditions. He bombed from 12,000 feet at 22.38, and saw the impact of his all-incendiary bomb load. Six crews, those of S/L Searby, P/O Edmonds, Sgt McDonald, F/L Hayward, Sgt Markland and Sgt

Price all brought back an aiming point photo, which was a record in 5 Group, and prompted a message of congratulations from the A-O-C, AVM Coryton. Gibson stooged around for twenty minutes after bombing, while his camera operator shot a movie, and he brought back a bombing photo plotted at a mile-and-a-half from the aiming point. The operation was highly destructive, and crews were able to see the glow of fires a hundred miles into the return journey.

The campaign against Lorient concluded on the night of the 16/17th after eight attacks totalling more than eighteen hundred sorties. 106 Squadron contributed eight Lancasters to this night's effort, of which two contained commissioned pilots, F/O Edmunds and P/O Brodrick. They took off between 18.15 and 18.45 to join an overall force of 377 aircraft, and all reached the target to deliver their bombs from between 9,500 and 12,000 feet in a five-minute slot to 20.53. Weather conditions were good, and three crews, those of Burpee, Brodrick and Markland, brought back aiming point photos. All returned safely to Syerston, leaving behind them a once proud town that was now a deserted ruin. Later on the 17th it was announced that P/O Cassels had been awarded a DFC, and his navigator, F/S Woollard, a DFM. Wilhelmshaven hosted its second raid of the month on the night of the 18/19th, which 106 Squadron supported with nine Lancasters in an overall force of 195 aircraft. F/L Hayward and the newly-promoted F/L Picken were the senior pilots on duty as they took off in a twenty-minute slot from 18.00, and all from the squadron reached the target area to find clear visibility and potentially good bombing conditions. F/L Picken located the target both visually and by a red marker bomb, and the target indicator was in his sights as his cookie and SBCs fell from 14,000 feet and burst in a built-up area. Burpee was 7,000 feet higher when he let his load go, too high to observe the results, but his bombing photo revealed fires, roads, canals and fields covering an area five miles from the aiming point. The other crews also claimed to have had the target indicators in their sights as they released their bombs, but most of the effort was found to have fallen west of the town into open country. Pathfinder claims of accurate marking were found to be mistaken, and the outcome was a major disappointment, which confirmed that all was still not well with regard to target identification and marking. The return to Syerston of R5750 was awaited in vain, and it would be confirmed later that the Lancaster had crashed into the North Sea in the general target area, killing the experienced and popular crew of Sgt Markland RNZAF. Five bodies were recovered by the Germans on the 21st, and the others eventually came ashore for burial. It will be recalled that both gunners had been awarded a DFM following an operation to Berlin in the previous month.

A considerably larger force returned to the port on the following night, without a 106 Squadron contingent, and this time delivered its bombs to the north of the town, again causing little damage. Part of the problem was traced to out of date maps, and this led to a general updating of those held by the Command. The night of the 21/22nd found nine 106 Squadron Lancasters outbound for Bremen as part of an overall force of 130 of the type, with a number of Pathfinder Stirlings and Halifaxes to supplement the marking. They had taken off from Syerston in a ten-minute slot to 18.20, with S/L Searby the senior pilot, backed up by F/Ls Shannon, Curtin and the newly promoted Edmunds. Complete cloud cover hid the target, and crews faced intense opposition as they made their bombing runs at 14,000 to 18,000 feet. All except Sgt Renshaw dropped their bombs within seconds of each other at 20.52, and he was last from the squadron to let his go six minutes later. All crews were diverted to the 6 Group station of Topcliffe on return because of fog at Syerston. No bombing photos were brought back, and, therefore, no assessment of results could be made.

Invariably, when the Command went to Nuremberg, it failed to achieve its aims, and frequently came off second best. On the night of the 25/26th a force of over 330 aircraft included thirteen Lancasters from 106

Squadron, led by W/C Gibson in ED649 and S/L Searby in ED593. F/L Curtin was among the first to take off at 19.00, and all were off the ground by 19.20, climbing to cruising altitude and forming up before setting course for the French coast. All were unanimous in their assessment of the conditions, which they described as good for bombing, with no cloud and excellent visibility. The Pathfinders were late arriving, and this forced the main force crews to orbit while they waited for the markers to go down. It was "squeaky bum" time, because no crew wanted to stooge around among hundreds of others and face the very real risk of collision. The squadron participants bombed from between 12,000 and 17,000 feet either side of 23.30, and all described a concentrated attack on the Pathfinder markers, with many fires and explosions all over the city. In fact, only a proportion of the bombing had hit the city, mostly on the northern fringes, and three hundred buildings were damaged. Most of the bombing was wasted, however, much of it on neighbouring communities up to eight miles away. Only nine aircraft failed to return on this occasion, but the squadron lost an experienced and popular crew, that of the American F/L Don Curtin DFC & Bar, a New Yorker, who had enlisted in the RCAF to get into the war. He and his crew, which included S/L McGrath RNVR, who was on attachment from HMS Daedalus, were just three operations short of completing their first tour, and died in the wreckage of W4886, after it crashed eight miles north of the target.

On the following night over 420 aircraft were sent to Cologne, among them ten Lancasters from 106 Squadron, once more led by Gibson in ED649 on his twenty-eighth and penultimate operation since taking command eleven months earlier. It was also his seventieth bomber operation in all, on top of the ninety-nine sorties he had accumulated as a night fighter pilot with 29 Squadron. Take-off at Syerston began at 18.35, and they were all climbing away within ten minutes for the relatively short trip to the target. Once more there were no early returns as the excellent run of perfect serviceability continued, and all reached the much-bombed city in good conditions with some ground haze. Burpee was the first to bomb, delivering his cookie and SBCs from 17,500 feet at 21.15. Gibson made a fast (220 i.a.s.), straight run at 16,000 feet, and dropped his bombs at 21.21 in the face of heavy and accurate flak. He saw them burst near the aiming point, and was satisfied that a concentrated raid was taking place. S/L Searby had an additional ten m.p.h on Gibson, as he raced across the city at 17,000 feet, and he saw the flash of his cookie's impact. As events were to prove, only around 25% of the bomb loads fell within the city, but they produced considerable damage to residential and city centre type buildings at a cost to the Command of ten aircraft. The night of the 27/28th was devoted to mining operations around the Frisians, for which the squadron contributed four freshman crews. F/O Wesley and Sgts Munro, Abel and Britton took off between 18.30 and 18.45, and delivered six 1,570 mines each into the correct location after pinpointing on Juist or using a Gee fix.

With Lorient now consigned to oblivion, the last night of the month brought the first of a number of attacks on the French port of St Nazaire in line with the January directive. 437 aircraft took off to attack the U-Boot pens, among them ten Lancasters from 106 Squadron, which began taking off shortly after 18.00. S/L Searby was the senior pilot on duty, and there was a first bombing operation for F/O Wesley. They all arrived in the target area to find no cloud, but smoke and haze impaired the visibility to an extent. Searby picked out the docks clearly, and had the TIs in his sights as he bombed from 14,000 feet at 21.17. All returning crews commented on the town being consumed by a conflagration, and Sgt Renshaw's crew reported still being able to see the glow from 5,000 feet as they approached Start Point on the Devon coast. The crews were correct in their belief that the operation had been an outstanding success, and reconnaissance revealed that an estimated 60% of the town's built-up area had been reduced to ruins. During the course of the month the squadron operated on fourteen occasions, and dispatched 117 sorties for the loss of five aircraft.

Another famous picture of 106 squadron, taken in March 1943. The dog strategically sitting next to Guy Gibson is Diny who belonged to S/Ldr Eric Hayward. Hayward was to lose his life two ops short of completing his second tour.

March 1943

The first major campaign of the year was beckoning in early March, and 106 Squadron welcomed a new A Flight commander, who would be a major influence on those taking part. S/L Peter Ward-Hunt, who was born on Gibraltar in 1916, was a man of small stature, but enormous personality, and someone who had gained operational experience since the very beginning of strategic bombing in May 1940. His operational career began with 49 Squadron at Scampton, and, at the end of a tour of thirty-two operations, he was awarded a DFC. After a period of screening he joined 207 Squadron to fly Manchesters, and took part in the attack on the Renault lorry factory in Paris, and later, while an instructor, he flew a training unit Manchester on the first thousand bomber raid on Cologne. His style was to lead from the front, and his opportunity to do so at 106 Squadron came with the first major operation of the new month. Berlin was selected to host a major operation on the night of the 1/2nd, for which 302 aircraft were made ready, a dozen of them Lancasters of 106 Squadron.

They took off between 18.25 and 18.50 on a night of good weather conditions, and headed for the rendezvous point, from where they would set course for the "Big City". The massive urban sprawl of Germany's capital produced confusing images on the Pathfinder H2S screens, which were difficult for the navigators to interpret. This made it impossible to establish a concentration of target indicators around the intended aiming point, and, even though the target was easily identified both visually and by markers, the high-flying bombers were presented with a variety of choices. S/L Ward-Hunt had red markers in his bomb sight as he delivered his cookie and twelve SBCs from 17,000 feet at 22.12, and although he did not observe the detonation, he saw several large fires. He brought back a bombing photo showing a built-up area plotted at five thousand yards from the aiming point. S/L Searby bombed from 20,000 feet at 22.13, and described large areas of the city on fire, and the other returning crews had similar stories to tell. Only Sgt Glaholm failed to reach the target after his compass became unserviceable. Bombing was spread over a wide area, but the south-western districts attracted the most loads, and severe damage was caused to housing and industrial premises, in what was the most destructive attack to date on this target. Seventeen aircraft failed to return, but 106 Squadron's participants came through unscathed.

Two nights later over four hundred aircraft set out for Hamburg, ten of the Lancasters provided by 106 Squadron. F/Ls Hayward and Picken were the senior pilots on duty, and other than that of F/O Wesley, the remaining crews were captained by sergeants. Take-off began at 18.40, and the crews enjoyed favourable weather conditions all the way out. Some crews pinpointed on the River Elbe, and confirmed their position by the Pathfinder red and green target indicators, and most had these in their bomb sights as they delivered their cookies and SBCs between 21.27 and 21.40 from an average height of 17,000 feet. F/Ls Hayward and Picken both commented on the fact that most of the bombing appeared to be falling to the west of the aiming point, and their observations were proved to be correct when bombing photos were plotted. Interpreting the H2S images had again proved problematic, and the small town of Wedel, thirteen miles downstream on the northern bank of the Elbe, had borne the brunt of the attack. Some bombs did fall within Hamburg itself, however, and the city's fire-fighters had to deal with a hundred conflagrations before lending their assistance to their neighbour. Crews reported the glow of fires still visible up to a hundred miles into the return flight. 106 Squadron's R5731 failed to return after crashing near Hohenaspe on the Schleswig-Holstein peninsular, north-west of Hamburg, and there were no survivors among the crew of F/O Wesley RCAF, who had only recently begun their first tour of operations.

The way was now clear for Harris to embark on the first campaign for which Bomber Command was adequately prepared and equipped, and the fearsome Ruhr Valley, Germany's industrial heart, was to be the battleground. Harris had tried before in 1942, unleashing thousands of sorties against Essen, Duisburg, Dortmund and Düsseldorf, and failing to establish the concentration necessary for success. He had been left frustrated by the inability of his crews to see through the blanket of industrial haze that protected them. Now, though, not only did Harris have available to him a predominantly four-engine heavy bomber force capable of carrying ever-increasing bomb-tonnages, he also had the electronic wizardry of Oboe, now tried and tested and close to its design capability. With a margin of error of four hundred yards, it no longer mattered that the ground was hidden from the crews. It mattered only that the high-flying Oboe Mosquitos reached the target with functioning Oboe equipment.

The Battle of the Ruhr opened on the night of the 5/6th, and was hosted by the much-visited industrial city of Essen, home of the giant Krupp armaments works. The squadron put up twelve Lancasters for this operation, led by S/Ls Searby and Ward-Hunt in ED593 and ED596 respectively. F/L Bill Picken DFC was among the first to take off at 18.30 to join up with an overall force of 440 aircraft. An unusually high number of early returns reduced the size of the force reaching the target to 362 aircraft, and among those aborting were three of the eight participating Oboe Mosquitos, upon whose performance the success of the operation depended. Also turning back with an unserviceable rear turret was 106 Squadron's Sgt Munro, and this was not the first time that W4156 had manifested that particular fault. The five serviceable Mosquitos marked the centre of the city to perfection, and the Pathfinder heavy brigade backed up on time to maintain the aiming point. The main force arrived in three waves, with the Lancaster element coming in last, and the result was the most accurate and destructive attack of the war to date on this formerly elusive city. S/L Ward-Hunt described hazy conditions and a thin layer of cloud over the target as he ran in to bomb on a red marker from 18,000 feet at 21.18. He was unable to see the impact of his bombs, but reported concentrated fires, one very large explosion, and many searchlights accompanied by heavy flak. S/L Searby made a timed run from yellow route flares over Dorsten, just north of the Ruhr, and bombed from 20,000 feet at 21.20. He echoed the comments of S/L Ward-Hunt, and added that the glow from the burning city was visible at the Dutch coast. In all ten crews returned with similar stories of a highly successful attack, and their confidence was confirmed by photographic reconnaissance, which revealed 160 acres of built-up area between the city centre and the Krupp works to have been destroyed. This amounted to more than three thousand houses, and there was damage to fifty-three buildings within the Krupp works itself.

Missing from debriefing was the crew of F/L Picken DFC, who had all been killed when W4918 crashed in the general target area. It was the sixth operation of Rhodesian Bill Picken's second tour, and he was considered to be one of the squadron's outstanding captains. There is a degree of uncertainty concerning the precise location of the Lancaster's crash, Bill Chorley, in his superb and indispensable Bomber Command Losses series, placing it to the north of Düsseldorf at 21.15. This location, south of Essen, would suggest that they were on the way home when the end came, but the time is a fraction too early for that to be the case. Another source claims the Lancaster came down onto farmland at Bönninghardt, north of the Ruhr and west of Dorsten, with its bombs still on board, and this would harmonize better with the timing. The explosion of the cookie apparently killed the farmer, Herr Schlootz, and four members of his family, and only a six-month-old baby girl survived.

It would be a full week before the next Ruhr operation, and in the meantime Harris turned his attention upon targets in southern Germany, beginning with Nuremberg on the night of the 8/9th. S/Ls Searby and Ward-Hunt took another opportunity to lead from the front by heading the 106 Squadron contingent of a dozen Lancasters, which were to join up with more than 320 others for the outward flight south-east across France. They got away from Syerston between 19.10 and 19.20 on a clear but moonless night, and all arrived in the target area dependent upon the Pathfinders to identify and mark the aiming point through the darkness and haze. Beyond the range of Oboe, the Pathfinders had to rely on H2S and visual means to do their work, but the conditions rendered visual identification impossible. The usual difficulties with H2S interpretation led to the marking being spread along the line of approach up to ten miles short of the city boundaries. Peter Ward-Hunt did make out some ground detail and also green target indicators, which he bombed from 20,000 feet at 23.36. He saw one very large fire in the east of the city, and several scattered fires, and returned home to report an uneventful trip. F/L Edmunds brought back a bombing photo plotted at 3,000 yards from the aiming point, while Burpee saw his bombs burst near the aiming point, and was one of a number to report two distinct concentrations of fire. P/O Brodrick's bombing photo was plotted at 1¾ miles from the aiming point, and he claimed the glow of fires was visible 120 miles into the homeward flight. Photo-reconnaissance revealed that half of the bombs had fallen outside of the city, mostly in a creep back along the line of approach, but six hundred buildings had been destroyed and fourteen hundred damaged, including some important war industry factories, among them those of the M.A.N. (Machinenfabrik Augsburg Nürnberg) and Siemens companies.

Twenty-four hours later it was the turn of Munich to face the Command, which put together a force of 264 aircraft, of which nine Lancasters represented 106 Squadron. S/Ls Searby and Ward-Hunt took the lead, and all were safely airborne by 20.30. Ward-Hunt was taken ill during the outward flight and he turned back, and Sgt Burton's rear turret became unserviceable putting an end also to his sortie. The others pressed on to the target, which they found under clear skies and slight haze. F/L Edmunds located the target by Pathfinder flares, but was also able to pick out ground detail. He bombed from 16,500 feet at 00.17, and brought back a photo plotted at 4½ miles from the aiming point. He described a good concentration of bombing, and reported one particularly large explosion, which was noted also by the other crews, whose photos were similarly plotted at 3,000 yards and more from the aiming point. Reconnaissance revealed later that a strong wind had pushing the main weight of the attack into the western half of the city, where considerable damage had been inflicted upon business and military premises, in addition to which the aero-engine assembly shop at the BMW factory was put out of action for six weeks.

The 10th brought news of decorations for a number of squadron personnel, including some who had been members of Gibson's crew. There was a Bar to his DFC for F/L Oliver, a DFC for F/Ls "Wimpy" Wellington, Scrivener and Drew and F/Os Burnside, Ruskell and Wickens, and DFMs for F/S Kennedy and Sgts Robin, Evans and Herbert. There were no major operations that night, but thirty-five Lancasters and Stirlings were sent on wide-ranging gardening sorties from the French coast to the Baltic. 106 Squadron selected four crews who hadn't operated over the previous two nights, those of F/S Burpee and Sgts Renshaw, Price and Yackman, and dispatched them to the Baltic to mine the waters in the Pollock garden, off the Island of Bornholm, east of Denmark and south of Sweden. They took off either side of 18.30, and each successfully found the garden area to plant five 1,570lb mines.

On the following night the series of attacks on Germany's southern cities concluded at Stuttgart. 106 Squadron supported the three hundred aircraft-strong operation with a dozen Lancasters, led by Gibson in ED649. Having been with the squadron for twelve months, Gibson must have known his time was up, and he probably recognised that this would be his final operation before being posted. Gibson had a second pilot on board, F/O Walter Thompson, a Canadian, who had arrived that very day from a conversion unit. Also on the Order of Battle on this night were S/Ls Searby and Ward-Hunt, and they took off either side of 20.00 for the three-and-a-half-hour outward flight. Gibson lost most of the starboard-outer engine's power after being hit by flak at the French coast, but continued on to the target mostly at 4,000 feet, before climbing to 12,000 feet for the bombing run. He delivered his cookie and twelve SBCs at 23.20, and watched them burst near a concentration of fires. S/L Ward-Hunt bombed target indicators two minutes after Gibson, but from considerably higher, 18,500 feet, and observed his bombs bursting. S/L Searby noted a large concentration of fires well to the north-west of the aiming point, and this was probably the result of the defenders employing dummy target indicators for the first time. They were successful in luring away much of the bombing, which fell harmlessly in open country, but some loads did find a number of south-western districts, where some housing was destroyed. Gibson and crew arrived home safely along with the squadron's other participants, and brought back a bombing photo plotted at four miles from the aiming point. Gibson now had the happy prospect of well-earned leave with his wife Eve in Cornwall, but it would be a few more days before his future was revealed to him.

Harris resumed his campaign against the Ruhr on the night of the 12/13th, with a return to Essen, for which a force of 457 aircraft was made ready. Syerston, as usual on any day of an operation, was a hive of activity, with riggers and fitters crawling over Lancasters, preparing them for an air-test to prove their fitness to take part. That established it was the turn of the armourers to fill the bomb bays and replenish the racks with fresh belts of .303 ammunition, before the tankers arrived to top up the fuel to the required level. On this evening thirteen 106 Squadron Lancasters snaked their way to the runway threshold, before taking off safely either side of 19.00 led by S/Ls Searby and Ward-Hunt. Weather conditions were good, with clear skies over the target, and the Pathfinders experienced no difficulty in identifying and marking the Krupp works aiming point. S/L Ward-Hunt had a green TI in his bomb sight as he delivered his cookie and SBCs from 22,000 feet, and watched them explode in a concentration of fires. He also observed one large explosion, as did a number of other crews. Sgt Irvine was at 18,000 feet as he made his bombing run on a red TI at 21.35, and was approaching the release point when the Lancaster was coned by searchlights, dazzling every member of the crew. The bombs were jettisoned live, but Sgt Irvine stated at debriefing that he believed they fell within the target area. F/S Burpee brought back a bombing photo plotted at three miles from the aiming point, and commented on the ferocity of the defences and abundance of searchlights. P/O Brodrick was at 14,000 feet as he bombed, and must have been at risk of being hit by the hardware falling from above. He, like many others, brought back a photo of fire tracks, and reported a great concentration of fires and two large explosions, both comments backed up by F/L Hayward. Post-raid analysis confirmed that the initial Oboe marking by Mosquitos had fallen across the Krupp complex, and the subsequent bombing had produced 30% more damage to the plant than the attack of a week earlier. Five hundred houses were also destroyed, but a proportion of the bombing still managed to find its way into nearby towns. It was a relatively expensive night for the Command, which registered the loss of twenty-three aircraft. Essen invariably claimed a 106 Squadron aircraft, and true to form, R5749, "Admiral Filha da Puta", failed to return after being torn apart by flak over the target. F/S McDonald RAAF and five of his crew were killed, and only the Australian bomb-aimer, F/S Lindsay, escaped with his life after falling through the smashed Perspex nose. He landed right in the centre of the Krupp works and became a PoW.

A welcome lull in operations now lay ahead for the crews as fog rolled across the Bomber counties of eastern England. Minor operations would hold sway for the next week and a half, and Sgt Price and crew were sent mining in the Privet region of the Baltic on the night after Essen. Conditions were good until just before the garden was reached, when ten-tenths cloud was encountered with a base at 100 feet. Sgt Price opted to head for the secondary target area of Silverthorn in the Kattegat Channel, and here he successfully delivered four mines before returning safely.

To his surprise Gibson found himself posted to 5 Group HQ at St Vincents in Grantham on the 14th, and believed, initially, that he was to assist in the writing of a book. On the 15th Harris met with the recently appointed A-O-C 5 Group, AVM Sir Ralph Cochrane, to tell him to form a special squadron under Gibson to train for an attack on the Ruhr Dams. On the 18th Gibson met with Cochrane, initially to establish his willingness to cancel his leave and take on one more operation. On the following day he was recalled to Cochrane's office, where he met base commander, G/C Whitworth, and was told to form a new squadron at Whitworth's main base at Scampton. Given a degree of autonomy in selecting his crews, Gibson naturally called upon a number of those with whom he had shared part of the past twelve months. Hopgood, having completed his tour back in October, was an automatic choice, as was Shannon, who by this time was about to begin training as a Pathfinder, and had barely had time to unpack at Wyton when Gibson's call came through. Canadian P/O Lewis "John" Burpee and crew also departed 106 Squadron and found their way to Scampton to join the new unit. Other current and former sons of the squadron would also answer the call to Scampton, and thereby gain a unique place in RAF Bomber Command history.

Pilot Officer Walter Thompson in March 1943. After his tour with 106 squadron he later joined 83 Squadron for his second tour. Walter Thompson DFC survived the war and subsequently published his memoirs as a book, 'Lancaster to Berlin'.

S/L Searby, who was very much a protégé of Gibson, was promoted on the 15th to step into his shoes as the squadron's new commanding officer. Although his time in office would be relatively brief as a result of his burgeoning reputation and career, he would continue to provide the outstanding leadership that had been a hallmark of the squadron since the earliest days. His promotion allowed F/L Hayward to step up one rank and take over as B Flight commander. A much refreshed bomber force returned to operations on the night of the 22/23rd, when St Nazaire and its U-Boot facilities were the target for an initial force of 357 aircraft. 106 Squadron detailed fourteen Lancasters, all but one of which would be carrying a new record load of eleven 1,000 pounders, one of them fitted with a delay fuse of between six and 144 hours. The odd man out was Sgt Munro, who had an 8,000 pounder in his bomb bay. S/Ls Ward-Hunt and Hayward were the senior pilots on duty, and the former carried a passenger in the person of the new Syerston station commander, G/C Odbert. The squadron's association with the Fleet Air Arm continued on this night with Lt Jess and Sub Lt Lee DSO flying as bomb-aimers. Lt Muttrie was already serving with the squadron, currently as a member of F/O Brodrick's crew. They took off in a thirty-minute slot from 19.00, and made their way south in excellent conditions with clear skies and just a little haze. The number of aircraft converging on the target was reduced by the recall of the majority of the Stirling element, and P/O Browne was also forced to turn back after losing two engines. He, ultimately, carried out a skilful landing on two engines at Downham Market. The other squadron participants were among 283 crews claiming to have bombed the target as briefed. S/L Ward-Hunt took a long run-up at 11,000 feet after easily identifying the target, and he brought back a bombing photo plotted at four miles from the aiming point. P/O Thompson was flying as crew captain for the first time, and he described an uneventful trip, which ended with a diversion to the O.T.U station at Wellesbourne-Mountford in Warwickshire because of fog at Syerston. Peter Page reported one particularly large explosion, which he believed to be of an oil-storage facility, and he found himself diverted on return to Desford in his home county of Leicestershire. F/O Brodrick and Sgt McGregor each brought back an aiming point photograph, which showed the target to have been well-plastered.

Over 450 aircraft took off for Duisburg on the evening of the 26th to continue the Ruhr offensive, and with the intention of emulating the recent successes at Essen. Eleven 106 Squadron crews were briefed, and S/L Ward-Hunt was again the senior pilot on duty. They took off either side of 18.30, but Sgt Abel returned early with W/T failure. It was a night of unhelpful weather conditions, which saw the target hidden under ten-tenths cloud with tops at between 12,000 and 20,000 feet. This would not normally have been a problem, but of the nine Oboe Mosquitos operating, one ditched in the North Sea and five turned back with equipment malfunctions. The remaining three Mosquitos were unable to provide adequate skymarking, and the bombing was consequently scattered and ineffective. Crews were able to see the parachute flares in the distance, but they quickly fell out of sight, and most bombed on timed runs. S/L Ward-Hunt bombed from 20,000 feet at 21.43, and observed several glows from fires, but he, like the others, could make no meaningful assessment of results.

Duisburg was the first of four operations to involve the squadron on consecutive nights. On the following night a force of almost four hundred aircraft was prepared for a major assault on Berlin, and among them were a dozen Lancasters representing 106 Squadron. They took off in an impressive ten-minute slot between 19.40 and 19.50, with F/O Brodrick the senior pilot on duty, and headed for the rendezvous point. F/S Page's Lancaster developed supercharger problems two hours out, and he was forced to turn back. The others pushed on to find clear skies over the target and good visibility with a little haze. The main force crews relied on the Pathfinder markers as their point of aim, and the 106 Squadron crews delivered their loads between 23.04 and 23.20, before returning with reports of large fires, the glow from which could be seen a hundred miles into the homeward flight. In fact, the Pathfinders had failed to find the city centre aiming point, and marked instead two areas on the south-western fringes. As a result most of the bombing fell well short of the city limits, with the main concentration around eleven miles from the centre, where, by good fortune alone, a secret store of valuable electronic equipment was hit and severely damaged.

On the following night St Nazaire hosted its third raid of the series, for which just two 106 Squadron crews, those of Sgts Howells and Robbins, were detailed. The former successfully completed his sortie, while the latter abandoned his for an unrecorded reason. Berlin was again the target for the night of the 29/30th, when a dozen 106 Squadron Lancasters contributed to an overall force of over 320 aircraft. They departed Syerston between 21.00 and 21.35 on a night of difficult weather conditions, which included severe icing. For the second operation running F/S Page turned back early, this time with pneumatic system failure, while Sgts Irvine and Yackman fell victim to the icing conditions, and were unable to maintain height. The force was routed in over the Baltic, where the weather improved and the cloud dissipated to leave clear skies over Berlin. The Pathfinders provided a pinpoint north of the target, and some crews used that, while others found the target easily by the cascading TIs. The winds were stronger than forecast, which delayed the arrival of the main force, but there seemed to be no awareness that the attack was misplaced. Sgt Robbins, on his first bombing operation as crew captain, had a red target indicator in his bomb sight as he delivered his cookie from 21,000 feet at 01.16 at the tail-end of the 106 Squadron effort, and saw the flash of its impact. He described the whole of Berlin being patterned, with fires running in all directions. The other crews echoed the impression of many fires and an effective attack, but, in fact, the Pathfinders had delivered the markers well to the south of the planned aiming point, and the subsequent bombing turned over a lot of earth in open country. A bitter blow for the squadron came with the failure to return of S/L Hayward DFC and crew, who were all killed when ED596 "Himself King" was shot down on the way home by Lt August Geigner of III/NJG/1. The Lancaster crashed at 04.29 near Lichtenvoorde in Holland, a few miles from the frontier with Germany. S/L Hayward was just two sorties short of completing his second tour of operations, both of which had been served with 106 Squadron. Among his crew were navigator F/O Young DFC, wireless operator P/O Mantle DFM & Bar and mid-upper gunner F/S Pryor DFM.

During the course of the month the squadron established three new records. 350 tons of bombs and mines were delivered over fourteen nights of operations, 134 sorties were dispatched and 834 hours of operational flying took place, all for the loss of four aircraft.

April 1943

April was to be the least rewarding month of the Ruhr campaign, largely because of the number of operations directed at targets outside of the region, and, therefore, beyond the range of Oboe. As Bomber Command was about to be released from its obligation to attack the French ports, small-scale operations took place against St Nazaire and Lorient on the night of the 2/3rd, and 106 Squadron supported the latter with two Lancasters, captained by Sgts Ridd and Rosner, who were both on their first operations as crew captain. The latter failed to complete his sortie because of intercom problems, but Sgt Ridd bombed the target from 13,000 feet and returned home safely. Meanwhile, Sgt Robbins was sent to the Deodars garden in the Gironde Estuary, and after making a timed run from the Ile de Cordouan, he delivered six mines into the correct location.

Essen was again in the bombsights on the night of the 3/4th, the first occasion on which more than two hundred Lancasters had operated together, a sign of the ever-increasing bomb-carrying capacity that could be brought to bear on the enemy's heartland. 225 Lancasters actually took off, among them fourteen provided by 106 Squadron. They began to leave Syerston at 19.00, with F/L Brodrick the senior pilot on duty, but Sgt Yackman lost the use of his starboard-outer engine, and had to turn back. The remainder pressed on to find the target clear of cloud, something which had not been guaranteed by the "met" man at briefing. The Pathfinders had prepared both a sky and ground marking plan, and ultimately employed both, leaving it to the crews to choose for themselves what to aim at. The force had been routed in north of the Ruhr, with guide markers provided at Dorsten, followed by a due south run to the target, where the 106 Squadron crews arrived between 22.01 and 22.10. Bombing took place from between 17,000 and 20,000 feet, and all but one returned to report a concentrated attack with many large fires and clouds of smoke. Widespread damage was caused in central and western districts, where more than 630 buildings were destroyed. The flak and searchlight defence had been very strong and accurate, and twenty-one aircraft failed to return, among them 106 Squadron's ED542, which crashed near Haltern, just north of the Ruhr, killing Sgt Ridd and his crew, who were operating together for just the second time.

Kiel was the target for the largest non-1,000 force to date of 577 aircraft, which took off in mid-evening on the 4th with fourteen 106 Squadron Lancasters among them. W/C Searby was the senior pilot on duty, and there was a first operation as crew captain for F/O Stephens. They began departing from Syerston shortly after 20.30, and headed into very unfavourable weather conditions in the target area, which included heavy cloud and strong winds. All of the 106 Squadron participants reached the target, and bombed between 23.23 and 23.46, mostly on red and green skymarkers, which would have been drifting across the target at speed and disappearing into the cloud. There were reports of glows beneath the clouds, but no one was able to say with any certainty where the bombs had fallen, and a decoy fire site may also have been a factor in drawing the bombing away from the intended aiming-point. Local authorities reported just a few bombs falling within the town, and damage was consequently slight.

Almost four hundred aircraft were sent against Duisburg on the night of the 8/9th, for which 106 Squadron dispatched seven Lancasters led by F/L Brodrick. Another mid-evening take off would bring them to the target area shortly after 23.30, but Sgt Burton and F/S Page were unable to get that far, both having to turn back early, the former with an unserviceable rear turret and the latter with compass trouble. The force encountered layers of thick cloud over the Ruhr with tops as high as 20,000 feet, and this inevitably compromised the accuracy of the Pathfinder markers. Sgt Munro bombed on e.t.a from his last Gee fix, and F/L Brodrick and Sgt Glaholm did exactly the same after seeing no flares or markers. F/L Edmunds dropped his cookie and SBCs from 20,000 feet on dead reckoning at 23.37, and all came home with a feeling of disappointment and expectation of failure. Reconnaissance confirmed their pessimism and revealed that the scattered attack had produced only modest damage. W4156 failed to return to Syerston, having crashed in the target area, and P/O Irvine and his crew, who were now well into their first tour, were all killed.

A return to this target was made on the following night by an all-Lancaster heavy force of 104 aircraft, six of them representing 106 Squadron. They were all off the ground by 20.30, led by F/Ls Edmunds and Brodrick, the latter having on board as second pilot the newly arrived S/L Young, who was the new B Flight commander. Thick cloud hung over the Ruhr, the effects of which Oboe should have negated, and marker flares were clearly seen by the crews as they started their bombing runs. F/L Edmunds was approaching the aiming point at 20,000 feet, when attacked by an enemy night fighter, which the gunners drove off. The bombs were jettisoned before the fighter made a second attack, and both aircraft were hit during the engagement, which ended inconclusively. F/L Brodrick had a green marker in his sights when he delivered his cookie and twelve SBCs from 19,000 feet, while F/S Page made a timed run from a red flare, and bombed from 20,000 feet a minute later. Two crews made mention of one large explosion, but otherwise the clouds concealed what was going on below. It was another scattered and disappointing attack, which destroyed fifty houses, but still fell well short of what might have been expected.

Temporarily shifting focus from the Ruhr, Harris targeted Frankfurt on the night of the 10/11th with a force of five hundred aircraft, of which just five Lancasters belonged to 106 Squadron. They were all off the ground shortly before midnight, four carrying the standard bomb load for city-busting of a cookie and twelve SBCs of 4lb incendiaries, while F/O Thompson had an 8,000 pounder on board. They reached the target area shortly before 03.00 to find heavy cloud again preventing any view of the ground, and four of the 106 Squadron contingent bombed on green skymarkers from 16,000 feet, while Sgt Reid chose an altitude of 19,000. There was a hint of an explosion and fires beneath the cloud, but, in truth, returning crews had no idea where their bombs had fallen. Photographic reconnaissance later revealed that a few loads had landed in southern suburbs, but that the rest had missed the city altogether. Three 106 Squadron crews supported a mining operation in the Bay of Biscay on the night of the 11/12th, F/L Browne, F/S Page and Sgt Burton departing Syerston in mid-evening for the eight-hour round trip. They found excellent conditions in the Furze and Elderberry target areas, with bright moonlight, and they had no difficulty in picking up pinpoints from which to make a timed run. F/L Browne found pinpoints all along the French coast, and selected San Sebastian on the Basque coast as his reference, from where he delivered five mines at three-second intervals. Sgt Burton arrived over the dropping zone, only to be frustrated by the failure of the bomb doors to open.

Another long-range operation involved a dozen Lancasters from the squadron on the night of the 13/14th. The target was the naval docks and warships at berth in the port of La Spezia on Italy's north-western coast, for which the 106 Squadron contingent began departing Syerston at 20.00. The station commander, G/C Odbert, hitched a ride with F/L Edmunds, and three other aircraft carried second pilots, including S/L Young with F/L Brodrick. It was approaching 02.00 as the two-hundred-strong force closed in on the target, which was found in good conditions under clear skies. Peter Page had been unable to climb through engine trouble, and continued to the target at low level, eventually reaching it at 4,700 feet. He had the docks in his bomb sights, and watched his 1,000 pounders burst across them before turning for home. The engines continued to behave erratically, however, and it was decided unwise to try to cross the Alps. The alternative option was to make for North Africa, and after pinpointing on Corsica, the Lancaster eventually reached Maison Blanche, where a safe landing was made at 06.20. The other squadron participants bombed from between 6,500 and 12,000 feet in a slot from 01.42 to 02.10, and helped to inflict severe damage upon the docks.

The busy month continued with a major operation against Stuttgart on the night of the 14/15th, which involved 460 aircraft, seven of them provided by 106 Squadron. F/Ls Browne and Brodrick were the senior pilots on duty, and the latter had with him S/L Latimer DFC, who was on board as an observer, but may have been posted in as the A Flight commander elect to succeed S/L Ward-Hunt. They were all airborne by 22.00, and climbed away before heading south to the rendezvous point and entry into Fortress Europe at the French coast. F/L Browne experienced severe icing about three hours into the outward leg, and decided to turn back, but the others continued on to approach the target from the north-east. It seems that not all of the Pathfinder backers-up pressed on to the city centre aiming point, but re-marked the first target indicators they came upon. This encouraged a creep-back along the line of approach, which was a regular feature of a heavy Bomber Command raid. There was no cloud over the city, and F/O Thompson was able to pick out ground detail before bombing from 16,000 feet at 01.29, and afterwards came down to low level to shoot up a train and an aerodrome. He would bring back a bombing photo plotted at two miles from the aiming point. Sgt Munro had factory buildings in his sights as he bombed from 17,000 feet three minutes later, and he was the only one from the squadron to bring back an aiming point photo. Sgt Reid arrived later than the others after being coned by searchlights, and by the time he bombed at 01.43, no target markers were visible. The creep-back could work for or against the success of an operation in a purely arbitrary way, and on this night there was a positive outcome as the bombing spread across the industrial suburb of Bad Canstatt, where some useful damage was achieved. Adjacent districts were also hit, and almost four hundred buildings were destroyed and more than nine hundred severely damaged. The squadron's ED752 crashed in France on the way home, and five of the eight occupants were killed, including the previously-mentioned S/L Latimer DFC. F/L Brodrick, his bomb-aimer and rear gunner survived as guests of the Reich, and the presence of such an experienced crew would be missed at Syerston.

An attempt to knock out the Skoda armaments works at Pilsen in Czechoslovakia on the 16/17th involved a force of over three hundred Lancasters and Halifaxes, while a predominantly Wellington and Stirling diversion took place at Mannheim. The main raid was a disaster waiting to happen because of the complexity of the plan. The idea was to identify the target visually in the anticipated bright moonlight, after first pinpointing on Pathfinder route markers. Take-off of the fourteen 106 Squadron Lancasters from Syerston began at 21.00, with S/L Young taking the lead for the first time, and all got away safely for what would be a nine-hour round trip. They had been told to cross the fighter belt at around 1,500 feet, before climbing to a minimum bombing height of 6,000. P/O Rosner was forced to jettison his bomb load and turn back early after ED649 began to judder uncontrollably, but the others pushed on in excellent conditions, precisely as those forecast at briefing. The squadron participants became somewhat spread out during the outward flight, and their bombing took place between 01.44 and 02.12 at altitudes ranging from 5,000 to 10,000 feet. Alarm bells should have rung at debriefing when returning crews began to describe bombing on target indicators. These were, in fact, the route markers, which were dropped seven miles from the aiming point, and by sheer ill-luck, over an asylum building. Sgt Reid admitted to a conviction at the time that he had bombed a dummy target, but that other aircraft were attacking it also. His bombing photo was plotted at 6½ miles from the Skoda factory, and others from the squadron were plotted at seven miles. S/L Young made three runs across the asylum at 5,000 feet before bombing on green target

This fine rendering of a Lancaster, celebrating the trip to La Spezia of P/O Walter Thompson and crew, was signed by W/C Guy Gibson and Air Vice Marshal (later Air Chief Marshal, Sir) Ralph Cochrane, AOC, 5 Group.

indicators, but he was unable to determine any results. The attack was a dismal failure, compounded by the loss of thirty-six aircraft, split evenly between the two types, and this amounted to a massive 11% of those dispatched. The Mannheim force also suffered heavy casualties amounting to eighteen aircraft, and the combined figure of fifty-four failures-to-return represented the heaviest loss to date in a single night.

A return was made to La Spezia by a Lancaster main force on the night of the 18/19th, with a contribution from 106 Squadron of thirteen aircraft led by S/L Young. They took off either side of 21.00, and arrived in the target area around four-and-a-half hours later to find excellent conditions, but an effective smoke screen blotting out most of the dockyard. The squadron participants had again become spread out during the flight to the target, and bombing times ranged from 01.42 to 02.12. S/L Young made two runs across the aiming point, and reported being able to pick out the battleships at berth. He bombed from 8,000 feet at 01.53 without observing the results, but he did bring back an aiming point photo. He was one of two from the squadron carrying a 5,500lb capital ship bomb, and Sgt Munro was the other. Munro found the dockyard completely obscured, but made a visual identification of the town and island before carrying out a timed run of sixty-six seconds, and bombing from 8,000 feet also at 01.53. His bombing photo was plotted at 1¼ miles from the aiming point. Sgt Abel reported a large explosion at 01.54, which he took to be an ammunition dump going up. P/O Thompson, Sgt Robbins and Sgt Howell were the others to bring back an aiming point photo, and all from the squadron returned safely. Photo-reconnaissance revealed the main weight of the attack to have fallen north-west of the aiming point, and it was the town, rather than the docks, that suffered most damage.

Later on the 19th awards were announced to a number of squadron members. There was a DFC for W/C Searby and also for F/O Margach, F/L Edmund's bomb-aimer, and P/O Lewis. F/S Leavesley received a Bar to his DFM, and there was a DFM also for Sgt Burcher.

The Baltic port of Stettin, today in Poland, would suffer a torrid time at the hands of Bomber Command throughout the war, and perhaps its coastal location was the key to its apparent vulnerability. 339 aircraft took off in the late evening of the 20th, among them a contingent of thirteen Lancasters from 106 Squadron which was adding a new target to its ever-increasing catalogue. F/L Browne was the senior pilot on duty as they departed Syerston either side of 21.30 and headed for Denmark, which they were to cross at around 5,000 feet in an attempt to avoid night fighters. The target was found to be clear of cloud and basking in bright moonlight, and most crews made a timed run from a lake on the north-western approaches. F/O Thompson was among these, and delivered his cookie and SBCs from 14,000 feet at 01.13 in the face of intense flak. They evaded a night fighter over the target, and then came down low to shoot up three trawlers off the Danish coast. F/O Stephens was making a timed run when coned in searchlights, which forced him to break off and go on to bomb visually. His aircraft was badly holed by shrapnel. Sgt Munro had an 8,000 pounder on board, and on his first run across the target it failed to release. As he approached a second time it fell out of the bomb bay, and was seen to burst short of the target. F/O Thompson arrived home with a Lancaster showing significant shrapnel damage, and a rear gunner with a leg wound, and it is not known whether this resulted from flak over the target or from one of the many uncharted light flak batteries and flak ships dotted along the Danish coast. Over twenty fires were still burning when photo reconnaissance took place thirty-six hours later, and it revealed an estimated one hundred acres in the centre of the city to be devastated, with thirteen industrial buildings and 380 houses completely destroyed.

On the 22nd F/S Page returned from North Africa, having been pressed into service as a taxi driver to transport Field Marshal Wavell and Air Marshal Sir Richard Peirse to Gibraltar, where he picked up a number of staff officers requiring a lift back to the UK. Minor operations occupied the following five nights, before the Ruhr offensive resumed at Duisburg on the night of the 26/27th. This operation by more than five hundred aircraft, including thirteen from 106 Squadron, which departed Syerston either side of midnight led by F/Ls Edmunds and Browne. Sgt Brown and his freshman crew were forced to turn back early with oxygen system failure, leaving the others to press on to the target. For once Duisburg was clear of cloud as the bombers approached from the north, and the red and green Pathfinder markers were clearly visible. The target was well alight by the time the 106 Squadron crews bombed between 02.18 and 02.46 in the face of a hostile searchlight and flak defence. Sgt Yackman was coned by at least thirty searchlights during the bombing run, forcing him to jettison his bombs in order to escape. Returning crews all commented on the volume of fire around the aiming point, and they were confident that this was the most successful raid yet on the city. F/L Edmunds and Sgt Burton brought back aiming point photos as proof of their efforts, and photographic reconnaissance confirmed that three hundred buildings had been destroyed, but even so, it also showed that the marking and the majority of the bombing had fallen short of the target to the north-east.

The largest mining effort of the war to date was mounted on the night of the 27/28th, when 160 crews were briefed to plant their vegetables in the sea lanes off the Biscay and Brittany ports and the Frisians. 106

The crew of P/O Clifford 'Steve' Stephens (back row, third from right), along with colleagues. This is possibly to celebrate the end of the crew's tour of operations.

Squadron contributed four Lancasters for Nectarines, off the Frisians, captained by Sgts Abel, Howell and Yackman, and F/L Browne, who were all on their way by 01.30. They found poor weather in the target area, with a cloud base at 600 feet, and three of them made a timed run after gaining a Gee fix, while Sgt Howell pinpointed on Juist. All successfully carried out their assigned tasks and returned safely. Twenty-four hours later a new record was set when 207 aircraft were sent mining in northern waters. The six 106 Squadron participants, which were all captained by NCOs, were briefed for the Hollyhock, Silverthorn, Verbena and Daffodil gardens in the Baltic, while others were off Heligoland and the Elbe. A record number of 593 mines were laid, but at a cost of twenty-two aircraft, the most ever sacrificed to a gardening operation, and these were largely the victims of light flak while seeking their target area at low level.

The final operation of the month was directed at Essen on the night of the 30th, when Oboe skymarking was planned in the face of expected cloud cover. The three hundred-strong force included thirteen 106 Squadron Lancasters, led by F/Ls Edmunds and Browne. They took off either side of midnight, and arrived at the target to find conditions as forecast. F/L Edmunds set off on a timed run from red and green markers, and bombed from 20,000 feet at 03.10. There was no chance of assessing the results, but a red glow beneath the clouds was indicative of a large fire. The other crews reported similar experiences, and most commented on the heavy flak barrage. The Essen jinx struck 106 Squadron again, when accounting for

Sgt Abel and his crew, who were all killed when ED451 crashed north-east of Dorsten. This town, on the northern fringe of the Ruhr, was often used as a route marker for the final run-in, and it seems likely, therefore, that this experienced crew was still outbound at the time of its demise. This operation did cause some fresh damage, but concentration was lacking, and this was perhaps the least effective attack on this city since the campaign began.

This was the squadron's most successful month since becoming equipped with Lancasters a year earlier. During the course of the month the squadron operated on sixteen nights, dispatching a total of 150 sorties and delivering a record bomb tonnage for the loss of four aircraft.

May 1943

Squadron Leader John Searby at the controls of a 106 Squadron Lancaster. The photograph is taken from the entrance to the bomb aimer's compartment.

May would bring a return to winning ways with some outstanding successes, and broken records, although it would be less demanding in terms of the frequency of operations. Operations were planned for each of the first three nights of the new month, but were cancelled, and it was not until the 4th that briefings took place for what would be a record-breaking operation that night. Dortmund was to be the target for a new record non-1,000 force of 596 aircraft, of which fifteen were to be provided by 106 Squadron, led for the final time, as events were to prove, by W/C Searby. They took off from Syerston either side of 22.00 and headed towards the North Sea crossing, but F/S Foulsham turned back with an engine problem and Sgt Howell with a failed oxygen system. The other squadron participants became spread throughout the bomber stream, some arriving early and others much later. The newly-commissioned P/O Glaholm described perfect weather conditions as he made a timed run from a yellow route marker, and had a green target indicator in his sights as he bombed the target from 19,000 feet at 01.03. He would bring back a bombing photo plotted at two miles west-north-west of the aiming point. He also described searchlights concentrated in one solid mass over the target, and heavy predicted flak. It was a full thirty minutes later before W/C Searby bombed from 23,000 feet, and his photo showed only fire tracks. Sgt Robertson and crew were operating with the squadron for the first time, and delivered their cookie from 18,000 feet at 01.20. The incendiaries were jettisoned over the sea, and they returned on two engines, suggesting that, perhaps, the engine problems had begun during the outward flight, and the incendiaries had been dumped to save weight to enable them to carry on. As they arrived over the English coast they found an air raid in progress, and landed at the first station they could find, which turned out to be Docking in Norfolk. They had contributed to a highly effective attack, despite the fact that only half of the bomb loads fell within three miles of the city centre aiming-point. A

Dinghy drill at Syerston in Lancaster R5611 and the wreckage of the same Lancaster, shot down at Rossum, Holland, on 13th May 1943.

decoy fire site was partially responsible for diverting some of the effort, and a number of Pathfinder backers-up also delivered their markers short with inevitable consequences. Even so, more than twelve hundred buildings were destroyed, and two thousand others severely damaged. Losses were high, at thirty-one aircraft, and this was to become a regular feature of operations over the Ruhr.

W/C Searby's brief spell of command came to an end on the 9th, when he was posted to 8 Group to command 83 Squadron, whose previous commander, W/C Gillman, had been lost on the Dortmund operation. Searby had undertaken twenty-six sorties with 106 Squadron, and he would go on to gain fame as the Master Bomber for the operation against Germany's rocket research and development centre at Peenemünde in August. Later on he would be appointed station commander at Warboys and then Upwood. His replacement as commanding officer of 106 Squadron was W/C "Ronnie" Baxter, who arrived from 50 Squadron. He was an officer under whom the squadron would continue to display its efficiency and esprit de corps. Baxter had learned to fly at Cambridge in the early thirties before joining the RAF. He was already an experienced pilot and a squadron leader when he was posted to Bomber Command to serve at 1 Group HQ in early 1942. In May of that year he moved on to 24 O.T.U as a wing commander, and served also in the BAT Flight at Abingdon. By the time he reached 1660 Conversion Unit at Swinderby on the 22nd of February 1943, he already had more than 950 hours in his log book. After conversion on a Halifax he undertook Lancaster training, and arrived at Skellingthorpe on attachment to 50 Squadron on the 2nd of April with 993 hours to his credit. His first operation was undertaken as second pilot to S/L Birch with Essen as the target on the following night.

There were no operations after Dortmund until the night of the 12/13th, when 572 aircraft took off to carry out the fourth raid of the Ruhr campaign on Duisburg, Germany's largest inland port. Fourteen 106 Squadron Lancasters lined up for take-off either side of midnight, with F/Ls Browne, Edmonds and

Hartley the senior pilots on duty. The newly-commissioned P/O Page turned back early after a gunner reported being ill, but the remainder carried on to find clear skies, good visibility and unambiguous marking. They were greeted by the usual hostile response from flak and searchlights, but pushed through to bomb on the concentration of red and green ground markers. P/O Rosner found himself in the vanguard of the main force element, and was the first from the squadron to deliver his load, which was a single 8,000 pounder at 02.02. The crew members were unable to assess the results of their work, but the fires were just starting as they turned away from the target. F/L Browne and crew were one of five from the squadron carrying ten 1,000 pounders, which they dropped from 20,000 feet at 02.11, and as they headed for home they witnessed a huge explosion at 02.16. P/O McGregor and crew were the others with an 8,000 pounder on board, and they confirmed the above-mentioned explosion, and brought back an aiming point photo. Sgt Brown was the last from the squadron to bomb, which he did at 02.32 as one of six crews carrying the standard city-busting bomb load of a cookie and twelve SBCs. By the time he wheeled away from the scene, the city centre was a mass of flames, and photo reconnaissance would confirm the success of the attack. This was the first time that the marking and bombing had been concentrated on the centre of Duisburg and its docks, and the result was the destruction of almost sixteen hundred buildings, and the sinking or damaging of many thousands of tons of shipping. Thirty-four aircraft failed to return, a new record for the campaign, but 106 Squadron welcomed all of its aircraft home.

While Bochum was being attacked by over four hundred aircraft from the other groups on the following night, 120 Lancasters from 5 Group acted as the main force in a return to the Skoda works at Pilsen, to try to rectify the failure of a month earlier. 106 Squadron put up fifteen aircraft for this operation, and they took off either side of 21.30 led by S/L Young. His rear turret became unserviceable, forcing him to turn back, and P/O Stephens and Sgt Davidson were others with technical problems that prevented them from continuing. F/Ls Hartley, Edmunds and Browne were left as the senior pilots, and the first-mentioned was shot up by flak as he flew over Münster. He arrived in the target area four hours after take-off, and bombed on a red target indicator from 11,500 feet at 01.26. He saw his 8,000 pounder burst in a built-up area, and brought back a bombing photo plotted at two miles north of the aiming point. F/L Edmunds watched his cookie and ten 500 pounders burst alongside the markers, which his bombing photo revealed to be three miles west-north-west of the target. F/L Browne bombed the centre of five markers from 10,000 feet at 01.23, and the point of impact was plotted at 2¼ miles from the aiming point. The night was clear with a little haze, and the defences were not particularly daunting, but still the target escaped damage, and this well illustrated the continuing problem of target locating and marking beyond the range of Oboe. Among nine missing aircraft was 106 Squadron's R5611, which was shot down over Holland by a night fighter flown by Hptm Herbert Lütje of III/NJG.1. The crash took place at 23.42, while the Lancaster was outbound, and there were no survivors from the crew of Sgt Howell.

There followed a nine-night rest from operations for the heavy brigade, and it was during this period, on the night of the 16/17th, that W/C Gibson assured his place in history, by leading the epic Operation Chastise against the Möhne, Eder and Sorpe Dams. There was good news in the form of a Victoria Cross for Gibson and a DFC for Shannon, but sadness at the loss of former 106 Squadron stalwarts, Hopgood, who was shot down over the Möhne, and Burpee and his crew, who crashed onto the Luftwaffe aerodrome at Gilze-Rijen. It was ironic that the newly-commission P/O Burpee had heard of the award of a DFM on the very day he flew to the Dams. The long lay-off for the squadrons had allowed time for an expansion programme to take place, which would substantially boost the numbers of aircraft available for operations from this point on.

106 Squadron Pilots on the Dams Raid

W/C Guy Gibson

P/O Lewis 'John' Burpee

F/L Dave Shannon (Simon Sanders).

F/L John 'Hoppy' Hopgood

Having played host to a record non-1,000 force at the start of the month, Dortmund was chosen to host the resumption of the Ruhr offensive at the hands of a new record force on the night of the 23/24th. This time the Ruhr giant would face more than eight hundred aircraft, of which sixteen Lancasters represented 106 Squadron. They lined up for take-off shortly before 22.00, with W/C Baxter taking the lead for the first time, and P/O Crowe DFC and crew back to start a second tour. Sadly, W/C Baxter lost his port-outer engine while over the North Sea, and was forced to return early having jettisoned his bombs. This was one of five early returns to afflict the squadron on what was clearly a poor night for engine serviceability. Peter Page came back with a dead starboard-inner engine, while P/O Munro and Sgt Robbins both lost their port-inners while climbing out over base. Finally Sgt Davidson and his crew believed for some reason that their bomb load had been prematurely dropped while over the North Sea, and they arrived back at Syerston to discover it was still intact in the bomb bay. One wonders how they explained that one! The target was found to be free of cloud, and F/L Edmunds made a timed run from a yellow target indicator. He had a red one in his bomb sight as he let his cookie and SBCs go from 20,000 feet at 01.03, but saw no bursts. The fires were beginning to take hold as he turned away, and he then spent a minute shaking off a cone of twenty-five searchlights that had ensnared him. His experiences were echoed by the other crews, all of whom returned safely. Reconnaissance revealed the marking and bombing to have been accurate and concentrated, causing the destruction of two thousand buildings in central, northern and eastern districts, while important war industry factories were also hit with a consequent loss of production. It was not a one-sided affair, however, and the defenders hacked down thirty-eight aircraft, another new record for the campaign.

Two nights later it was the turn of Düsseldorf to face a force of more than seven hundred aircraft, for which 106 Squadron contributed fifteen Lancasters. They began taking off shortly after 23.00 led by S/L Young, but the gremlins intervened again to bring three crews back early. For his second operation running S/L Young had a turret become unserviceable, this time the mid-upper, F/O McGregor lost his air speed indicator (a.s.i.), while P/O Yackman lost most of his instruments. The others reached the target to find the weather conditions less favourable than of late with up to eight-tenths cloud, and there were complaints that a profusion of condensation trails had further reduced visibility. The 106 Squadron contingent bombed from between 16,000 and 20,000 feet over a period of forty-two minutes from 01.43, but only F/O Stephens saw the impact of his own bomb. W4242 was attacked by an unidentified enemy fighter, which illuminated the Lancaster with a searchlight. F/O Crowe's mid-upper gunner, Sgt Christie, took exception to this, and fired a burst which knocked bits off the offender, and sent it down in flames to be claimed as destroyed. In the event, cloud, along with decoy markers and fire sites, contributed to scattered marking and confused the main force participants, with the result that bombs were scattered over a wide area with no point of concentration. Damage within the target city was modest, and the failure cost a further twenty-seven aircraft, although none again from 106 Squadron.

It had been a good month for the squadron thus far, with only one missing crew, but the Essen jinx struck again on the night of the 27/28th, when 106 Squadron put up thirteen Lancasters as part of an overall force of more than five hundred aircraft. Peter Page was the first to take off at 21.50, and the others followed over the ensuing forty minutes. There was one early return, and for once it wasn't S/L Young, but F/O Crowe, who had problems with three engines. Cloud over the target was anticipated, and it turned out to be between six and nine-tenths when the 106 Squadron crews began to arrive. The Pathfinders had prepared for the use of skymarkers, and the crews picked these up easily as they ran the gauntlet of intense and accurate flak, and dodged the searchlight concentrations. P/O Yackman was at 22,000 feet, and spent an uncomfortable few minutes trying to avoid the flak. In that regard he was not entirely successful, as his ground crew discovered when he handed back to them a badly-holed Lancaster. Sgt Whyatt was on his first operation as crew captain, and he bombed the target from 20,000 feet at 01.17, before returning safely home to describe the trip as uneventful. Reconnaissance showed that bombing was once again scattered and, in many cases, short of the intended aiming point. Even so, almost five hundred buildings were destroyed, and before this campaign began, that would have been considered a major success at this target. Twenty-three aircraft failed to return, and among them was the squadron's W4842, "Fema Dora", containing the crew of Sgt Robbins. It was learned later from the International Red Cross that they had made an emergency landing on Dutch soil, and all had survived to become PoWs.

Two nights later 719 aircraft took off for Wuppertal, a conurbation on the south-eastern fringe of the Ruhr consisting of the towns of Barmen and Elberfeld. Eleven 106 Squadron Lancasters began taking off at 22.30 led by S/L Young, and there were no early returns. The aiming point for this operation was the centre of Barmen, and it was one of those relatively rare occasions when all facets of the plan came together in perfect harmony. Accurate marking was followed by concentrated bombing, which probably caused a mini-firestorm in the narrow streets of the town's central districts. When F/L Hartley bombed from 19,500 at 01.01 the fires were just beginning to gain a hold around the markers, and it was immediately clear that this was a successful raid. The other crews echoed his comments, and all but one of them returned safely home. The absentee at debriefing was Sgt Whyatt and his crew, whose R5677, "Admiral Chattanooga", had crashed in the target area on just their second operation together, and all on board were killed. Reconnaissance revealed an estimated one thousand acres, or 80% of the built-up area, reduced to ruins, with four thousand houses destroyed, along with five of the six largest factories, and over two hundred other industrial premises. It was a tragedy also in human terms, which saw the deaths of around 3,400 people, by far the heaviest casualty figure inflicted by the Command to date. The shocked and now homeless residents may have been cheered to know that thirty-three aircraft had been brought down, and that more than 220 of their tormentors would not be returning to their homes either. This was the final operation of the month, during the course of which the squadron had operated on just seven occasions, dispatching ninety-nine sorties for the loss of three aircraft.

June 1943

The Pathfinder and main force units remained on the ground for the first ten nights of June, as the weather intervened. 106 Squadron offered aircraft for operations on all but two occasions, but cancellations came through to keep them grounded. From a positive perspective this allowed the squadrons time to refresh and replenish, and to ease the new crews into their maiden tour. It was not until the night of the 11/12th that the first major operation of the month was mounted, and it involved almost eight hundred aircraft, whose crews were briefed to attack Düsseldorf. 106 Squadron put fifteen Lancasters into the air, led by W/C Baxter, with S/L Young in support. S/L Williamson had recently been posted in to take over as A Flight commander, and he was flying as second pilot with F/L Edmunds. They began taking off at 22.20, but it would be a full hour before the whole squadron was off the ground, and there would be no early returns. They climbed into heavy cloud with tops at 24,000 feet, but this thinned as the target hove into sight, and was at three to four-tenths at 5,000 feet as the attack began in bright moonlight. F/L Hartley was the first from the squadron to bomb, which he did at 01.28 from a little over 19,000 feet. He described the target burning furiously, and knew already that this was a successful attack. W/C Baxter saw red markers cascading ahead of him, and bombed from 19,000 feet at 01.33, without being able to see the impact. P/O Burton and crew bombed from 20,000 feet and took a photograph of the docks before heading home to complete their first tour of operations. Sgt Brown and crew were the last squadron participants over the target, and they bombed at 02.19 before also returning safely home. Reconnaissance revealed this to be the most punishing attack of the war thus far on this Ruhr city. But for a stray marker dropped fourteen miles north-east of the city, which inevitably attracted some bomb loads, it could have been far worse for the city's residents, even so, almost nine thousand fires were recorded, 130 acres of built-up area were destroyed and 140,000 people were bombed out. The squadron negotiated the operation without loss, but a total of thirty-eight aircraft failed to return, and this equalled the highest loss of the campaign to date. To put this figure into context, it represented the equivalent of two standard squadrons plus reserves lost in a single operation.

106 Squadron was able to contribute sixteen Lancasters to a force of five hundred aircraft made ready for an attack on the Ruhr town of Bochum on the following night. S/Ls Young and Williamson were the senior pilots on duty as they began taking-off at 22.10, but P/O Munro, Sgt Barker and F/L Browne all returned early with failed engines. The others found the target under varying amounts of thin cloud and bright moonlight, and S/L Williamson, who was undertaking his first operation as crew captain since joining the squadron, bombed from 19,000 feet at 01.31. F/L Hartley was having problems with stability as he approached the target, and jettisoned four of his SBCs of incendiaries to avoid stalling. He bombed from 17,000 feet at 01.23 with little manoeuvrability available to him, but got home to land at Wittering. All returning crews gave similar reports of scattered bombing early on, becoming concentrated later, with many large fires taking hold and at least one very large explosion. Heavy predicted flak was accurate up to 20,000 feet and beyond, but defence was described by some as not up to usual Ruhr standard. Reconnaissance confirmed that the town centre had sustained severe damage, and the Command claimed 130 acres of destruction. This time twenty-four aircraft were missing, although again none from 106 Squadron. Later on the 13th awards were announced to a number of squadron personnel, and among the recipients of the DFM were the now P/Os Glaholm and McGregor.

An all-Lancaster heavy force of 197 aircraft was prepared for an operation to Oberhausen on the night of the 14/15th, of which thirteen were provided by 106 Squadron. They took off either side of 22.30 led by S/L Williamson, but it wasn't long before some of them turned back with technical difficulties. F/L Crowe was thwarted by a failed port-inner engine, F/O Hoboken had his guns freeze up and P/O Robertson lost his rear turret to a hydraulics failure. F/L Edmunds located the target, situated to the east of Duisburg, by means of Pathfinder route markers, but as they passed by Duisburg they were coned for three minutes in searchlights, and it became necessary to jettison the bomb load in order to escape. Sgt Brown and crew experienced a torrid time after being attacked three times by a JU88 while on approach to the target. Both combatants sustained damage, and the Lancaster's rear gunner was slightly wounded, but the JU88 was seen to dive down with black smoke pouring from it, and was claimed as damaged. The other squadron participants bombed between 01.22 and 01.37 from 18,000 to 20,500 feet, and all but two returned home. The operation was a success at a cost of seventeen aircraft, over 8% of the force, and this time 106 Squadron did not escape retribution from the enemy defences. The two failures to return represented the first multiple loss to afflict the squadron since the middle of January. Veteran R5551, which had a bulged bomb bay to accommodate an 8,000 pounder, and had been the first Lancaster to carry an 8,000lb bomb over the Alps, fell victim to a night fighter over Holland, and crashed near Arnhem, killing P/O Brown RCAF and six others of the eight men on board, the sole survivor falling into enemy hands. ED649 crashed in the target area, and the crew, captained by the forty-year-old F/O Oates, who were only a couple of operations into their tour, all lost their lives.

While the above operation was in progress, five crews carried out a special night exercise, the significance of which would be apparent a few days hence. The night of the 16/17th brought something of an experimental raid on Cologne, where, rather than employing Oboe Mosquitos to mark the target with sky flares, the job was handed to sixteen Pathfinder heavies with H2S. The force of 202 Lancasters and ten Halifaxes from 1, 5 and 8 Groups contained ten aircraft representing 106 Squadron, and they departed Syerston either side of 22.30 led by S/L Williamson. Sgt Davidson returned early with intercom failure, and P/O Robertson was attacked by a JU88 soon after crossing the enemy coast. The combat lasted eight minutes, during which both aircraft sustained damage and the bomb load was jettisoned. The others pressed on to find the target under seven to ten-tenths cloud, and tracking and release point flares in evidence. Not all of the H2S sets functioned properly, and the skymarking was consequently late and sparse. S/L Williamson delivered his mixed load of a cookie, four 500 pounders and 30lb and 4lb incendiaries from 22,000 feet at 01.02, but saw no results. He observed a large red glow beneath the clouds and scattered fires, but was more occupied by a frozen gun in the rear turret, severe icing conditions and condensation trails, the last-mentioned advertising the bomber's presence to enemy night fighters. He arrived home safely, but described it as "altogether an uncomfortable trip". Bombing was scattered, but four hundred houses were destroyed and many thousands of others damaged to some extent, at a cost to the Command of fourteen aircraft.

A hectic round of five operations in six nights now tested the Lancaster squadrons' air and ground crews alike. It began with an all-Lancaster attack on the Zeppelin works at Friedrichshafen on the shores of Lake Constance, close to the border with Switzerland. The plant was manufacturing Würzburg radar sets, as fitted to Luftwaffe night fighters, and used to facilitate the interception of RAF bombers. This was the operation for which the five 106 Squadron crews had been training a few nights earlier. The attack by the sixty-strong force made up predominantly from 5 Group squadrons, was to be controlled by VHF radio by a Master Bomber, in the manner recently adopted by Gibson at the Dams, and the man selected was the highly experienced former commanding officer of 49 Squadron, G/C Leonard Slee. The 106 Squadron element consisted of S/L Young, F/Ls Browne and Hartley and P/Os Reid and Yackman, and they took off at 21.45 to join up with the rest of the force. G/C Slee's Lancaster developed engine problems while outbound, and he was forced to drop back into the gaggle and hand over control to his deputy, W/C Cosme Gomm, the very popular and well respected commanding officer of 467 Squadron RAAF. *Gomm's career was eerily similar to that of Gibson, in that both were born overseas, Gibson in India and Gomm in Argentina, and both slotted a tour on night fighters between bomber tours.)* It was planned to attack from between 5,000 and 10,000 feet to aid accuracy at this small and compact target, but a fierce searchlight and flak defence persuaded Gomm to order the crews to climb a further 5,000 feet, where stronger winds acted against them. The skies were clear and the visibility good as the first wave aimed their bombs at Pathfinder target indicators on the instructions of the Master Bomber. S/L Young released his cookie and seven 500 pounders from 13,000 feet at 02.48, and watched them burst in the target area. He described very accurate bombing, observing one stick to burst right across the aiming point, and the other crews echoed his remarks. The second wave carried out a "time and distance" run from the lake, and reconnaissance revealed that about 10% of the bombs had hit the factory, causing extensive damage, and other nearby industrial buildings were also afflicted. No aircraft were lost, and they avoided the night fighters waiting for their return over France by flying on to bases in North Africa. The 106 Squadron crews landed at Maison Blanche in what was the first of what became known as "shuttle" operations.

The intense flurry of operations continued at Krefeld on the night of the 21/22nd, when a force of seven hundred aircraft was made ready, among them ten 106 Squadron Lancasters. They took off either side of

23.30 led by F/Ls Edmunds and Crowe, and all arrived to find the target clear of cloud under a half-moon and in good visibility. All reported seeing the Pathfinder markers cascading, and they bombed on these between 01.33 and 02.19, before returning home safely. This was an outstandingly accurate and concentrated attack, which led to the destruction of over five and a half thousand houses, and the deaths of a thousand people. In return for this the Command lost forty-four aircraft, mostly to night fighters in the moonlit conditions, and this was the heaviest casualty figure of the campaign to date. On the following night it was the turn of Mülheim to host a major operation, for which 557 crews were briefed, among them eleven from 106 Squadron. Situated on the Rhine east of Duisburg and just south of the recently-attacked Oberhausen, the city was most associated with the coal industry, and also had an important and vibrant docks area. W/C Baxter put himself on the Order of Battle for this one, and took off at 22.30 to head for the east coast in generally good weather conditions. As usual, the outward route took them north of the Ruhr, before turning south to pass between Duisburg and Essen, where the flak was ferocious, and crews would later report observing Krefeld still burning over to the south-west. The Pathfinders opened the attack bang on time, employing ground markers that were clearly visible through the thin veil of cloud. One of the squadron's new crews, captained by Sgt Leonard, turned back with engine trouble, but the others reached the target and experienced no difficulty in identifying the aiming point. F/L Crowe bombed from 18,500 feet at 01.18, and noted that bombs were falling all around the markers, indicating that the attack was concentrated and accurate. Sgt Barker and crew arrived at the tail end of the raid with their 8,000 pounder, and found a red target indicator to aim at, thus demonstrating the effectiveness of the Pathfinder backers-up, who continued to maintain the aiming point. The blockbuster went down from 18,000 feet at 01.56, and added to the destruction that was evident from the many fires. Photo-reconnaissance confirmed the crews' impressions, and revealed that eleven hundred houses had been destroyed, while a further twelve thousand were damaged. On the debit side, this success cost the Command another thirty-five aircraft, but all from 106 Squadron made it back.

While the Pathfinder and main force squadrons recovered from their exertions on the following night, the Lancasters from the Friedrichshafen raid returned from North Africa, bombing the docks at La Spezia on the way. The crews had been briefed to bomb on instructions to be issued on arrival at the target, which took place some time after 23.30. They found an oil storage facility had already been hit, and thick black smoke was ascending, adding to the smoke screen, which was the only effective official defensive measure. P/O Reid was the first from the squadron to arrive, and decided not to hang around in case the smoke blotted out the target. He made a timed run from the headland, and delivered his 1,000 and 500 pounders at 23.57 from 9,500 feet. F/L Hartley was instructed to bomb five hundred yards north of the oil fire, and he complied at 00.05 from 12,500 feet. S/L Young received no instructions, and let his load go at 00.06 from 11,000 feet, while F/L Browne circled for forty-five minutes before being ordered to bomb at 00.07. P/O Yackman heard no instruction, and after circling for thirty minutes, bombed of his own accord at 00.22.

After their night's rest, the Command gathered in force again to attend to the Elberfeld half of Wuppertal, whose neighbour, Barmen, had been reduced to rubble a month earlier. 630 aircraft took off, 106 Squadron represented by thirteen Lancasters. They departed Syerston either side of 22.30 led by S/L Williamson, and flew to the target in five-tenths cloud, which had cleared by the time they arrived shortly before 01.30. The Ruhr defensive ring forced the crews to run the gauntlet of flak well before any individual town or city was reached, and there was a myth that a gap existed between Mönchengladbach and Cologne when a southerly route was in use as on this night. Sgt Davidson was driven off course by intense flak and huge searchlight concentrations, and bombed Düsseldorf as an alternative, and Sgt Leonard was attacked by a night fighter south-south-west of Düsseldorf, and jettisoned his bombs while successfully evading it. The Pathfinder markers were well placed, and P/O Robertson was the first from the squadron to bomb at 01.07, by which time fires were already taking hold. S/L Williamson watched a red TI cascade at 01.32 before bombing on it from 19,000 feet two minutes later. Sgt White was the last from the squadron to bomb at 01.40, and all returned safely to report a highly successful attack, the glow from which could be seen from the Dutch coast. Reconnaissance confirmed the crews' impressions, and although a creep-back along the line of approach from the west had allowed some bombs to fall on other urban areas, the destruction within Elberfeld was even more devastating than in Barmen, and around 90% of its built-up area was estimated to have been levelled. Approximately three thousand houses were destroyed along with 171 industrial premises, and many more sustained damage. In return for this success a further thirty-four aircraft failed to return, giving a combined loss over these three consecutive Ruhr operations of 113 aircraft and crews, which represented almost two percentage points above what was considered to be sustainable. 106 Squadron posted no crews missing from these operations, but the balance was about to be redressed.

The oil refinery town of Gelsenkirchen had always proved to be an elusive target to identity and hit, and a force of 473 aircraft was dispatched late on the evening of the 25th to attempt to rectify the matter through the use of Oboe. Fourteen 106 Squadron Lancasters lined up for take-off led by S/L Young, and they all got away safely between 22.30 and 23.00. There was complete cloud cover over the target, where the spearhead of the main force arrived before the Pathfinders, and had to circle to await the markers. It was during this period that P/O Rosner's aircraft was hit by flak, which knocked out the oxygen system, and he turned for home, bombing what he believed to be Essen on the way. For once, Oboe failed to provide accurate marking, after almost half of the Mosquitos found their equipment malfunctioning. The result was a scattering of bombs on various Ruhr locations in an echo of past experiences, and the intended target escaped with scant damage. The 106 Squadron crews bombed between 01.21 and 01.53, and those returning commented on the ferocity of the flak defences and the abundance of night fighters. Thirty aircraft were missing, and 106 Squadron equalled its worst reversal of the war to date, with four failures to return. R5572 crashed in central Holland, and produced the only survivor from among the four crews. The fact that it was the pilot, Sgt Davidson RCAF, who escaped with his life, suggests that the Lancaster may have broken up in the air and thrown him clear. W4256 crashed in northern Holland with the crew of Sgt White, while EE125 was lost without trace with the crew of the B Flight commander S/L Young, and presumably found the sea. W4367 was hit at the Dutch coast and came down in the Ijsselmeer, taking with it the crew of P/O Peter Page. After the war the land was reclaimed, and the actual crash site is now in the village of Dronten, north-north-east of Harderwijk. Peter came from the Leicestershire town of Lutterworth, where a few years earlier, Frank Whittle had formed Power Jets Ltd and built his first jet engine. Peter had only recently married, and his widow, Joan, would remain single for the rest of her life, which ended in the early 2,000s.

A series of three raids on Cologne spanning the turn of the month began on the night of the 28/29th, for which a force of six hundred aircraft was prepared, thirteen of them from 106 Squadron. F/Ls Hartley, Browne and Crowe were the senior pilots on duty, the last-mentioned now having stepped up temporarily to fill the vacancy of B Flight commander following the loss of S/L Young. They took off into cloudy skies either side of 23.00, and headed for the rendezvous point. The prospects of success diminished when the Oboe Mosquitos arrived on target seven minutes late, and only six of the original twelve were able to release their skymarkers over the cloud-covered city. F/L Crowe was among the first from the squadron to reach the city, having struggled with an engine problem that prevented him from climbing as high as he would have liked. He bombed at 01.50 from 16,000 feet before he saw the first TIs go down, and he made his way home in cloud at 4,000 feet. F/L Hartley picked up the tracking flares, and then the red flare with green stars over the target, and he had these in his bomb sights as he delivered his load from 19,500 feet at 01.50. He saw no results, but witnessed a large explosion two minutes later. F/L Browne's port-outer engine started to give trouble soon after take-off, and eventually had to be feathered. Just as he opened the bomb doors to run across the target, a night fighter attacked, and the bomb load was jettisoned over Euskirchen, south-west of the target, during evasive action. Despite these setbacks, the attack developed into the most destructive of the war thus far against this much-bombed city. 6,500 buildings were destroyed, 4,300 people were killed, and a further 230,000 bombed out in return for the loss of twenty-five aircraft. This was the last of eleven operations conducted by the squadron during the month, which resulted in 125 sorties for the loss of six aircraft and crews.

July 1943

106 Squadron began the new month with a mining operation on the night of the 1/2nd, involving three new crews, for whom it would be their maiden operation together. The target area was Nectarines, a much visited garden off the Frisians, and F/S Hendry, P/O Hayley and F/O Harvey all used a Gee fix to locate their drop zones and successfully deliver six mines each. The first major operation for the Command as a whole took place on the night of the 3/4th, and brought a return to Cologne. 650 aircraft were made ready, of which thirteen Lancasters were provided by 106 Squadron. S/L Williamson was the senior pilot on duty as they got away from Syerston between 22.15 and 23.15, and the spearhead of the squadron contingent began to arrive within sight of the target shortly after 01.00. The aiming point was on the heavily industrialized east bank of the Rhine, and it was easily identified by the well-placed Pathfinder markers. Fires had already taken hold when F/L Hartley, the point of the 106 Squadron spear, bombed from 20,800 feet at 01.18, a minute ahead of F/L Browne and two ahead of F/S Foulsham, and both Hartley and Browne brought back an aiming point photo. There was the usual flak defence along with a new Luftwaffe tactic, the introduction of Wilde Sau (wild boar). This employed single-engine day fighters of JG300, commanded by Major Hajo Hermann, to operate over the target. Their brief was to seek out and destroy individual bombers silhouetted against the burning city. Returning crews were unanimous in their appraisal that it had been a successful operation, and this was confirmed by photo-reconnaissance, which revealed the destruction of many industrial buildings and more than two thousand houses, which deprived a further 72,000 people of their homes. Thirty aircraft failed to return, and as one might expect, this was a little down on recent experiences when operating further north over the heart of the Ruhr.

The third and final raid of the current series was carried out on the night of the 8/9th by an all-Lancaster heavy force of 280 aircraft, including fourteen from 106 Squadron. F/Ls Browne and Crowe were the senior pilots on duty as they began taking off at 22.10, and a number of new crews were on the Order of Battle. F/S Bristow and crew had only recently embarked on their first tour, and they took off in ED360 at 22.25, before heading for the east coast. It was not long before an engine fire developed, however, forcing them to turn for home. The Lancaster made it as far as the Cambridgeshire Fens before crashing about five miles north-west of Wisbech at 01.40 with a 4,000 pounder still on board. The flight engineer and bomb-aimer were the only survivors after the cookie went up and totally destroyed the Lancaster along with all trace of F/S Bristow and his wireless operator, Sgt Worthington, who are commemorated on the Runnymede Memorial. F/L Crowe reached the target to find ten-tenths cloud and no markers, and bombed on e.t.a from 20,000 feet at 01.10, confident in his position because of a Gee fix obtained by his navigator, also named Crowe, just before. He described the route as excellent, and added that the trip had presented no special troubles. None of the crews was able to assess the results of their own bombs, but a glow beneath the clouds suggested that it was another punishing blow, and this was confirmed by photographic reconnaissance. The bombing had fallen largely onto hitherto less-severely afflicted districts, and almost 2,400 domestic buildings were destroyed along with a score of others of an industrial nature. A bonus was the loss of just seven aircraft, but of these, two were from 106 Squadron. R5573, "Admiral Foo Bang III", fell victim to a night fighter over Belgium on the way home, and crashed at 01.30 north-north-east of Liege. There were no survivors from the crew of Sgt McLean, who were on their first operation together. ED720 exploded over Cambrai in France while homebound, again as the result of an encounter with a night fighter, and only one man survived as a PoW from the eight-man crew of American 1st Lt Rosner, the squadron veteran, who had recently transferred to the USAAF from the RCAF. When the Cologne city authorities were able to assess the cost of the three raids, they catalogued eleven thousand buildings destroyed, 5,500 people killed, and a further 350,000 made homeless.

On the following night another attempt was made to hit the Nordstern synthetic oil plant at Gelsenkirchen. A force of 418 aircraft included eleven Lancasters from 106 Squadron, led by F/L Browne, and they began taking off at 22.30 to form up over base before heading for the North Sea. The target, as forecast, lay under ten-tenths cloud, and crews located it by means of tracking flares and then release point flares. P/O Robertson was the first from the squadron to deliver his payload, which he did at 01.14 from 21,000 feet, and F/L Browne and F/S Brown followed up a minute later. None was able to see the results of their efforts, but a glow beneath the clouds encouraged them to be optimistic about the success of the attack. Unfortunately, equipment failure afflicting five of the Oboe Mosquitos caused the main weight of the attack to hit an area to the south of the intended aiming point, and while some damage was caused in Gelsenkirchen, it was Bochum and Wattenscheid that suffered most. Flak was intense and a number of 106 Squadron Lancasters sustained damage, but all returned home to fight another day.

A two night rest preceded the tenth raid of the war on Turin, which was undertaken by an all-Lancaster force of 295 aircraft from 1, 5 and 8 Groups. 106 Squadron put up thirteen aircraft, led for the first time by the 24 year-old S/L Philip Brandon-Trye, who had been posted in on the 1st, presumably to replace S/L Young. He had previously served with 207 Squadron, but it is not known whether he had come to 106 Squadron directly from there. Whatever, this night's events would alter any original intentions. They departed Syerston in a fifteen minute slot to 22.30, and headed into heavy cloud and violent storms over France. F/L Crowe had his a.s.i. freeze up, and he was unable to climb above the cloud to escape the icing conditions. He tried three times to fly round the high cumulo-nimbus cloud, but was thwarted each time, and, accepting that he had insufficient altitude to safely cross the Alps, he jettisoned his load and turned back. The others reached the target shortly before 02.00 to find little or no cloud, and they were able to identify ground detail and clearly see the Pathfinder markers. The squadron crews bombed between 01.46 and 02.20 from 15,000 to 20,000 feet in the face of very weak opposition, and all but one made it safely home after ten hours and more aloft. Thirteen Lancasters failed to return, and 5 Group posted missing one of its heroes, W/C Nettleton of 44 Squadron, who had worn the VC since the epic Augsburg raid of April 1942. He had been shot down into the sea off the Brest peninsular, and no trace of the aircraft or crew was ever found. Also missing from this operation was 106 Squadron's DV181, from which an indistinct wireless message was received at 06.30 stating, "We are being attacked by enemy f". The broadcast was cut off at that point, and it seems certain that P/O Hayley and his crew suffered the same fate as Nettleton, and disappeared into the sea off the French coast. Photo-reconnaissance revealed that both crews had contributed to an accurate attack, that fell predominantly to the north of the city centre, and produced the highest death toll to date at this target of 792 people.

On the 14th awards were announced to a number of 106 Squadron members, including F/L Edmunds, who received a DFC and F/L Oliver, whose DFM was probably in recognition of his time serving in Gibson's crew while an NCO. There was also a DFM for the now tour-expired P/O Burton. On the 15th the squadron bade farewell to S/L Williamson, who was posted to Dunholme Lodge to fill the vacancy for a commanding officer at 44 Squadron following W/C Nettleton's loss. This allowed S/L Brandon-Trye to step into his shoes as A Flight commander, rather than replace S/L Young as B Flight commander. This also provided the opportunity for F/L Crowe to become the permanent successor to the latter, and he would shortly be promoted to acting squadron leader rank. During a lull in major operation during the mid-month period, 5 Group targeted a number of electricity transformer stations in northern Italy, in an attempt to disrupt electricity supplies to railways ferrying troops and supplies to the battle in Sicily. 617 Squadron carried out its first operation since the Dams on the night of the 15/16th against transformer stations near Bologna and Genoa, and similar targets at Cislago and Bologna were selected for eighteen Lancasters from the group on the following night. 106 Squadron contributed three aircraft to Bologna, captained by F/L Crowe and P/Os Munro and Yackman, and each made a number of runs across the target at around 2,500 feet, releasing a few of their fourteen 500 pounders each time. The bombs were seen to straddle the aiming point, and the crews followed up with machine gun fire. There were no losses, and the three 106 Squadron crews landed safely at Blida in Algeria after a ten-hour trip.

Tragedy struck on the afternoon of the 18th, when a number of senior officers attended a gunnery course demonstration run by 1485 Bombing and Gunnery Flight at Fulbeck. G/C Odbert, the Irish station commander at Syerston, and 106 Squadron's S/L Brandon-Trye, were among those invited to witness the "5 Group corkscrew" evasive manoeuvre, and it was decided that they should do this at first hand rather than from the ground. The students, who had been intended to fly on this fighter affiliation exercise were dismissed, and the four officers climbed aboard to join the pilot, W/O Heard, and the gunnery instructor, Sgt Breslin. The fighter was a Miles Martinet, piloted by F/O Jordan, and as he made his approach to simulate an attack, and while still two hundred yards behind the Wellington, he watched the Wellington's starboard wing break off outboard of the engine. It immediately went into a dive, and crashed near Appleby in Lincolnshire, killing all on board.

Although two further operations to the Ruhr would take place towards the end of the month, the offensive had now effectively run its course, and Harris could look back with pride at the successes of the past five months, and, as a champion of electronic aids, take particular satisfaction from the vital role played by Oboe. Germany's industrial heartland now lay in ruins, giving lie to Goering's proud, but ill-judged boast, that no bombs would fall on German soil. It is true that the campaign had taken a heavy toll on the Command, but the factories and the Empire Training Schools had more than kept pace with the rate of attrition, and new aircraft and crews were being fed into the squadrons on demand, with sufficient left over to continue the gradual expansion. With confidence high in his Command's ability to deal effectively with any area target, Harris sought an opportunity to deliver a knockout blow against an important industrial city, which would send shock waves reverberating around the Reich.

Hamburg, as Germany's second city, had the necessary political status to suit Harris's needs, and was a centre of industry, particularly, U-Boot construction. It also satisfied Harris's criteria in operational respects, in being close to a coast for navigational purposes, and easily reachable during the few hours of darkness afforded by midsummer. Finally, beyond the range of Oboe, which had proved to be so decisive at the Ruhr, Hamburg had the wide River Elbe to provide a good H2S signature for the navigators high above. In each year of the war to date Bomber Command had visited Hamburg during the last week of

July, and this was the period selected for Operation Gomorrah, a short series of maximum effort raids, designed to erase Hamburg from the map under the weight of ten thousand tons of bombs.

The bell sounded for round one on the night of the 24/25th, when the 790 aircraft were to receive the benefit of the first operational use of Window, bundles of tinfoil-backed strips of paper, which, when dispensed into the air to fall in dense clouds, swamped the enemy night fighter, searchlight and gun-laying radar with false returns, and rendered them effectively blind. The device had been available for a year, but its use had been vetoed in case the enemy copied it. The enemy had, in fact, already developed its own version, known as Düppel, and it had been withheld from operational use for the same reason. There was a late evening departure, and W/C Baxter was the last of the 106 Squadron contingent to take off at 23.00. Weather conditions were good throughout the operation, and crews began to release Window at a predetermined point over the North Sea. The effects of the device were made immediately apparent by the lack of combats taking place during the outward leg. A number of aircraft were shot down during these early stages, but they were well off track, and beyond the protection of the Window screen, and may even have been early returns. Once in the target area, the crews witnessed a rare lack of co-ordination between the searchlights and flak batteries, and defence was at best random and sporadic.

The conditions were in place to concentrate the markers on the planned aiming point and deliver a crushing blow upon the city, but the Pathfinders wasted the opportunity to an extent, and the markers were somewhat scattered, although close enough to the city centre to make little difference if the main force did its job. Those from 106 Squadron reaching the target early on were able to identify ground detail, and saw the Pathfinder target indicators cascading. F/O Hoboken bombed first at 01.03 from 19,000 feet, and a number of other crews from the squadron followed up during the ensuing two minutes. By the time that W/C Baxter arrived to bomb at 01.37, there was a concentration of fires and smoke rising to 16,000 feet. F/O Harvey was the last to bomb at 01.42, and he joined the others in a safe return. Reconnaissance revealed that only 50% of the bombs had been delivered within three miles of the aiming point, and an extensive creep-back had developed, which cut a six-mile swathe of destruction along the line of approach across the north-western districts and out into open country. It was, however, an effective attack, in which 2,284 tons of bombs had been delivered, and it was a promising start to the campaign, which also left fifteen hundred people dead. Only twelve aircraft failed to return, an indication of the success of Window. While this operation was in progress, the shuttle force, including F/L Crowe and P/O Munro returned from North Africa, having bombed the docks at Leghorn on the way. F/L Crowe lost an engine during the attack, and made the entire return journey from the target on three. A 61 Squadron crew brought back P/O Yackman's Lancaster with two members of his crew, while the others remained at Blida suffering from some form of sickness.

Harris decided to switch his force to Essen on the following night, possibly because of reports of dense smoke still lingering over Hamburg, but also because of an expected cold front moving in to create unfavourable weather conditions. He could also take advantage of the body blow dealt to the enemy's defensive system by Window. 705 aircraft took off, among them seventeen Lancasters representing 106 Squadron led by F/Ls Stephens, Browne and Hartley. They got away between 22.00 and 22.25, but F/Os Hoboken and Harvey were forced to return early with technical failures. The others arrived in the target area to find conditions ranging from clear to three-tenths thin cloud, and there was a general consensus that searchlights were ineffective and flak not as heavy as might be expected at this target. F/S Foulsham was the first from the squadron to arrive, to see red TIs cascade at 00.26, and he bombed four minutes later from 19,700 feet. There was already a concentration of fires, and this was clearly visible on his aiming point photograph. 106 Squadron crews continued to pass over the target and bomb for a further forty minutes, and for once, the Essen jinx did not claim a 106 Squadron crew. The industrial eastern districts of Essen were hit particularly hard on this night, and the Krupp works sustained its heaviest damage of the war. Almost three thousand houses were also destroyed, along with fifty industrial premises, and this at a cost of twenty-six aircraft.

After a night's rest 780 aircraft set off for Hamburg late on the 27th, to deliver what in the event would turn out to be the most devastating attack of the war on a German city. 106 Squadron provided eighteen Lancasters, led by F/Ls Crowe, Hartley and Stephens, who were among the first to take off at 22.20. Crowe was in ED819, whose starboard-inner engine cut at just 100 feet and caught fire. The fire was extinguished with difficulty, and Crowe made two complete circuits of the airfield before landing in the dark with a full fuel and bomb load on board. The weight of the aircraft was 62,000lbs, a full 9,000lbs above the safe landing weight. F/O Hoboken turned back early for the second operation running, and freshmen Sgt Large and crew were also unable to complete their sortie. The others pressed on, and what followed the force's arrival over Hamburg was both unprecedented and unforeseeable, and was the result of a conspiracy of random factors. A spell of unusually hot and dry weather during July had left tinderbox conditions within parts of the city, and when the Pathfinders dropped their markers, they did so with unaccustomed concentration, but two miles to the east of the planned city centre aiming point. They fell into the densely populated working class residential districts of Hamm, Hammerbrook and Borgfeld, and attracted the 729 main force crews, which followed up with uncharacteristic accuracy and scarcely any creep-back. They delivered most of their 2,300 tons of bombs into this relatively compact area, creating individual fires, which took hold and joined together to form one giant conflagration, which sucked in oxygen from surrounding areas at hurricane velocity to feed its voracious appetite. Such was the ferocity of this meteorological phenomenon, that trees were uprooted and flung bodily into the flames, along with debris and people. The temperature at the seat of the inferno reached a thousand degrees Celcius, and it was only once all of the combustible material had been consumed, that the fire began to subside.

None of this was evident to the crews high above, who were focussed on delivering their bombs onto the Pathfinder markers, obtaining a photo and then getting the hell out of the target area as quickly as possible. F/L Hartley found the visibility to be poor as he watched TIs cascade at 00.55. He bombed four minutes later from 19,000 feet, then remained on course until the photo-flash confirmed a picture. He returned home to report not seeing his bombs burst, and to comment on the volume of searchlights and their lack of effectiveness. His bombing photo was plotted at four miles east-north-east of the aiming point, as was F/L Browne's, and all returning crews were of one opinion, that the target area was a mass of flames, the glow of which was visible from two hundred miles away, and that by the time they turned away from the inferno, smoke was rising to bombing altitude. An estimated forty thousand people perished on this one night alone, and on the following morning the first of an eventual 1.2 million inhabitants began to file out of the tortured city. Seventeen aircraft failed to return, and among them were two from 106 Squadron. ED303, "Flag Day", crashed in the target area with the crew of Sgt McLeod, who were all killed on just their second operation together, and ED708 was shot down into the North Sea by a night fighter on the way home, taking with it the crew of F/S Charters, who were on their eighth operation.

A force of 777 aircraft set out again for Hamburg on the night of the 29/30th, sixteen of them provided by 106 Squadron led by W/C Baxter. They took off between 22.10 and 22.50 with the intention of approaching the city on a north-south heading, after the Pathfinders had marked the previously untouched northern and north-eastern districts. Sgt Reid returned early with a dead engine, but the others continued on, W/C Baxter arriving to find no cloud, but considerable smoke at 14,000 feet from the previous attack. He bombed on green TIs at 00.57 from 19,800 feet, and noted that the flak and searchlight activity had increased. He was some ten minutes behind the earliest 106 Squadron arrivals, and squadron aircraft would continue to pass over the target until F/Os Cole and Harvey delivered their loads at 01.25. F/O Harvey reported the glow of fires again visible from two hundred miles away. Reconnaissance revealed that the Pathfinder markers had again fallen two miles to the east of the planned aiming point, and south of the firestorm area. The creep-back from the 707 aircraft to arrive on target spread across these already devastated districts, before creating a new large area of fire further north in the Barmbek and Wandsbek districts, which the exhausted local fire units were unable to reach through rubble-strewn streets. Twenty-eight aircraft were missing from this operation, to demonstrate that the Luftwaffe was beginning to recover from the effects of Window, but all from 106 Squadron returned safely.

The string of successful attacks continued on the night of the 30/31st at Remscheid, a town on the southern fringe of the Ruhr just below Wuppertal. A mixed force of 273 aircraft consisting of roughly equal numbers of Halifaxes, Stirlings and Lancasters was made ready, with Oboe Mosquitos to carry out the marking. This was the operation that would bring down the final curtain on the Ruhr campaign, and for which the squadron's original contribution of fifteen Lancasters was reduced to just four. F/Os Hoboken, Wodehouse, Claridge and Sgt Reid took off shortly after 22.00, and all of them bombed in a nine-minute slot a little after 01.00 before three of them returned home to report a highly successful operation. R5665 fell victim to a night fighter near the target shortly after bombing, and P/O Reid RCAF, who, it is believed, was American, stayed with the aircraft while his crew parachuted into captivity, and sacrificed his life. The bomb-aimer, P/O Gold RCAF, discovered that his parachute had been burned, and decided to jump to his death from 18,000 feet rather than die in the fire or the crash. Remarkably, he regained consciousness on the ground, and found he had suffered only a dislocated shoulder and knee. The attack on Remscheid destroyed over three thousand houses along with many industrial premises, while killing over a thousand people. During the course of the month the squadron was involved in twelve operations, including the two "shuttle" raids, and dispatched 128 sorties for the loss of six aircraft.

August 1943

The new month began for 106 Squadron with a training accident on the afternoon of the 1st involving veteran Lancaster R5614. Sgt Fred Mifflin touched down heavily, and opened up the throttles to go round again. At the same time a cross wind caused him to lose control, and the aircraft ended up in the overshoot area off the runway, where it was destroyed by fire. The entire crew managed to escape, but all sustained injuries to some degree. Sadly, Mifflin would be one of the casualties on a bad night for the squadron nine months hence. Operation Gomorrah drew to a less than satisfactory close on the night of the 2/3rd of August, when violent electrical storms, severe icing and huge cumulus cloud formations during the outward flight persuaded many crews to abandon their sorties, and either jettison their bombs or attack alternative targets. Of 740 aircraft taking part, ten were provided by 106 Squadron, and they began taking off from Syerston at 23.20 with no senior officers on duty. F/S Barker found his rudder was sticking, and in turning to bypass a particularly evil area of storm, it jammed and sent the Lancaster into a diving turn to port. The bomb load and some of the fuel were jettisoned, and the sortie was abandoned. F/O Wodehouse reached the German coast before the conditions defeated him, while F/S Foulsham got as far as the target area, where he found his aircraft threatened by lightning, pounded by hail stones and ringed by static. The engines began to behave erratically, and two had to be feathered, whereupon the bombs were jettisoned and the sortie abandoned. There was very little Pathfinder marking, and those crews 02.44.

Intensive maintenance in the open air at Syerston in 1943.

actually delivering their bombs did so mostly on e.t.a based on a Gee fix. Somehow, F/S Hendry saw a concentration of green markers on the ground from 19,000 feet, and bombed these, while P/O Whetter picked up red route markers, but saw nothing over the target, and bombed on e.t.a. from 17,800 feet at 02.44. ED358 was attacked by a night fighter after bombing, and had a large hole in a wing to show for it, but F/O Poore and crew came home without further incident. Bombing was scattered around the general area, with the main weight perhaps falling on the little town of Elmshorn, some twelve miles from Hamburg. Hamburg itself barely noticed the event, but the damage had already been done.

Italy was now teetering on the brink of capitulation, and a mini campaign was mounted during August, to help nudge it over the edge. 1, 5 and 8 Groups went to Genoa, Milan and Turin on the night of the 7/8th, and former squadron commanding officer, W/C Searby, acted as Master Bomber for the Turin element, as a rehearsal for the approaching Peenemünde operation, although this was as yet unknown to Searby. The Master Bomber technique, involving voice control, required him to remain over the target for the duration of the operation, exposed throughout to the defences. He would assess the accuracy of the markers, and advise the main force as to which to aim for. Once the attack was well under way he would exhort and encourage the crews to press through with their bombing run and not drop short. From this point on the use of a Master Bomber would be a regular feature of Bomber Command operations. 106 Squadron put up ten Lancasters for Milan on this night, and they took off either side of 21.00, again with no senior officers present. The target was located without difficulty in good weather conditions, and F/O Ham and Sgt Trill brought back aiming point photos. The squadron participants bombed between 01.15 and 01.24, and all but one returned safely. DV196 was the exception, and was shot down by a night fighter over France on the way home. F/O Wodhouse and his bomb-aimer were killed, but five of the crew did survive, and four of them ultimately evaded capture.

A medium-sized force of 450 aircraft was sent to Mannheim on the night of the 9/10th, when cloud contributed to a poor Pathfinder marking performance. The subsequent attack was described as scattered, but the local authorities listed over thirteen hundred building as destroyed or seriously damaged, 133 large and 417 medium fires, along with a whole catalogue of other damage, including that inflicted upon locomotives and rolling stock. 106 Squadron provided a dozen Lancasters for this operation, which took off either side of 23.00, and among them was P/O Robertson, who was back for a second tour, and had flown on the previous operation as a second pilot to F/S Harris. Most crews found TIs to aim at, and described the trip as uneventful with little opposition, except at the French coast, where it was a little more lively.

Nuremberg was the destination for 653 aircraft on the following night, for which 106 Squadron detailed ten Lancasters led by W/C Baxter. They took off either side of 22.00, and found the target under eight-tenths cloud, through which the pathfinder ground markers were barely visible. Even so, W/C Baxter had green ones in his sights as he bombed from 19,100 feet at 01.05, and he could make out the glow of fires. They may have been the same TIs that F/O Ham aimed at from 700 feet lower at exactly the same time, and he saw several explosions as well as the fires. F/S Hendry arrived thirty six minutes later to find the target by means of Pathfinder flares, but saw no TIs on the ground, and bombed on e.t.a from 18,000 feet. His was one of nine crews to return safely from what was generally described as a quiet trip. P/O Perry was attacked by a JU88 on the run-in to bomb, but his rear gunner, Sgt Groombridge, claimed to have shot it down. The absentee at debriefing was the crew of F/S Harris RAAF, whose DV195 had crashed into a north-western suburb, about four miles from the city centre, possibly after colliding with a 619 Squadron Lancaster, and all on board lost their lives. *(The ranks are those specified in the ORB, and may, therefore, not harmonize with those recorded in Bill Chorley's Bomber Command Losses series, in which Harris is shown as P/O).* Reconnaissance showed that the operation had been successful, and had caused serious damage in central and southern districts.

The campaign against Italy was drawing to a conclusion, and the final effort came in a series of operations against Milan and Turin during a five-night period. The night of the 12/13th took a force of five hundred Lancasters and Halifaxes to Milan, while a smaller, predominantly 3 Group force of Stirlings attacked Turin. 106 Squadron supported the former with eleven Lancasters, and they took off in a thirty minute slot to 21.50 in the absence of a senior officer. They arrived in the target area shortly after 01.00, guided by route markers, and located the city without difficulty in good visibility and weather conditions. P/O Whetter bombed from 18,500 feet at 01.17, and brought back an aiming point photo, as did F/S Barker and Sgt Trill, and all from the squadron contributed to a concentrated assault before returning safely. Two nights later 140 Lancasters of 1, 5 and 8 Groups returned to Milan, this time with six aircraft from 106

Squadron amongst their number, and Sgt Trill, F/S Callan and F/S Hay all returned with aiming point photos from another successful and uneventful operation.

199 aircraft went back twenty-four hours later to end 1 and 5 Group's involvement with Italy. This time 106 Squadron contributed eight Lancasters, and the senior officer present was Syerston's new station commander, G/C Hodder, who was with the crew of P/O Robertson. Also flying with the squadron for the first time, as second pilot to F/S Barker, was S/L Howroyd, who had been posted in on the 19th of July to replace S/L Brandon-Trye, who, it will be recalled, had been lost in the same accident as G/C Hodder's predecessor. It was an earlier take-off than of late, either side of 20.30, but all other details of the operation were similar to those experienced during the two previous attacks on this city. P/O Robertson bombed at 00.11 from 15,000 feet, and impressed his new station commander by bringing back an aiming point photo. P/O Perry did likewise, and all returned safely having contributed to another effective attack. Later that day the award of a DFC was announced to F/L Hartley and to P/O Crowe, the navigator in the crew of his namesake, F/L Crowe. Elements of 3 and 8 Groups conducted the very last operation of the war against Italy by Bomber Command on the night of the 16/17th, when Turin was the objective, but many of the 3 Group Stirlings were diverted on return, and by the time they got back to their home stations, it was too late to prepare them for that night's vitally important operation.

Since the very start of the war, intelligence had been filtering through, much from anonymous sources, concerning German research into rockets. Scant regard was given to the reports, but by mid 1943, it had been clear for some time that most of the activity centred upon Peenemünde, a secret establishment on the island of Usedom just off the Baltic coast. The brilliant scientist, Dr R V Jones, had been monitoring trials of the V-1 flying bomb by reading the data gleaned from German Enigma signals traffic, and he now knew the weapon's range. He would ultimately use what he learned to feed disinformation back to the enemy. In June a PRU Mosquito had managed to photograph a V-2 on a trailer, but, despite the evidence, Churchill's chief scientific adviser, Professor Lindemann, or Lord Cherwell as he became, refused to give credence to rocket weapons, and claimed the photo was of an airship-type craft. It took the combined urgings of Duncan Sandys and Dr Jones to convince Churchill of the need to act, and an operation was scheduled for the first available opportunity under the codename Hydra. This arose on the night of the 17/18th, for which a force of 597 aircraft was made ready, the numbers somewhat depleted by the unavailability of some 3 Group Stirlings for the reason already mentioned.

The complex plan called for three aiming points to be attacked, the housing estate, wherein lived the scientists and workers, the V2 assembly sheds, and finally the experimental site, each assigned to a specific wave of bombers, with the Pathfinders bearing the responsibility for shifting the point of aim accordingly. 3 and 4 Groups were assigned to the first aiming point, 1 Group to the second, and 5 and 6 Groups were to bring up the rear, 5 Group authorized to employ its "time and distance" method of aiming, if it seemed that smoke might obscure sight of the aiming point. Take-offs were scheduled between 21.00 and 22.00, and as the bombers approached the target area, G/C Len Slee, former 49 squadron commanding officer and now commander of the Pathfinders' 139 Squadron, would lead a spoof raid by eight of his Mosquitos on Berlin, with the intention of misleading the German night fighter controller into thinking that this was the main raid.

F/L Hartley was first away from Syerston at 21.15, and the remaining eight Lancasters were off the ground by 21.35, most, but not all, carrying a cookie, six 1,000 pounders and two 250 pounders. They flew to the target in excellent weather conditions, and arrived off the Baltic coast to find the operation well under way. Throughout the operation 83 Squadron's G/C Searby remained overhead and in range of the defences, directing the marking and bombing, and there were early problems for him to solve when some misplaced markers fell onto the Trassenheide forced workers camp, a mile or so south of the housing estate. Trapped inside their wooden barracks, many of these "friendly" foreign nationals were killed or injured by the 3 and 4 Group bombs, but once rectified, the operation proceeded more or less according to plan, and some important members of the V-2 technical team were killed. The 1 Group second phase experienced a strong cross-wind, but had, never the less, inflicted damage on the assembly sheds. W/C Baxter ran in from the island of Rügen, and was directed by G/C Searby to a cluster of green TIs, which he bombed from 7,000 feet at 00.49. F/L Hartley bombed the same markers from the same altitude at the same time, and commented on the lack of flak but evidence of many night fighters. This was true, because it was while the 5 and 6 Group aircraft were in the target area, that the night fighters arrived belatedly from Berlin, and they proceeded to shoot down bombers, both in the skies above Peenemünde, and on the return journey towards Denmark. They were employing their "Schräge Musik" (jazz music) upward-firing cannons for the first time, and these would prove to be lethal to Bomber Command aircraft over the ensuing eight months. F/O Ham saw at least two bombers shot down, and of the forty failing to return, twenty-nine were from 5 and 6 Groups, seventeen and twelve respectively, and this represented 14.5% and 19.7% respectively of those dispatched. Remarkably, all of the 106 Squadron aircraft landed safely back at Syerston to report what they believed was a successful operation. When the bombing photos were plotted the aiming point had been captured by P/O Yackman and Sgt Storer. The operation was sufficiently effective to push back the development programme of the V2 by a number of weeks, and the testing was transferred eastwards into Poland, beyond the range of Harris's bombers, while construction moved to hastily-built underground facilities in central Germany, where slave labour was employed.

The Ruhr town of Leverkusen, situated on the southern edge of the Ruhr north of Cologne, was home to a factory owned by the I.G. Farben company, which was engaged in the manufacture of synthetic oil and other substances. It would also be established after the war that it, too, relied heavily on slave labour. A force of 462 aircraft was made ready for an operation on the night of the 22/23rd, and the crews were told that the factory was the intended aiming point. 106 Squadron supported the operation with eleven Lancasters, led for the first time by S/L Howroyd as A Flight commander, and they took off either side of 21.00, and arrived over the target to find thick cloud with tops as high as 20,000 feet. The conditions forced the use of skymarkers, the least accurate method of target marking, and S/L Howroyd aimed for these as he bombed from 19,000 feet at 00.20. He saw the glow of fires beneath the clouds, and a number of other crews reported large explosions, but, in reality, no one had a clue where their bombs had fallen. F/O Cole and crew had a very close encounter with another Lancaster, and P/O Forsyth was attacked four times by a night fighter, but evaded each time. A modest five aircraft failed to return, and among them was 106 Squadron's JA871, which crashed near Düsseldorf, killing F/O Kain RCAF and his crew, who had only recently embarked on their first tour. Reconnaissance suggested that the cloud and a partial failure of the Oboe signal had resulted in a scattered attack that deposited bombs onto a dozen other Ruhr towns, but missed the factory.

Harris now wanted to turn his attention to a target, the destruction of which, he believed, would bring an early conclusion to the war. As the seat and symbol of Nazi power, Berlin held the key to ultimate victory. The psychological blow to the German people would be immense, and a similar belief had fuelled Hitler's determination to capture Stalingrad, a quest which had culminated in a humiliating defeat earlier in the year. What some believed was an obsession of Harris, which blinded him to all other considerations, would occupy much of the Command's resources for the next eight months. There is also debate as to when the campaign actually began. Was it with the three-raid series about to take place, or was it in November, which heralded the start of a sixteen raid series that would last until the end of March 1944? The ORB for 1 Group's 103 Squadron at Elsham Wolds has no doubts, and heralds the coming operation with the words, "Twenty-four aircraft were detailed to attack this target, which begins the so-called "Battle of Berlin". The 106 Squadron ORB describes it as the long-awaited assault on Berlin, so, clearly, it had been rumoured for some time. Whatever the answer, the attempt to bring Berlin, and, thereby, Germany to its knees, would become the Command's most bitter struggle of the entire war, and come closest to breaking its spirit.

The long and arduous road to Berlin, was joined by over 720 crews on the night of the 23/24th of August, for which 106 Squadron put up thirteen Lancasters led by the newly promoted B Flight commander, S/L Crowe, who was undertaking his first operation of the month. Take-off times were getting earlier as the days shortened, and it was 20.10 when the first departures took place from Syerston. They headed for the east coast and the North Sea, with the intention of crossing the enemy coast via the known gap in the defences at Egmond. From there they would adopt an almost due-easterly course to the target, with a slight dogleg to the south-east north of Hanover. This was to be the first area raid to be controlled by a Master Bomber, a job handed to the grizzled and tough former Canadian bush pilot and brawler, W/C Johnny Fauquier, who had twice commanded 405 (Vancouver) Squadron, and would see 617 Squadron through to the end of the bombing war as a group captain in 1945. The sheer size of Berlin made identification of a specific area by H2S a challenge of the greatest magnitude.

On this night the Pathfinders were unable to locate the centre of the city, and the target indicators fell well to the south onto the fringes. The main force arrived late, and some crews opted to head directly for the markers from the south-west, rather than follow the planned route, and swing past the southern edge of the city to approach from the south-east. The skies were clear and the visibility good as S/L Crowe arrived in the target area, and he located it by means of red and green target indicators and visual identification of a built-up area. He bombed from 19,000 feet at 23.51, and brought back a photo plotted at 3½ miles south-west of the aiming point. P/O Robertson and F/O Poore were the last from the squadron to bomb at 00.20, the latter directed to three green TIs by the Master Bomber, whose contribution he described as "very helpful". P/O Robertson commented on the lack of flak but abundance of night fighters, and he observed a number of combats. There was a good concentration of fires as they turned away from the target, by which time smoke had drifted up to 15,000 feet. On the way home F/Os Cole and Harvey were each attacked by a JU88, which their gunners shot down after short combats. Despite the presence and efforts of the Master Bomber, a proportion of the bombing fell into open country, and many outlying communities reported bombs falling around them, something that would become a feature of the entire campaign. Never the less, in the face of all of the failures in procedure, over 2,600 buildings had been destroyed, and this was the best result yet at Germany's capital. The cost was enormous, however, and at fifty-six aircraft was the largest loss to date, with the Halifaxes and Stirlings suffering particularly high percentage losses.

106 Squadron had come through unscathed on this night, and was able to put fifteen Lancasters into the air for a trip to Nuremberg on the night of the 27/28th as part of an overall force of 674 aircraft. S/L Howroyd was the senior pilot on duty, and there was a first operation for Canadian F/S Don Cheney and crew, who had arrived on the squadron on the day of the Peenmünde operation, and who, like their colleagues, F/O Poore and crew, were destined one day to join 617 Squadron. They departed Syerston in good weather conditions either side of 21.00, and headed for the rendezvous point over the Channel. The Pathfinders found the city clear of cloud, but difficult to locate on what was a very dark night. H2S did

not perform well, and although the initial marking was accurate, a creep-back developed, and problems with communications prevented the Master Bomber's instructions from getting through to the majority of the main force. F/L Hartley was on his fiftieth operation, and the final one of his second tour, and he was among the early arrivals over the target, delivering his cookie and incendiaries at 00.31, and observing many large fires. In contrast, P/O Roper and crew were another on their first operation, and they bombed at 00.47, also noting a good concentration of fires already burning. S/L Howroyd was among the last from the squadron to arrive in the target area, and he aimed his bombs at the centre of three cascading green TIs from 21,000 feet at 01.02. Thirty-three aircraft failed to return, but 106 Squadron came through unscathed, and crews were quietly confident that the raid had been successful. However, when their bombing photos were plotted, they were seen to be between 1½ and five miles south-south-east of the aiming point, and it seems that most of the bombing was wasted on open country.

When the twin towns of Mönchengladbach and Rheydt were revealed as the targets at briefings on the 30th, the crews would no doubt have been cheered by the prospect of a short-haul operation to the south-western fringes of the Ruhr Valley. Again the force comprised over six hundred aircraft, including fifteen Lancasters from 106 Squadron, which took off after 23.00 with no senior officers on duty. The plan was to attack in two phases, separated by two minutes as the Pathfinders shifted the point of aim from one town to the other. F/O Roper lost his port-inner engine while outbound, and this ended the recent run of excellent serviceability. The early arrivals among the 106 Squadron contingent found varying amounts of thin or broken cloud with tops at 10,000 feet, and bombed Mönchengladbach shortly after 02.00 on clearly visible Pathfinder markers. Those reaching the target area around 02.30 and beyond attacked Rheydt, but by the time F/O Poore and crew turned up at 02.50 after a navigational error delayed them, there were no markers to aim at, so they chose the centre of three fires, and let their cookie, four 1,000 pounders and 964 incendiaries go at 02.54. As far as the operation as a whole was concerned, everything proceeded according to plan, and both towns sustained heavy damage, with a combined total of around 2,300 buildings destroyed. Twenty-five aircraft were lost, but for the third consecutive operation, all of the 106 Squadron participants arrived home safely.

The last night of the month brought a return to Berlin by a force of 622 aircraft, of which fourteen represented 106 Squadron. They began taking off shortly after 20.00 in the absence of any senior officers, but F/O Roper didn't get away until 20.55, and he ultimately abandoned his sortie once it became clear he would be alone over the target if he continued. P/O Yackman also returned early after his port-outer engine gave trouble. The route to the target took the force over Texel and south of Hanover, and they began arriving in the target area shortly after 23.30 to find varying amounts of cloud, some describing it as low with gaps, and others as thin six to seven-tenths with tops at 8,000 feet. The reliability of H2S was again called into question as the Pathfinders delivered their markers onto the southern outskirts of the city, and the problem was compounded for the main force crews by an abundance of night fighters in the target area, some deploying flares to highlight the routes being used by the bombers to and from the target. Inevitably a creep-back occurred, which stretched thirty miles back along the line of approach.

P/O Whetter was probably the first from the squadron to make an attack, having been guided to the target by route markers and red and green TIs. He bombed at 23.38, and described the defences as heavy and accurate. F/O Ham was on his bombing run when JD146 was hit by flak and severely damaged, and he and his wireless operator sustained serious wounds. They turned for home, streaming fuel from ruptured tanks, and we will pick them up again later. The majority of the squadron's aircraft arrived over the city in a fifteen-minute slot either side of midnight, and bombed from between 17,500 and 20,000 feet, and were largely untroubled by the defences. One exception was P/O Storer, who lost his hydraulics system to flak, but he skilfully carried out a forced-landing at home, without causing any crew casualties or further damage to DV229. Now back to JB146, which despite crippling damage, loss of fuel and a badly injured pilot, made it back to home airspace, and crash-landed on Romney Marshes in Kent at 03.00. F/O Ham's heroics had saved five members of the crew, but he and wireless operator Sgt Weight succumbed to their injuries before help came. Forty-seven aircraft failed to return home after this dismal failure, the vast majority falling victim to night fighters. This was certainly the cause of the demise of 106 Squadron's ED409, although it was brought down near the Mittelland Canal north-east of the Ruhr in the Münsterland region shortly after crossing into Germany during the outward flight. F/S Hendry RNZAF and three of his crew were killed, but the flight engineer, navigator and bomb-aimer managed to save themselves before falling into enemy hands. The Halifaxes and Stirlings had again borne the brunt of the enemy defences, and alarm bells were beginning to sound concerning their vulnerability compared with that of the Lancaster. Reconnaissance and local reports revealed that only eighty-five houses were destroyed in the capital. During the course of the month 106 Squadron operated on thirteen occasions, launching 144 sorties for the loss of five aircraft.

September 1943

Having closed the August account, it was Berlin that opened September's, and it was an all-Lancaster heavy force of 316 aircraft that winged its way towards Denmark during the evening of the 3rd, with the intention of approaching the target from the north-east. 106 Squadron put up eleven aircraft for this operation, led by S/L Howroyd, and they took off either side of 20.00, and headed for the Dutch coast at Den Helder and a direct route to the target. The outward journey was undertaken over cloud, but this had almost cleared by the time the target hove into sight shortly before 23.30, and this allowed the Pathfinders to employ ground markers. They went down over the aiming point, before creeping back five miles along the line of approach, which, fortunately, intersected the Siemensstadt industrial district. P/O Large bombed from 20,000 feet just to starboard of a cluster of green TIs at 23.36, and reported seeing the glow of fires from 150 miles into the return journey. His bombing photo would be plotted at six miles from the aiming point. Don Cheney was down at 14,000 feet when he bombed at 23.27, and described a big concentration of fires along with heavy and accurate flak and many searchlights. He had an engine fail over the target, and undertook the long flight home on three. S/L Howroyd had just bombed from 20,000 feet at 23.37, when JA893 was attacked by a night fighter. A fierce combat ensued, during which the enemy aircraft was shot down, and the Lancaster severely damaged. There were also crew casualties, the bomb-aimer, P/O Saxby, being killed, while the rear gunner, Sgt McKenzie, sustained serious wounds. The Lancaster was ditched 150 miles off the English coast, and the crew scrambled into the dinghy, leaving the body of P/O Saxby behind. Within hours a Hudson of 279 Squadron had dropped a lifeboat, and a naval launch completed the rescue, but, sadly, not before Sgt McKenzie had succumbed to his wounds. They were put ashore at Immingham on the north Lincolnshire coast at 05.45. The operation had been partially successful, through a proportion of the effort causing destruction in a number of residential and industrial districts, but at a cost of twenty-two Lancasters, 7% of those dispatched. 106 Squadron's ED385 crashed into woods while east-north-east of Hanover on the way home, and F/O Roper RAAF died with his crew.

Possibly because of the severe losses incurred over the three raids, a massive 125 aircraft and crews, Berlin was shelved until the long dark nights of winter could provide better protection. In the meantime, there were plenty of other targets to occupy the Command, and the twin cities of Mannheim and Ludwigshafen, facing each other astride the Rhine in southern Germany, were selected as ideal candidates to exploit the creep-back phenomenon. The plan placed the aiming point in the eastern half of Mannheim, after an approach from the west, which would take the bombers directly over Ludwigshafen. In this way the bombing would spread back across the western half of Mannheim, over the Rhine, and spill into Ludwigshafen on the west bank. A force of 605 aircraft was made ready, which included a contribution from 106 Squadron of just eight Lancasters. The squadron ORB states, "No replacements being forthcoming to build up our depleted resources, the squadron could offer only eight aircraft for tonight's raid". The next sentence reads, "The night proved disastrous". They departed Syerston either side of 20.00, with no senior pilots on duty, but the station commander, G/C Hodder, was taking part and flying with P/O Robertson. F/S Hart had to return early with a dead engine, and F/S Turnor touched down five minutes later with an unserviceable rear turret, The other pressed on towards the target, and P/O Trill was the first from the squadron to arrive, finding almost clear skies and good visibility, and a cluster of five cascading green TIs to aim at. He bombed from 18,700 feet at 23.05, and brought back an aiming point photo, something that he seemed to do on a regular basis. Sgt Mifflin bombed another cluster seven minutes later, and his bombing photo was plotted at three miles from the aiming point. Sgt Gibbs arrived much later on, and bombed at 23.38, by which time he was able to describe, "a very fine concentration of fires".

The success of the operation was confirmed by photo-reconnaissance, which revealed that the plan had worked perfectly. Both cities sustained heavy damage, the Ludwigshafen authorities alone recording three large areas of fire, and almost two thousand individual conflagrations. There was a high cost to pay for the success, however, and thirty-four aircraft failed to return home. For the second operation running 106 Squadron had two empty dispersals to contemplate on the morning after. W4922 had crashed in or on the banks of the Rhine at Ludwigshafen, killing F/S Taylor RAAF and his crew, and DV182 was attacked by a night fighter, the first burst of fire from which killed the pilot, P/O Robertson, and mortally wounded his flight engineer, Sgt Cunliffe. A fire broke out as the Lancaster went down, and only the bomb-aimer, F/O Willatt, was able to escape before it crashed north-west of Karlsruhe. In all, seven men died, including Syerston's station commander, G/C Hodder.

Over four hundred Lancasters and Halifaxes took off for Munich on the evening of the 6th, among them seven Lancasters provided by 106 Squadron. They took off either side of 20.00, and there were no early returns. The target was mostly cloud-covered, and neither the ground marking nor skymarking was effective. The Pathfinders marked the Ammersee to the city's south-west, and most crews made a timed run from there. It is believed that 106 Squadron's ED819 was on this leg, approaching the target to bomb, when it crashed less that ten miles from the centre of Munich, killing P/O Large and his crew. The others completed their attacks between 23.34 and 23.50 from around 20,000 feet, and contributed to a scattered attack, which fell mainly into southern and western districts with indeterminate results. Sixteen aircraft failed to return, thirteen of them from the Halifax contingent. There followed a two-week break for most 1 and 5 Group squadrons, while a series of operations was mounted against specific precision targets in France, which included a factory, coastal batteries and railway installations. Stirlings and Halifaxes of 3 and 4 Groups respectively provided the bulk of the main force on these occasions. 617 Squadron also carried out its ill-fated attack on the Dortmund-Ems Canal during this period on the night of the 15/16th, and former 106 Squadron member, F/L Bob Hutchison, was killed while flying with Gibson's successor, W/C Holden.

Main force operations resumed on the night of the 22/23rd, when over seven hundred aircraft were dispatched on the first of a four-raid series against Hanover. 106 Squadron put thirteen Lancasters into the air either side of 19.00, led by W/C Baxter. The route took the bomber stream out over the north German coast across the Schleswig-Holstein peninsular, and some aircraft came within range of the Emden flak defences. P/O Barker's ED420 was hit, and the damage included an unserviceable rear turret. The bombs were dropped on Emden, and the Lancaster turned for home, where a safe landing was carried out. The others completed the two-and-a-half-hour outward flight, and arrived in the target area to find good weather conditions. W/C Baxter bombed a concentration of seven green TIs from 21,000 feet at 21.33, and described good fires, well concentrated, and visible for over two hundred miles. He also reported being attacked by a single engine fighter, which his gunners drove off. F/O Cooper and crew were on their first operation together, and they, too, commented on the fires covering a large area. F/O Harvey was attacked by a JU88 while on the bombing run, and the bombs were dropped unsighted. F/O Poore brought back an aiming point photo, while, for once, P/O Trill's showed only fire tracks, but all crews returned with reports of many fires and a highly successful attack.

The marking had, indeed, been very concentrated, as had been the bombing, and this should have resulted in an effective operation. However, stronger than forecast winds had shifted the main weight of the effort to an area between two and five miles south-south-east of the city centre, and, according to Martin Middlebrook and Chris Everitt's indispensable tome, The Bomber Command War Diaries, rendered it ineffective. There was no report from Hanover to support this, but photographic reconnaissance confirmed that the attack was misplaced and south-east of where it should have been. Even so, in a city the size of Hanover, an area two to five miles from the centre would be built-up, and the fact that at least one aiming point photo was brought back, and that fires were visible from two hundred miles away, suggests that the attack was a tad more successful than we have come to accept.

The second raid of the month on Mannheim took place on the following night, for which over six hundred aircraft were detailed. 106 Squadron supported the operation with fifteen Lancasters, led by S/Ls Crowe and Howroyd, which departed Syerston either side of 19.00. The plan was to hit the northern districts of the city, which had escaped serious damage in the past, and the clear skies and good visibility helped the pathfinders to find the aiming point and leave it well-marked. P/O Barker and S/L Crowe were among the first from the squadron to reach the target, and they bombed at 21.53 and 21.54 respectively, by which time large fires were already beginning to take hold. By the time P/O Gibbs bombed from 20,000 feet at 22.13, there were many fires and a pall of smoke was rising into the air. The aim of the attack had been achieved, and the northern half of the city had suffered massively by the time a creep-back spilled over the Rhine into Ludwigshafen, Oppau and Frankenthal. Around a thousand buildings were destroyed in Mannheim, and an important I G Farben factory in Ludwigshafen sustained serious damage. In all, two thousand fires were reported, and more than thirty thousand people were rendered homeless. It proved to be an expensive success for the Command, however, after thirty-two aircraft failed to return. 106 Squadron's DV271 crashed near Neuleiningen, a few miles to the north-west of Mannheim, and only the bomb-aimer, P/O Heatherington, escaped with his life from the crew of P/O Trill.

The campaign against Hanover continued on the night of the 27/28th, when fourteen 106 Squadron Lancasters joined up with over 650 other aircraft. They took off between 19.10 and 19.50 led by S/L Howroyd, and a number of new crews, those of F/O Lee and F/L Ginder, were undertaking their first operation with the squadron, while F/L Poore was on his first since being promoted. F/O Cooper and P/O Storer returned early with turret malfunctions, but the others reached the target to find clear skies and good visibility. P/O Barker arrived in the first wave after identifying a lake north-west of the target. He bombed at 22.00 from 20,000 feet, and reported that fires were just starting as he turned away. P/O Holbourn was attacked by an FW190 over the target, and claimed it as damaged, and P/O Hanavan brought back an aiming point photo. They arrived back home to find appalling weather over Syerston, but all got down safely to report what appeared to be another highly successful operation, with fires visible from 150 miles away. It was, indeed, another very concentrated attack, but wrongly forecast winds again pushed it away from the intended aiming point, and the main weight of bombs had fallen into open country a few miles to the north.

The final operation of the month was mounted on the night of the 29/30th against the Ruhr town of Bochum, which fell within the range of Oboe. 106 Squadron provided thirteen Lancasters to the force of 350 aircraft, and two others to mine the waters of Danzig Bay. F/O Hoboken and the newly-promoted F/L Claridge got away first at 18.00, and they would successfully complete their sorties, each laying five mines in the correct locations and returning safely after ten hours aloft. Those participating in the main operation began taking off at 18.10, with F/L Ginder the highest-ranking pilot on duty. P/O Hay returned early with an unserviceable rear turret, while the remainder headed for the target via the northern point of Texel, and arrived to find clear skies and good visibility. The 106 Squadron participants bombed either side of 21.00, and contributed to the successful execution of the plan, which resulted in heavy damage within the town and its environs. During the course of the month the squadron operated on seven occasions, dispatching eighty-three sorties for the loss of five aircraft. The ORB mentions also that the squadron had been operational for three years by this point, and had dispatched 3,050 sorties since the 9th of September 1940.

October 1943

Having closed the September account, the Ruhr provided the destination to open the new month's operational proceedings, and the attack on Hagen would prove to be the first of six operations for the Lancaster squadrons in the space of eight nights. Situated at the eastern end of the Ruhr, south of Dortmund, Hagen was a relatively small town associated with the steel and coal industries, and was to be targeted on the night of the 1/2nd by an all-Lancaster heavy force of 243 aircraft of 1, 5 and 8 Groups, with Mosquitos to provide the Oboe marking. 106 Squadron provided fifteen aircraft led by W/C Baxter, which began taking off at 18.10. Rather than entering Fortress Europe via the Lincolnshire coast, the force departed England over Dungeness in order to not run the gauntlet of the Ruhr defences. There were, of course, no genuine gaps in the defences ringing the region, and W/C Baxter reported fierce flak on the way in over ten-tenth's cloud. The marking was spot on, and W/C Baxter bombed from 19,000 feet at 21.03 on cascading red and green target indicators. The town wilted under an accurate and concentrated assault, to which all of the squadron's aircraft contributed, and almost all returned to comment on a quiet trip. Reconnaissance revealed the usual residential damage, in addition to which, forty-six industrial businesses were destroyed, including a U-Boot accumulator battery factory, and the loss of production here considerably slowed U-Boot output.

The following night brought an attack on Munich, for which 106 Squadron provided thirteen Lancasters as part of a force of almost three hundred from 1, 5 and 8 Groups. S/L Howroyd was the senior pilot on duty, on a night when all of the pilots were officers. They took off safely between 18.30 and 19.10, but F/O Forsyth lost his starboard-outer engine while outbound, and had to turn back. The skies were clear over the target, and the visibility good with ground haze as S/L Howroyd bombed on a cluster of green target indicators from 20,000 feet at 22.41. P/O Hanavan brought back an aiming point photo, while F/O Cole's was plotted at five-and-a-half miles away, but for the 106 Squadron crews, at least, it proved to be another quiet trip. Reconnaissance showed that many bomb loads had fallen into southern and south-eastern districts, where 339 buildings were destroyed, and this was the result of scattered marking, and the use by 5 Group of its "time and distance" method, which delivered most of its effort up to fifteen miles short of the city.

Halifaxes and Stirlings joined forces with the Lancaster brigade on the night of the 3/4th, when Kassel was the target for a force of 547 aircraft. 106 Squadron contributed nine Lancasters, which departed Syerston in a ten-minute slot from 18.45, and headed for the northern tip of Texel. The target was situated to the east of the Ruhr, and a little beyond the now famous Edersee, where the repairs to the dam were nearing completion. A local sub-camp of the Dachau concentration camp provided slave labour for the city's Henschel aircraft factory. The skies were clear as the initial target indicators went down from the H2S-equipped blind marker aircraft, but they overshot, and ground haze prevented the visual markers from correcting the error. As a result many bombs fell onto the city's western fringes and outlying communities. However, it is believed that a stray bomb hit an ammunition dump at Ihringshausen, east of the city centre, which attracted many bomb loads, and the nearby district of Wolfsanger was devastated. Damage included large fires at the Henschel and Fieseler aircraft factories, but, unknown to all, this was but a prelude to the ordeal in store for this city in less than three weeks time. The 106 Squadron crews all reached the target to bomb between 21.17 and 21.36 from an average of 20,000 feet, and although none was able to observe the results of their own efforts, P/O Holbourn brought back an aiming point photo.

Twenty-four hours later Frankfurt was selected to host a raid by an initial force of 406 aircraft, including eleven Lancasters from 106 Squadron, led by S/L Howroyd. They all got off the ground safely between 18.15 and 18.45, but P/O Lee turned back with a failed engine, and P/O Holbourn lost the use of his mid-upper and rear turrets. F/O Latham and crew were on their first operation together, and they lost their port-inner engine soon after take-off, but elected to carry on. S/L Howroyd located the target easily by ground detail and Pathfinder route markers, and delivered his bombs from 20,000 feet at 21.41. The other crews had similar stories to tell of clear marking and little opposition, and all returned safely. F/O Latham and crew were late arriving on their three good engines, and there were no markers to aim at. They had been unable to climb above 14,500 feet, and bombed a concentration of fires from that altitude before turning for home. They were picked up by an enemy night fighter, but the gunners drove it off, and they arrived home last at 02.00, having undertaken almost the entire round trip on three engines. They had contributed to a highly successful attack, the first of the war at this hitherto elusive target, which left its docks area and eastern districts a sea of flames.

A two night rest allowed the crews some respite, before 343 of them, including fourteen from 106 Squadron, were called to briefings on the 7th for an all-Lancaster attack on Stuttgart. It was on this night that 101 Squadron's radio countermeasures (RCM) aircraft would operate for the first time in numbers. The equipment, known to the squadron as ABC (airborne cigar), was, in fact "Mandrel", which was designed to jam night fighter ground-to-air communications. Each of the ABC-equipped Lancasters carried an extra man, whose knowledge of German had only to be sufficient to recognise the language. He would then use the device to broadcast engine noise across the radio channels in use. They would also carry a normal bomb load, reduced by 1,000lbs to compensate for the weight of the equipment and operator. Once proved to be effective, a number of 101 Squadron ABC Lancasters would accompany every major operation, whether or not the rest of 1 Group was operating. F/Ls Claridge and Poore were the senior pilots on duty as the 106 Squadron contingent began to take off at 20.15, and, after forming up, they headed for the Sussex coast to exit England over Beachy Head. Some time later P/O Richards turned back with an unserviceable rear turret. The skies were clear for most of the outward flight, but cloud began to build up fifty miles from the target, obscuring the ground. The target was located by Pathfinder route markers and TIs, and F/L Poore aimed at a cluster of greens from 19,000 feet at 00.13. He described the routing as good and the opposition slight, but a number of others commented on the flak being heavy. F/L Claridge dismissed the whole affair as "devoid of interest". The marking had developed in two main areas, and the attack caused substantial damage to the city, with 344 buildings destroyed and more than four thousand damaged to some extent. Whether ABC was responsible, or a Mosquito diversion at Munich, the remarkably low figure of just four aircraft failed to return.

The third operation of the series against Hanover took place on the night of the 8/9th, when five hundred aircraft lined up for take-off very late in the evening. 106 Squadron had enjoyed an excellent start to the month with five successive loss-free operations, but this night was to bring a stark reminder of the realities of war. The squadron was called upon to provide just eight Lancasters, which were all safely off the ground by 23.10. P/Os Gibbs and Richards turned back with engine failures, but the others pressed on to reach the target shortly after 01.30. The attack took place in fairly clear skies, and for the first time the bombs fell where intended in central and eastern districts from north to south. The 106 Squadron contingent bombed between 01.34 and 01.39 from an average of 20,000 feet in the face of only slight opposition. On return they commented on the success of the diversionary raid on Bremen, which seemed to some to have diluted the defences. The operation was an outstanding success, which completely destroyed almost four thousand buildings, and damaged to some extent thirty thousand others, but night fighters arrived on the scene while the attack was still in progress, and contributed to the loss of twenty-seven bombers. 106 Squadron's W4242 crashed on approach to the target, about twenty-five miles to the north-west, and P/O Hay and his crew were killed. S/L Howroyd, who had survived a ditching on return from Berlin a month previously, was in DV272, which crashed about seven miles south-west of the city, probably after bombing, and only the bomb-aimer, P/O Cromb RCAF, survived to fall into enemy hands.

Minor operations occupied the middle third of the month, providing the crews with nine nights to catch up on sleep and visit the local hostelries. 106 Squadron had been informed of an impending move from Syerston to a new home at Metheringham. This was an airfield still under construction, hewn out of the farmland a few miles west of Woodhall Spa, and it was bereft of the permanent buildings and comfortable accommodation so treasured by its soon-to-arrive occupants. An advanced party left for Metheringham in mid month to begin the process, and they found conditions to be very basic. They endured a cold and miserable existence, and had to sleep wherever they could find a convenient spot, mostly in the cookhouse and the messes. On the 15th the award of a DFC was announced to P/O Yackman, and a DFM to F/S Foulsham.

Elsewhere, the oasis of peace was brought to an end on the night of the 18/19th with the final raid of the series on Hanover. This was an all-Lancaster affair involving 360 aircraft, thirteen of which were provided by 106 Squadron. F/L Ginder was the senior pilot on duty as they departed Syerston either side of 17.30, and there was a maiden operation for P/O Anderson and crew. They all reached the target to find almost complete cloud cover, and this thwarted the Pathfinders' attempt to find the intended aiming point. However, their markers were visible to the main force crews through the clouds, and were bombed accordingly. The 106 Squadron crews bombed from between 20.16 and 20.23 from an average of 20,000 feet, and most found the defences to be light to moderate but not troublesome. This was not the case for R5609, which underwent a torrid time, beginning with an attack by a BF110 during the bombing run. The Lancaster sustained severe damage, as did the rear gunner, and was then hit by flak. The bombs were jettisoned, before a JU88 tried its luck and was beaten off, and there was a final encounter with a flak shell before leaving the target area. Both enemy aircraft were claimed as damaged, and P/O Richards brought the Lancaster home to a safe landing. Reconnaissance suggested that most of the bombing had missed the city altogether. Eighteen Lancasters failed to return, 5% of the force, and it was a high price to pay for a failure. In all, the series of four operations against Hanover cost the Command 110 aircraft, in return for one spectacularly effective attack.

Another new target for 106 Squadron was Leipzig, the large city situated midway between Kassel and the Czechoslovakian frontier in eastern Germany. A force of 358 Lancasters was made ready on the 20th, representing 1, 5, 6 and 8 Groups, of which thirteen belonged to 106 Squadron. They would be led for the first time by the new A Flight commander, S/L Dunn, who had just been posted in to replace the missing S/L Howroyd, and he was first away at 17.00. The weather conditions outbound were appalling, with cloud tops up to 25,000 feet, violent electrical storms and icing, and this would cause problems that curtailed a number of sorties. P/O Anderson had all of his instruments fail when he was around ninety minutes out, and he was the first to land back at 20.15. P/O Mifflin lost his intercom soon after take-off, but continued on to Holland, where he bombed Bergen-Alkmaar airfield before turning back and touching down an hour later. P/O Perry lost both inner engines three hours into the flight, when he was already struggling to maintain height through severe icing, and he also came back. He had the added pressure of having the new station commander, G/C Pleasance, on board.

F/O Jardine was the first from the squadron to reach the target area, and he bombed from 22,000 feet at 21.06 on the glow of fires reflected in the clouds, without seeing any route or target markers. He returned to describe it as a long, tedious trip, which achieved doubtful results. P/O Callan and F/O Latham were a minute behind, and the latter did see a yellow TI and two "Wanganui" flares (skymarkers), and bombed the second flare from 14,500 feet. As on a previous occasion, F/O Latham had been forced to feather an engine while outbound, and carried out most of the operation on three. On approach to the target S/L Dunn's bomb-aimer believed he saw a red target indicator, and they headed in that direction to bomb from 20,000 feet at 21.12. That proved to be the only suspicion of Pathfinder activity seen by this crew, and they returned with a pessimistic assessment of the likely results. F/L Boyle had a similar story to tell of the absence of route markers and target flares, and they bombed on estimated position at 21.13. ED358 failed to arrive back with the others, and news eventually came through that it had crashed in northern Germany, with no survivors from the crew of P/O Hanavan, which included an additional air-bomber.

The final operation of the month took place on the night of the 22/23rd, and was directed at Kassel, which, therefore, was hosting its second attack in three weeks. A force of 569 aircraft was prepared, of which fourteen Lancasters were provided by 106 Squadron. They began taking off at 17.55, with F/L Boyle the senior pilot on duty. F/O Harvey had his a.s.i and altimeter ice up shortly after take-off, but pressed on in the hope that it would rectify itself. When this had not happened by the time they reached the Scheldt Estuary, it was decided to turn back, and the bombs were dropped on a flak battery on the island of Schouwen. P/O Barker also came home early after suffering supercharger problems. The others pushed on to find clear skies over the target, where the Pathfinder blind markers had overshot the aiming point. The visual markers rescued the operation, however, by identifying the city centre and delivering their markers accurately onto it. The main force followed up with extreme accuracy, and despite the presence of a decoy fire site, which may have drawn off a few bomb loads, the majority contributed to one of the most devastating attacks of the war on a German city. The 106 Squadron crew bombed between 21.05 and 21.19 from an average height of 20,000 feet, some finding the defences light, while others described the flak as accurate. P/O Callan's DV274 was hit during the bombing run, and ED593 was attacked by a night fighter on the way home and severely damaged. Six members of the crew, including the pilot, F/O Hoboken, were wounded, the rear gunner seriously. The enemy was driven off once, but came back and inflicted further damage, before it was finally evaded. The pilot skilfully brought the crippled Lancaster back to Syerston, where the weather conditions had deteriorated, and a safe landing was deemed impossible. F/O Hoboken ultimately pulled off a masterful landing at nearby Coleby Grange, and there were no further crew injuries to report.

Reconnaissance revealed that over four thousand apartment blocks had been destroyed in Kassel, with many thousands more seriously damaged, and this represented 63% of the city's living accommodation. Scores of industrial and public buildings were also afflicted, and the death toll in the ensuing firestorm, which was not as extensive as that at Hamburg, exceeded six thousand people. Many RAF airmen also lost their lives on this night, as night fighters penetrated the bomber stream and took a heavy toll. Forty-three aircraft failed to return, which represented 7.6% of those dispatched. Beginning on the 23rd stores and equipment began to move eastwards from Syerston to Metheringham, and this would continue for the next two weeks. During the course of the month the squadron operated on eight nights, dispatching 109 sorties for the loss of three aircraft.

November 1943

On the 3rd Harris sent a memo to higher authority, in which he stated he could "wreck Berlin from end to end", and added a proviso concerning an American participation in the campaign. He went on to say that it would cost between them five hundred aircraft, but that it would cost Germany the war. There was never the slightest chance of gaining American support, committed as they were to a land invasion, where the newsreels could record the heroic events. Harris probably guessed this, and in his own stubborn way would resume the Berlin campaign, begun back in August, with or without the support of the USA. In the meantime the new month's operations would begin with an attack on Düsseldorf on the night of the 3/4th, for which a force of 589 aircraft was made ready. 106 Squadron had sixteen Lancasters lined up for take-off at Syerston at 17.00, led by S/L Dunn, and they all got away safely over the ensuing forty minutes. There were no early returns, and they arrived in the target area to find clear skies and good visibility. Searchlights were plentiful, but the flak was described by most as slight and not troublesome. The 106 Squadron crews bombed between 19.43 and 20.02 from an average of 20,500 feet, and P/O Perry brought back an aiming point photo. The marking and bombing proved to be highly accurate and concentrated, and inflicted enormous damage upon housing and industry in central and southern districts. The eighty-eight tons of bombs for this operation was amongst the highest yet carried by the squadron. This was the final operation with the squadron for Don Cheney and crew, who found themselves posted to the newly-formed 630 Squadron at East Kirkby.

The following week passed by without operations, and on the 5th an advance party of five officers and sixty-one NCOs and airmen moved to Metheringham to prepare the way for the remainder of the squadron. The squadron was warned on the 7th to be prepared for the aircraft and main party to move on the 8th, followed by the farewell party on the 9th and the completion of the whole process on the 10th. However, plans were changed when operations were scheduled on the nights of the 8th and 9th, only to be cancelled at the last minute. The aircraft were then expected to fly to Metheringham on the 10th, but another operation was called and the squadron was told to prepare instead for that. 313 Lancasters from 1, 5 and 8 Groups were to attack marshalling yards serving the main route into Italy at Modane in southern France. 106 Squadron put up fourteen Lancasters for the distant target, that would be difficult to identify in awkward terrain. Take-off took place between 20.30 and 21.10 with F/L Claridge the senior pilot on duty, and after

A 'Cookie' is loaded onto a 106 Sqn Lancaster at Syerston prior to delivery to Stuttgart. The bomb, weighing either 4,000 or 8,000 lbs, was devastating as an 'area weapon' and was used extensively against industrial targets inside Germany (Crown Copyright).

forming up they headed for the south coast at Selsey Bill, before making for the Normandy coast at Cabourg. The Pathfinders slightly overshot the aiming point, but F/O Cooper, who was the first from the squadron to deliver his nine 1,000 pounders a few seconds before 01.00, aimed at the centre of six red TIs from 16,700 feet, and he brought back an aiming point photo. P/O Perry was another to capture the aiming point with his camera, and, in all, two hundred crews brought back photographs showing them to be within one mile of the target, which suffered extensive damage.

On return from this nine-hour round trip the 106 Squadron contingent landed back at Syerston, before flying over to Metheringham later in the day. The first training and familiarisation flights took place on the following day, and on the 13th W/C Baxter took S/L Dunn's crew on a fifty minute inspection from the air and to test the airfield approach equipment after a number of complaints from crews. Among awards announced on the 14th was a DFC for the now tour-expired F/L Stephens. A lull in operations after Modane allowed a brief settling-in period at their new home, and an opportunity for the squadron to swap its Lancasters for a new batch equipped with H2S. These were ready for action on the 18th, the day that would herald the resumption of Harris's war against Germany's capital city.

The main Battle of Berlin began with the dispatch of an all-Lancaster heavy force numbering 440 aircraft, of which thirteen represented 106 Squadron, led by W/C Baxter. He was amongst the first away at 17.10, and the others followed in his wake over the ensuing twenty-five minutes. They made for the Lincolnshire coast and a direct route to the target passing north of Hanover to attack Berlin from west to east. In order to split and confuse the defences, almost four hundred mostly Halifaxes and Stirlings headed south for Mannheim and Ludwigshafen. Both forces found cloud concealing their targets, and blind marking had to be employed. The 106 Squadron crews all reached Berlin, and aimed at the skymarkers from between 20,000 and 25,000 feet in a ten-minute slot from 21.00. They were unable to assess the results of their efforts, but the general opinion was of a scattered attack. Flak over the target was light, but F/O Forsyth ran into heavy and accurate flak on the way home, which knocked out an engine. P/O Gibbs' mid-upper gunner, Sgt Smith, passed out and sustained severe frostbite after his oxygen tube broke, and they came back at the unheard-of altitude of 29,000 feet with an unserviceable rear turret, before eventually landing safely at Tangmere on the south coast. Reconnaissance showed the bombing to be scattered with no point of concentration, and it was a similar story at Mannheim, but it seems at least that the diversion was successful, and only nine Lancasters were lost raiding the capital. The Mannheim contingent fared less well after night fighters arrived on the scene, and twenty-three aircraft failed to return.

A maximum effort was called for on the night of the 22/23rd, and the squadrons responded with 764 aircraft, the largest force yet sent to Berlin. 106 Squadron contributed sixteen Lancasters, led by S/L Crowe, who would be operating for the first time since September. They took off either side of 17.00, and after forming up over the North Sea adopted a route similar to the previous one with a reciprocal return. JB566 was hit by flak about thirty-five minutes short of the target, and the resulting engine fire persuaded P/O Garnett to jettison his load and turn for home. P/O Gibbs also had a problem that forced the curtailment of his sortie, and F/O Harvey was the third to turn back after his navigation equipment failed. The others pressed on to reach the target in poor weather conditions, and found it once more under complete cloud cover. S/L Crowe located the target by means of Pathfinder red flares with green stars, and bombed on these from 19,000 feet at 20.05. As before it was impossible to assess what was going on beneath the clouds, but the impression was of a concentrated attack, with the glow of fires penetrating the clouds, and those still in the target area at 20.22 witnessed a massive explosion. It was, in fact, a massively successful raid, which cut a swathe of destruction from the centre to the west, mostly across residential districts, and created large areas of fire, some of which developed along the lines of a firestorm. The catalogue of destruction included three thousand houses and twenty-three industrial premises, while the human cost was over two thousand people killed and 175,000 rendered homeless. The weather kept most of the night fighters on the ground, and twenty-six failures to return was quite modest in view of the target and the size of the force. Of these only a relative few were lost in the target area. The continuing disproportionately high losses of Stirlings could no longer be tolerated, and once the survivors returned on this night, the type was withdrawn from future operations over Germany.

Most of the squadron's participants had been diverted on return from Berlin because of bad weather at home, and by the time they arrived back at Metheringham, orders had already come through for a return to Berlin that night. This placed an insuperable burden upon the ground crews and armourers to get a full complement of aircraft ready in time, and despite their Herculean efforts, only six could be offered as part of the all-Lancaster heavy force of 365 aircraft. They set out shortly after 17.00 to return to the "Big City", with F/L Ginder the senior pilot on duty, and adopted the now familiar route. The German night fighter controller correctly guessed Berlin to be the destination, but the recently-introduced Sahme Sau (tame boar) running commentary system was compromised by spurious instructions broadcast from England. For the second operation running F/O Harvey was forced to return early, after severe icing prevented him from climbing above 12,000 feet. He was one of forty-six to turn back, a massive 12% of those dispatched, and this may have been a symptom of the strain of back-to-back operations to Berlin. Guided by the glow of fires still burning through the clouds, the Pathfinders easily located the target, and the main force crews had plenty of target indicators to aim at. The 106 Squadron crews bombed between 20.01 and 20.14 from 19,000 to 21,000 feet, before returning safely home. They had contributed to another accurate raid, which destroyed a further two thousand houses along with industrial buildings, and led to more than fourteen hundred people losing their lives at a cost to the Command of twenty Lancasters. These two operations were the most successful of the entire campaign.

Before the next assault on the "Big City", Frankfurt was subjected to a scattered but moderately successful raid on the night of the 25/26th, but this did not include main force Lancasters. 106 Squadron had now operated for five weeks without having to post missing any crews, but this was about to change. For the fourth time in nine nights Berlin was selected as the target, this time for an all-Lancaster heavy force of 443 aircraft, of which eighteen were provided by 106 Squadron. The planners decided it was necessary to make the target less predictable, and laid on a simultaneous diversionary operation on Stuttgart by a Halifax main force, along with a more complex route. The plan called for both forces to exit England over Beachy Head before making for the French coast, and then adopt an easterly course across Belgium to a point north-east of Frankfurt, where the two forces would diverge, one due south, and the other to the north-east. The bombing run at Berlin would be roughly west to east across the city, with a 180° turn and a direct flight back between Hanover and Bremen to exit the Dutch coast near Egmond.

The Metheringham contingent began taking off at 17.00 on the 26th, with F/Ls Boyle and Ginder the senior pilots on duty. While outbound, ED873 developed a surging starboard-outer engine, which prevented the Lancaster from climbing. The bomb load was jettisoned, and P/O Neil returned to Metheringham on three engines, but overshot the landing and crashed near the airfield, fortunately with only an injury to the rear gunner. JB592 crashed in Germany north-east of Frankfurt on the way to the target, and F/O van Hoboken DFC, was killed with his crew. At thirty-two years of age, Brussels-born Jaques van Hoboken was considerably older than most of his contemporaries, and was well into his first tour of operations. His presence and that of his crew would be greatly missed by the squadron. P/O Hinckley was probably in the same general area, when his navigator reported sick, and an attack was made on Koblenz as an alternative. Approaching Berlin from the south the Pathfinders missed the aiming point by some distance to the north-west, but the skies were clear and the markers plentiful, and F/O Harvey noted that the bombing was concentrated around the markers. While running across the target at 22,000 feet, flak caused slight damage to his bomb doors, and he saw a JU88 diving over the target with a trail of black smoke behind it. He also watched a Pathfinder Lancaster being shot down at 21.15, before bombing three minutes later, and returning home safely. P/O Pezaro had only recently joined the squadron, and he described the target area as a mass of flames, with smoke rising up to 10,000 feet. F/O Forsyth saw an explosion at 21.18, which was seen to cause a building to disintegrate. P/O Mifflin had remained at 23,000 feet during the outward leg, and he commented on a lot of bomb loads being jettisoned by aircraft below him. This observation was backed up by F/O Cole, who specified "outside the searchlight belt" as the location of most of this activity. In his book, The Berlin Raids, Martin Middlebrook makes the point that 1 Group Lancasters were more heavily loaded than those of 5 Group. The 1 Group A-O-C, AVM Rice, had conducted tests to find the absolute maximum bomb tonnage that a Lancaster could carry before its undercarriage began to fail. This prevented 1 Group crews from climbing to safer altitudes, and it was well-known that many dumped some of the excess once over enemy territory.

All returning crews spoke of the mass of fires and dense smoke, and some saw explosions well after leaving the target. Weather conditions at home caused major diversions, and 6 Group stations had to deal with landing the majority of returning aircraft, commendably achieving this feat with only one collision. Despite missing the intended aiming point, the bombing still managed to land within the city, and by sheer good fortune, some fell across the industrial suburbs of Siemensstadt and Tegel, where thirty-eight war industry factories were destroyed. The Command could again claim a successful operation, but in the absence of the poorer performing Halifaxes and Stirlings, the Lancasters suffered a 6.2% loss rate amounting to twenty-eight aircraft. This was the final operation of a month in which 106 Squadron had operated on six occasions, dispatching eighty-three sorties for the failure to return of a single Lancaster and the loss of a second one at home.

December 1943

Having closed the November operational account, it fell to Berlin to open the one for December on the night of the 2/3rd, when an all-Lancaster main force of 378 aircraft was made ready. 106 Squadron contributed sixteen aircraft led by F/Ls Claridge and Ginder, and all got away safely by 17.00. There was a return to the straight-in route across Holland to the target and a reciprocal return with no feints and no diversions. The German night fighter controller established in good time that the Capital was the objective, and was, therefore, able to have units on station awaiting the bombers' arrival. Inaccurately forecast winds led to the bomber stream becoming spread out, and this would impact upon the accuracy of the attack. P/O Richards turned back with severe icing issues, and F/O Jardine got as far as Brandenburg, on Berlin's western approaches. He had lost his intercom early on, and now had a frozen windscreen that he couldn't see through, so bombed Brandenburg and headed for home. The others all reached the target to bomb on the "Wanganui" flares and ground markers, which could be seen through the thin veil of cloud. P/O Mifflin's JB612 was attacked and severely damaged by a night fighter over the target after bombing at 20.20 from 20,500 feet, and was then hit by heavy flak, and the whole return journey was made on three engines. There was too much cloud to determine the results, but the impression was of an initially scattered attack, which became more concentrated as it developed. The squadron participants bombed between 21.19 and 21.32, and all but one returned safely. At debriefing some reported persistent, accurate flak, while others saw little or none, but a number of references were made to night fighter activity, and the use of rocket projectiles, which seemed to have a range of about one mile. Reconnaissance confirmed a scattering of the bombing, mostly in southern districts and in open country, although some useful industrial damage was caused both east and west of the city centre. The winds continued to spread the bomber stream out during the homeward leg, and the night fighters scored steadily. Forty aircraft failed to return, including one dispatched from Metheringham. Having used up their ration of luck a week earlier, P/O Neil and his crew were killed, when ED874 was brought down to crash about ten miles north-east of the centre of Berlin. The sixty-seven tons of bombs dropped by the squadron was the best in 5 Group.

On the following night 527 Lancasters and Halifaxes set out for Leipzig, which had been spared the possible ramifications of a Bomber Command assault by atrocious weather conditions back in October. 106 Squadron briefed thirteen crews, for whom there was to be a later take-off, beginning with S/L Dunn at a minute past midnight. All got away safely to cross the Lincolnshire coast and adopt a direct course for Berlin as a feint. The night fighter controller assumed Berlin to be the target, and was able to intercept the stream, before losing it as it turned south for Leipzig. The Pathfinders employed both sky and ground markers in the face of what most found to be ten-tenths cloud, and crews aimed for concentrations of release-point flares. The 106 Squadron crews bombed between 03.58 and 04.11 from 20,000 to 23,000 feet, and all safely negotiated the long southern return route to arrive home and report a successful attack. Not all were so fortunate, however, and many of the twenty-four failures to return stumbled into the Frankfurt defence zone and were shot down. Reconnaissance confirmed that the city had been subjected to a heavy and damaging attack, which destroyed residential and industrial buildings alike. For the second night running 106 Squadron topped the bomb-tonnage ladder for the group with fifty-seven tons.

Thereafter, the weather and the "moon period" kept the main force on the ground for almost two weeks, during which period the opportunity was taken to train crews on the use of H2S. Among awards announced to 106 Squadron personnel on the 11th was a DFC for P/O Barker. When the crews next went to briefing on the 16th they discovered the red tape on the wall map once again terminated at Berlin. An all-Lancaster main force and Pathfinder heavy brigade of 483 aircraft was to be accompanied by ten Mosquitos, and they would once more adopt a direct route to the target. The concession to diversionary measures was incorporated into the return flight, which would take the retreating bomber stream in a north-westerly direction to the Baltic, to gain the North Sea by way of southern Denmark. 106 Squadron contributed fifteen Lancasters, with no pilots above flight lieutenant rank, and they began taking off at 16.20, on a night which would forever be remembered for what happened when the tired crews arrived home. Night fighters picked up the bomber stream early, and there were combats all the way to Berlin and over the city itself. It was during the outward flight that 106 Squadron sustained its only casualty of the night, JB638 crashing at Achmer, north of Osnabrück, in the region of the Mittelland Canal, and P/O Storer and his crew were killed. F/L Harvey and F/O Cole were the first 106 Squadron crews to arrive at the target, and they bombed on release point flares from 21,000 feet at 20.01. The others from the squadron followed up over the next nine minutes, and only F/O Forsyth reported trouble from the defences in the form of a JU88, which his gunners drove off and claimed as damaged. The operation was moderately effective, the bombing falling mainly into residential areas, but without any recognisable point of concentration. Twenty-five aircraft failed to make it back, but a nightmare scenario awaited many crews on their return to home airspace, as a blanket of fog descended upon the stations principally of 1, 6 and 8 Groups. Exhausted after eight hours aloft, and short of the fuel necessary to take them to distant diversion airfields, crews stumbled around in the murk, desperately seeking somewhere to land. During a two-hour period, either side of midnight, twenty-nine Lancasters crashed or were abandoned by their crews, and around

150 airmen lost their lives. It was a tragedy that they should battle their way to and from Berlin only to be sacrificed to the weather conditions at home.

5 Group had been lucky to have clear conditions to land, while the 1 Group squadrons in the north of the county had suffered grievously, and it was only later on the 17th that the fog began to roll in across Metheringham. The crews were next called to briefings on the 20th, when they were told that Frankfurt would be their target that night. It was to be a major operation involving 650 aircraft, of which seventeen were to be provided by 106 Squadron. W/C Baxter put himself on the Order of Battle, and there were maiden operations for P/O Dickerson and crew and P/O Leggett. They were led away by the commanding officer at 17.00, the others following in his wake over the ensuing twenty-five minutes, and there would be no early returns. It was becoming routine for the enemy night fighter controllers to plot Berlin as the destination for large bomber fleets. A southerly approach to the Capital would take the force past Frankfurt to the north, as had been the case with the recent operation, when Stuttgart had been used as a diversion. The intention was to keep the enemy guessing as to the final destination, Stuttgart, Munich, Mannheim or Frankfurt in the south, or Kassel, Hanover or Berlin to the north. If not deceiving the enemy entirely, the ploy might dilute the strength of the night fighter numbers brought to bear. On this night a small 8 Group diversionary raid was to take place at Mannheim, but it would not succeed in its purpose. The night fighter controller began to plot the bomber stream as soon as it crossed the English coast, and was able to feed his aircraft into it early on, which resulted in combats all the way to the target.

The Pathfinders had been briefed to expect clear skies, but were met by up to eight-tenths cloud cover. W/C Baxter found five-tenths cloud over the target, but good visibility, and aimed his bombs at two green target indicators from 20,000 feet at 19.43. He saw a good concentration of fires and smoke rising to above the cloud tops, and was complimentary about the route. That last comment was echoed by P/O Holbourn, who described his trip as “devoid of incident”. The final 106 Squadron crew bombed at 19.51, and all returned safely, many of them commenting on the abundance of night fighters, but only F/O Jardine and crew had to fight one off. The Germans were employing dummy target indicators, and also lit a decoy fire south-east of the city. This attracted some bombs, but the creep-back found its way into the city, where over 460 houses were destroyed and many more damaged. Many public and cultural buildings were also hit, including scores of schools. Forty-one aircraft failed to return, but there was none missing from Metheringham. 106 Squadron delivered ninety-two tons of bombs, including five minol cookies, and this exceeded all other 5 Group squadrons by a clear thirteen tons[3].

Briefings took place on the 23rd for another operation to Berlin, conducted by a three hundred-strong all-Lancaster main force and eighty-four Pathfinder heavies with a small Mosquito element. 106 Squadron had fifteen aircraft ready for take-off, led away by S/L Dunn at 23.35, but one Lancaster became bogged down off the perimeter track, and five sorties had to be scrubbed. The route took the force south-east across the Scheldt Estuary to the Belgian/German frontier, then due east to a position south of Frankfurt, where a Mosquito element peeled off to carry out a diversionary raid on Leipzig. Berlin would be approached from the south-west, and after bombing the crews were to continue to the north, before turning sharply west for the direct route home across Holland. The weather outbound was not helpful to the enemy night fighters, and the Mosquito feint helped to draw them off. The target area was largely cloud-covered, and a proportion of the Pathfinder force experienced technical problems with their H2S sets. Marking was consequently scattered and sparse, but S/L Dunn found release-point flares and cascading green TIs to

[3] Minol was an explosive substance developed for use in mines, but was a useful supplement to TNT and RDX when they were in short supply.

Wing Commander Baxter and crew in earlier days, with a Wellington.

aim at, and delivered his minol cookie and incendiaries from 20,000 feet at 04.04. He reported two good fires, the glow from which was still visible fifty miles into the return journey. F/S Milne was only a few sorties into his first tour, and as an NCO pilot, was a very rare animal indeed in a squadron that had for some time been populated exclusively by officer pilots. He confirmed S/L Dunn's observation of two good fires, and commented on the presence of night fighters, but no contact with them. Only F/O Leggett had an actual encounter with night fighters, and had to evade three separate attacks. Reconnaissance confirmed the scattered nature of the bombing, and only two districts in the south-east of the city sustained meaningful damage to the tune of 287 houses destroyed. Sixteen Lancasters were lost, but all ten from Metheringham made it back.

Christmas passed in relative peace before another operation was launched against Berlin on the night of the 29/30th. This was to be the first of three raids on the city in a five night period spanning the turn of the year. This night's effort was a major undertaking involving more than seven hundred aircraft, of which sixteen belonged to 106 Squadron. Led by S/L Crowe, they took off either side of 17.00, and, after forming up, adopted a route that took the bomber stream over Texel on a long, straight leg aimed at Leipzig. There a Mosquito element peeled off to carry out spoof raids on that city and Magdeburg, while another spoof took place many miles to the west over the Ruhr. Berlin was cloud-covered, and the Pathfinders had to employ Wanganui flares, which tended to lead to a lack of concentration. S/L Crowe confirmed the ten-tenths cloud with tops at 14,000 feet, and he bombed on red and green release-point flares from 20,500 feet at 20.09. The others from the squadron had all bombed by 20.26 and were on their way home to report what they believed had been a fairly successful and relatively uneventful operation. When F/O Leggett got back to Metheringham, he had a different story to tell. The route home had been via a point south of Bremen, to exit the enemy coast over the Frisians, but it seems that ED593 was perhaps a little north of track and strayed too close to Bremen. It was hit by flak, and, the crew believed, rocket projectiles, and was severely damaged. Worse, however, the flight engineer, Sgt Braid, was killed, and the wireless operator, P/O Worthy, was wounded. They struggled back to England on two engines, and landed at Coltishall in Norfolk without further mishap. Reconnaissance revealed that most of the bombs had fallen into southern and south-eastern districts and outlying communities, where almost four hundred houses had been destroyed, but this was a poor return in view of the size of the effort. Losses, however, were comparatively low at twenty, just 2.8% of those dispatched. During the course of the month 106 Squadron operated on six nights, dispatching eighty-seven sorties for the loss of two aircraft. Of particular pride was the fact that it topped the bomb tonnage ladder on four of those six occasions.

January 1944

There is no doubt that the winter campaign was hurting the Command, but over in Berlin the inhabitants were experiencing their own winter of discontent. Priding themselves in being Berliners first and Germans second, they were a hardy people, and just like their counterparts in London during the Blitz of 1940, they bore their trials with fortitude and with humour, and no amount of bombing would break their resolve to stand firm. Banners were paraded through the streets proclaiming, "You may break our walls but not our hearts", and the most popular song of the day, Nach jedem Dezember kommt immer ein Mai, After every December comes always a May, was played endlessly over the radio, hinting at a change of fortunes with the onset of spring. The crews of Bomber Command and the citizens of Berlin shared a common wish for the New Year, that the Capital would cease to be the focus of Harris's attention. The winter of 1943/44 was an inauspicious period for new crews to embark upon their first tour of operations. Up to a year earlier a crew might have been eased into operations with freshman trips to French coastal targets or leafleting over Occupied Europe, but now a maiden operation could mean Berlin, and some crews would make this hazardous journey a dozen times or more. In the event, both camps were to be disappointed, and the new year was barely twenty-four hours old before the bombers once more appeared overhead, arriving in the early hours of Sunday the 2nd of January.

There were fifteen 106 Squadron aircraft among the 421 Lancasters detailed for the operation, and they began departing from Metheringham at 23.59 led by S/L Dunn. It had been intended to set off much earlier, but doubts about the weather pushed the start time back, and, as a result, there were insufficient hours of daylight left to employ the planned route. The original outward route had called for a wide swing over Denmark and the Baltic, with a southerly return south of the Ruhr and over Belgium, but the outward leg had to be shortened. The bomber stream formed up over the North Sea and crossed the Dutch coast at Egmond, before passing over the northern tip of the Ijsselmeer. From there it was an almost direct route to the Capital, to which a strong tail wind would push them in less than ninety minutes. There was heavy cloud all the way out, with tops at cruising altitude, but this did not prevent the night fighters from making contact after the enemy controller easily identified the target, and he totally ignored the Mosquito feint at Hamburg. It is believed that sixteen Lancasters were shot down on the way out, and among them was 106 Squadron's JB642, which crashed north-west of Hanover, and only the rear gunner from P/O Garnett's crew survived to fall into enemy hands. S/L Dunn closed on the target at 20,000 feet at 03.00, and saw release-point flares and target indicators ahead. He bombed on a cluster of flares at 03.08, but was unable to observe any results. He thought the marking was somewhat scattered, and this observation was echoed by many others. For most it was a relatively uneventful trip, but P/O Dickerson was attacked by a night fighter, and ND332 was slightly damaged at a time when its rear turret was unserviceable. P/O Banfield and crew watched a combat between a Lancaster and a JU88, which resulted in the enemy aircraft losing an engine. Banfield's gunners also fired at it and claimed it as damaged. The bombing found no point of concentration, and most of it was scattered around the southern fringes of the city and into wooded country. Twenty-eight Lancasters failed to return, and 106 Squadron lost a second one, when JB645 came down near Berlin with the crew of P/O Holbourn, who all lost their lives.

There was another late take-off on the following night for 383 aircraft bound for Berlin. A dozen 106 Squadron Lancasters lined up at Metheringham, led by F/Ls Ginder and Harvey, and they began taking off at 23.50. Eight were safely airborne before one Lancaster put a wheel off the peri-track and became bogged down, and this led to four sorties being cancelled. The outward route was directly across Holland to a point south of Bremen, where a dogleg took the bombers to the north-west of Berlin for the run-in.

Against the odds, some crews made it. F/O Victor Cole and his crew celebrate the end of their tour of ops. Cole survived the war.

On the way home they would pass south of Hanover and north of the Ruhr to exit at the entry point on the Dutch coast. The presence of the bomber stream was quickly spotted by the night fighter controller, who accurately predicted its destination. A trap was set between Hanover and Bremen, but the two factions failed to come together, and it was not until the night fighters were sent to Berlin that the combats began. ND331 was attacked by a night fighter and damaged, and F/O Cole lost control temporarily, until regaining it at 12,000 feet. In the meantime he had ordered his crew to prepare to abandon the aircraft, and by the time it was rescinded, the mid-upper gunner, Sgt Harding, had baled out. The bombs were jettisoned, and, on return, the crew claimed the enemy aircraft as damaged. There was ten-tenths cloud over the target, and F/L Harvey bombed a concentration of release-point flares from 22,000 feet at 02.49. No crew was able to see the results of their efforts, but most observed the glow of fires through the clouds, and all from Metheringham returned safely. The attack was only marginally more effective than that of the previous night, and the number of buildings destroyed could be counted on two fingers. Twenty-seven Lancasters were lost, mostly in the target area, and ten of them were Pathfinders, half of them from 156 Squadron.

It had been a punishing round of operations, but Berlin would now be spared a visit from Harris's heavy brigade for almost three weeks. To compensate, however, he would send regular Mosquito nuisance raids to rob the inhabitants of their sleep. After two nights at home eleven 106 Squadron crews were briefed on the 5th for an attack that night on the Baltic port of Stettin, where the Command had a good record of success. A force of 348 Lancasters and ten Halifaxes took off either side of midnight, the 106 Squadron contingent led by F/Ls Claridge, Harvey and Poore. A Mosquito feint at Berlin succeeded in drawing off the majority of the night fighter force, and the Metheringham Lancasters arrived safely in the target area to find clear skies over the port and bright moonlight. They bombed between 03.49 and 03.57 from between 18,000 and 22,000 feet, and turned for home convinced by the many large fires, the glow from which could be seen from 150 miles away, that the operation had been a success. F/Ls Claridge and Poore each brought back an aiming point photo, while P/O Kirkland and crew reported being attacked by three separate night fighters, one of which they claimed as damaged. Reconnaissance confirmed the effectiveness of the marking and bombing, and that the early stages of the attack by the Lancaster main force had hit the city centre, before drifting towards the western districts. Over five hundred houses were destroyed along with twenty industrial buildings, and a further eleven hundred houses and twenty-nine industrial buildings sustained serious damage, while eight ships were sunk in the harbour.

The arrival of the moon period allowed further respite from operations, and batches of crews were given a forty-eight hour pass over the ensuing week. Snowfalls and freezing conditions made life difficult for ground personnel, but they were able to keep Lancasters flying for training purposes. It was the night of the 14th before the next operation was mounted, and there must have been a degree of relief when the red tape on the wall maps at briefings terminated some way short of Berlin. It landed, in fact, on the medieval city of Brunswick, situated around fifty miles south-east of Hanover. Almost five hundred Lancasters took off in the late afternoon for the first major attack on this target, and among them were thirteen representing 106 Squadron. The German night fighter controller became aware of the approaching bomber stream while it was still over the North Sea, and assembled a reception committee at the German frontier near Bremen. A running battle then ensued all the way to the target and back as far as the Dutch coast. Most crews found complete cloud cover over the target, and identified it by means of Pathfinder release-point flares. Those from Metheringham bombed between 19.14 and 19.23 from 20,000 to 22,000 feet, and all returned safely, persuaded by the glow of fires beneath the clouds that it had been an effective attack. In fact, the bombing had missed the city and fallen onto outlying communities to the south, and the disappointment was compounded by the failure to return of thirty-eight aircraft. These first two weeks of 1944 had been particularly bad for the Pathfinders, and 156 Squadron alone had lost fourteen aircraft, the equivalent almost of two complete flights. Such losses could not be sustained, and many sideways posting took place to maintain a leavening of experience in each 8 Group squadron.

F/L Ian Harvey, photographed on 8th January 1944, during the monthly 'moon period, which usually brought a brief respite from ops.

Fog kept the Lincolnshire squadrons on the ground for the next few days and nights, and during this period, on the 16th, the award of a DFC was announced to the popular W/C Baxter. Berlin's turn came again on the night of the 20/21st, and it was to be a maximum effort raid involving 759 Lancasters and Halifaxes, including a contribution from 106 Squadron of sixteen aircraft. Take-off from Metheringham began at 16.30, and it was something of a novelty for the crews to be aloft in sufficient daylight to be able to see the other participants funnelling towards the rendezvous point over the North Sea. Recent heavy losses had pointed to the need to adopt diversionary tactics, and abandon the straight-in straight-out routing. The plan for this night was to enter German airspace near Bremen, and approach Berlin from the north-west, while small Mosquito feints at Kiel and Hanover hopefully caused confusion in the minds of the night fighter controller. This did not happen, and night fighters infiltrated the bomber stream south of Kiel. They were employing the tame boar system, based on night fighters assembling around radio beacons and being directed to the bombers by running commentary. All of the 106 Squadron aircraft reached the target, and found it covered by ten-tenths cloud with tops at somewhere between 10,000 and 18,000 feet, depending on whose report one reads. Both sky and ground markers were used by the Pathfinders, but most crews aimed at clusters of release point flares (skymarkers) in a ten-minute slot from 19.35, before turning south-west to a point north of Leipzig. From here they headed due east, with the night fighters still very much in evidence until south of Brunswick, where most peeled off. North-east of the Ruhr they turned to the north-west to cross northern Holland and exit enemy territory over Terschelling. By this time, twenty-two Halifaxes and thirteen Lancasters had been brought down, but again 106 Squadron came through without loss. Returning crews could only speculate as to the results of their efforts. The consensus was that the eastern districts bore the main weight of bombs, but a further four raids had taken place before photographic reconnaissance was possible, and by then specific damage could not be apportioned to a particular attack.

On the following night over six hundred aircraft were prepared for an attack on Magdeburg, a new target sixty miles west of Berlin, while twenty-two 5 Group Lancasters and a dozen Mosquitos carried out a spoof raid on Berlin. 106 Squadron briefed fourteen crews for the main operation, and two for Berlin, and they lined up for take-off shortly before 20.00. Seven crews got away safely for Magdeburg, and one for Berlin, before the second Berlin-bound Lancaster became bogged down while taxying in the darkness, and prevented all others from taking off. They headed out over the Lincolnshire coast for the three-hour flight to the target, which was undertaken over thick cloud that prevented sight of the spot-fire route markers. The German night fighter controller was not deceived by the spoof, and the main bomber stream was picked up by the night fighters before it even crossed the north German coast. Conditions improved as Magdeburg hove into sight, and the cloud thinned to between three and six-tenths with tops up to 6,000 feet. Some crews, who, like those of 106 Squadron, now had their own H2S, arrived ahead of the Pathfinders because of stronger than forecast winds, and rather than wait for zero hour, they began to bomb. The fires caused by this, along with very effective enemy decoy markers, compromised the Pathfinder efforts to achieve concentration after their initial red target indicators went down at 22.50. The 106 Squadron participants bombed on clusters of cascading green TIs between 22.59 and 23.13, and all returned home to describe large fires and a fairly uneventful trip. A massive fifty-seven aircraft fell victim to the defences, thirty-five of them Halifaxes, and this was a new record for a single target, in return for which, it is believed, most of the bombing was wasted.

Seventeen Lancasters were manned and ready to go from Metheringham on the evening of the 25th, when Frankfurt was the intended destination, but a scrub signal came through twenty-five minutes before take-off. The end of the month brought the final concerted attempt to destroy Berlin, with an unprecedented three operations in the space of four nights beginning on the 27/28th. An all-Lancaster heavy force of 515 aircraft included seventeen from 106 Squadron, led by F/L Ginder. They began to roll at Metheringham at 17.40, and all were safely away within fifteen minutes, although P/O Anderson would return early with inoperable mid-upper and rear turrets. There was a complex plan in place, which involved the main force following a small mining diversion towards the German Bight, before turning south-east towards central Germany, suggesting an attack on Hanover, Brunswick, Magdeburg or Leipzig. At a predetermined point the stream would swing to the north-east to run in on Berlin, while a Mosquito element maintained the original course and dropped dummy route markers. The ruses worked to an extent, and fewer fighters infiltrated the outbound stream than of late. Berlin was cloud-covered, and the Pathfinders employed skymarkers, which were bombed by the first 106 Squadron crews shortly after 20.30, from between 20,000 and 22,000 feet. F/L Ginder saw a large explosion at 20.33, and F/O Perry reported the glow of fires being visible 150 miles into the return journey. Sgt Moxey and crew, who had just joined the squadron, became lost on the way home, and required four fixes from Southampton before they found the south coast and landed at Middle Wallop. They were joined by P/O Rosser and crew, whose navigator had become ill soon after leaving the target, and it was the bomb-aimer who took over his duties to guide them home. The bombing had been scattered over a wide area, much of it falling once more into outlying communities. Never-the-less, some fresh damage was created within the city for the loss of thirty-three Lancasters.

Halifaxes joined in for the next operation on the following night, when a total of 677 aircraft took off, including seventeen Lancasters from 106 Squadron, led by S/L Crowe. They began to take off shortly after midnight to join a bomber stream, which, this time, was routed in and out over Denmark on a more-or-less reciprocal course. Its departure had been preceded by various spoof and diversionary efforts earlier in the evening, including a Mosquito attack on Berlin, minelaying in Kiel Bay and a spoof attack on Hanover. One feature of this operation was the high rate of early returns, amounting to sixty-six aircraft, or almost 10% of those dispatched. Among them were F/S Milne, whose JB663 developed an engine problem, and P/O Pezaro, who had an unserviceable rear turret. The night fighter controller concentrated his forces over Berlin, where the 106 Squadron crews began to arrive a few minutes after 03.00 to find cloud cover and the employment of skymarkers. S/L Crowe saw one very large explosion in the distance as he closed on the city at 03.15, and he bombed ten minutes later from 20,000 feet. He thought it was the most concentrated attack that he had witness at this target, and believed that fires were still burning from the previous night's attack. Some crews bombed on release-point flares, while others could see the ground markers through gaps in the clouds, but all were of one mind, that this appeared to be a highly concentrated and destructive operation. Reconnaissance revealed that many bombs did, indeed, fall into western and southern districts, where around 180,000 people were bombed out of their homes, and scores of administrative and public building were damaged. Much of the attack, however, was again wasted on outlying communities, and the Command paid the heavy price of forty-six missing aircraft.

Before briefings took place for the final operation of the month on the 30th, W/C Baxter carried out a thirty-minute flight to test "Fishpond", an updated H2S system that alerted the crew to the approach of a night fighter. Then it was back to the war for an operation involving 534 aircraft taking off for Berlin in the early evening. For the third time in a row 106 Squadron put seventeen Lancasters into the air, led by W/C Baxter with an experienced all-NCO crew, who were first off at 17.15. For the second operation running, P/O Pezaro was forced to turn back, this time with a defective engine. The Metheringham contingent joined up with the others over the North Sea, before heading for the Schleswig-Holstein peninsular, and an approach to the target from the north-west. The return route would take them south of Brunswick, followed by a dash for the Dutch coast via the northern tip of the Ijsselmeer. The 106 Squadron contingent arrived in the target area to find complete cloud cover and skymarkers in use, and they bombed on clusters of these during an eight-minute slot from 20.25. Returning crews mostly reported large areas of fire and a successful attack, and only F/O Forsyth had a brief encounter with a night fighter, which hit and slightly damaged the bomb bay directly under his seat. It was reckoned that the odds of surviving a tour were lowest during the first half-dozen sorties, and once through these, chances were that a crew would reach the mid-twenties. Then the odds shortened again for the final five, and tension among these crews must have been very high. F/O Forsyth and his crew were on their penultimate operation on this night, and their hearts were surely racing until the enemy fighter broke off the engagement. Reconnaissance showed that further grievous damage had been inflicted upon the city and its outlying communities in return for the loss of thirty-three aircraft. This time one of them was from Metheringham, ND336, which crashed into the North Sea, and took with it P/O Kirkland RAAF and his crew. His body would wash ashore on the Frisian island of Vlieland some five weeks later, and was the only one from the crew to be recovered.

There is no question that Berlin had been sorely afflicted since the resumption of the campaign in November, and although there would be two further heavy attacks on the city during the next seven weeks, they would be in isolation, and this series at the end of January, which had cost the Command 112 heavy bombers, proved to be the last concerted effort to bring the Capital to its knees. Berlin had not been wrecked from end to end, as Harris had predicted, but there had never been a realistic chance that it could be. Berlin was no Hamburg, developed over centuries with narrow streets and tightly-packed residential districts. It was a modern city of concrete and steel, with wide thoroughfares and open spaces that acted as firebreaks. More firebreaks were created with each attack, invoking the law of diminishing returns. It was also too distant, too big and too well defended, and the campaign came at a time when the Luftwaffe Nachtjagd was at its most efficient and lethal. During the course of the month 106 Squadron operated on nine nights, dispatching 123 sorties for the loss of three aircraft.

February 1944

The main force spent the next two weeks on the ground, and it provided an opportunity to draw breath and replenish after the intense period of long range operations. The moon period began on the 4th, and from then a programme of training was carried out, which covered H2S, high level bombing, fighter affiliation and night cross-counties (bull's-eyes). When the crews were next called to briefings on the 15th, they learned that they were to be part of a record-breaking effort that night to the "Big City". The operation would involve the largest non-1,000 force to date, comprising 891 aircraft, and it would be the first time that over five hundred Lancasters and over three hundred Halifaxes had been committed to a single target. The weight of bombs reaching the target would also be a new record 2,642 tons. There would be a new record also for 106 Squadron with the dispatch of nineteen Lancasters. They began taking off at 17.10 led by S/L Dunn, and, after forming up, they joined the bomber stream over the North Sea for the outward leg, which took them in a north-easterly direction to cross southern Denmark, before a turn to the south-east led directly to the target. A minelaying operation had taken place in Kiel Bay before the giant fleet passed over the region, and there had also been a spoof attack by Mosquitos on Berlin and Frankfurt-an-Oder further to the east. The return route was almost direct from south of Berlin, with a slight dogleg to pass south of Bremen and out over Egmond on the Dutch coast. The attack was timed to begin at 21.13, and F/L Poore was the first from 106 Squadron to arrive, in the spearhead of the main force, and he bombed the skymarkers at 21.15 from 21,000 feet. The attack was supposed to be over by 21.35, and all of the Metheringham crews had delivered their bombs by then, although others continued to arrive right up until almost 22.00. It was impossible to assess the results of the operation because of the complete cloud-cover, but much of the tonnage was delivered to good effect within the Capital's built-up area. A thousand houses were destroyed, along with five hundred temporary wooden barracks, some important industrial buildings were hit, while the emergency services had to deal with over eleven hundred fires. It was another expensive night for the Command, however, with a final tally of forty-three missing aircraft.

106 Squadron lost no aircraft to the defences, but there was another scare for F/O Forsyth and crew after JB641 was hit by incendiaries from above and severely damaged. Fate was determined to give this crew a hard time on their final sortie, but they brought the Lancaster home, where it was declared category AC, which meant beyond unit repair, but could be repaired on site by another unit or contractor. On board with Forsyth and flying as second pilot was P/O Bill Carey, the young Australian who would join 617 Squadron later in the year, and end up temporarily in luxurious internment in Sweden following the second attack on the Tirpitz. The overlapping circuits of the neighbouring bomber airfields in the region provided numerous opportunities for collisions, and this meant that the tired crews had to maintain vigilance right down to the runway. JB534 had just joined the circuit, and was at around 1,000 feet when the bomber-aimer called a terse warning about another aircraft ahead. P/O Dickerson pushed the nose down to avoid a collision, but the Lancaster impacted the ground near Metheringham ten minutes after midnight, and broke in two. The pilot and three others in the forward section were killed instantly, and the wireless

operator succumbed to his injuries later in the day, but both gunners were taken to hospital and survived. Later on the 16th the award of a DFC was announced to five pilots, F/Ls Claridge and Harvey, and F/Os Cole, Perry and Forsyth.

Preparations were made for operations on each of the ensuing three days, but each was cancelled. The potential for disaster attended every major Bomber Command operation, and on three occasions before the end of the winter campaign it would be realized in horrific fashion. The crews were called to briefings on the 19th, and informed that the target for the night was Leipzig, for which 823 aircraft were made ready, including seventeen Lancasters of 106 Squadron. After consideration of the weather and the target, however, two inexperienced crews were withdrawn. A route was planned that took the bomber stream across the Dutch coast, while a mining diversion took place in Kiel Bay to hopefully draw off the night fighters. The bombing was to take place in well-defined waves, and 106 Squadron aircraft were assigned to the first, second, third and sixth. It was 23.45 when S/L Dunn led them away from Metheringham for the four-hour outward leg, which was intended to have them over the target between 04.00 and 04.19. To get there many had run the gauntlet of enemy night fighters, which met the bomber stream at the Dutch coast, and stayed in contact all the way to the target. A stronger-than-forecast tail wind had driven some of the leading main force aircraft to Leipzig ahead of schedule, and around twenty of them were shot down by the local flak as they orbited, awaiting the Pathfinder markers to go down. Four others were involved in collisions and crashed as a result. S/L Dunn located the target by means of Pathfinder markers confirmed by his own H2S, and bombed on release-point flares bang on 04.00 from 21,500 feet, along with a number of others from the squadron. A couple of minutes behind, F/L Ginder had S/L Murdoch alongside him as second pilot, who would shortly assume command of B Flight. The cloud cover made it impossible to assess the results of the attack, and no photo-reconnaissance was possible before an American raid took place. Returning crews believed the attack was concentrated, and described large fires and explosions. It would never be determined whether or not it had been an effective operation. What was not in doubt, however, was the scale of the Command's losses, and when all returning aircraft had been accounted for, there was a shocking shortfall of seventy-eight. Among them was 106 Squadron's ME630, which was caught by a night fighter at 21,000 feet as it approached the target and shot down, although not before F/O Leggett and his crew had managed to take to their parachutes. Sadly, it appears that the pilot fell into water and drowned, while his crew was rounded up and taken into captivity. The less efficient Mk II and V Halifaxes in particular took a beating on this night, and had demonstrated their vulnerability by losing a disproportionately high figure of over 13%. This could not be tolerated any longer, and Harris withdrew them from further operations over Germany, as he had the Stirlings in November.

Despite the horrendous losses, almost six hundred aircraft took off on the following night for Stuttgart, among them thirteen Lancasters from 106 Squadron. F/L Ginder was the senior pilot on duty as they took off either side of midnight. The crews had been assigned to specific waves, four in the first, and three each in the second, third and fourth. F/O Penman and P/O Anderson returned early with technical problems, but the others pressed on to the south coast and beyond. A large exercise over the North Sea by aircraft predominantly from the training units, and a Mosquito diversion at Munich, successfully drew up many night fighters two hours before the main raid made landfall over France, and this allowed the crews to attack the city unmolested. Complete cloud-cover prevented an assessment of the outcome, but photo-reconnaissance revealed that central districts had sustained substantial damage, as had others in the north-east and north-west, and an important Bosch factory was severely damaged. A very modest nine aircraft failed to return, and there were no absentees from among the 106 Squadron contingent.

A new tactic was introduced for the next operation, which took place on the night of the 24/25th against the town of Schweinfurt, the centre of Germany's ball-bearing production. The overall force of 734 aircraft was divided into two waves of 392 and 342 aircraft, separated by two hours in an attempt to catch the night fighters on the ground refuelling and rearming as the second wave passed through. Seventeen Lancasters represented 106 Squadron, six in the first wave and the remainder in the second, and these were assigned once more to specific waves within each force. W/C Baxter took the early shift with the recently arrived New Zealander, S/L Murdoch and F/L Sprawson, who were both undertaking their first operations with the squadron as captains, and also in this first wave were F/O Latham and P/Os Hinkley and Starkey. They got away from Metheringham in a five-minute slot from 18.30, but S/L Murdoch was unable to complete his sortie because of W/T failure. The remainder pressed on to find the target under clear skies with good visibility, and W/C Baxter located the target by means of Pathfinder markers, fires and smoke. He bombed a cluster of red TIs from 22,500 feet at 23.22, and witnessed three large explosions in the target area. F/L Sprawson described a great column of smoke rising to 10,000 feet, and concurred with the others in the first phase of the operation, that it had been successful. There were no senior officers among the second phase crews, who took off between 20.30 and 20.40, three of them briefed to support the Pathfinders as backers-up. P/O Richards was one of these, and he delivered his five 2,000 pounders at 01.09 from 22,500 feet, before bringing back a bombing photo plotted at two miles from the aiming point. He described the target as a mass of flames, the glow from which could be seen two hundred miles into the return journey. Over 2,200 tons of bombs were delivered, but it seems that most fell short of the town, and photographic reconnaissance was unable to distinguish the RAF results from those of the US Eighth Air Force attack during the previous day. All from Metheringham returned safely from what had been a trip of about eight hours, but thirty-three others failed to return. However, the second wave lost 50% fewer aircraft than the first, suggesting that there was some advantage to be gained from dividing the force.

On the following night the target was Augsburg, the beautiful and historic city deep in southern Germany, which will be remembered for the epic daylight raid on the M.A.N diesel engine factory there in April 1942, for which the late and previously-mentioned S/L Nettleton earned a VC. Thirteen 106 Squadron crews were assigned to the first wave taking off either side of 18.30, after which they headed for the exit point at Beachy Head to join up with the rest of the force. P/O Rosser and the recently commissioned P/O Milne would take off three hours later as the only squadron representatives in the second-phase force. The station commander, G/C McKechnie, was the senior pilot on duty, and he was backed up by S/Ls Dunn and Murdoch. There were no early returns, and all reached the target to find clear skies and good visibility. The recently-promoted F/L Gibbs was one of three from the squadron acting as a Pathfinder backer-up, and he bombed a concentration of red and green TIs from 20,000 feet at 22.45. P/O Hinkley brought back an aiming-point photo, and nine others were plotted within a short distance of the target. By the time the second wave swept in shortly after 01.00 the target was a sea of flames, with smoke rising to 15,000 feet. In contrast to the outcome on the previous night, the Augsburg raid was an example of Bomber Command at its most awesomely destructive, and the cultural heart of this historic city was torn out by fire, destroying for ever centuries of history. A more modest twenty-one aircraft failed to return, and the practice of splitting the force would become a regular feature of major operations from this point on.

The end of the month was characterized by snowfalls, and many of the residents of RAF Metheringham were kept busy wielding shovels. During the course of the month the squadron operated on five nights, dispatching seventy-nine sorties for the loss of two aircraft, one of them crashing at home. The author of the ORB completed the summary for the month by compiling statistics covering the period of operations from the 9th of September 1940 to the 29th of February 1944. Number of nights operated, 368, days 14, sorties 3,531, losses 136, loss rate 3.8%. Bomb tonnage, 8,001.1. Enemy aircraft claimed, (to end of January 1944 only), destroyed 14, probables 3, damaged 23.

March 1944

Lancasters taxiing at Metheringham 24th March 1944

Stuttgart opened the March account, when a force of over 550 aircraft set out very late on the night of the 1st with a contingent of sixteen 106 Squadron Lancasters among them. The Metheringham aircraft took off between 23.10 and 23.30, with S/Ls Dunn and Murdoch taking the lead. Heavy cloud outbound protected the bomber stream from night fighters, and, once at the target, the bombs were aimed at Pathfinder skymarkers, giving the crews no opportunity to assess the accuracy of their work. S/L Dunn was among the first from the squadron to arrive, and he described the visibility above the cloud, the tops of which were at 15,000 feet, as good. He saw no Pathfinder flares, and fixed his position by H2S, before delivering his five 2,000 pounders at 03.01 from 20,000 feet. He turned for home in the belief that the attack was scattered and ineffective, and, despite observing a number of large explosions beneath the cloud, most crews returned with the same disappointing impression. In fact it was an effective attack, which fell predominantly into central, western and northern districts, where further extensive damage resulted, and a bonus was the remarkably low casualty figure of just four aircraft. 106 Squadron had dropped sixty-six tons of bombs, and this was the highest in 5 Group.

106 Squadron official photograph taken in March 1944 (Crown Copyright).

W/C E K Piercy and crew. Third from the left is navigator P/O Philip George.

Thereafter, for the following two weeks, minor operations held sway, a number of which were significant in regard to the Allied plans to invade Europe three months hence. It was necessary to dismantle the French and Belgian railway systems under the "Transportation Plan", to prevent their use by the enemy to move men and equipment to the battle areas. The first salvoes in this campaign of interdiction were fired by elements of 4, 6 and 8 Groups at Trappes marshalling yards on the night of the 6/7th, and le Mans twenty-four hours later, and it provided an opportunity to employ the Stirlings and older Halifaxes that had been removed from operations over Germany. Also of great significance, as a result of developments in bombing techniques at 617 Squadron involving low-level marking, 5 Group undertook a number of small-scale operations during this period to test the method's efficacy. W/C Baxter took part in an attempt to strike at the Michelin tyre factory at Clermont-Ferrand on the night of the 6/7th, but the crews were recalled when ten minutes from the target because of a fear of inflicting casualties on French civilians. Baxter commented, "A pity", in his log book, but the operation would be rescheduled.

His time in command was coming to an end, and on the 8th W/C Piercy arrived from his Lancaster conversion at 5LFS Syerston as the new commanding officer elect. The outgoing commander undertook his final operation with the squadron on another small-scale 5 Group trial operation on the night of the 10/11th, when ten 106 Squadron Lancasters joined twenty others from 61 and 619 Squadrons to attack an aircraft factory at Chateauroux in central France, while other elements from the group were active at three other locations. W/C Baxter flew with S/L Dunn, so that he could concentrate on controlling the marking and bombing, and W/C Piercy flew as second pilot with F/O Latham. They took off between 20.00 and 20.25, and arrived in the target area to find clear skies with ground haze. S/L Dunn identified the target visually, and dropped three red spot-fires from 6,000 feet right on top of the factory. It was the accuracy

Group Captain McKechnie and crew.

of these and the controlling by W/C Baxter which was responsible for the success of the operation. The squadron participants bombed in a ten-minute slot from 22.44, from between 7,000 and 8,000 feet, and S/L Murdoch brought back an aiming point photo. Reconnaissance confirmed the accuracy of the attack, and it brought a fitting conclusion to the tour of the highly popular and greatly respected W/C Baxter.

W/C Baxter departed 106 Squadron on the 13th with a total of 1,170 hours 50 minutes flying time in his log book. His successor, W/C Edmund Keith Piercy, had served in the Middle-East on Wellingtons, and most recently had completed a spell as an instructor at 1661CU at Winthorpe, which had Stirlings on charge. It was here that he inherited his new crew, whose original pilot, F/O Hinton, had failed to return from an operation as a second pilot shortly after they were posted to 9 Squadron. Now headless, they were shipped back to Winthorpe to complete their training and find a new driver. Piercy was a shy man, who was secretive about his Christian names, and never revealed them to his crew. He was also known to be an accomplished drinker, but he did not allow this to impact upon his operational efficiency, and he was recognised to be a first rate pilot. He quickly acquired the nickname Pluto, which he also applied to his favoured Lancaster. His passion, though, was his Matchless 1,000cc motor cycle, which he raced up and down the runway, much to the consternation of the station commander, G/C McKechnie.

When major operations resumed on the night of the 15/16th, Stuttgart faced its third attack in a little over three weeks. A massive force of 863 aircraft departed their stations either side of 19.00 hours, and among them were eleven Lancasters from 106 Squadron, led for the first time by W/C Piercy, with S/L Murdoch also on the Order of Battle. They headed south over Reading to Selsey Bill, before making for the French coast, and then flew over France as far as the Swiss frontier before turning north-east to the target. It was at this point that the night fighters caught up and many combats took place. The attack began late, possibly because of head winds, and, despite clear conditions, the marking fell short. There was a choice of sky and ground markers to aim at, and 106 Squadron crews bombed between 23.15 and 23.31 from an average of 22,000 feet. Some bombs hit the city centre, but the majority fell into open country to the south-west. Thirty-seven aircraft failed to return, but 106 Squadron's recent excellent record of loss-free operations continued, although the Lancasters of F/L Sprawson and P/O Bartlett were hit by incendiaries from above, and needed some repair work. While this operation was in progress six others from Metheringham joined a small-scale 5 Group effort against an aero-engine factory at Woippy near Metz in north-eastern France, led by 617 Squadron. The plan was for the 106 Squadron crews under S/L Dunn to illuminate the target, but ten-tenths cloud obscured the ground, and the operation was abandoned.

On the following night six of the squadron's Lancasters joined others from 617 Squadron to attack the Michelin tyre factory at Clermont-Ferrand, in the Auvergne region of central France. S/L Dunn led them away at 19.15, and it took almost four hours to reach the target, which lay under ten-tenths cloud with a base at 13,000 feet. Dropping below, S/L Dunn identified the factory visually and by red spot-fires, and delivered marker flares to illuminate it. He then flew back across it to deliver his ten 1,000 pounders from 12,000 feet at 23.10. The other squadron representatives also carried out accurate attacks, and left the target in flames with smoke rising to 12,000 feet. They returned safely, confident in the effectiveness of their efforts, and F/L Gibbs had an aiming-point photo as evidence.

The first of two heavy raids on Frankfurt was mounted on the night of the 18/19th, for which a total of 846 aircraft were detailed, including thirteen Lancasters from 106 Squadron, led by W/C Piercy with S/L Murdoch in support. F/L Sprawson was among the first to take off, at 19.10, but both starboard engines overheated while outbound, and he was forced to turn back. P/O Bartlett mistook release-point flares for route markers and overshot Frankfurt, so turned south and attacked Mannheim instead. The remaining eleven squadron participants arrived to find the target enveloped in thick ground haze, and W/C Piercy picked out three red ground markers, which he bombed from 23,000 feet at 22.04. On return he would comment on the late arrival of the Pathfinders and sparseness of the marking. The other crews had similar stories to tell, and P/O Hinkley described the Pathfinders as very late. The impression given by all at debriefing was of a widely scattered and general ineffective attack, with few fires. How wrong they were! Reconnaissance revealed, that accurate Pathfinder marking had led to a swathe of damage from west to east across the city, afflicting five and a half thousand houses and a hundred industrial premises along with dozens of public buildings. In return twenty-two bombers failed to return, a sustainable 2.6% of those dispatched.

While this operation was in progress six 106 Squadron Lancasters, led by F/Ls Gibbs and Ginder, joined thirteen from 617 Squadron to destroy the Poudrerie Nationale explosives factory at Bergerac, east of Bordeaux in south-western France. It took almost four hours to reach the objective, but once there, the squadron participants illuminated the aiming point for the 617 Squadron crews to bomb, six of them with 12,000lb blockbusters (not to be confused with Wallis's 12,000lb Tallboys, which were not yet in use), as used against the Dortmund-Ems Canal in September of the previous year. The 106 Squadron crews followed up with incendiaries between 23.10 and 23.16 from medium level, and all returned home safely from another highly successful precision attack. Two nights later the target for 617 Squadron and six

Lancasters of 106 Squadron was the nitro-cellulose explosives factory at Angouléme, situated to the north of Bergerac. The 106 Squadron element, led by F/Ls Gibbs and Ginder, were to perform the Pathfinder role again, and took off at 19.10 to head for the south coast. There was no cloud over the target, and visibility was good as they established their position first by H2S and then visually by the light from their own flares. They circled to watch 617 Squadron pound the aiming point with high explosives, before going in themselves to drop their incendiaries either side of 22.30 from an average of 12,500 feet. Reconnaissance later revealed that most of the factory buildings had been destroyed, and those still standing were damaged to some extent.

Another 816 aircraft were made ready for a return to Frankfurt on the night of the 22/23rd, of which eighteen belonged to 106 Squadron. They began to take off at 18.45, with S/L Murdoch the senior pilot on duty. The force headed for the Dutch coast in a departure from the normal routine for a target in southern Germany, and once over enemy territory a direct course was adopted to the target. In the face of five-tenths cloud the Pathfinders opened the attack with skymarkers, and the early arrivals bombed on these, but once delivered the ground markers were clearly visible, and they became the focus. The first of the 106 Squadron crews arrived in the minutes before 21.45, and all had bombed on the ground markers by 22.00. Returning crews described an outstandingly concentrated attack, and spoke of the glow of fires being visible from two hundred miles into the return journey. The level of destruction was even greater than that inflicted four days earlier, and half of the city would now be left without electricity, gas and water for an extended period. At 948 people the death toll on the ground was more than twice that of the earlier raid. A further 120,000 people were bombed out of their homes, and this figure had to be added to the 55,500 who had been de-housed as a result of the earlier attack. Bomber losses were heavier on this night, amounting to thirty-three aircraft, and among them was one of the Lancasters provided by 106 Squadron. JB648 crashed in the target area after exploding in the air, and only the mid-upper gunner from the crew of P/O Rosser RAAF managed to escape by parachute to fall into enemy hands. The total of 99.2 tons of bombs delivered by the squadron on this night represented a new record for a single target.

The squadron continued its Pathfinder work on behalf of 617 Squadron on the night of the 23/24th, when the target was the Signa aero-engine works at Lyon in south-east-central France. F/Ls Gibbs, Ginder and Lee, F/O Latham and P/Os Anderson and Milne were all safely airborne by 19.30, and arrived in the target area at around 22.45 to find clear skies but poor visibility caused by thick ground haze. They remained in the target area at 13,000 feet dropping illuminator flares at intervals during a twenty-minute slot either side of 23.00, and used up all of their flares trying to keep the aiming point visible. The plan was for the 106 Squadron crews to then illuminate and attack the nearby transformer station, but having exhausted their supply of flares, they were unable to identify it, and were ordered to abandon the attempt and head for home. According to 617 Squadron records the 106 Squadron crews actually illuminated the wrong area, firstly four miles to the north, then ten miles to the south and finally ten miles to the north. There was also an element of unreliability in the flares themselves, which were supposed to burst at 4,000 feet, but often did so at 8,000 feet or on impact with the ground.

The nineteenth and final operation of the campaign against Berlin since the previous August, and the sixteenth since the resumption in November, was mounted on the night of the 24/25th. It would prove to be the last time that RAF heavy bombers would target Germany's capital city, and, thereafter, it would be the Mosquitos of 8 Group's Light Night Striking Force that maintained the pressure on the resident population, right up until the time that Russian ground forces arrived in the suburbs. 811 aircraft were made ready, including fourteen Lancasters at Metheringham, with W/C Piercy taking the lead for the second time since his appointment. The force was routed out over southern Denmark and the Baltic to aim for a point north-east of Berlin, before turning to approach the city from north-east to south-west. After running across the city they were to carry out two doglegs to starboard to take them north of Magdeburg and south of Hanover, and then a shallow turn to port to cross Holland and gain the North Sea via Egmond. W/C Piercy took off at 18.35, and landed back an hour-and-a-quarter later after his instruments failed. The others got away safely, and climbed to cruising altitude, where they began to meet unfamiliar wind conditions.

The Command had developed a system, which was designed to keep crews abreast of wind strength, and ensure that all navigators were working off the same data to maintain the cohesion of the bomber stream and adherence to the timing schedule. Selected crews in each squadron were designated "windfinders", and their task was to ascertain the wind speed and direction, and transmit their findings to the operation controllers at home, who, after making any necessary adjustments, would broadcast new instructions to the entire force. The problem on this night was the presence of an unknown phenomenon, which we know today as a "jetstream". It blew from the north, pushing the bomber stream continually south of its intended track and breaking its cohesion. The windfinders had never encountered such powerful winds before, and, distrusting their own readings, modified them down for fear of being disbelieved. The raid controllers in turn, disbelieved the modified data, and modified it further before broadcasting the figures to back to the bombers. As a result all of the navigators were working with incorrect information, and the bomber stream became spread out over northern Germany. A scattered bomber stream inevitably led to a scattered attack, and this was the common theme in the post raid reports from the Metheringham crews. They bombed between 22.28 and 22.50 from an average of 22,000 feet, some on release-point flares and others on ground markers seen cascading through the partial cloud cover. F/O Richards used an H2S fix because the markers were too scattered, and there were no instructions coming through from the Master Bomber. F/S Hall and crew were on their first operation together, and their first run across Berlin was determined to be south of the city. They made a second run in the face of heavy flak, which knocked out an engine, and were the last from the squadron to deliver their bombs before turning for home. The entire homeward journey was carried out on three engines, and they eventually landed safely at Wing in Buckinghamshire at 02.40. For his perseverance and flying skills F/S Hall received the immediate award of the DFM.

Reconnaissance showed that some fresh damage had been inflicted upon Berlin, sufficient to de-house around twenty thousand people, but 126 other communities also reported bombs falling. It was another disaster, however, which cost the Command seventy-two aircraft, many of them falling to flak batteries when the winds drove the returning bombers over heavily defended areas including the Ruhr. Fourteen others fell victim to night fighters over the target. During the Berlin offensive, nineteen major operations and one diversion were directed at the Capital, and 106 Squadron was present at every one, producing an impressive record. It despatched 281 sorties, the equal second highest number in the group, and only one less than 57 Squadron, and lost just eight Lancasters, the equal second lowest in the group. Fifty-six crewmen were killed, and four survived as PoWs. (The Berlin Raids, Martin Middlebrook).

On the following night six 106 Squadron crews joined forces yet again with 617 Squadron for a return to the Signa works at Lyons. This time W/C Piercy was on the Order of Battle, and led them off at 19.30. The visibility in the target area proved to be better on this night, and the target was identified visually. W/C Piercy dropped flares for ten minutes, then circled for twenty minutes before bombing on the raid leader's (Cheshire) instructions on red spot-fires. He reported the glow of fires to be visible a hundred miles into the return journey. F/L Gibbs delivered his flares between 23.06 and 23.14, and then circled for thirty-one minutes before dropping his all-incendiary load from 6,000 feet at 23.45. So accurate did the illumination seem, that F/O Anderson was not called upon to employ his, but he did deliver his incendiaries at 23.52 before turning for home. F/Ls Gibbs and Ginder and P/O Milne all brought back aiming point photos. Over at Woodhall Spa there was a debate about the accuracy of the 617 Squadron spot-fires delivered by Cheshire, Shannon and McCarthy, and whether or not the crews had bombed the correct ones. By the time Hadland had dropped the last bombs at 00.06, and hour after the raid began, smoke obscured the target, and it was not possible to see if the factory had been hit. Cheshire reported that there were fires covering approximately one square mile, and reconnaissance ultimately revealed that the attack had been concentrated to the south-west of the factory.

The period known as the Battle of Berlin, or more accurately the winter campaign, still had a week to run, and contained two more major operations for the crews to negotiate. The first of these was against the old enemy of Essen on the night of the 26/27th, when over seven hundred aircraft were made ready, seventeen of them Lancasters from 106 Squadron. F/Ls Gibbs, Ginder and Lee were the senior pilots on duty as the squadron contingent got away in an eighteen-minute slot to 20.00. This was the final operation of F/L Gibbs' first tour. There were no early returns, and the target was reached in the expectation of finding "Parramatta" (ground marking) markers to aim at. However, ten-tenths thin cloud made it difficult for some to locate the markers, although most found cascading red TIs or the glow of them as a useful reference point, and, failing that, they relied on an H2S fix. Almost all crews commented on the presence of spoof skymarker flares dropped by the enemy, but they were unsuccessful in drawing away the bombing. The 106 Squadron crews bombed between 22.00 and 22.17, and all returned safely with varied reports, some observing no fires, some the glow of fires, others describing a scattered attack and a large explosion or two. It was clear that none had any real idea of what was happening on the ground, but, in fact, the bombing had found the mark, and over seventeen hundred houses were destroyed, and many industrial buildings sustained severe damage. Thus was continued the remarkable run of successes against this important centre of war production since the introduction of Oboe to main force operations a year earlier. An added bonus was the loss of only nine aircraft, but this was to be more than redressed when the final operation of the winter campaign took place four nights later.

A third attempt to destroy the Signa aero-engine works at Lyons was mounted on the night of the 29/30th, for which 106 Squadron detailed four crews, led again by W/C Piercy. They took off at 19.40, each carrying twenty flares, and arrived in the target area to find clear skies and visibility assessed at eight miles. F/L Ginder was the first to release his hooded flares, the first batch of three going down at 22.56. The delivery by three 106 Squadron aircraft was co-ordinated to ensure a constant illumination, and W/C Piercy dropped three flares at 23.05, six at 23.13, six more at 23.20 and, finally, four at 23.26. By the time of F/O Hinkley's arrival, W/C Cheshire was satisfied that the illumination had achieved its aim, and he was told to retain his flares. They returned safely home, and were informed later that the bombing by 617 Squadron had been on the mark, and that sixteen of the twenty-two key buildings on the site had been destroyed.

When the group commanders came together on the 30th to plan for that night's operation to Nuremberg, AVM Cochrane of 5 Group suggested a direct route to the target, which involved a long, straight leg from Belgium across Germany to a point fifty miles north of the target, from where the final run-in would commence. The other Lancaster group commanders backed the idea, and it was the only departure from an otherwise standard deep-penetration operation, which would normally be expected to incorporate feints and diversions as devised by the Pathfinder planners. As a Halifax operator, AVM Roddy Carr of 4 Group was less enamoured with the idea, but he was outvoted. 8 Group's AVM Don Bennett bitterly opposed the plan and predicted a disaster, but his protestations went unheeded. There was also some doubt about the forecast weather conditions, which had suggested cloud at cruising altitude to conceal the bomber stream. When a Met Flight Mosquito crew radioed in to cast doubt on this, the warning was also ignored. Many expected the operation to be cancelled, but it was not to be, and almost eight hundred aircraft took off late in the evening to head towards an unmitigated disaster.

At Metheringham seventeen Lancasters lined up for take-off, and they were airborne by a little after 22.30. F/Ls Ginder, Lee and Sprawson were the senior pilots on duty on what was to be the blackest night in the Command's history. It was not long before the crews began to notice unique, almost freak meteorological conditions, which included bright moonlight and crystal clear visibility. Instead of being cocooned in darkness, ostensibly alone in the sky, they were able to see dozens of other aircraft, which, in the absence of the forecast cloud at cruising altitude, were silhouetted like flies on a table cloth against the layer of white cloud below. Condensation trails formed in the cold night air to further advertise the presence of the bomber stream, which was handed on a plate to the enemy night fighters orbiting their beacons close to the chosen route. F/L Lee and P/O Warren would miss the approaching carnage after engine failures forced them to return early. The battle for survival began over Charleroi in Belgium, and F/O Penman and crew found themselves to be the quarry of two night fighters, which made a number of attacks, that caused extensive damage and knocked out the rear turret. The mid-upper turret then also became unserviceable when the engine providing its power failed. The bombs were jettisoned and the fighters evaded, and ND332 was brought back to a landing at Manston, where the undercarriage collapsed on touch-down. The crew walked away from this one, but their reprieve was to be short-lived. The massacre of the bomber stream continued all the way to the target, the track marked by the burning wreckage on the ground of Lancasters and Halifaxes. More than eighty were lost before the target was even reached.

What was not immediately appreciated was the presence of a jetstream wind, like the one that had compromised the Berlin operation a week earlier. This time it blew from the south, pushing a proportion of the bomber stream up to fifty miles north of the intended track. The windfinder system again failed to cope, leaving many crews unaware of the inaccuracy of their navigation. As a result aircraft turned onto the final leg from a false position, and more than a hundred of these bombed Schweinfurt in error. F/O Lee was among these, having arrived at what was believed to be the approximate location of the target, and finding no markers. Over to the north, however, there were searchlights and incendiaries, and he altered course to bomb there at 01.20, later realising that it was probably Schweinfurt. Combined with the losses, this substantially reduced the numbers reaching Nuremberg, and little useful damage was inflicted. The twelve 106 Squadron crews reaching the intended target located it mostly by means of release-point flares, and bombed between 01.03 and 01.27, a number after surviving attacks by night fighters. F/O Anderson was intercepted first by an ME210, which his gunners claimed as damaged, and later by an FW190, which they claimed as destroyed. Ninety-five aircraft failed to return, and many more were written off with battle damage, or in crashes while landing. Three Metheringham crews were missing, among them JB566, which exploded near Berghausen, north-west of Frankfurt on the way to the target, and F/S Hall DFM and four of his crew were killed. ND535 "Queen of Sheba" suffered a similar fate after an encounter with Oblt Martin Becker, and also blew up, in its case eight miles north-west of the centre of Giessen, north of Frankfurt, and throwing clear the pilot, P/O Starkey, and his bomb-aimer, F/S Paris, who both survived to fall into enemy hands. It seems that ND585 had drifted a little north of the intended track while crossing Belgium on the way home, and was unfortunate enough to fall into the clutches of a night fighter, which shot it down south-west of Namur with no survivors from the crew of P/O Moxey RAAF.

During the course of the month the squadron operated on thirteen nights, and launched 156 sorties for the loss of four aircraft. The sorties represented the highest monthly figure since converting to Lancasters in May 1942. It was also announced that the statistics for February meant that the squadron had won the 5 Group bombing competition for the third month in a row.

Unquestionably, this six-month long campaign was the toughest faced by the crews during the entire war, and it was their "winter of discontent", probably the only time when the morale of the crews was in question. Harris had failed to wreck Berlin from end to end, and the cost had been greater than he anticipated, and certainly he had not come close to bringing about a collapse in the German will to continue the fight. Now a new campaign lay before the crews, one which had begun, as already mentioned, with attacks on marshalling yards at Trappes and le Mans during the first week of March. Since then other marshalling yards at Amiens, Laon, Aulnoye, Courtrai and Vaires had been added to the list and systematically targeted, generally to good effect. The time had now come for the rest of the Command to turn its attention in this direction, and officially from the 14th of April, Harris's bomber force would become subject to the requirements of the Supreme Headquarters Allied Expeditionary Force (SHAEF), under General Eisenhower, and would remain thus shackled until the Allied armies were sweeping towards the German frontier at the end of the summer.

April 1944

That which now lay before the crews was in marked contrast to what had been endured over the preceding months. In place of the long slog to distant German targets on dark, often dirty nights, shorter range trips to the occupied countries would become the order of the day in improving weather conditions. These would prove to be equally demanding in their way, however, and would require of the crews a greater commitment to accuracy, to avoid unnecessary civilian casualties. The main fly in the ointment was a pronouncement from on high, which decreed that most such operations were worthy of counting as just one-third of a sortie towards the completion of a tour, and until this flawed policy was rescinded, an air of discontent pervaded the bomber stations. With Harris at the helm city-busting would never entirely be shelved in favour of other considerations, but it was to take a back seat for the time being. The size of the force now available to Harris enabled him to succeed in an area where his predecessor had failed, namely, to strike effectively at multiple targets simultaneously. Targets could now be assigned to individual Groups, to Groups in tandem or to the Command as a whole, as operational requirements dictated, in the sure and certain knowledge that each force had the capacity to deliver a knockout blow at the first attempt.

The first week of the new month was devoted to small-scale operations, one of which enabled 106 Squadron to open its account on the night of the 5/6th. The target was an aircraft repair factory at St Martin du Touch, Toulouse, in south-western France, for which 144 Lancasters and a single Mosquito from 5 Group took off. As previously mentioned 617 Squadron had been experimenting with a new method of accurately marking precision targets, and this was the first occasion on which other elements of the group, other than 106 Squadron, had been involved. The system was based on low-level visual marking, and its success would lead to 5 Group becoming largely independent from the main force. On this night W/C Cheshire went to war for the first time in a Mosquito, and delivered two red spot-fires at 00.17 onto the well-defended factory buildings from under 1,000 feet. Such was their accuracy, it was unnecessary for Munro and McCarthy to back up, and they acted as a beacon to the approaching main force. The dozen Lancasters from 106 Squadron had been led off from Metheringham at 20.30 by W/C Piercy, but he landed back seventy-five minutes later with some kind of technical problem. The weather at departure was very poor, but clear skies greeted the crews over France, and this enabled them to locate the target easily. The main force crews, who had no special training in precision bombing, plastered the site and destroyed the factory with only limited collateral damage to civilian housing. The 106 Squadron element bombed from between 12,000 and 15,000 feet from 00.22 to 00.41, and P/O Anderson brought back an aiming point photo, while F/L Lee's was plotted at fifty feet away. The success of this operation convinced Harris that low-level visual marking was viable, and he now authorized 5 Group to operate independently under appropriate conditions.

The new campaign got under way in earnest on the night of the 9/10th with attacks on the Lille-Delivrance goods station by elements of 3, 4, 6 and 8 Groups, and the marshalling yards at Villeneuve-St-Georges in Paris by elements from all of the groups. Each operation involved over two hundred aircraft, and the former at least was highly successful, and destroyed over 2,100 items of rolling stock. However, both attacks caused widespread collateral damage in residential districts, in which over five hundred people were killed, and this was a problem that would never satisfactorily be addressed. 106 Squadron was not involved in either operation, but sent eight Lancasters instead to lay mines in the "Privet" garden in the Baltic. They were all airborne by 21.30 with W/C Piercy taking the lead, and S/L Murdoch also on the Order of Battle. Each was carrying five 1,570lb mines to be delivered from high level, and this was new territory for 106 Squadron, which had carried out its many previous mining operations exclusively from low level. The operation was entirely successful, and all crews delivered their stores into the allotted locations by means of H2S from 15,000 feet, between 01.37 and 01.49, before returning safely home.

Meanwhile, F/Os Anderson and Latham and P/O Milne were engaged in the low-level mining of the Köningsberg Seekanal, a fifty-four yard-wide stretch of water, which provided the only access to the Baltic from the German naval base in the port of Königsberg. Flying as second pilot with F/O Latham was S/L de Belleroche, who had been posted in as a flight commander elect. They took off from Metheringham at the same time as the others for their one thousand-mile outward leg, and found the target without difficulty under clear, moonlit skies. In the interests of accuracy, the mines had to be delivered from low level, 150 feet, and this would require running the gauntlet of formidable defences. Light flak and heavy machine guns were positioned on both banks of the canal, and many searchlights were brought to bear, some laid horizontally to present an impenetrable dazzle trap to blind the pilots, bomb-aimers and gunners. Despite this, each Lancaster ran without deviation along the waterway and two of them deposited five mines each into the briefed location. P/O Anderson had a single "hang-up", which he was able to drop in an alternative location, and all returned to land safely after more than nine hours aloft. The ORB proudly states; "The whole operation was completed with skill, resolution and outstanding courage, and resulted in many congratulatory messages…"

On the following night five separate railway targets were assigned, and 5 Group sent 178 Lancasters to Tours in west-central France to attack its marshalling yards. 106 Squadron contributed eleven aircraft, which took off in a thirty-minute slot from 22.10, with station commander, G/C McKechnie, the senior pilot on duty, S/L de Belleroche flying as crew captain for the first time, and S/L Crowe, who was now the station navigation officer, on board with P/O Harper. They approached the target from the west in clear skies and bright moonlight, and were instructed to overshoot the red spot-fires by six hundred yards, after they had been delivered short. G/C McKechnie found the target easily, made the necessary adjustments and bombed from 5,000 feet at 01.35. F/O Crosier brought back the best bombing photo, plotted at 250 yards from the aiming point, and the others were within 500 and 1,300 yards. All returning crews reported fires and explosions, and were confident that the bombing had been concentrated around the aiming point, which reconnaissance confirmed to be true.

Aachen was the main target on the night of the 11/12th, for an all-Lancaster force of 340 aircraft from 1, 3, 5 and 8 Groups. The town had two major marshalling yards, one in the west and the other in the east, and these were the preferred aiming points for the attack, although the numbers of aircraft involved dictated that this would develop as a standard area raid. Seven 106 Squadron crews were briefed, with S/L Murdoch taking the lead, and, with thunderstorms over Lincolnshire, they took off between 20.30 and 21.15. P/O Durrant turned back with a failed engine, but the others reached the target to find a thin veil of eight-tenths cloud, through which the red and green ground markers were clearly visible. The squadron crews bombed between 22.42 and 22.58 from an average of 17,000 feet, and F/L Lee brought back a photo plotted at 1,200 yards from the aiming point. Most of the bombing fell into central and southern districts causing massive damage in what was the town's heaviest attack of the war, and more than fifteen hundred people lost their lives. Much damage was inflicted upon the town's railway system, but it would be necessary to go back to finish the job. Among awards announced on the 15th were DFCs for S/L Dunn and navigator F/O Greenhalgh.

Within hours of the attack on the Toulouse aircraft factory earlier in the month, Harris had authorised the transfer of 83 and 97 Squadrons from the Pathfinders on permanent loan to 5 Group. They were to perform the heavy illuminator and marking role, and were to be joined by 627 Squadron's Mosquitos, which would take over the low-level marking function from 617 Squadron. The loss of three of his finest squadrons to 5 Group was a slap in the face for Pathfinder chief Bennett, whose ideas on target marking were diametrically opposed to those of Cochrane at 5 Group. Both possessed brilliant minds and were passionate in their pursuit of bombing accuracy, but Bennett believed that the low-level concept exposed the crews to unnecessary danger. The transfers exacerbated the tensions between the two men, but 83 and 97 Squadrons were actually going home to the group they had served so well before joining the Pathfinders in August 1942 and April 1943 respectively. The crews, however, despite their squadrons' 5 Group heritage, and the fact that the majority had found their way to the Pathfinders via 5 Group, were less than enamoured by the move, and were fiercely protective of their 8 Group status and the one step up in rank that they enjoyed over their non-Pathfinder counterparts. In the event they were allowed to retain their ranks and the coveted Pathfinder badge, and never officially left 8 Group.

The heavy brigade remained on the ground for the following week, and it was during this period on the 17th, that 83 and 97 Squadrons arrived at Coningsby, two days after 627 Squadron had taken up residence at nearby Woodhall Spa. The new crews had barely tumbled out of their Lancasters before they were summoned to a briefing by the base commander, Air Commodore Bobby Sharp, who, rather than welcoming them as brothers-in-arms, proceeded to harangue them about their bad 8 Group habits, and told them to buckle down and learn the ways of 5 Group. This was an insult to highly qualified and experienced crews, who were accustomed to handling the most complex tasks under operational conditions. Had the introduction to 5 Group been handled more delicately, the integration of the new units might have progressed more smoothly. In the event W/Cs Deane and Carter, of 83 and 97 Squadrons respectively, dug their heels in and refused to allow their crews to participate in the operation planned for the night of the 18/19th, on the basis that they were not yet ready.

Four railway targets had been selected, with 5 Group assigned to Juvisy, a major railway junction situated some dozen or so miles south-east of Paris. 202 Lancasters took off alongside four Mosquitos from 617 Squadron, which would benefit from the high-level contribution of three Oboe Mosquitos from 8 Group to provide an initial reference for the low-level contingent. 106 Squadron detailed nine Lancasters for this operation, but one swung off the runway during take-off, before careering across the grass and bursting a tyre. The others took off without mishap either side of 21.00 led by S/Ls Murdoch and de Belleroche, and headed for the south coast in good weather conditions, which would persist throughout the trip. The target was located easily by flares and spot-fires, and the 106 Squadron crews bombed from an average of 7,500 feet between 23.32 and 23.50. All returning crews commented on the volume of thick smoke rising up from the target, and it was clearly a very successful operation, which reconnaissance confirmed had all but destroyed the town. While this operation was in progress, W/C Piercy led a further nine Lancasters to conduct high-level mining sorties off Swinemünde in Stettin Bay (Geraniums). The skies were clear, but thick haze made pinpointing difficult, and they had to select alternative positions from which to make their runs. Never the less, all nine crews successfully delivered their five mines in the correct locations between 00.28 and 00.45, and returned home safely.

On the night of the 20/21st, while over 350 Lancasters of 1, 3, 6 and 8 Groups attended to Cologne, the development of the 5 Group method would continue in a two phase attack on the marshalling yards at la Chapelle, situated just north of Paris. This would be the first fully-orchestrated performance of the independent group, and would be the first outing in their new roles for 83 and 97 Squadrons, while 627 Squadron assisted and observed. The plan called for three high-level 8 Group Mosquitos to drop cascading flares by Oboe to provide an initial reference, while six Mosquitos of 627 Squadron laid a window screen ahead of the approaching main force. Once the aiming point had been identified, the first of the 83 and 97 Squadron flare force would illuminate it for the low-level 617 Squadron Mosquitos. They would mark it with red spot-fires for the main force to aim at, and the whole process would be repeated at a second aiming point an hour later. At Metheringham eighteen Lancasters waited at the threshold as part of the second phase, and G/C McKechnie was the first to roll at 23.00 closely followed by F/O Penman. S/Ls Murdoch and de Belleroche were also on the Order of Battle, and S/L Crowe was flying with F/O Anderson. Communications problems slightly compromised the first phase, and some aircraft returned with their bombs still on board, but by the time the 106 Squadron crews arrived on the scene, matters seemed to be proceeding according to plan. They found clear skies over the target, but ground haze and smoke from the first attack threatened to impair sight of the markers. Despite this, most were able to see the red spot-fires without difficulty, and they dropped their fourteen 1,000 pounders each from 7,000 to 11,000 feet between 01.21 and 01.45, and brought back ten photos plotted at between six hundred and 2,000 yards from the aiming point. The 113.4 tons of bombs delivered, in the form of 254 X 1,000 pounders, was a new record for the squadron. Reconnaissance on the following day confirmed that both halves of the yards had suffered massive destruction, and a bridge at the southern end was also severely damaged.

The real test of the 5 Group method would come at a heavily defended urban target in Germany, for which Brunswick was selected on the night of the 22/23rd, while almost six hundred other aircraft raided Düsseldorf. 106 Squadron put up a record twenty Lancasters as part of a 5 Group heavy force of 238, plus seventeen Mosquitos from 617 and 627 Squadrons, and ten 101 Squadron Lancasters to perform a radio countermeasures (RCM) role. The Metheringham contingent got away in a twenty-two-minute slot from 23.05 led by W/C Piercy, with S/Ls Murdoch and de Belleroche in support. F/L Lee was also on the Order of Battle, undertaking the twenty-ninth and penultimate operation of his first tour. P/O Durrant turned back with engine failure, but the remainder pressed on to find the target, according to some, under clear skies, and to others, beneath thin layers of cloud, but all were in agreement concerning ground haze. They bombed on the Pathfinder ground markers from 17,000 to 20,000 feet between 01.56 and 02.07, and all but one returned safely with no particular comments to make, and photos showing only fires and smoke. F/S Cunningham was singled out for particular mention for completing his sortie after losing an engine while outbound, and covering the entire homeward leg on three. The operation was not entirely successful for a number of reasons, largely to do with communications difficulties and some misplaced markers to the south. Some bombs found the city centre, but the majority probably fell onto outlying communities to the south, and the likelihood is that Brunswick escaped serious damage. On the credit side, only four Lancasters were lost, but one of these was 106 Squadron's JB567, which fell to a combination of flak and a night fighter over Germany, and resulted in the deaths of F/L Lee and five others on board, including a second pilot, P/O Tucker. The flight engineer, F/S Simes and bomb-aimer, F/O Beven, survived to be taken into captivity.

The night of the 24/25th brought over eleven hundred sorties by the Command, of which 637 were assigned to Karlsruhe. 5 Group, meanwhile, committed 234 Lancasters and sixteen Mosquitos to Munich, where 617 Squadron Mosquitos were to carry out the marking for the final time before handing the job over to 627 Squadron. If any city would be an acid test for the efficacy of the 5 Group method, then the heavily-defended Munich was it. 106 Squadron put up seventeen Lancasters for this operation, led by W/C Piercy and S/L de Belleroche, and they got away from Metheringham either side of 21.00, before settling onto a devious route to try to outwit the defences. F/L Sprawson returned early with a dead engine, but the others pressed on across south-western France, which, along with a feint by six 617 Squadron Lancasters dropping flares and target indicators over Milan, suggested Italy as the destination. Meanwhile, eleven 627 Squadron Mosquitos were on a more direct route to drop window two-and-a-half minutes ahead of the flare force. At 01.40 Cheshire dived through the searchlights and fire from two hundred light flak guns to deliver his markers from 1,500 feet, before racing across the rooftops to make good his escape. The first 106 Squadron crews delivered their bombs thirteen minutes later, and all were on their way home shortly after 02.00, bringing back ten bombing photos plotted at one to three miles from the aiming point. The operation was an outstanding success that resulted in much damage to residential and municipal property, and it was probably this operation that sealed the award of the Victoria Cross to Cheshire at the conclusion of his tour.

Up to this point, the newly-arrived 627 Squadron had been training and observing, in preparation to take over from 617 Squadron as the group's low-level markers. Now it was time to step up to the plate and assume the role, and this it did at Schweinfurt on the night of the 26/27th, when 106 Squadron waved off sixteen Lancasters from Metheringham as part of an overall heavy force of 206 aircraft from the group. S/Ls Murdoch and de Belleroche were the senior pilots on duty as they departed Metheringham either side of 21.30. They battled an unexpectedly strong head wind and enemy night fighters all the way to the target, where they found mostly clear skies and thick haze. They were able to pick out the target by means of flares, spot-fires and ground markers, and delivered their bombs from 15,000 to 20,500 feet between 02.26 and 02.44. Numerous photos were brought back, three of them plotted within two miles of the aiming point, and the best, by F/S Cunningham just half a mile away. On this occasion the 627 Squadron marking was not accurate, and the head wind delayed the arrival of the heavy markers and the main force. Most of the bombing fell outside of the town, and night fighters continued to harry the bombers throughout the period of the attack. It was a costly failure, with twenty-one Lancasters missing, and five empty dispersals

Flying Officer Freddie Mifflin (left), who tragically died when his Lancaster was shot down leaving the target area at Schweinfurt. His flight engineer, Sgt Norman Jackson, (right, with GC Leonard Cheshire) received the VC for climbing out onto the wing of their burning Lancaster is an attempt to extinguish the flames, in what was one of Bomber Command's most famous episodes. Cheshire was also the recipient of the VC for sustained gallantry in the course of 102 operations.

at Metheringham next morning told a sorry tale of the squadron's fortunes, which were its unhappiest to date.

The eight man crew of B Flight commander, S/L Murdoch, produced just one survivor, the second pilot, Sgt Bradley, after JB601 "Victory" was brought down over north-eastern France while outbound. S/L Murdoch was a Kiwi from Christchurch, who had joined the pre-war regular RAF. P/O Harper died with four of his crew in JB562, which crashed south-east of Mannheim, and well to the south-west of the target. P/O Fraser's ND850 was attacked by a BF110 over north-eastern France while outbound, and may have been hit by a rocket projectile. Whatever the cause, the bomb load caught fire, and the pilot and three others managed to parachute to safely, ultimately to evade capture. ND853 crashed in the general target area, killing P/O Bishop and four of his crew, while the navigator and bomb-aimer were taken into captivity. F/O Mifflin was bringing ME669 out of the target area having bombed, when it came under attack from a night fighter. A fire took hold in the starboard wing, inboard of the engines, and F/S Norman Jackson, the flight engineer, undertook the hazardous task of climbing onto the wing with a portable extinguisher, to try to quell the flames. His parachute had accidentally deployed during his exit, and his colleagues inside the aircraft hung on to the rigging lines to secure him. The extinguisher was whipped away by the 200 mph airflow, and, as the fire intensified, Jackson found himself in danger of being engulfed by the flames. He began to sustain burns to his face, hands and clothing, and unable to maintain his tenuous hold, he slid off the trailing edge, followed by his canopy, which showed signs of being alight. As he fell to earth, F/O Mifflin gave the order for the remainder of his crew to abandon the aircraft, and four of them did so safely. Sadly, Mifflin and the rear gunner were killed, and Jackson broke an ankle on landing, leading to a ten month spell in hospital recovering from his various injuries. On his return to England, he was awarded the Victoria Cross for his outstanding gallantry.

This was the final operation of the month for 106 Squadron, during which it had operated on nine nights, dispatching 129 sorties for the loss of six Lancasters. Awards of the DFC were announced on the 29th to F/Os Anderson and Latham and P/O Milne for their outstanding performance earlier in the month when delivering mines at low level in the Königsberg Canal in the face of the most fearsome opposition.

May 1944

As the invasion of Europe drew ever closer, airfields, fuel and ammunition dumps and coastal defences were added to the railway targets. 5 Group continued its attacks on precision targets with the bombing of an aircraft assembly factory and the Proudrerie Nationale explosives factory at Toulouse on the night of the 1/2nd, for which 106 Squadron contributed a dozen Lancasters to an overall heavy force of 131. The 106 Squadron contingent was led by W/C Piercy, backed up by the newly-promoted and freshly appointed B Flight commander, S/L Sprawson. They began taking off at 21.30 to attack the explosives factory, and the spearhead arrived in the target area some four hours later in clear skies and good visibility. They identified the target visually in the light of flares, and bombing took place on spot-fires from between 6,000 and 8,000 feet in a seven-minute slot from 01.32. Eleven bombing photos showed the target area, with plots up to 1,400 yards from the aiming point. The best performance was by F/O Bellingham and crew, whose photo was plotted at one hundred yards. Both targets were severely damaged, and there were no losses to report afterwards.

1 and 5 Groups joined forces on the 3/4th to carry out a complex attack on an important German military camp at Mailly-le-Camp in north-central France. It was home at the time to a Panzer Divisional HQ, and a number of Panzer battalions and MT units that could be brought to bear in defence against the invasion. The operation was led by W/C Deane of 83 Squadron, with 617 Squadron's W/C Cheshire acting as marker leader in a Mosquito. There were two main aiming points, one for each group, and a third for 1 Group's Special Duties Flight, the group's own target finding and marking unit. The plan called for Cheshire to follow the flare force in at low-level, and drop red spot-fires on the first aiming point, and for Shannon to back-up. The 5 Group main force would then be called in, before a distinct pause allowed the second aiming point to be marked for 1 Group. 106 Squadron contributed a dozen Lancasters led by S/L Sprawson, and they got away safely either side of 22.00, arriving a little over two hours later in the target area to find clear skies and bright moonlight.

The operation was well under way by this time, Cheshire having delivered his spot-fires at 00.00½, and Shannon at 00.06, after which a 97 Squadron Lancaster also backed them up accurately. The operation was bang on schedule, and Cheshire handed proceedings over to Deane to call in the 5 Group heavies. It was at this point that matters began to go awry, as Deane found himself unable to pass on instructions because of communications problems, which would later be sourced to interference from an American broadcasting station and a wrongly tuned VHF transmitter. In the absence of instructions the 5 Group force began to bomb the markers, and were still doing so as the time arrived for the second aiming point to be marked. Cheshire called for a halt in the bombing to allow the second pair of 617 Squadron Mosquitos to run across the target at low level, but bombs were still falling as they ran the gauntlet, and, at 2,000 feet, they were lucky to survive the multiple blasts of 4,000 pounders. As predominantly 1 Group Lancasters milled around the target area awaiting instructions, night fighters got amongst them, and began shooting them down. The sight of burning aircraft falling all around got the better of some crews, who became guilty of R/T indiscipline in their frustration and anxiety. Despite the problems the bombing was accurate and caused much damage, destroying thirty-seven tanks and almost seventy other vehicles, along with barracks and transport sheds. The 106 Squadron contingent bombed from 5,500 to 8,000 feet between 00.09 to 00.30, and escaped the carnage to bring back eleven bombing photos plotted within half a mile of the aiming point. Forty-two Lancasters were lost, however, two-thirds of them from 1 Group, and recriminations abounded afterwards, with many accusations being unjustly directed at Cheshire.

106 Squadron enjoyed a three-night break from operations thereafter until the night of the 7/8th, when a number of airfields, a coastal battery and an ammunition manufacturing and storage facility were assigned to small forces. 106 Squadron contributed a dozen Lancasters to a 5 Group force of fifty-eight plus four Mosquitos, whose crews were briefed to attack the last-mentioned at Salbris, east of Tours in central France. W/C Piercy led them off at 22.00, each carrying a cookie and sixteen 500 pounders, which were destined for specific buildings within the complex. They arrived in the target area to find clear skies, bright moonlight and visibility described by W/C Piercy as thirty to forty miles. They bombed in a seven-minute slot shortly after 00.30 from 5,000 to 7,000 feet, and left the target largely in a state of ruin. The success was gained at a cost of seven Lancasters, four of them from Metheringham, and all came down in the area of Loir-et-Cher, just south of Tours, where a second 5 Group operation had been conducted that night against the airfield. They were almost certainly the victims of night fighters, and the crews of P/O Bartlett in JB292, P/O Rose in JB612, F/O Penman in LL891 and P/O Warren in ND870, were all posted missing. On board LL891 as second pilot to F/O Penman was F/O Steylaerts, a Belgian, and the bomb-aimer, F/O Aaron, was an American from Philadelphia. News would eventually filter through that the bomb-aimer from JB612, Sgt Smith, was the sole survivor from among the twenty-nine crew members involved, and he ultimately evaded capture.

Two nights later 5 Group sent fifty-six Lancasters with Mosquito support to attack two factories. One of them was a foundry and stamping works, and the other the Gnome & Rhone aero-engine factory, both located in Gennevilliers, a north-western district of Paris. The latter had been bombed previously by elements from the squadron in April and May 1942, but its target on this night was the former. A dozen 106 Squadron Lancasters departed Metheringham in a fifteen-minute slot from 22.10 led by S/L Sprawson, and they arrived in the target area in clear skies, with bright moonlight, but the presence of ground haze. The River Seine provided a strong reference point, and the target was easily identified and bombed from 7,000 to 8,000 feet between 00.35 and 00.42. Ten crews returned safely home, bringing back nine bombing photos showing the target. Both operations were successful, but at a cost of five Lancasters, and 106 Squadron again had the sad task of posting missing two of its own. ND851 is believed to have exploded and crashed near Brionne, a location within striking distance of the Normandy coast, and it is reasonable to assume from the manner of its loss that the bombs were still on board and it was heading south-east to the target. P/O Woodhams RAAF and five of his crew lost their lives, and only the bomb-aimer, Sgt James, survived to become a PoW. ND511 also came down on French soil, and there were no survivors from the crew of P/O Sutherland.

The group dispatched a force of 190 Lancasters late on the evening of the 11th to deal with a military camp at Bourg-Leopold in Belgium. 106 Squadron detailed eight Lancasters led by S/L de Belleroche, and they were all on their way by 22.25. The main force element arrived late at the target because of inaccurately forecast winds, and by this time the flares had become scattered and unable to provide adequate illumination. Haze added to the difficulties in identifying the target, and only a single red spot-fire was available as a reference. In view of the close proximity of civilian housing, the Master Bomber called a halt to proceedings after ninety-four aircraft, including six from 106 Squadron, had bombed.

Having lost six crews before the first two weeks of the month were out, there was no doubt some relief for 106 Squadron as it spent the following seven nights at home. The night of the 19/20th was busy indeed for the Command as nine hundred sorties were dispatch on a variety of operations, including attacks on five major railway yards in France, and a number of coastal batteries. 5 Group was assigned to the yards in the centre of Tours, having destroyed those on the outskirts on a previous occasion. The operation by over a hundred Lancasters and four Mosquitos would require great care and patience, particularly on the part of the Master Bomber, who had to ensure that residential areas were left untouched. 106 Squadron contributed sixteen Lancasters, all of which were safely on their way by 22.25, led by W/C Piercy and S/L Sprawson. F/S Browne returned early with defective radio equipment, but the others pushed on into central France, and arrived in the target area to portray a confusing picture of the conditions from ten-tenths cloud to no cloud. A reasonable interpretation is that a layer of cloud covered the region, with a base at around 7,000 feet, and below that it was clear with ground haze. The Master Bomber brought them below the cloud base, where the target was easily identified, and the squadron contingent aimed at red spot-fires from 5,200 to 7,500 feet between 00.50 and 01.02. The operation took longer to complete than had been intended, but it seems that collateral damage was kept to a minimum, and the yards were badly damaged. All aircraft returned without incident, but fog at Metheringham led to most being diverted, although the recently-installed FIDO fog dispersal system was put into use for the first time, and aided at least one landing. Seven bombing photos were plotted within 750 yards of the aiming point, the best, by P/O Thompson, at a mere two hundred yards.

It had been a year since Harris had last targeted Duisburg, and on the night of the 22/23rd he renewed acquaintance with the industrial giant, when sending over five hundred Lancasters and Mosquitos from 1, 3, 5 and 8 Groups. 106 Squadron supported the operation with six Lancasters, while sending a dozen more to lay mines in the Forget-Me-Not garden in Kiel harbour. It was the latter force that took off first with a much greater distance to cover, and was made up of the squadron's more experienced crews, including those of S/Ls de Belleroche and Sprawson. They began taking off at 22.00, each carrying six mines for delivery from high level, and all but one located the target area, and made timed runs from whichever pinpoint they selected. The ORB timings show F/O Taylor delivering his mines at 00.36, and completing the round trip in six hours, while F/S Fox did not release his until 01.50, and his flight time was six hours-forty-five minutes. F/O Bellingham searched long and hard for his target area, but was unable to find it and brought his mines back.

Meanwhile, back at Metheringham the weather was poor as the bombing brigade, consisting of inexperienced crews, took off at 22.45, and adopted the well-trodden path out over the Lincolnshire coast. The conditions remained unfavourable all the way to the cloud-covered Ruhr, where Oboe skymarking was employed to identify the aiming point. F/S Kitto was attacked by a night fighter ten miles from the target, and jettisoned his bomb load to successfully evade it. Four of the other crews bombed on Pathfinder release-point flares, and the fifth on a searchlight concentration, and they were all on their way home by 01.30 to report what they felt was a scattered attack. The loss of twenty-nine aircraft demonstrated that the Ruhr was still a dangerous place for heavy bombers, but they had at least caused substantial damage within the city's southern districts, where 350 buildings were destroyed, and more than six hundred others severely damaged.

106 Squadron had no casualties to report, and was able to offer eighteen Lancasters on the following night for another attempt at the difficult target of Brunswick. This was just one of a number of operations taking

place, which, in total, would commit more than a thousand sorties to the fray. The largest effort was against Dortmund, which like Duisburg, was to receive its first raid for a year. 5 Group sent 225 Lancasters and ten Mosquitos to Brunswick, of which eighteen Lancasters were from 106 Squadron, led by S/Ls de Belleroche and Sprawson. Take-off began at 22.30, and on arrival in the target area they encountered unexpected cloud, estimated at between five and ten-tenths. The 5 Group method relied heavily on good visibility and communications, and neither attended this operation, as a result of which, most of the bombing missed the city. The conditions forced the markers to use everything available, red spot-fires and green TIs at first, and then Wanganui flares towards the end, and the squadron participants chose individually which to aim for. They delivered their mixed loads of HE and incendiaries between 01.16 and 01.43, and all but one returned home, S/L Sprawson to claim a JU88 as damaged. The squadron was represented among the thirteen missing Lancasters by ME790, which crashed in Germany, killing F/L Houlden and six others of the eight occupants, including the second pilot, F/S Scott RCAF, who was probably operating for the first time. The wireless operator, W/O Pringle RAAF, one of four Australians on board, was the sole survivor, and he became a PoW. It was announced on the 25th that S/L Crowe had been awarded a Bar to his DFC.

A railway junction at Nantes, on the Loire, inland from St Nazaire, provided the target for a hundred Lancasters and four Mosquitos from the group on the night of the 27/28th. 106 Squadron supported the operation with ten Lancasters, all containing relatively inexperienced crews. They took off either side of 23.00, and found the target easily in good conditions and excellent visibility. Despite this, only four crews saw markers, and they bombed between 01.43 and 01.46 on red spot-fires from an average of 9,000 feet. The others circled for up to twenty-five minutes, before receiving a W/T message at around 02.10 to abandon the operation. P/O Monaghan did bomb, before LM549 was attacked and extensively damaged by a night fighter on the way home. His gunners claimed the enemy as damaged, and P/O Monaghan pulled off a masterly one-wheel landing at the emergency strip at Carnaby on the Yorkshire coast. He and his crew walked away from the scene, apparently none the worse for their experience. An even more testing experience was to come the way of this pilot within six weeks, one that he would also negotiate without dire consequences.

While the above operation was in progress, five experienced crews went mining in the Rosemary garden in the Bay of Biscay. They took off just before midnight led by S/L de Belleroche, and they found their respective release points without difficulty by H2S fix. Each delivered six mines into the briefed locations from 15,000 feet, and returned safely. A dozen Lancasters departed Metheringham late on the evening of the 31st to join others from the group in an attack on a coastal battery at Maisy. Situated on the Normandy coast, it looked down on the beaches that would shortly become famous as Omaha and Utah, where American invasion forces would struggle to gain a foothold on D-Day. They took off in a violent thunderstorm either side of 23.00, led by W/C Piercy and S/L Sprawson, and the unfavourable conditions persisted most of the way to the target. At 00.53, shortly before reaching the target, they received a general recall signal, and all returned to base after jettisoning part of their bomb loads. In the event, only six of the sixty-eight participants had bombed by the time that cloud compelled the Master Bomber to abandon proceedings. It was announced that night that S/L Sprawson was to receive the immediate award of a DFC. During the course of the month the squadron carried out ten bombing and two mining operations, dispatching 145 sorties for the loss of seven aircraft and crews.

June 1944

June was to be a hectic month as the Command became embroiled in a variety of important campaigns, each competing for attention. The priority at the start of the month was the impending invasion, Operation Overlord, which was to be launched as soon as the unsettled weather over the Channel relented. In the meantime, the Command continued its attacks on coastal defences in the Pas de Calais region to maintain the deception concerning the actual landing grounds, and 106 Squadron opened its month's account with fifteen Lancasters detailed to support one of these on the night of the 2/3rd. The target was a heavy railway-mounted battery at Marquise, for which the squadron representatives departed Metheringham in ten-tenths low cloud and drizzle shortly before midnight led by S/L de Belleroche. The unfavourable weather persisted all the way to the target, where F/Os Bellingham and Mather and W/O Kipfer bombed on the glow of red target indicators between 01.40 and 01.42. The other 106 Squadron crews were either awaiting instructions over the target or were on final approach, when they received a message to stop bombing and return home. Two nights later fifteen 106 Squadron crews were briefed for a return to the battery at Maisy, but worsening weather as take-off time approached caused the withdrawal of all but the three most experienced crews. W/C Piercy, S/L Sprawson and W/O Cunningham got away by 02.00, and reached the target ninety minutes later to find eight to ten-tenths cloud. W/C Piercy came down to 6,200 feet to get under the cloud base, and bombed on the glow of red target indicators, confirmed by H2S, at 03.39. S/L Sprawson remained above the cloud at 9,000 feet, and bombed on the faint glow, the location of which was confirmed by Gee and H2S. W/O Cunningham relied on Gee, and his location was confirmed by the observation of red TIs on the ground. All three returned safely to report an apparently concentrated attack. Later on the 3rd the award of the DFC was announced to six squadron officers, including F/L Poore, who was now at 617 Squadron.

The Command was up in force on the evening of the 5th, D-Day Eve, to further disrupt coastal defences, and mount a variety of spoof and feint operations to disguise the precise landing points. 106 Squadron dispatched sixteen Lancasters on this night to target a battery at St Pierre du Mont, perched on a promontory to the west of Omaha beach and the east of Utah. In total the Command committed a new record of 1,211 sorties to the night's operations. There was no reference to the invasion at briefings, but crews were instructed to maintain strict flight levels, and under no circumstances to jettison bombs over the sea. Aircraft were taking off throughout the night, and those returning in the grey light of dawn may have been lucky enough to catch a glimpse, through occasional breaks in the cloud, of the greatest armada in history, ploughing its way sedately across the choppy Channel below. The 106 Squadron contingent was led away by S/L de Belleroche at 02.35, and they reached the target area to find a layer of cloud at around 10,000 feet. The Master Bomber called for them to drop beneath the cloud base, from where the red and green target indicators could be easily seen. The Metheringham crews were each carrying 13,000lbs of bombs, made up of eleven 1,000 pounders and four 500 pounders, and S/L de Belleroche delivered his from 8,250 feet at 04.50. The other crews had all bombed from between 6,500 and 11,500 feet by 05.00, and turned for home in the grey, lightening skies of morning. The ORB states; "As our crews were returning across the Channel, they saw a vast fleet of miscellaneous craft from battleships to barges, heading towards the coast of Normandy. "D-DAY" HAD ARRIVED!!!"

Huts at dispersal at Metheringham, 1944.

Crew of F/O F. Clement

On D-Day Night, over a thousand aircraft were aloft for the second day running, attending to communications targets behind the beachhead, in an attempt to prevent reinforcements from reaching the battle area. 5 Group sent 120 Lancasters, including sixteen from 106 Squadron, and four Mosquitos to attack road bridges at Coutances near Caen to prevent their use by the enemy to bring resources to the beachhead. They began to depart Metheringham at 00.25 led by S/L Sprawson, and arrived in the target area to find ten-tenths cloud at 5,000 feet, with a full, bright moon above. The Master Bomber called them down to beneath the cloud base, where the targets were easily identified by flares, red spot-fires and target indicators. The bombing was very concentrated in the face of considerable light flak, but smoke and fires made an accurate assessment difficult. The 106 Squadron crews bombed from between 3,000 and 5,000 feet either side of 02.45, and fourteen of them returned home safely. Six Lancasters were lost during the course of the operation, and when it was all over there were two more empty dispersals at Metheringham. They should have been occupied by ND680 and NE150, which had both come down on French soil, the former close to the target. By this time S/L Sprawson had been B Flight commander for a little over five weeks. He and his navigator and bomb-aimer arrived safely on the ground and were able to evade capture, while the flight engineer and wireless operator were picked up by the enemy. Both gunners failed to survive, and P/O Arnold, the mid-upper, at forty years of age, was among the oldest officers to lose his life on operations. The latter Lancaster was captained by P/O Warren, and it came down well to the north-east of the target, probably after an encounter with a night fighter. The pilot and four others died in the wreckage, the bomb-aimer succumbed to his injuries four days later, while the navigator, F/O Drylie, managed to retain his freedom. In some compensation, F/O Mather's gunners claimed the destruction of a BF110. Photo-reconnaissance confirmed that both bridges had been put out of action, and congratulatory messages were received from the C-in-C Army Group.

The night of the 8/9th was devoted to attacks on five railway centres, again to prevent German reinforcements from reaching the beachhead. 5 Group targeted installations at Rennes, on the Brest peninsular, with ninety-seven Lancasters and three Mosquitos. 106 Squadron supported the operation with a dozen aircraft, which began taking off at 23.05 with F/L Clement the senior pilot on duty. They were each carrying eighteen 500 pounders, two with delayed action fuses varying from six to thirty-six hours, and they were assigned to three waves, four in each. They arrived in the target area to find complete cloud cover, but excellent visibility beneath. The markers were accurately placed, and the squadron aircraft bombed them at heights ranging from 6,000 to 8,500 feet between 01.34 and 01.50, and all returned safely with six aiming point photos.

It was railways again two nights later, when four targets were attacked, including one at Orleans in north-central France, which was assigned to a 5 Group force of 108 Lancasters and four Mosquitos. Eighteen

106 Squadron Lancasters were made ready, eight for the main raid and ten for a subsidiary operation involving only Metheringham crews. F/L Taylor DFM was the first away at 21.50, and his was one of the crews briefed to attack a ten-mile stretch of railway line running north from Orleans to Chevilly, while the others took care of the marshalling yards. Taylor would act as Master Bomber for his element, and after bombing was to direct the efforts of the other nine. The last Lancaster departed Metheringham at 22.35, and only P/O Thompson was forced to turn back early with engine failure. There was little cloud in the target area, and visibility was good, enabling the marshalling yards to be identified easily, both visually and by the red spot-fires burning in their midst. Seven 106 Squadron aircraft bombed from altitudes of 3,000 to 6,500 feet either side of 00.45, and F/S Futcher and P/O Easby brought back aiming-point photos, which showed the target to have been obliterated. F/L Taylor assessed the visibility as twenty-to-thirty miles as he closed on the marshalling yards, which he used as a reference before turning north and flying up the railway line. He dropped hooded flares at 00.38, but two of them failed to ignite, and he would not be alone in experiencing problems with malfunctioning flares of this type. Fortunately, sufficient ignited, and were supplemented by reconnaissance flares, to provide adequate illumination of the track, and F/L Taylor bombed from 1,200 feet at 00.50 just south of Cercottes, towards the northern end of the stretch. He then spent the next eight minutes cruising up and down directing the efforts of the other crews, and he observed a number of sticks falling along the tracks. F/L Williams came down to 800 feet, and watched his bombs straddle the line south of Artenay. W/O Cunningham dropped the first of his sixteen 500 pounders three miles north of Orleans, and the last of them ten miles north. Reconnaissance photos confirmed that the track was cratered, and that a number of goods trains had sustained damage.

F/O PJ Richards after a raid in a good mood. His mood was no doubt lightened even further by the award of a DFC.

Later on the 11th awards of the DFC were announced to the missing F/L Lee, and to F/Os Richards and Lee. Road and rail communications were targeted on the night of the 12/13th, when 5 Group was involved at Poitiers and Caen. Seventeen Lancasters from Metheringham supported the former as part of an overall force of 112 Lancasters and four Mosquitos, and they got away in an eighteen-minute slot from 22.25, led by W/C Piercy. It took almost three-and-a-half hours to form up and reach the target area in western France, where the force encountered patchy cloud but good visibility. The target was easily located by means of red spot-fires and green TIs, and the squadron element delivered their four 1,000 pounders and twelve 500 pounders at heights ranging from 5,500 to 10,000 feet, and no fewer than thirteen, including W/C Piercy, brought back aiming point photos. The accuracy of the attack was confirmed by reconnaissance, and it was the most successful of the six operations carried out that night against railway objectives. A new oil campaign opened on this night, with a successful attack on the Nordstern plant at

Gelsenkirchen by elements of 1, 3 and 8 Groups. All production was halted for several weeks at a cost to the enemy of a thousand tons of aviation fuel per day.

The first daylight operation since the departure of 2 Group a year earlier took place on the evening of the 14th against enemy naval units sheltering in the port of le Havre. Elements predominantly from 1, 3 and 8 Groups took part, but Lancasters of 617 Squadron were on hand as the sole representatives of 5 Group, and their job was to bomb the concrete E-Boot pens with the recently introduced 12,000lb Tallboy. There was considerable collateral damage in districts close to the port, but few E-Boots remained intact to threaten the Allied shipping supplying the beachhead. 106 Squadron was not involved, but supported a 5 Group effort by 214 Lancasters and five Mosquitos against tank and troop concentrations at a road junction in the village of Aunay-sur-Odon, a few miles south of the beachhead. Metheringham dispatched twenty Lancasters in twenty-two minutes from 22.30 led by S/L de Belleroche. They found the target in excellent bombing conditions, and all delivered their eleven 1,000 pounders and four 500 pounders from 6,000 to 10,000 feet on and around the aiming point. F/O Crosier was the last to bomb, at 01.04, and he was one of sixteen to bring back an aiming-point photo. There was considerable night fighter activity, and F/S Fox had to fight off the attentions of two JU88s and two FW190s, his gunners claiming one of the former as damaged. In all, 1,200 tons of bombs were dropped, 106 Squadron delivering a new squadron record of 116 tons, the most by any individual unit involved.

Boulogne hosted an attack on the evening of the 15th in a repeat of the previous night's events at le Havre, and again much destruction was wrought in the port and neighbouring districts. Later that night twenty 106 Squadron Lancasters joined ninety others and four Mosquitos from the group to attend to an ammunition and fuel dump at Chatellerault, near Poitiers. The 106 Squadron contingent was airborne in twenty-one minutes from 21.10 led by S/L de Belleroche and the newly-arrived and appointed B Flight commander, S/L Marshall DFC. The Metheringham aircraft were divided equally among the four waves, and they bombed on Pathfinder markers between 00.55 and 01.03 from 7,000 to 10,000 feet. All returned safely, fourteen with aiming-point photos, and reconnaissance confirmed that the attack had destroyed eight of thirty-five fuel storage sites in the area. The ORB justifiably commends the squadron on launching a total of forty aircraft on consecutive nights, with no early returns and thirty aiming-point photos.

The month's second new campaign began on the night of the 16/17th, when four hundred aircraft from 1, 4, 5, 6 and 8 Groups accurately attacked four V1 flying bomb launching sites in the Pas de Calais. Such targets were to occupy much of the Command's attention over the next three months, and the ORB entry for the 19th mentions that southern England had "for some days now been subjected to an assault by the much-heralded "secret weapon", variously described as pilotless aircraft, Buzz Bombs or Doodle-Bugs". 106 Squadron stayed at home on this night and the next few, before dispatching sixteen Lancasters to a site at Watten, south-east of Calais, on the evening of the 19th, only to recall them ten minutes later because of the expectation of a dangerously low cloud base at the scheduled landing time. On the 20th preparations were made for a planned daylight operation on the following day, and in anticipation of regular daylight operations during the summer, tail fins were painted white with a green stripe, and the aircraft letter was also painted in white. In the event, the daylight operation did not take place, but the new colour scheme remained.

5 Group entered the new oil campaign on the night of the 21/22nd, when dividing its forces between the plants at Wesseling, on the west bank of the Rhine south of Cologne, and Scholven-Buer, situated in the north-western quarter of Gelsenkirchen at the eastern end of the Ruhr. It sent 120 Lancasters to each, along

with a handful of Mosquitos to carry out the low level marking. A number of ABC Lancasters from 1 Group's 101 Squadron were also in attendance to jam the enemy ground-to-air communications with their "Mandrel" equipment (RCM). The 106 Squadron contingent took off in a twenty-minute slot from 23.10, led by S/L Marshall, and all but one arrived safely in the Gelsenkirchen target area. F/L A L Williams (not to be confused with F/L A G Williams) had turned back after a navigational error caused him to fall fifteen minutes behind the others, all of whom had been assigned to specific waves with strict timings. Clear skies had been expected, but the presence of ten-tenths cloud threw a spanner in the works and rendered the Mosquito low-level marking plan unworkable. This was, in fact, the one flaw in an otherwise highly successful method. The same situation had also arisen at Wesseling, where the bombing had to carried out by H2S, while over Gelsenkirchen Oboe sky marking had to suffice. Seventeen 106 Squadron aircraft bombed on the Pathfinder release-point flares from 17,000 to 20,000 feet, and although it was impossible to assess the outcome, returning crews reported fires and smoke. The flak over the Ruhr was heavy and accurate as always, and night fighters were out in numbers also. It was the latter that gave the Command a bloody nose on this night by bringing down thirty-seven aircraft from the Wesseling contingent, almost 28% of those dispatched, and four 5 Group squadrons, 44, 49, 57 and 619 each lost six aircraft, although one of the 57 Squadron casualties ditched off the East Anglian coast and the crew was rescued. There were nine failures-to-return from Scholven-Buer, and two of these belonged to 106 Squadron. LM570 was outbound over central Holland's Gelderland when it was intercepted by a night fighter and shot down, killing F/O Bellingham and his crew. On board as a second pilot was S/L Loughborough, who had just been posted to the squadron to succeed S/L de Belleroche as A Flight commander. LL955 suffered a similar fate, probably also while outbound, and crashed a little further north in the Gelderland, about eleven miles south-west of Zwolle, with no survivors from the crew of P/O Brodie.

Over seven hundred aircraft were committed to attacks on seven flying bomb launching sites on the night of the 24/25th, when 106 Squadron contributed seventeen aircraft to a 5 Group force of 102 Lancasters and four Mosquitos bound for one at Pommereval, south-east of Dieppe. The Metheringham brigade was safely on its way by 22.35, with F/L A G Williams the senior pilot on duty, and they were again allotted to specific waves, six in the first and second, and five in the third. The operation was favoured by excellent weather conditions of clear skies and good visibility, and the 106 Squadron crews passed over the aiming point between 00.04 and 00.12 to deliver their eighteen 500 pounders, two in each load containing delay fuses. The medium level bombing of between 6,500 and 9,000 feet ensured accuracy, and thirteen aiming-point photos of what the ORB describes as "constructional works" were taken. There were no fighters reported on this night, but flak was quite heavy and accurate, and four Lancasters failed to return. It is believed that LL975 crashed in the target area, probably the victim of flak, and P/O Wright RAAF and four of his crew perished. The flight engineer and bomb-aimer, Sgts McPhail and Knaggs respectively, parachuted to safety, and both ultimately evaded capture.

It was back to railways on the night of the 27/28th, when 103 Lancaster crews from 5 Group were briefed to attack the marshalling yards at Vitry le Francois in north-eastern France. The 106 Squadron contingent of sixteen departed Metheringham either side of 22.00, with W/C Piercy the senior pilot on duty. Visibility in the target area was good, and the markers well-placed, but smoke began to obscure them, and twenty aircraft from the final wave were instructed by the Master Bomber not to bomb. Eleven of the squadron's crews had released their nine 1,000 pounders and three 500 pounders by this time, from 4,800 to 7,500 feet between 01.45 and 01.57, and five aiming-point photos were brought back. The operation was only moderately successful, causing damage to the western end of the yards, and it cost two Lancasters, both of which belonged to 106 Squadron. LL974 was shot down by a night fighter, and crashed near Thibie, north-west of the target, killing F/S Fox and his crew. JB664 crashed near Nemours, north-east of Orleans, also after an encounter with a night fighter, and P/O Easby perished with his crew.

The month's hectic schedule concluded for 106 Squadron with participation by fourteen of its Lancasters in a daylight attack on a flying bomb site or "constructional works" at Beauvoir on the 29th. This would be the squadron's first daylight foray since Milan on the 24th of October 1942. The target was situated in the Burgundy region of north-central France, and the force of eighty-five Lancasters was to fly out in loose formation, with crews once more assigned to specific waves. There would also be a large and comforting fighter escort to keep them safe from the attentions of the Luftwaffe. W/C Piercy was the senior pilot on duty, and he was supported by S/L Marshall and the newly promoted S/L A L Williams, who had replaced the tour-expired S/L de Belleroche as A Flight commander, and was now well into his second tour with the squadron. They began taking off ten minutes after midday, and located the target easily in good conditions, although there was partial cloud cover. S/L Williams was in the first wave, and reported being able to visually pick out concrete buildings and the "ski site", and released his eleven 1,000 pounders and four 500 pounders on them, confirmed by a Gee fix, from 17,000 feet at 13.46. Some of those arriving a few minutes later found the aiming point obscured by smoke, but all but one from the squadron carried out an attack at altitudes ranging from 14,000 to 19,000 feet, and were on their way home by 13.55. F/O Mather was unable to pin-point the target, and jettisoned his bombs over enemy territory. Flak was heavy and accurate, and F/S Netherwood's ND868 was hit and severely damaged. The pilot displayed fine airmanship by bringing the Lancaster and crew back to a safe landing at the emergency strip at Woodbridge in Suffolk. During the course of the month the squadron operated on fourteen occasions, dispatching 220 sorties for the loss of seven aircraft and crews. There were also thirty-eight awards to squadron members past and present, including a Bar to the DFC, twenty-two DFCs and fifteen DFMs.

July 1944

106 Squadron enjoyed a gentle introduction to the new month's activities, and took no part in large-scale attacks on flying bomb related sites on the 2nd and 4th. It was not until the final hour of the 4th that sixteen Lancasters departed Metheringham to join others from the group for an attack on a large cave complex at St Leu d'Esserent, some thirty miles north of Paris, which was being used to conceal and store flying bombs. Originally used to grow mushrooms, the site covered a large area, and the task for the 211 main force crews was to cut all communications to the main dump, while 617 Squadron directed its Tallboys against the tunnel complex at Creil, three miles away. They took off between 23.15 and 23.30, led by S/L Marshall, and arrived in the target area two hours later to find favourable conditions, but considerable flak and fighter opposition. The markers were both accurate and concentrated, and the 106 Squadron crews bombed them from 15,000 to 18,000 feet between 01.33 and 01.41, before returning home to report an effective attack. Both elements of the operation were considered successful, but night fighters got amongst the Lancasters, and thirteen were brought down. 106 Squadron was represented among the missing by ME832 "Hare's Hound", and ND339, and the fortunes of the two crews differed markedly. P/O Futcher and five of his crew lost their lives in the former, which was shot down about five miles west-south-west of Beauvais while approaching the target. F/S McNaughton, the Canadian bomb-aimer, was the only survivor, and he ultimately evaded capture. In contrast, there were six survivors from the crew of F/O Crosier, and four of them also retained their freedom. The fact that F/O Crosier was the single fatality in this crew suggests that he may have remained at the controls in the finest traditions of the service, to allow his crew time to save themselves.

The first major operation in support of the advancing Allied ground forces took place during the evening of the 7th, when over 450 bombers attacked an area of open ground north of Caen, delivering almost 2,300 tons of bombs somewhat ineffectively onto enemy troop concentrations. Late that night 5 Group returned to St Leu-d'Esserent with two hundred Lancasters, of which sixteen belonged to 106 Squadron. They began taking off at 22.30, with S/L Marshall the senior pilot on duty, and many other experienced crews in support. They found the target easily by means of the Pathfinder markers, and on this occasion flak was negligible, probably because an estimated 130 night fighters had been concentrated exclusively on this area. The 106 Squadron crews delivered their ten 1,000 pounders and four 500 pounders each from 12,000 to 15,000 feet accurately into the mouths of the tunnels between 01.16 and 01.22, blocking access to the flying bombs within. Eleven Lancasters returned to Metheringham, and their crews reported a concentrated attack, confirmed by P/O Durrant's bombing photo, which was plotted at thirty-five yards from the aiming-point. F/O Mavaut reported having to orbit the target three times waiting for the time to bomb, and there were echoes of Mailly-le-Camp in his comments. The night fighters took a heavy toll, amounting to twenty-nine Lancasters and two Mosquitos, a massive 14% of the force, and five of the victims belonged to 106 Squadron, thus equalling its previous blackest night.

It was a particularly bitter blow to Metheringham, because they were all experienced crews, and represented the backbone of the squadron. Although most fell victim to night fighters, it was flak that brought down PB144 as it was leaving the target area and heading towards Beauvais. It crashed at 01.30 and burst into flames with no survivors from the crew of S/L Marshall DFC, a New Zealander, who had joined the RAF before the war, and had been B Flight commander since the loss of S/L Sprawson a month earlier. He left a widow, Doris, who came from Bradford. F/L Clement DFC and his crew, which included two other holders of the DFC, were in JB641, which, it is believed, was shot down by a night fighter just after crossing the Normandy coast on the way to the target, and again there were no survivors. ME789 and ME381 ran into night fighters at about the same time as each other as they headed for the target, and the former had both port engines and rear fuselage ablaze as F/O Mather RCAF and his predominantly Canadian crew took to their parachutes north-west of Beauvais at around 01.00. This was the same time that P/O Monaghan RAAF and his crew hit the silk near Oulins, west of Paris, and both crews arrived safely on the ground. The navigator from ME789, F/O Evans RCAF, managed to evade capture, but his crew mates were picked up by the enemy and packed off to a PoW camp. The bomb-aimer and wireless operator from ME381 suffered a similar fate, while their five colleagues slipped through the net and retained their freedom. ME668 had all four engines on fire by the time F/L Marchant RAAF, his flight engineer and bomb-aimer left it to its fate to be taken prisoner. The remaining four crew members, whose positions were aft of the flight deck, were still on board when the Lancaster crashed. Just three days hence news would come through that S/L Sprawson and his navigator, F/O Barker, had just returned home after evading capture.

There was no immediate opportunity for the squadron to "get back on the horse", and there must have been a sombre air, while the population of RAF Metheringham came to terms with the loss of thirty-five familiar faces in one night. A special congratulatory message was received from A-O-C, AVM Sir Ralph Cochrane, who considered it the finest effort by the group, successfully pressing home the attack in the face of the fiercest opposition. S/L John Grindon was appointed as the new B Flight commander, and in view of the record of previous incumbents, it could well have been regarded as a poisoned chalice. In the event, and unlike many of his predecessors, he would survive. Born in Cornwall in September 1917, he had served with 150 Squadron in the Advanced Air Striking Force (AASF) in France during the "Phoney

War". He was posted home to take a navigation course just as the German advance crushed the Low Countries, and, thereby, he missed the carnage that effectively knocked the Fairey Battle squadrons out of the conflict. Thereafter he served two tours as an instructor in Canada, before taking up a staff job at Bomber Command HQ. He volunteered for operational duty, and was sent to undergo Lancaster training at 5 LFS.

There was a four night break from operations for the squadron until the night of the 12/13th, when elements from 1 and 5 Groups were assigned to railway targets at three locations. 5 Group sent 157 Lancasters and four Mosquitos to Culmont-Chalindrey in eastern France to attack two aiming points. Just six 106 Squadron Lancasters were involved, and they took off at 21.50 with F/L Taylor the senior pilot on duty. They found the target in clear conditions with no defensive activity, but a problem with VHF communications meant that only the western aiming point could be attacked. The Metheringham crews delivered their eight 1,000 pounders and three 500 pounders from medium level, 5,000 to 8,000 feet, between 02.10 and 02.14, but the high proportion of delayed action fuses in use prevented an immediate assessment of results. All returned safely, four of them with aiming-point photos. Later on the 13th, on the delivery of the 2,800th Lancaster, A.V. Roe presented 5 Group with a silver model of a Lancaster. Cochrane decided it should be awarded to the squadron with the best non-accident record between January and June 1944, which proved to be 106 Squadron as a result of its magnificent record of just one accident in 6,848 hours of flying.

The night of the 14/15th was devoted largely to attacks on railways and flying-bomb-related targets, and 106 Squadron made ready ten Lancasters for an attack on the railway yards at Villeneuve-St-Georges in the south-eastern suburbs of Paris. In all 111 Lancasters, six Mosquitos and a P38 Lightning were detailed to take part, and they began taking off at 22.05, with F/L Lines the senior pilot on duty, having just arrived as an experienced replacement to cover recent losses. There was some cloud over the target, and the Master Bomber called the crews down to ensure accuracy, and, hopefully, avoid civilian casualties. The marking was accurate and concentrated, and the Metheringham crews bombed on red spot-fires or red and green target indicators from 5,500 to 8,000 feet. The last one bombed at 01.53, and all arrived safely home with six aiming point photos between them. On the following night nine 106 Squadron Lancasters were among 104 from the group to take off to attack railway yards at Nevers in central France. The squadron contingent got away either side of 22.00, led by W/C Piercy, and S/L Grindon undertook his first operation as second pilot to F/L Taylor. They reached the target some four hours later to find favourable conditions and prompt and accurate marking. They delivered their seven 1,000 pounders and eight 500 pounders from 4,000 to 5,000 feet between 01.58 and 02.13. The entire force was carrying delayed-action ordnance, and no immediate assessment could be made. Photo-reconnaissance later in the day revealed that the site had been all but obliterated, and there was much damage to rolling stock.

The 17th was spent by the crews in intensive training for an operation to be mounted on the following morning. As dawn arrived over the British Second Army on the 18th, so did more than nine hundred RAF bombers, whose crews had been briefed to attack five fortified villages to the east and south-east of Caen. It was the start of the ground forces' Operation Goodwood, which, Montgomery hoped, would be a decisive breakout into wider France as a prelude to the march towards the German frontier. 106 Squadron was back to full strength, and it was still dark as nineteen Lancasters took off from Metheringham either side of 04.00, with G/C McKechnie and W/C Piercy taking the lead, and S/L Williams in support. The specific aiming point for the squadron was the Mondeville steel works, which the Germans had converted into a strongly defended fortress, and the destruction of which would be of huge benefit to the advancing ground forces. They located the target with ease, and bombed either visually or on target markers from 6,000 to 10,000 feet between 05.43 and 06.07. They were each carrying eleven 1,000 pounders and four 500 pounders, and as one crew commented on return, "Bombing concentrated, no loose sticks seen". The RAF dropped five thousand tons of bombs to good effect on two German divisions in just half an hour, and the Americans followed up with a further two thousand tons.

That night 5 Group was sent to destroy a railway junction at Revigny, which 1 Group had twice failed to hit. This time the lines were cut, but, in the absence of a 106 Squadron participation, the group received a bloody nose to the tune of twenty-four Lancasters, as night fighters enjoyed an orgy of success. A V1 supply dump at Thiverny provided the objective for 104 Lancasters from 5 Group, which were to attack in daylight, in mid-evening, on the 19th. Metheringham provided seventeen aircraft for this target, situated between the recently-visited sites at St Leu-d'Esserant and Creil, north of Paris. There were no senior pilots on duty as they took off at 19.30 and headed for the south coast to pick up a Spitfire escort. All from the squadron reached the target in fine weather conditions, but ground haze and late preliminary marking by the Pathfinder element led to most of them having to bomb visually. They were over the target between 21.29 and 21.37 at altitudes ranging from 14,000 to 18,000 feet, and although there was moderate to intense heavy flak, no fighters appeared, and no aircraft were lost. Reconnaissance revealed some loose bombing, but nine 106 Squadron crews brought back an aiming-point photo.

Railway yards and a triangle junction at Courtrai provided the target for a joint effort by 1, 5 and 8 Groups on the night of the 20/21st, for which 106 Squadron contributed twenty Lancasters. F/L Taylor was the senior pilot on duty as they departed Metheringham after 23.00, and they found the target to be free of cloud, but slightly obscured by ground haze. The marking was well-placed, and the squadron participants delivered their eleven 1,000 pounders and four 500 pounders each onto them from 10,000 to 12,500 feet between 00.56 and 01.30, before returning home safely with seventeen aiming-point photos. There was considerable night fighter activity in the target area, and two unnamed 106 Squadron crews had encounters, one claiming a twin-engine enemy aircraft as destroyed. Reconnaissance revealed that both aiming points had been obliterated in return for the loss of nine Lancasters.

The first attack on a German city for two months was mounted against Kiel on the night of the 23/24th, when more than six hundred aircraft appeared with complete surprise from behind a 100 Group-laid RCM screen[4]. The original call for twenty aircraft from Metheringham was reduced to twelve, and they were all safely off the ground by 23.00 with S/L Grindon taking the lead for the first time. They arrived in the target area to find a thin layer of cloud, through which the target markers were clearly visible, and they bombed from 17,300 to 20,000 feet in a nine minute slot from 01.27. The attack created massive damage in all parts of the town, particularly in the port area, where U-Boot yards and naval facilities were hit.

On the night of the 24/25th came the first of three raids in five nights on the southern city of Stuttgart. Six hundred aircraft were involved, including nine from 106 Squadron, while nine others from Metheringham joined in an attack by a hundred Lancasters on an oil storage depot at Donges on the north bank of the Loire inland from St Nazaire. The Stuttgart-bound Lancasters took off first, and were airborne from Metheringham by 21.50 led by F/L Taylor. They arrived in the target area around four hours later to find complete cloud cover and "Wanganui" flares in use. The 106 Squadron aircraft were each carrying one

---

[4] In November 1943 100 Group was formed to take over the Radio Countermeasures (RCM) role, which had been the preserve of 101 Squadron since its introduction a number of months earlier. 101 Squadron, however, would remain in 1 Group and continue to provide RCM for the remainder of the war.

2,000 pounder and twelve "J" clusters of incendiaries, which they delivered from 16,000 to 20,000 feet between 01.48 and 01.57, before returning with reports of fires beneath the clouds, but no genuine clue as to actual results. The second 106 Squadron element took off at 22.25, with F/Ls Jones, Lines, Parry and Williams the highest-ranking pilots on duty. They were carrying the regular load of eleven 1,000 pounders and four 500 pounders, which they delivered onto Pathfinder markers from 9,000 to 11,000 feet between 01.43 and 01.52. The clear skies and good visibility enabled the crews to assess the outcome, and they all returned safely home confident in the success of the operation. This was confirmed by photo-reconnaissance, which revealed the site to have been devastated.

F/O Philip George, navigator for W/C Piercy, in front of a Lancaster.

The evening of the 25th found a 5 Group force of ninety-four Lancasters and six Mosquitos setting off for an airfield and signals depot at St-Cyr, situated near Limoges in south-western France. Twenty of the Lancasters belonged to 106 Squadron, and they were airborne by 18.00 led by S/Ls Williams and Grindon. They arrived in the target area two hours later to find ten-tenths cloud with a base at 13,000 feet, and good visibility beneath. The target was easily identified, and the Metheringham crews bombed from 9,000 to 12,000 feet in a five-minute slot to 20.00, and all returned safely for their crews to claim an accurate attack. They also had a magnificent twenty aiming-point photos to back up their claim! Before the night was out the second operation against Stuttgart was under way at the hands of 550 aircraft. This was a particularly destructive attack, which left much damage in hitherto less-severely afflicted central districts.

5 Group continued the railway campaign at Givors, south of Lyon in south-eastern France on the night of the 26/27th, when 170 Lancasters were detailed to carry out an attack on the marshalling yards. 106 Squadron contributed twenty Lancasters, and among the crews taking off between 21.15 and 21.30 was that of P/O Durrant, embarking on the thirty-sixth and final operation of their first tour. S/Ls Grindon and Williams were the senior pilots on duty as the squadron contingent made its way to the French coast in appalling weather conditions of heavy cloud, rain, hail, violent thunderstorms and bad visibility. Most crews came beneath the 7,000 foot cloud base to bomb, and aimed at green target indicators or red spot-fires in accordance with the Master Bomber's instructions. S/L Williams was actually at 5,500 feet when he delivered his seven 1,000 pounders and four 500 pounders at 02.20, and he reported observing sticks of bombs falling across the tracks. He was also one of three crews to bring back an aiming point photo, along with F/L Lines and F/L Jones. F/L Taylor searched for half an hour, but was defeated by the

conditions and abandoned his sortie. All came safely home to Metheringham after what many described as a most unpleasant trip, but their efforts were rewarded with a successful outcome at the westerly of the two aiming-points.

Crew of F/O DW Meredith in July 1944.

The final attack of the Stuttgart series took place on the 28/29th, at the hands of almost five hundred Lancasters from 1, 3, 5 and 8 Groups, while over three hundred other Lancasters and Halifaxes from 1, 6 and 8 Groups targeted Hamburg for the first time since Operation Gomorrah a year earlier. 106 Squadron put up eighteen Lancasters for Stuttgart, and they took off in an eighteen minute slot from 22.00 with the senior pilots of flight lieutenant rank. They flew across France in bright moonlight above the cloud layer, and night fighters infiltrated the stream, taking a heavy toll of bombers. Five 106 Squadron crews reported being engaged inconclusively, and F/O Browne's gunners claimed one enemy aircraft as damaged. There was a layer of thin cloud over the city, and the Pathfinders initially employed skymarker flares (Wanganui), at which the squadron crews aimed their single 2,000 pounder and twelve "J" cluster incendiaries from 14,000 to 18,500 feet between 01.55 and 02.02. ME778 was one of thirty-nine aircraft failing to return, after it was intercepted by a night fighter. F/O Pemberton RAAF and his crew actually made it across the border into Germany before the end came, and they were all killed in the ensuing crash a few miles to the south-west of Karlsruhe and about fifty miles short of the target. Although it was difficult to make an accurate assessment of this night's attack on Stuttgart, the series had severely damaged the city, particularly its central districts. Most of the public and cultural buildings had been destroyed, and almost twelve hundred inhabitants had lost their lives. Night fighters also caught the Hamburg force on its way home, and a further twenty-two aircraft were shot down, bringing the night's casualty figure to sixty-one aircraft.

A daylight operation in support of largely American ground forces was mounted in the Villers Bocage-Caumont area of Normandy in the early morning of the 30th. Six aiming points and a total of 692 aircraft were involved, and the 5 Group contingent of 185 Lancasters was assigned to attack Cahagnes. 106 Squadron detailed twenty-one Lancasters, which took off at 06.00 led by W/C Piercy and both flight commanders. They arrived in the target area to find low cloud obscuring the ground, and the Master Bombers at four aiming points had little choice but to call off the attacks. The weather at Metheringham was marginal for the task of safely landing twenty-one Lancasters, so the returning crews were told to adopt a circuitous route home to give time for a forecast improvement in conditions. They arrived safely over England with their eighteen 500 pounders still on board, and it was then that tragedy struck PB304. At around 10.15 the aircraft was seen to dive out of low cloud and explode on impact on the banks of the River Irwell at Pendleton near Salford, Greater Manchester. F/L Lines and his crew perished, along with two civilians on the ground, one of them a seventy-two year old grandmother.

On the evening of the 31st 5 Group dispatched ninety-seven Lancasters, including a dozen from 106 Squadron, to attack a railway tunnel at Rilly-la-Montagne, just south of Reims, which was being used to store flying bombs. G/C McKechnie and S/L Grindon were on the Order of Battle for this one, the former taking with him F/O Markes as second pilot and S/L Crowe, the station navigation leader, which meant that JB665 was groaning under the weight of nine crew members, eleven 1,000 pounders and three 500 pounders. Despite this it took off safely at 17.25, and headed for the south coast, joining up with the rest of the force somewhere near Reading. F/O Fyson returned early with a defective bomb sight, but the remainder arrived in the target area to find clear conditions and 617 Squadron, whose Lancasters were also in attendance with their Tallboys to seal the tunnel entrances. The task for the remainder of the force was to crater the approaches, and the 106 Squadron crews, assigned to the northern end of the target area, delivered their hardware from 15,000 to 18,000 feet between 20.19 and 20.22.

While this operation was in progress, a second force of 1 and 5 Group Lancasters was on its way to attack locomotive facilities and railway yards at Joigny-la-Roche, situated north-west of Auxerre, and some ninety miles south east of Paris. Eight 106 Squadron Lancasters took off either side of 17.30 led by W/C Piercy and S/L Williams, and arrived in the target area to find clear skies and good visibility. The marking was concentrated, as was the bombing, and the squadron crews delivered their standard bomb loads from 12,000 to 15,000 feet in just three minutes from 20.19 under the umbrella of a fighter escort, and all brought back an aiming-point photo. This proved to be the final activity of a second successive hectic month for Metheringham, which had required the squadron to operate on ten nights and five days against sixteen targets. 242 sorties represented a new squadron record, as did the 1,070 tons of bombs delivered. Nine aircraft and crews were lost, but although no one on the squadron could know, the worst was, in fact, now behind them, and in the remaining nine months of the bombing war, there would be only two incidences of multiple losses.

August 1944

If July had been a busy month operationally, August was about to place even greater demands on the squadrons, as focus remained upon the multiple campaigns against flying bomb sites, oil, railways, and tactical support for the land forces. The first week of the month was dominated by the push to eradicate the flying bomb menace from the Pas de Calais, and operations were mounted on each day from the 1st to the 6th. 106 Squadron was involved at two targets on the 1st, launching sites at la Breteque and Siracourt, to which it dispatched five and twelve Lancasters respectively in the late afternoon. 777 aircraft were committed to numerous attacks on this day, but weather conditions proved to be unfavourable, and 106 Squadron's crews were among 698 to receive a recall signal. On the following afternoon almost four hundred aircraft were sent to attack one launching site and three supply sites. 106 Squadron contributed nineteen Lancasters to the underground storage facility at Trossy-St-Maximin, north of Paris, and they were ready for take-off at 10.45, but were held back until eventually departing Metheringham at 14.10 led by W/C Piercy, with S/Ls Williams and Grindon in support. Conditions in the target area were good, and the aiming point was identified visually by all crews, who delivered their standard bomb loads from 15,000 to 18,000 feet between 17.01 and 17.03. Flak was fairly intense and accurate, and five aircraft returned bearing the scars of battle, but there were no crew casualties, and the consensus was that it had been a concentrated and successful attack.

On the 3rd over eleven hundred aircraft took part in further operations against three flying bomb stores, and the 106 Squadron contingent of sixteen Lancasters took off shortly before noon to retrace its steps from the previous day and return to Trossy-St-Maximin. The weather was not so good on this occasion, and the crews, of which F/L Williams' was the most senior, were greeted with complete cloud cover and further intense flak activity. The squadron bombed on Pathfinder markers from 18,000 feet between 14.30 and 14.32, but the crews were unable to make any assessment of the results. The impression was of a scattered attack, and eleven Lancasters returned to Metheringham with flak damage.

The squadron was not involved in the next round of operations against two of the same targets on the 4th, but was back in action on the 5th with eighteen Lancasters as part of a large 5 Group force attacking the cave storage complex at St-Leu-d'Esserent. This was, as will be recalled, a target with recent painful memories for Metheringham of seven missing crews. They took off at 10.30 led by S/L Grindon, and there was a first operation for the newly arrived F/L Stewart. F/O Boivin returned early with engine failure, but the others approached the target area shortly before 13.30 in conditions of four-to-six-tenths cloud. A number of crews, including S/L Grindon, commented that the lead squadron was too far south of track, and this would compromise the bombing run of a number of 106 Squadron aircraft. The target was identified easily through gaps in the cloud, and the squadron aircraft delivered their standard bomb loads from 17,000 to 19,000 feet between 01.31 and 01.33, without being able to observe results. F/O Mavaut was among those unable to line up on the target in time, and he retained his bombs, while F/O Meredith bombed marshalling yards north of the target for the same reason. There were celebrations on landing for W/O Cunningham DFC and crew, who had now completed their first tour of operations on a total of thirty-five, achieved in under five months.

On the 6th sixteen of the squadron's crews were briefed for an attack on the U-Boot pens at Keroman (Lorient), during which they would support 617 Squadron, who would be employing Tallboys. On the previous day, while attacking a similar target at Brest, 617 Squadron's F/O Don Cheney and crew, who had begun their operational career at 106 Squadron a year earlier, had been shot down by flak off the French coast, and although three members of the crew lost their lives, Cheney and the others were assisted by local people, and soon returned home. It had been their thirty-ninth sortie. W/C Piercy was the senior pilot on duty as they departed Metheringham at 17.30, each carrying thirteen 1,000 pounders. F/O Kitto turned back with engine failure, but the others pressed on in excellent weather conditions and picked up an escort of Mosquitos provided by 100 Group. The use of "Serrate" Mosquitos of 100 Group was a new idea, and a departure from their usual role, which was to hunt down enemy night fighters as they stalked RAF bombers. Through their skill and effectiveness they quickly became feared as the scourge of the Nachtjagd. There were two aiming points for this evening's attack, the northern end for 617 Squadron and the southern one for the boys from Metheringham. They identified it visually, and delivered their bombs from 15,000 to 19,000 feet between 20.28 and 20.30 in the face of an intense flak defence. It was a concentrated and accurate attack, and the squadron participants brought back fourteen aiming point photos. 617 Squadron had achieved two direct hits with Tallboys, but would go back on the following day, suggesting the job had not yet been done. In the event they were recalled because American forces were moving into the area.

Over a thousand aircraft were involved in tactical support during the evening of the 7th, when targeting five aiming points ahead of Canadian forces. The operation had to be carefully controlled to avoid "friendly fire" incidents, and a Master Bomber and deputy would be on hand at each site. Fifteen 106 Squadron Lancasters were part of a 5 Group effort of 179 aircraft. They took off either side of 21.30 with

Crew of F/O Jack Netherwood. Back row: Glen Hendrey, Bomb Aimer; Al Parisani, Mid Upper Gunner;, Len Lucas, Wireless Operator. Front row: Bill Lloyd, Rear Gunner; Jack Netherwood, Pilot; Harry Winter, Navigator.

no senior officers present, and headed for Secqueville la Campagne, a village just to the south-east of Caen, which contained an enemy troop concentration. The target was located visually under clear skies, but the presence of considerable haze persuaded the crews to bomb on red target indicators, which they did from 6,000 to 9,500 feet between 23.18 and 23.22. F/O Bumford was unable to deliver his stores because of a bomb sight malfunction at the last moment, and LM641 failed to return with the crew of F/O Rabone RNZAF after crashing at Quetteville, north-east of the target and south of the Seine Estuary near Honfleur. The wireless operator and rear gunner lost their lives, but F/O Rabone and four of his crew parachuted to safety, and all but the flight engineer managed to evade capture. The attacks were generally effective, but the conditions dictated that 360 aircraft were sent home with their bomb loads intact.

During the mid-evening of the 9th 171 Lancasters and fourteen Mosquitos from 5 Group took off for an oil storage dump in the Foret de Chatellerault in western France, south of Tours. Fifteen of the Lancasters were provided by 106 Squadron, and an additional five ABC Lancasters from 101 Squadron spread themselves among the stream to give RCM protection. They departed Metheringham either side of 21.00 led by S/Ls Grindon and Allinson, the latter having just been posted in to succeed the tour-expired S/L Williams as A Flight commander. F/O Fyson and P/O Thompson and their crews were designated as "windfinders" for the whole force, a task which they would discharge successfully. They arrived in the target area to find no cloud, but the presence of considerable ground haze created poor visibility. Fortunately, the Pathfinder marking was accurate, and three large explosions were observed, along with much black smoke. All of the Metheringham crews carried out an attack from 4,500 to 8,000 feet between 00.04 and 00.20, and eight brought back an aiming-point photo.

On the 11th, while 617 Squadron took care of the U-Boot pens at la Pallice, thirty-five other Lancasters from the group, including six from Metheringham, attacked a similar target at Bordeaux under the protection of six Mosquitos of 100 Group. F/Os Browne, Harris and Kipfer and F/S Netherwood took off at 11.50 to place themselves ten minutes ahead of the main force as windfinders, while F/Os Meredith and Mavaut departed twenty minutes later. There were excellent conditions in the target area, and the four 106 Squadron "early birds" awaited the arrival of the others before bombing visually from 19,000 feet shortly after 16.30. There was heavy and intense flak, and LL948 was hit, causing a slight eye injury to F/O Harris's mid-upper gunner, F/S Long. They all arrived safely home between 19.30 and 19.45, each bringing back an aiming-point photo. Because of a shortage of Tallboys, even 617 Squadron was forced to employ 2,000lb armour piercing bombs, but photo reconnaissance later showed them to be ineffective against the reinforced concrete structures at both locations. This was the final operation of their tour for F/O Browne and crew, who no doubt filled the remainder of the evening with celebrations in the bar. Within an hour of their return from Bordeaux, a dozen other 106 Squadron Lancasters began taking off as part of a 189-strong force briefed to attack the marshalling yards at Givors, south of Lyon in eastern

France. S/L Grindon was the senior pilot on duty as they headed to the exit point over the south coast, and they arrived in the target area to find clear skies and good visibility. The Pathfinder marking was accurate, and the squadron participants bombed them from 6,000 to 9,000 feet between 01.14 and 01.20, before returning safely home with seven aiming-point photos and confident reports of a successful operation, which were confirmed by photo-reconnaissance.

The first operations of the month to be aimed at urban targets in Germany were mounted on the night of the 12/13th, when Brunswick and the Opel motor works at Rüsselsheim were the objectives for 379 and 297 aircraft respectively. The former was an experiment to ascertain whether or not main force crews could locate and bomb a target on H2S alone, without the presence of a Pathfinder element to provide marking. This was possibly an attempt to ease the pressure on 8 Group, which was having to support multiple operations by both day and night. 106 Squadron provided a dozen Lancasters for this operation, which W/C Piercy led away from Metheringham at 21.30. As they had been preparing to leave, a "rush" job was announced, and a further seven crews were briefed for an operation against German troop concentrations and a road junction north of Falaise in an area south of Caen. These crews would not take off until after midnight, and in the meantime the Brunswick-bound force made its way eastwards under clear skies, before encountering ten-tenths cloud in the target area with tops at 7,000 feet. This was not a problem, as the whole purpose of the operation was to locate and bomb the target blind. Ten of the 106 Squadron crews bombed from 18,000 to 22,000 feet between 23.58 and 00.08, and observed the glow of fires beneath the cloud, while two others bombed on e.t.a over a built-up area, which was believed later to be Hildesheim, a little over thirty miles short of Brunswick. Some of the bombing did hit Brunswick, but there was no concentration, and many outlying towns also reported bombs falling. It turned into an expensive night as forty-seven aircraft failed to return from the two main operations. This was despite the fact that the targets were located in different parts of Germany two hundred miles apart, and should have acted as an effective diversion for each other. W/C Piercy's ND682 was hit by heavy flak somewhere near Emden on the way home, but they got back without further incident.

The seven crews briefed for Falaise were led away at 00.15 by F/L Parry, to join up with the rest of the 144-strong mixed force. The target was located without difficulty, and the markers were plentiful and accurate. The 106 Squadron Lancasters were each carrying twelve 1,000lb GP (general purpose) or SAP (semi-armour piercing) bombs and a single 1,000lb MC (medium capacity) with a six hour delay fuse. These were delivered from 6,000 to 8,000 feet between 02.18 and 02.21, and all returned safely to report a successful operation. The ORB entry for the 14th states that; "After two months of severe fighting, the Allied armies have at last broken out from their Normandy bridgehead, and the German army is now in full retreat".

A major operation was mounted on the afternoon of the 14th to bomb seven German troop positions in the Falaise area ahead of the advancing Canadian 3rd Division. Over eight hundred aircraft were involved, including ten from 106 Squadron, whose crews were briefed to bomb at Quesnay, a village close to the previous night's effort north of Falaise. W/C Piercy led them away at noon, on what would be his final operation as the squadron's commanding officer. They located the target easily, and bombed on target indicators in accordance with the Master Bomber's instructions from 10,000 to 11,000 feet between 14.20 and 14.21, and returned safely with nine aiming-point photos. Master Bombers were on hand to control the bombing at each aiming-point because of the close proximity of the opposing armies, but despite the most stringent efforts to avoid friendly fire incidents, some bombs did fall into a quarry occupied by Canadian troops, and thirteen were killed. Later that evening 128 Lancasters from the group were sent to attack ships in Brest harbour. Thirty-one were assigned to a hulk, possibly the Clemenceau, thirty-seven to an oil tanker and fifty, including the 106 Squadron element, to the French cruiser Gueydon. This vessel had been attacked during the morning by elements from 617 and 9 Squadrons, but was found to be still afloat, as was its companion, the Clemenceau. Eight 106 Squadron Lancasters took part in the operation, departing Metheringham either side of 17.30 led by S/L Allinson. They found the vessels under clear skies but protected by intense and accurate flak, despite which they pressed home their attacks from 17,000 to 18,000 feet between 20.26 and 20.31, and returned safely with an aiming-point photo each. They reported smoke rising from the cruiser, and observing it to be "down at one end", and the tanker was also seen to be on fire. The Photographic Reconnaissance Unit (PRU) produced evidence on the following day that Gueydon had settled on the bottom and its decks were awash.

A view from the ground of Gilze Rijen airbase August 1944 as it is bombed by 106 squadron.

As Harris prepared to resume heavy raids on German urban targets, he dispatched more than a thousand aircraft on the morning of the 15th to attack nine fighter airfields in Holland and Belgium. A 5 Group force of 103 Lancasters, including seventeen from Metheringham, was briefed for Gilze-Rijen, situated west of Tilburg in southern Holland. The 106 Squadron contingent was selected to form the spearhead of the force, and S/L Allinson led them away from Metheringham either side of 10.00. On board with the A Flight commander was Mr V Lewis, a war correspondent with the Daily Sketch newspaper, while a Mr T Wilson represented the BBC in F/L Williams Lancaster, complete with state of the art recording equipment. They arrived in the target area to find clear skies and excellent visibility, and delivered their eleven 1,000 pounders and four 500 pounder across the airfield from 17,000 to 19,000 feet between 12.07 and 12.10. Returning crews brought back fifteen aiming-point photos and reported smoke rising to 6,000 feet over the target. The success was confirmed by PRU photos, which revealed eight hundred craters across the airfield and at least a hundred on the runways. Mr Lewis devoted several columns to the squadron in praise of its efforts, but Mr Wilson's recording equipment let him down, and there would be no broadcast by the BBC.

There were two main operations on the night of the 16/17th, both of them directed at German ports. The larger of the two forces, bound for Stettin, numbered 461 aircraft, ten of them provided by 106 Squadron, while six others from the squadron mined the approaches to the port. S/L Allinson led the main element away at 21.25, with the newly-arrived F/L Fee on board as a second pilot. After W/O Donkin turned back through an inability to climb, the remainder closed in on the target some three-and-a-half hours later to find between two and ten-tenths cloud with a base at 18,000 to 20,000 feet, but good visibility below, and the Pathfinder markers clearly visible. S/L Allinson bombed on a cluster of greens from 19,000 feet at 01.12, and reported good fires in the target. The rest of the squadron participants followed up over the ensuing twelve minutes from 17,000 to 19,000 feet, but were unsure as to the effectiveness of the attack, some suggesting it was scattered. In fact, it was highly successful, destroying or severely damaging 2,500 houses and fifty industrial premises, while also causing havoc amongst shipping in the harbour.

While this was in progress, over eighty aircraft were involved in mining duties in the Baltic region. Two of the 106 Squadron gardeners, F/L Stewart and F/O Kitto, had taken off late, and, unable to make up the time, abandoned their sorties on instructions from the controller. The remaining four made their way to the Young Geranium garden, the 150-yard-wide Stettin Canal, which required a low-level run-in to ensure accuracy. F/L Jones identified the target area first by flares and then by flame floats, and then, somehow, accidentally jettisoned two of his five mines. Pressing on, he approached at 300 feet and two hundred miles per hour i.a.s. (indicated air speed), and delivered the remaining three mines in the correct location in the face of intense light flak from both banks. F/O Sayeau RCAF went in at 250 feet and dropped two mines at 190 i.a.s. at 01.19. F/L Williams laid a single mine from 300 feet, while F/O Kipfer RCAF made two runs, both at 350 feet, delivering two mines on each occasion into the briefed locations. All returned safely, and there were immediate awards of the DFC to F/O Sayeau and F/O Kipfer, and also to the latter's bomb-aimer, F/O Redman. The Admiralty was impressed by the efforts of these crews, and sent a message of congratulations. The simultaneous attack on Kiel by 340 aircraft also produced heavy damage in the docks area, but a proportion of the bombing fell outside of the town to the north-west.

On the afternoon of the 18th 5 Group sent 158 Lancasters and eleven Mosquitos to bomb a flying bomb supply dump in the Foret de l'Isle-Adam north of Paris. 106 Squadron contributed fifteen aircraft, led by F/Ls Jones, Stewart, Parry and Fee, the last-mentioned on his first operation with the squadron as crew captain. They began taking off at 11.35, before flying in formation to the target, which they located easily in good conditions, and bombed visually from 9,000 to 10,000 feet between 14.10 and 14.12. F/O Meredith was about to bomb when cloud slid across the aiming point, and he abandoned his sortie. There was intense flak, causing damage to four 106 Squadron aircraft, and W/O Donkin's flight engineer was wounded in the foot. Shortly before they arrived home, four other Lancasters departed Metheringham either side of 15.30 to join up with sixty Lancasters and five Mosquitos from the group to attack an oil storage depot at Bordeaux. S/L Allinson was the senior pilot on duty as they headed for the south coast, and all was well until F/L Williams noticed an excessive oil leak in his port-inner engine, and decided to turn back. The others reached the target, which was easily identified under clear skies, and bombed it from an average of 15,500 feet at 20.10 in the face of intense flak. S/L Allinson's aircraft was holed, but made it home safely with an aiming-point photo to add to those of the other two crews.

Having operated against eighteen targets over fourteen days and nights, the squadron was happy to spend the following week at home, where it could rest and recuperate while minor operations held sway. In some ways it was an advantage to be so busy, as it allowed crews to complete a tour of operations in as little as two months, whereas earlier in the war it might have taken a year or more to amass thirty operations. W/C Piercy's time as commanding officer was up after completing his second tour of twenty-five operations. He had been with the squadron for just five months, and had put himself on the Order of Battle more frequently even than Gibson, and this at a time when commanding officers were expected to operate perhaps just once per month. He was officially posted out on the 25th, and would eventually be sent to the Middle East, where he apparently lost his life in an accident in 1945. He was succeeded on the 26th by W/C M M J Stevens.

When major operations were re-launched on the night of the 25/26th, the Command was up in strength committing over thirteen hundred aircraft to a variety of operations. The largest effort on this night, involving over four hundred aircraft from 1, 3, 6 and 8 Groups, was directed for the second time during the month at the Opel motor works at Rüsselsheim. The operation was partially successful, and a number of departments were temporarily put out of action, but lorry production was barely affected. 5 Group, meanwhile, was also over southern Germany at the virtually virgin target of Darmstadt. There were seventeen Lancasters from 106 Squadron among the 190-strong heavy element, and these set off either side of 21.00 led by F/Ls Jones, Stewart, Williams, Parry and Fee. They headed towards the south coast, rendezvousing on the way with the remainder of the force, before setting course across France. Matters began to go awry as the Master Bomber was forced to turn back, and his two deputies were then shot down after crossing into Germany. The illuminators dropped their flares too far to the west, and this prevented the low-level Mosquito element from finding the target. The main force crews reached the target to find clear skies but hazy conditions, and F/L Stewart orbited for twenty-seven minutes at under 9,000 feet waiting for markers to go down. In their absence, and without the benefit of H2S, which had failed, he could not positively identify the target, and bombed a concentration of incendiaries dropped by another aircraft at 01.53. F/O Mavaut arrived over Darmstadt at 01.15 to see some flares but no markers, and his H2S had also failed. At 01.20 he received orders by VHF to bomb, but no code word was mentioned, and he decided to bomb the first alternative target he came upon, which turned out to be scattered while lights and a fire at 01.44. Those with functioning H2S equipment were able to make an attack from 10,000 feet and below, between 01.20 and 01.41, mostly after waiting for many minutes for markers and instructions. One photo was plotted at fifteen hundred yards from the aiming-point, but others were between five and eight miles away. A few bombs did fall in Darmstadt, but many crews found other targets, some even joining in at nearby Rüsselsheim.

As matters turned out, this was to be but a temporary reprieve for Darmstadt. On the following night 1, 3 and 8 Groups returned to Kiel, while 174 Lancasters from 5 Group set out on the 950-mile slog to the port of Königsberg (now Kaliningrad in Lithuania), which was being used by the enemy to supply the eastern front. The full fuel load meant a reduction in bombs, and the 106 Squadron contingent of fourteen each carried a single 2,000 pounder and a dozen "J" clusters. They began taking off at 20.15 led by F/Ls Jones, Stewart, Williams and Fee, and it was five hours later when they closed on the target in clear conditions and good visibility. They mostly found concentrations of red target indicators to bomb, confirmed by their own H2S, and carried out their attacks from an average of 11,000 feet between 01.17 and 01.25. Returning crews reported large fires, explosions and smoke, and the glow could be seen up to 250 miles away on the return journey. Photo-reconnaissance revealed that most of the bombing fell into the town's eastern districts. While this operation was in progress, F/L Parry AFC and F/Os Thompson and Fyson were in the same area, off the coast, delivering mines into the narrow and well-defended Königsberg Seekanal. Thompson and Fyson represented the high-level element, and delivered their four mines each from 13,000 feet at 01.00 and 01.06 respectively. F/L Parry, meanwhile, went in at 90 feet in what were described as perfect conditions, and in the face of intense light flak from both banks, delivered five mines into the briefed locations. On his return, Parry received the immediate award of the DFC to add to the AFC (Air Force Cross) already in his possession.

The final operations in the flying bomb campaign were conducted on the 28th, and Allied ground forces took control of the Pas de Calais a few days later. 106 Squadron was not involved on this day, but its aircraft were being prepared for another go at Königsberg to be mounted on the night of the 29/30th. This time 189 Lancasters took off, among them sixteen from Metheringham, and because of the extreme range,

The new Station Commander at RAF Metheringham, Group Captain Maurice Heath, with WAAFs of the administration group.

they again carried between them only 480 tons of bombs to deliver onto four aiming points. Station commanders were not supposed to operate, but it was difficult to keep G/C McKechnie away from a Lancaster with a bomb load, and he was the senior pilot to depart Metheringham on this night, supported by S/L Grindon. They took off either side of 20.30, and arrived in the target area some five hours later to find excellent conditions below the cloud level. The Master Bomber kept the spearhead of the force circling for twenty minutes before the marking began, but the later arrivals could see the markers going down as they approached. F/O Marks orbited for twenty-four minutes, before eventually bombing from 10,000 feet at 01.44. S/L Grindon and a number of others bombed towards the tail end of the attack, following the Master Bomber's instructions to aim at a concentration of red and green TIs and allow a twenty-two second overshoot. LM215 was hit by light flak during the bombing run, and lost the use of its port-outer engine, but F/O Kitto brought it back on three.

Fourteen aircraft returned safely to Metheringham, some with photos of the target, and all with reports of large fires and explosions and a belief in the success of the operation. Two Lancasters were missing, however, including JB593 "Admiral Dombo", which contained G/Captain McKechnie and crew. McKechnie, who had been awarded a George Cross in 1940, had been an inspiration to the crews at Metheringham for putting his life on the line when he didn't have to. As no trace of the Lancaster and crew was ever located, it must be assumed that it went into the sea. On board was flight engineer Ron Clarke, who had been a member of W/C Piercy's crew. Also missing was ND331, from which the flight engineer and bomb-aimer managed to escape by parachute, but F/O Boivin and the rest of his crew also disappeared into the cold waters of the Baltic. The operation was a major success, which destroyed over

40% of the town's residential and 20% of its industrial buildings. Inevitably, the delay in starting the attack allowed night fighters to arrive on the scene, and fifteen Lancasters were brought down. While this operation was in progress, F/Os Mavaut and Archer delivered four MkVI mines each from 13,000 feet into the Königsberg Seekanal, and returned to report a successful outcome. W/C Piercy took temporary command of Metheringham pending the appointment of G/C Heath as the permanent successor to G/C McKechnie. This, of course allowed, him the freedom to ride his motor bike up and down the runway without any disapproving looks from higher up the food chain.

Although the threat from the V1 had now largely been nullified, the V2 remained a menace, and was a weapon against which, once launched, there was no defence. Six hundred aircraft set out in the early afternoon of the 31st to attack nine V2 storage sites in France. 5 Group sent contingents to three sites, including Auchy les Hesden, which was the target for forty-nine Lancasters, sixteen of them from 106 Squadron. F/O Marks was first away at 15.30, and take-offs were not completed until 16.10. S/L Allinson was the senior pilot on duty as they headed across the Channel and found their way to the target, situated a few miles inland from Berck-sur-Mer. Weather conditions were far from ideal with heavy showers and five to eight-tenths cloud, and the bombers were forced to orbit while the Master Bomber identified the target. The squadron crews bombed from between 10,000 and 16,000 feet in a ten-minute slot from 18.08, and the effort seemed to be fairly concentrated on the markers. There was little opposition, and all of the participants returned home safely with reports of an uneventful trip. During the course of the month the squadron had taken part in twenty-three operations, including mining, on ten days and eight nights, and had dispatched a record 288 sorties for the loss of three aircraft.

September 1944

The destructive power of the Command was now almost beyond belief. Each of its heavy bomber Groups was capable of laying waste to a German town at one go, and from now until the end of the war this would be demonstrated. Much of the Command's effort during the month would be directed towards the liberation of the French ports remaining in enemy hands, but operations began for 106 Squadron with participation in attacks on six Luftwaffe-occupied aerodromes in Holland. 5 Group detailed 103 Lancasters and two Mosquitos for an attack on Deelen, and 106 Squadron provided seventeen of the former, led for the first time by W/C Stevens. They were all airborne from Metheringham by 15.30 for the short-range operation, but F/O Archer was forced to turn back with a faulty bomb sight. The others arrived at the target to find varying amounts of cloud up to nine-tenths, and orbited while they awaited gaps through which to aim. Twelve aircraft bombed from 13,800 to 16,000 feet between 17.33 and 17.43 in the face of a spirited flak defence from the airfield, while four others were thwarted by the cloud and brought their bombs home. All returned safely, F/S Thomas's PB122 with damage from heavy flak, and there were eight aiming-point photos to confirm that the operation had been so successful, that the Luftwaffe abandoned the aerodrome. There were celebrations for the popular F/O Kitto RNZAF and crew, who, although bringing their bombs home on this occasion, had now completed their first tour of operations.

The first operation against enemy positions around le Havre took place on the 5th, and it was followed up on the 6th, 8th and 9th, although without participation by 106 Squadron. On the night of the 9/10th 5 Group sent a modest force of 113 Lancasters and fourteen Mosquitos to attack Mönchengladbach. 106 Squadron prepared eighteen aircraft, which took off between 02.30 and 03.00 led by S/L Grindon. The bombing was carried out in clear weather with good visibility, and under the control of a Master Bomber, and the squadron participants each delivered their cookie and incendiaries in a six-minute slot to 05.24 from 16,500 to 17,000 feet. As they withdrew from the target, they observed many fires and a large pall of smoke rising upwards. Photo-reconnaissance confirmed the success of the attack, which left the town centre devastated. Almost a thousand aircraft were committed to attacks on eight enemy strong points around le Havre on the 10th, and the final operation against the port took place on the 11th, this time with a 106 Squadron presence. Eighteen Lancasters had been detailed at Metheringham, and eleven got away safely by 06.20, before the next one became bogged and blocked access to the runway. W/C Stevens led the squadron contingent, and they located their aiming point, the outer defences at Cadillac, just after dawn in excellent weather conditions and visibility. Bombing took place from 11,500 to 12,000 feet between 07.34 and 07.42, and all returned safely with aiming point photos. Within hours of this operation the German garrison surrendered to British forces.

Later that night a 5 Group force of 226 Lancasters and fourteen Mosquitos set out for Darmstadt in southern Germany, a target attacked ineffectively by the group in late August. 106 Squadron dispatched twenty Lancasters, which departed Metheringham either side of 21.00 with no pilots above flight lieutenant rank on duty. It was approaching midnight as they closed on the target in good conditions, with perhaps a little thin cloud, and F/O Bumford was the first to bomb on red TIs, at 00.02, by which time the city was already burning. The others followed up over the ensuing ten minutes from 11,800 to 12,500 feet, and they reported the glow of fires still visible more than a hundred miles into the return journey. The conditions had been ideal for the 5 Group marking method, and photo-reconnaissance confirmed the main weight of the attack to have fallen in the centre and surrounding districts to the south and east, where a firestorm developed. It is believed that more than twelve thousand people lost their lives, 10% of the population, and seventy thousand were rendered homeless. There was considerable night fighter activity, and F/O Kipfer's Lancaster sustained extensive damage in an encounter. Twelve Lancasters failed to return, and among them was 106 Squadron's PB203, which crashed in the target area at midnight. F/L Mavaut RCAF was the holder of a DFC, and he died along with three others of his crew, while his navigator and bomb-aimer, both also Canadian, survived to become PoWs. Following on from the recent attack on Mönchengladbach, this raid must have sounded the alarm bells amongst German authorities with regard to other small and industrially insignificant towns, although it is unlikely that the Nazi machine allowed reports from the afflicted areas to spread far and wide. There was, indeed, just cause for concern, as worthwhile targets for Bomber Command were becoming increasingly scarce.

Two major operations were mounted on the night of the 12/13th, the larger to Frankfurt by over 370 Lancasters and nine Mosquitos from 1, 3 and 8 Groups, and the other to Stuttgart by over two hundred Lancasters and Mosquitos of 5 Group, with a sprinkling of 101 Squadron RCM Lancasters in support. W/C Stevens was the senior pilot on duty, supported by S/Ls Allinson and Grindon, and the thirteen 106 Squadron Lancasters began to depart from Metheringham at 18.55. They enjoyed an uneventful flight across France to the target, which they found under clear skies with ground haze. Bombing took place on well-placed Pathfinder markers from 17,000 to 19,000 feet between 23.12 and 23.18, and the glow of the fires could be seen from a hundred miles away. Both operations left massive damage in their wake, and at Stuttgart the northern and western districts were all but erased from the map as a firestorm took hold, and over eleven hundred lives were lost. The Frankfurt force lost seventeen Lancasters, but just four were missing from Stuttgart, and all thirteen from Metheringham returned safely, with aiming-point photos from W/C Stevens and F/L Fee.

After four years to the week of operating on the front line, 106 Squadron was given a new role, acting as a training unit for the group's Pathfinder element. It would continue to take part in the bombing offensive, but, perhaps, with a little less intensity, and its orders would come through principally from Coningsby, the home of 83 and 97 Squadrons and the base commander Air Commodore Bobby Sharp. In future it would receive crews recommended by their training units as suitable for entry to the Pathfinders, and they would complete five operational sorties with the squadron, before moving on to the Navigation Training Unit (NTU) at Warboys in Cambridgeshire for training in Pathfinder methods. Thereafter, they would return to Metheringham for further operations until being posted to either 83 or 97 Squadrons[5].

The squadron was not called into action again until the morning of the 17th, when 762 aircraft took off to attack enemy troop positions around the port of Boulogne. Sixteen Lancasters departed Metheringham, led away at 08.15 by S/L Allinson, who had the new station commander, G/C Heath, on board as second pilot. By the time they were all safely airborne, the operation, which would stretch over four hours, was just getting under way as the first of seven aiming-points was attacked at 08.30. The squadron contingent arrived to find clear skies and good visibility, and they delivered their standard loads of eleven 1,000 pounders and four 500 pounders from 8,000 to 9,000 feet between 09.46 and 09.52, before returning home with an aiming-point photo each. In all, three thousand tons of bombs were dropped, paving the way for Allied ground forces to move in, and shortly afterwards the German garrison surrendered. On the following evening 5 Group sent over two hundred Lancasters to Bremerhaven, along with seven Mosquitos to carry out the low-level marking. Sixteen 106 Squadron Lancasters stood ready for take-off from Metheringham at 18.15, with W/C Stevens taking the lead, supported by S/L Allinson. There were no early returns, and the squadron contingent went in at medium level, releasing their all-incendiary loads from 12,000 to 12,800 feet on Pathfinder markers in accordance with the Master Bomber's instructions. As they headed out of the target area at 21.10 they could see many large fires and a number of huge explosions, and the glow was still visible from 150 miles away. Reconnaissance confirmed that the operation had been stunningly successful, and had destroyed over 2,600 buildings with a modest nine hundred tons of bombs, at a cost of just two aircraft.

On the following night the group joined forces with 1 Group to return to Mönchengladbach, the scene of a successful operation earlier in the month. On this occasion its twin town of Rheydt was the principal target in the complex plan, and the Master Bomber for the occasion was the former 106 Squadron commanding officer and national hero, W/C Guy Gibson VC, who was currently base operations officer at 54 Base at Coningsby. The decision to allow Gibson to act as Master Bomber was somewhat surprising, as he was barely qualified, and there were many better qualified members of the 5 Group Master Bomber fraternity at Coningsby, like W/C Owen, who had controlled the recent attack at this target, and W/Cs Jeudwine and Woodroffe. Gibson had been agitating to get back into the war before it was over, and didn't want his service to end in a backwater, while others gained the glory by being in at the death. Gibson was a warrior, and the war had brought out of him qualities, which, in peacetime, may have lain dormant. War had also given him a direction, and he revelled in the company of fellow operational types, particularly those of the officer class. Having been torn away from the operational scene following the Dams operation, his direction had gone, and he had become listless, frustrated and discontented. His time in the operational wilderness had not, however, deprived him of his arrogance and self-belief, and when the opportunity to fly as Master Bomber on the coming raid presented itself, he grabbed it. As Master Bomber he would fly a Mosquito borrowed from 627 Squadron, an aircraft with which he had only a fleeting acquaintance. The

[5] It should be remembered, that although these squadrons were now on permanent loan to 5 Group, they remained officially Pathfinder/8 Group units.

requirements of the operation, involving three aiming points, would have taxed an experienced Master Bomber, which Gibson was not, and he apparently brushed aside the advice which was offered, and also refused to accept the Mosquito prepared for him by 627 Squadron, insisting on another, which was duly provided.

W/C Stevens again took the lead as the eighteen 106 Squadron Lancasters began departing Metheringham at 19.00, and S/L Grindon was also on the Order of Battle. The squadron's aiming point was the town centre of Rheydt, and it was here that Gibson experienced some difficulty in maintaining control. They arrived to find clear skies and good visibility, but W/C Stevens commented that the TIs were late in going down. F/O Kelley was instructed to bomb on green TIs, but none was visible, and he aimed instead at fires burning in the centre of the target area. F/L Stewart received the same instruction, but he found greens to aim at, and brought home an aiming-point photo. F/O Sayeau was ordered to bomb greens, only to have that instruction cancelled and changed to reds. Others also commented on the lateness of the marking, and some crews bombed markers not assigned to them. The squadron crews each delivered their single 2,000 pounders and dozen 500lb incendiary bombs in an eight-minute slot just before 22.00 from 12,000 to 12,800 feet, and sixteen of them returned home. F/L Barron used Gee to find Metheringham, but was unable to locate it precisely in cloudy conditions, and while circling to get his bearings, had to take evasive action to avoid another aircraft. He was unable to maintain control, and pulled off a successful crash-landing near Fulbeck airfield. Although he and his crew walked away unscathed, PB298 was written off. The operation cost four Lancasters, two of which belonged to 106 Squadron. PB347 crashed on the west-north-westerly approach to the target shortly after crossing the frontier with Holland. F/O Brindley and five of his crew lost their lives, and only the bomb-aimer, F/O Ayres, escaped to become a PoW. PB359 crashed east-south-east of the target after bombing, and F/L Fee RAAF managed to evade capture, while the three other survivors did not. Generally the operation was a success, and much damage was inflicted on both towns. Gibson did not return, and his Mosquito crashed on the outskirts of Steenbergen in Holland, where he now rests in the Catholic cemetery, alongside his navigator, S/L Warwick, who it seems, was pressganged by Gibson into taking part. No satisfactory explanation for Gibson's loss has been forthcoming, but the wife of a Lancaster rear gunner claimed after her husband's death in the nineties, that he believed he had inadvertently shot down the Mosquito, believing it to be an enemy night fighter.

The first of a series of operations to liberate Calais was mounted on the 20th, the day on which the award of a DFC was announced to W/C Piercy and F/O Durrant. AVM Cochrane visited the station on the 21st, accompanied by the 54 Base commander, Air Commodore Sharp, and the former squadron commanding officer, W/C Baxter. Germany's canal system was a vital component in the transport network, and facilitated the import of raw materials and the export of finished goods to support the war effort. Its wide thoroughfares allowed the passage of large barges, and as the slack in Germany's war production was taken up during 1944, traffic was being pushed through at increasing levels. The section of the Dortmund-Ems Canal near Ladbergen had been an occasional target for 5 Group since June 1940, and, always well defended, it had cost the lives of many good crews. The raised earthen banks south of Ladbergen had last been attacked by 617 Squadron in mid September 1943 with disastrous results for the squadron. Now it was time to attack the twin aqueduct section closer to Ladbergen, which had been the scene of the epic attack by Hampdens in August 1940, during which S/L Learoyd of 49 Squadron had earned a Victoria Cross. 136 Lancasters were prepared for this operation on the night of the 23/24th, including a contingent from 617 Squadron carrying Tallboys, and sixteen from 106 Squadron. An operation by 113 other aircraft from 5 Group against the nearby night fighter airfield at Münster/Handorf was intended to act as a diversion, as would the night's main operation by more than five hundred aircraft of 1, 3, 4 and 8 Groups against Neuss in the Ruhr.

W/C Stevens again put himself at the top of the Order of Battle, thus maintaining the tradition of 106 Squadron commanding officers to lead from the front, and was supported by S/L Allinson. They were airborne in ten minutes from 19.10, but F/O Kelley returned early after his mid-upper gunner reported sick. The others arrived in the target area shortly before 22.00 to find complete cloud cover over the canal, but good visibility below the cloud base at around 8,000 feet. 617 Squadron went in first, and direct hits by two Tallboys breached both branches of the section, leaving a six mile stretch of the waterway drained. The problem of identification in this region was made difficult by the presence nearby of the Mittelland Canal, which joined the Dortmund-Ems Canal in Das Nasse Dreieck (the Wet Triangle) near Ibbenbüren a few miles further north, and the Glane, a river which passed under the Dortmund-Ems Canal in the same locality. Features were easily confused, and some aircraft strayed north of the intended aiming point, to a spot beyond the town of Ladbergen, where a similar-looking section of the Mittelland Canal was attacked. The crews arriving first bombed on the glow of markers through the cloud, while later arrivals were brought below the cloud base. Four of the 106 Squadron crews bombed from between 14,000 and 15,000 feet on target markers, while W/C Stevens, F/O Meredith and S/L Allinson were below 8,000 feet over what they believed to be the correct location, but their bombing photos were plotted six miles north of the intended aiming point. F/O Symes bombed Handorf airfield as an alternative, while F/L Sexton abandoned his sortie over the target on instructions from the Master Bomber. Night fighters were active towards the end of the raid, and contributed to the loss of fourteen Lancasters, more than 10% of those dispatched. 106 Squadron was represented among the missing by ND868, which crashed near Ibbenbüren, killing seven of the eight men on board, including the newly-arrived second pilot, F/O Isaac, and only the pilot, F/L Jones, survived to fall into enemy hands. F/O Meredith RCAF and crew arrived back in a night fighter-damaged PB248, and thus completed their first tour of operations.

Further operations against enemy positions around Calais were mounted on the 24th, 25th and 26th, while 106 Squadron stayed at home. 216 Lancasters of 5 Group took off after midnight on the 27th for Karlsruhe in south-western Germany, and among them were thirteen representing 106 Squadron. They departed Metheringham either side of 01.00, led once more by W/C Stevens, and found the target under eight to ten-tenths cloud cover, which necessitated skymarking. This was assessed as accurate, and the Master Bomber called the force in in two waves, the 106 Squadron element being divided between them, eight in the first and five in the second. They all bombed from 10,700 to 12,300 feet in an eight-minute slot to 04.10, before returning safely to report the glow of fires a hundred miles into the return journey. There were no plottable photos, but reconnaissance confirmed that the bombing had been spread throughout the city.

On the following night it was the turn of Kaiserslautern, also in south-western Germany, to host a visit from a 5 Group force numbering over two hundred Lancasters, including thirteen from 106 Squadron. S/L Allinson was the senior pilot on duty, and he had the station commander, G/C Heath, with him as second pilot. They took off shortly after 22.00, and arrived in the target area to find a thin layer of cloud at 3,000 feet. The railway workshops were of particular interest to the 106 Squadron crews, but this was an area attack, and most carried all-incendiary loads, while some others had a single 2,000 pounder and a dozen 500lb incendiaries. The squadron contingent bombed on well-placed Pathfinder markers from 4,000 to 5,000 feet between 01.03 and 01.10, and all returned safely. The attack led to the destruction of an estimated 36% of the town's built-up area, at a cost of a single Lancaster and one Mosquito. Once again there were no casualties from Metheringham. On the following day the final operations to clear enemy forces from Calais took place, and Canadian ground forces moved in to accept the surrender. There was no further activity for 106 Squadron during a month that had seen eleven operations on three days and eight nights, involving 171 sorties, and the loss of five aircraft and four crews.

October 1944

The new month began operationally for 106 Squadron on the night of the 4/5th, with participation in a mining effort in northern Waters. The target areas for over seventy Lancasters and Halifaxes were the Kattegat Channel and Oslo Fjord. The five 106 Squadron participants were assigned to the former, the Silverthorn garden, in company with fifteen others from the group. W/C Stevens led them away at 17.15, and they arrived in the target area to find good conditions with a little low cloud. They delivered six mines each from 11,000 feet either side of 21.00, and returned safely as the only one of the four 5 Group squadrons involved to be 100% successful. On the following morning a 5 Group force of over 220 aircraft set out for Wilhelmshaven, among them nine representing 106 Squadron. S/L Allinson was the senior pilot on duty as they departed Metheringham at 07.55, and this would be the squadron's first experience of operating over Germany in numbers in daylight. The target was found under ten-tenths cloud, and the bombing took place by H2S. Nine of the 106 Squadron crews delivered their ten 1,000 pounders and four 500lb J incendiary bombs from 17,000 to 18,300 feet shortly after 11.00, but a mechanical problem prevented S/L Allinson from releasing his load. He tried repeatedly to jettison it on the way home, but ultimately had to land with it still on board. This was the final operation of this crew's first tour. There was no possibility of making an assessment of results, and the impression was of a scattered attack.

A new Ruhr offensive began on the night of the 6/7th, when 3, 6 and 8 Groups sent over five hundred aircraft to Dortmund, and inflicted severe damage for the loss of only three aircraft. 5 Group, meanwhile, was carrying out the last of thirty-two major attacks on the city of Bremen. 246 Lancasters made up the heavy brigade, and fourteen of these represented 106 Squadron led by S/L Grindon. There was also a final operation of their first tour for F/L Stewart and crew, who had F/L Barlow RAAF on board as second pilot. They took off at 17.45 and headed into crystal clear conditions with a three-quarter moon, which was ideal for the 5 Group low-level marking method. They passed over the aiming point at an average altitude of 16,000 feet, and delivered their bombs on the Master Bomber's instructions between 20.20 and 20.34. Returning crews reported large explosions, and the glow of fires still visible 150 miles into the homeward trip. The attack resulted in a devastating blow, which created a large area of fire in the city centre, and destroyed or seriously damaged almost five thousand buildings. Five aircraft failed to return, among them PD214, which crashed into the sea, taking with it the eight-man crew of F/L Stewart. It would have been a bitter blow to the squadron members to see one of their own crews robbed of the prize of survival at the final moment, and they were about to bid farewell also to S/L Grindon, for whom this had been the sixteenth and final operation with the squadron. He would be posted from the squadron on the 8th to take command of 57 Squadron at East Kirkby. At the end of April 1945 he would succeed G/C Johnny Fauquier as commanding officer of 617 Squadron. He was succeeded as B Flight commander by the newly-promoted S/L Parry DFC, AFC.

The squadron was not involved in any operations over the following week, when much of the Command's effort was directed towards coastal defences around the Scheldt Estuary, and the softening up of enemy resistance in the Eifel region of Germany ahead of the advancing Allied ground forces. During the few rest periods over the summer months the squadrons of 54 Base had competed for a handsome bronze sports trophy awarded for points won in cricket, swimming, athletics, badminton, rifle-shooting and other pursuits. On the morning of the 8th Air Commodore Sharp presented it to the winners, 106 Squadron. Early on the 14th more than a thousand aircraft set out for Duisburg to launch Operation Hurricane, a series of massive raids in tandem with the USAAF 8th Air Force designed to demonstrate to the enemy the overwhelming superiority of the Allied air power ranged against it. At breakfast time the RAF delivered over four and a half thousand tons of bombs into the already battered city, while over twelve hundred American heavies were active in the Cologne area. Bomber Command returned to Duisburg that night in similar numbers to press home the point about superiority.

Astonishingly, this enormous effort of launching 2,018 sorties in under twenty-four hours was achieved without the assistance of 5 Group, which took advantage of the night activity over the Ruhr to have another crack at Brunswick, which had, thus far, largely escaped serious consequences despite four earlier attempts. Of the 233 Lancasters dispatched, a dozen were provided by 106 Squadron, all containing a pilot of flying officer rank. They took off either side of 23.00, and arrived in the target area more than three hours later to find clear skies and good visibility. The marking was accurate, and, although the early stages of bombing tended to undershoot, the Master Bomber quickly brought it back on track, calling for crews to overshoot by nineteen seconds. The 106 Squadron contingent passed over the aiming-point at between 02.30 and 02.36, and delivered their loads of one 1,000 pounder and 2,400 4lb incendiaries from 17,400 to 18,000 feet, contributing to a highly effective raid, that destroyed the heart of this ancient and historic city. Returning crews reported fires visible from a hundred miles away, and bombing photos were plotted at between 1,300 and 3,300 yards from the aiming-point. Such was the level of destruction that local authorities believed a thousand bombers had taken part.

During the course of the month a number of operations had been mounted to assist ground forces in the capture of the island of Walcheren in the Scheldt Estuary, which guarded the approaches to the much-needed port of Antwerp some forty miles upstream. The sea walls on the western extremity at Westkapelle had been breached on the 3rd, but efforts would continue throughout the month, particularly against the coastal batteries, before the ground assault could be mounted. On the 17th a daylight attack was mounted by forty-seven Lancasters and two Mosquitos of 5 Group, of which eight were provided by 106 Squadron. They were on their way by 13.00 with loads of fourteen 1,000 pounders fitted with delay fuses of varying lengths. They arrived at the target in good conditions, and bombed from 4,500 to 6,000 feet shortly after 14.00, before returning safely home with an aiming-point photo each.

The night of the 19/20th brought two major operations against cities in southern Germany. The larger was directed at Stuttgart, and involved over 580 aircraft from 1, 3, 6 and 8 Groups in a two-phase attack, which caused severe damage in central and eastern districts. Meanwhile, 5 Group dispatched a force of 263 Lancasters and seven Mosquitos to Nuremberg, an operation supported by thirteen 106 Squadron aircraft. They were airborne by 17.45, led by W/C Stevens, and arrived in the target area a little over three hours later to find nine-tenths cloud, which impeded the low-level marking method. Blind marking had to be employed instead, and crews bombed on the glow of markers seen through the clouds. The 106 Squadron crews bombed either side of 21.00 from between 13,000 and 17,200 feet, and all returned home without incident. It was not possible to assess the outcome, but it seems that most of the bombing fell into southern rather than central districts. Fortuitously, this was where the bulk of the industry was situated, and forty-one industrial buildings were destroyed, along with four hundred houses.

The new Ruhr offensive continued at Essen on the night of the 23/24th, when a new record of 1,055 aircraft was dispatched to deliver over 4,500 tons of mostly high explosive bombs. 5 Group sat this one out, and operated next on the following night, when sending twenty-five Lancasters to lay mines in northern waters. The gardens were Kraut, Yew Tree and Silverthorn, and 106 Squadron contributed ten aircraft to the last-mentioned, the Kattegat Channel. They were all off the ground by 17.30, led by W/C Stevens, and encountered ten-tenths cloud in the target area with tops at 8,000 feet. H2S was used to locate Anholt Island, from where timed runs were made, and all aircraft dropped six mines each from an average height of 12,000 feet either side of 22.00. There was no opposition of any kind, and all landed safely at Lossiemouth after eight to nine hours in the air. A follow-up operation against Essen was carried out by over seven hundred aircraft during the afternoon of the 25th, but 5 Group played no part. Cologne's turn for further attention came on the 28th, and on the evenings of the 30th and 31st, and further massive destruction was heaped upon this now utterly rubble-strewn city.

The final major operation of the month for 5 Group took place on the night of the 28/29th, when 237 Lancasters and seven Mosquitos took off for Bergen in Norway, intending to attack the U-Boot pens. 106 Squadron contributed sixteen Lancasters to this operation, none of them piloted by a senior officer, but two South African Air Force pilots were on duty, Capt Pechey and Lt Addison, along with two almost all-Australian crews, whose flight engineers were RAF. They were all safely airborne by 23.00, and made their way to the target, where the anticipated clear conditions required for the low-level marking method did not materialize. The Master Bomber called the heavy force down to five thousand feet to gain a better view of the markers, but, even at this height, cloud was encountered. Five of the 106 Squadron aircraft bombed on red target indicators from 5,000 to 6,000 feet after making a number of runs across the aiming point, but the raid had to be called off after just forty-seven aircraft had bombed. While this was in progress, two others from the squadron successfully delivered six mines each into the waters of Oslo Harbour (Onions), before returning safely to Metheringham.

The final operation against the defences on Walcheren was mounted by a hundred Lancasters and eight Mosquitos of 5 Group at lunchtime on the 30th. Six Lancasters departed Metheringham at 10.35, and were in position ninety minutes later with loads of fourteen 1,000 pounders with delay fuses of thirty minutes to an hour. Visibility was poor, but the Zouteland battery was identified visually and by markers, and the squadron participants bombed on red TIs from 2,500 to 4,000 feet shortly after noon, before returning safely with five aiming-point photos. On the following day the ground forces went in, and, after a week of heavy fighting the island was taken. Even so, it would be a further three weeks before the Scheldt was cleared of mines, and the first convoy would not arrive at Antwerp until the 28th of November. It had been a good month for 106 Squadron, which had lost just a single Lancaster and crew from seven night operations, including two mining, and three in daylight involving a total of ninety-five sorties.

November 1944

5 Group was in action immediately at the start of the new month, with the Meerbeck synthetic oil plant at Homberg as the intended target. 226 Lancasters were detailed for the operation along with two Mosquitos, with other Mosquitos from 8 Group in support. The plant was situated just to the north-west of Duisburg, which made it a flak hot-spot for bombers, particularly in daylight. Twenty 106 Squadron Lancasters departed Metheringham either side of 14.00, led by S/L Parry, and on arrival in the target area they encountered complete cloud cover with tops reaching up to 9,000 feet. The skymarkers were scattered, and the first bombers to arrive on scene either failed to see the markers or watched them falling behind.

These brought their bombs home, but 160 aircraft did deliver their payloads, the 106 Squadron contingent doing so from 16,000 to 18,000 feet between 16.09 and 16.13 without being able to assess the results. Flak was intense and accurate, and a burst shot away one of PB303's engines, while probably inflicting other serious damage. This resulted in the Lancaster crashing near Steenbergen in southern Holland, the scene of Gibson's fatal crash six weeks earlier, and there were no survivors from the crew of F/O Symes, who were well into their first tour.

A massive operation to Düsseldorf in the early evening of the 2nd involved 992 aircraft, including sixteen Lancasters from 106 Squadron, which departed Metheringham in as many minutes up to 17.00. There were no senior pilots on duty as they made their way out for what would prove to be the final raid of the war on this much-bombed Ruhr city. The skies were cloudless and the visibility excellent as they approached the target to find the Pathfinder marking both accurate and concentrated. The 106 Squadron crews were at a variety of altitudes between 15,500 and 21,000 feet, and were well spread out in the bomber stream. F/O Scott, the pilot of an all-Australian crew, other than for the RAF flight engineer, was among the first to deliver his mixed payload of a cookie, six 1,000 pounder and six 500 pounders, which went down at 19.15, when it was too early in the raid to assess what was happening below. By the time F/O May RAAF dropped his bombs at 19.41, however, there were very large areas of fire and the whole city was covered by smoke. PB248 was severely damaged by cannon fire from a night fighter, but F/O Day and crew brought the Lancaster home. Many returning crews reported a large explosion, and the glow of fires still visible from up to two hundred miles away, and F/O Stansfield brought back an aiming-point photo. The operation was, indeed, highly successful, and left the northern half of the city with a further five thousand houses either destroyed or seriously damaged, along with twenty-five industrial premises.

While over seven hundred aircraft from 1, 4, 6 and 8 Groups pounded the centre of Bochum on the evening of the 4th, a 5 Group force of 170 Lancasters and Mosquitos attacked the embankments of the Dortmund-Ems Canal near Ladbergen, which had been partly repaired following the attack in September. As the ORB mentions embankment rather than aqueduct, it presumably refers to the section south of the aqueducts closer to Greven, which had been the target for the ill-fated 617 Squadron attack in September 1943. A dozen Lancasters lined up for take-off at Metheringham at 17.40, and all got away safely in around ten minutes. There was no cloud in the target area, and apart from some haze, visibility was good. The target was identified visually and by ground markers, and the squadron crews bombed in accordance with the instructions from the Master Bomber from 10,000 to 13,000 feet in a six-minute slot from 19.30. All returned safely, and there were four aiming-point photos. This was the hundredth operation for Lancaster JB663, which had been taken on squadron charge on the 18th of November 1943. The canal was again breached, leaving vital traffic stranded, and preventing much needed materials from reaching their end users, like, for example, smelting coke needed for the large steel-producing works at Salzgitter near Brunswick.

Two nights later a similar operation was mounted against the banks of the Mittelland Canal at its junction with the Dortmund-Ems Canal near Gravenhorst, ten miles or so north of the Ladbergen section. It was another 5 Group show, involving 235 Lancasters and seven Mosquitos. 106 Squadron supported the operation with eighteen Lancasters, which departed Metheringham at 16.30, and arrived in the target area to find complete cloud cover with a base at 4,000 feet and poor visibility. Low-level marking was not designed to take place in these conditions, but a single Mosquito eventually did deliver its target indicator accurately onto the aiming point, where it fell into the water and was extinguished. Thirty-one crews bombed before the Master Bomber called a halt to proceedings, and all of the 106 Squadron crews were sent home with their bombs. It became a rare failure for the group after difficulty was encountered in finding the target in an area criss-crossed by waterways. There was quite intense night fighter activity on the routes to and from the target, and ten Lancasters failed to make it home. Among the missing was 106 Squadron's LL953, which crashed on German soil, killing F/O Neale and his crew.

There were no further operations for the group until the early evening of the 11th, when the Rhenania-Ossag oil refinery at Harburg was the target for 230 Lancasters, including twenty from Metheringham. The target, on the southern bank of the Elbe opposite Hamburg, had been attacked by American bombers on a number of occasions, and was always well–defended. Fourteen of the 106 squadron crews were briefed to attack the refinery, while the remaining six focussed on the town, and W/C Stevens led them off at 16.25. There was no cloud over the region, and apart from some haze the visibility was good. The crews bombed from 16,300 to 19,000 feet on red TIs in accordance with instructions from the Master Bomber, and the last of the 106 Squadron contingent was heading away from the target by 19.30. Returning crews reported large fires and explosions, and dense smoke rising up to 10,000 feet. It was not possible to distinguish between the damage caused by this raid and the earlier ones by the Americans, but a local report suggests that the town bore the brunt of the attack.

The 16th was devoted to attacks on the towns of Düren, Jülich and Heinsberg in Germany's Eifel region east of Aachen, which were in the path of the advancing American Ninth Army. A total of 1,188 aircraft were involved, and 1, 5 and 8 Groups provided the heavy bombing and marking force of 485 Lancasters for the first-mentioned. 106 Squadron contributed nineteen aircraft, which got away from Metheringham either side of 13.00 with S/L Parry the senior pilot on duty, and no less than five pilots of the SAAF. They flew to the target over ten-tenths cloud, which cleared as they approached the aiming point in the final wave of the attack. They bombed on the instructions of the Master Bomber from 10,000 to 12,500 feet between 15.37 and 15.45, and returned confident in the success of the attack. All Metheringham crews claimed to have hit the target, but most of the photos were unplottable because of the smoke covering the area. The operation was a complete success, which all but erased the town from the map and killed over three thousand of its inhabitants.

The night of the 21/22nd was busy in the extreme, with more than thirteen hundred sorties dispatched on five main operations and a host of minor ones. 5 Group was involved in simultaneous operations against the Dortmund-Ems Canal at Ladbergen and the Mittelland Canal at Gravenhorst with a total of 260 Lancasters and eleven Mosquitos. 106 Squadron was assigned to the Dortmund-Ems Canal attack, which again focussed on the embankment south of the twin aqueduct section. The last of twenty-one Lancasters departed Metheringham at 17.55 to join up with 101 others, and they arrived in the target area to find six to nine-tenths cloud with a base at 4,000 feet. The Master Bomber brought them down to below the cloud, where the markers were clearly visible, and they bombed from 2,500 to 6,000 feet between 21.03 and 21.12. The attack seemed to be accurate, but no photographs were taken because of the low-level aspect of the operation. PRU photos, however, confirmed that the embankment had been breached again, and that section of the canal drained. There were no losses, but two Lancasters failed to return from the Gravenhorst operation, which was also successful. The Germans recognised that repairing the canals was an open invitation to Bomber Command to return, but so vital were they to the transportation system, that they could not be abandoned. The answer was to complete repairs, but to leave the sections drained to dupe RAF reconnaissance, until sufficient traffic had built up to push through in one night. At that point the canal would be flooded and then drained again to maintain the deception.

On the following night the group dispatched 171 Lancasters and seven Mosquitos to attack the U-Boot pens at Trondheim in Norway. 106 Squadron sent fourteen Lancasters on this operation, taking off from Metheringham either side of 16.00, and they arrived in the target area to find clear skies and excellent visibility. However, an effective smoke screen prevented the marker force from finding the aiming point, and the Master Bomber had no option but to send the force home. They were probably on their way to bed when a further six 106 Squadron crews took off at 04.50 to join others in laying mines in Heligoland Bay (Rosemary). F/L Marks found ten-tenths cloud in the target area, but good horizontal visibility, and, using H2S, made an eleven-mile run from the western tip of Wangerooge Island, and released six mines from 12,000 feet at 06.40. The other crews carried out similar runs of varying distances to leave a chain of mines across the important sea lane, and all returned without major incident. Later on the 23rd awards of the DFC were announced to F/Os Thompson, Harris, Browne Kitto, Fyson and Archer, and W/O Carmichael.

Munich was the objective for 270 Lancasters and eight Mosquitos of 5 Group on the night of the 26/27th, when 106 Squadron put up a record twenty-three aircraft. S/L Parry was the senior pilot on duty, and he was among the last to take-off at 23.59. Forming up and climbing to operational altitude was a time-consuming business, and it would be five hours before the target was reached. There was not a single early return from the Metheringham contingent, and all arrived in the target area in good shape and under clear skies with good visibility. They bombed the target indicators from an average of 17,000 feet in accordance with the instructions from the Master Bomber between 05.00 and 05.06, and all returned safely with reports of a successful operation. F/O Vallance brought back an aiming-point photo, and many others were plotted within two miles. This was the final operation of S/L Parry's first tour, and it was also the last of the month for 5 Group. Thereafter other elements of the Command carried out heavy and destructive attacks on Freiburg and Neuss on the 27/28th, Essen on the 28/29th and Duisburg on the 30th. 106 Squadron operated on seven nights and two days during the month, dispatching 169 sorties for the loss of two aircraft and crews. This was the second month in succession that the squadron had operated without a single early return.

December 1944

There were no operations for 5 Group for the first three nights of the new month, and in the meantime 1, 4, 6 and 8 Groups pounded the Ruhr town of Hagen on the 2/3rd. Worthwhile targets were becoming more and more scarce at a time when the Command was at its most powerful, and this final period of the war would bring the most devastating attacks to date on the German homeland. When 106 Squadron returned to action in the early evening of the 4th, it was to provide twenty-two Lancasters as part of a 5 Group force of 292 aircraft for an attack on the strategically unimportant town of Heilbronn. Situated thirty miles north of Stuttgart, the town had the misfortune to sit astride a north-south rail link. The main operation on this night was actually by 535 aircraft of 1, 6 and 8 Groups at Karlsruhe, some fifty-six miles west-south-west of Heilbronn, and the concentration of aircraft in this area would bring out the night fighters. Departure from Metheringham began at 16.30, and they arrived in the target area to find clear skies and good visibility. By the time F/O Scott and crew had fought off six attacks by night fighters, they were off track, and, in fact, had flown past the target. Too late to turn back, they jettisoned their cookie and incendiaries two miles south-west of the target and turned for home. The others bombed from an average of 11,000 feet on target indicators as instructed by the Master Bomber, and were also on their way home by 19.40. In a matter of just a few minutes over twelve hundred tons of bombs rained down onto the target, and an estimated 82% of its built-up area was reduced to ruins. Seven thousand people are believed to have lost their lives, the vast majority as the result of a firestorm. In return, the defences claimed twelve Lancasters, and among them was 106 Squadron's PB281, which came down near the target. Only the rear gunner survived as a PoW from the crew of F/O Thompson, which, apart from the flight engineer, was all-Australian. F/O Dodson was attacked by a JU88, which his gunners claimed as destroyed.

Crew of Flight Lieutenant (acting Squadron Leader) Arthur Barden

Two nights later the southern town of Giessen and its railway yards were the targets for 255 Lancasters and ten Mosquito of 5 Group, while other elements of the Command attacked Leuna and Osnabrück in what was a heavy night of activity involving over thirteen hundred sorties. 106 Squadron provided twenty Lancasters for Giessen, situated forty miles north of Frankfurt, and their crews were among eighty-seven briefed to attack the marshalling yards, while the remainder went for the town itself. It was shortly after 17.00 when the first ones began to roll, and they all got away safely to rendezvous with the other squadrons. F/O Hamilton was forced to make a rare early return after his rear turret became unserviceable, but the remainder pressed on to reach the target and find varying amounts of cloud between three and seven-tenths. Visibility was good, however, and the target indicators were clearly visible. The 106 Squadron crews were over the target between 20.18 and 20.26, and bombed in accordance with instructions from the Master Bomber from an average of 10,000 feet. Returning crews spoke of large fires, and F/Os Norton, Scott and Simpson brought back aiming-point photos, while several others were plotted within a short distance. Reconnaissance confirmed later that both aiming points had sustained severe damage.

As American ground forces continued their advance across the Eifel region of Germany, operations were mounted against the dam at the Urft Reservoir, to prevent its use by the Germans to flood the area. The first small-scale attack was mounted by 8 Group on the 4th, and this was followed up by 5 Group on the 8th, when the force of 205 Lancasters included fourteen from 106 Squadron and nineteen from 617 Squadron carrying Tallboys. The Metheringham crews departed at 09.00 in a sleet storm, and found the target under varying amounts of cloud ranging from four to ten-tenths. This prevented three crews from locating it, while the remainder managed to find sufficient gaps to bomb from 8,000 to 11,500 feet between 11.04 and 11.20. P/O Phelan RCAF and F/L Barden brought back aiming-point photos, and a number of others were plotted within two thousand yards. The conditions were too marginal for the 617 Squadron element, and they returned home with their valuable Tallboys still on board. 129 aircraft did release their bombs, but the attack was scattered and the dam escaped damage. The operation was rescheduled for the following day, and fifteen Lancasters took off from Metheringham at 04.30, but were recalled before they reached the coast because of unfavourable weather conditions. 233 Lancasters took off for the same target at lunch time on the 11th, among them fifteen from 106 Squadron, led by F/Ls Barden and Bretherton. Conditions were hardly improved, and up to nine-tenths cloud with tops at 8,000 feet made life difficult for the Master Bomber. He tried to bring the crews down to below the cloud base, and some complied, while others bombed through gaps. All but three of the 106 Squadron crews attacked from 4,000 to 7,500 feet either side of 15.00 without being able to assess the results, but aiming point photos were obtained by F/Os Arnot RAAF and Hamilton, and most of the others were plotted within a mile. Reconnaissance revealed a number of hits on the dam, but no breach occurred.

The award of a DFC was announced on the 12th to S/L Allinson and F/Os Netherwood and Coen. The final heavy night attack of the war on Essen was mounted that night without a 5 Group element, and on the following night a 54 Base force of fifty-two Lancasters and seven Mosquitos from 106, 83, 97 and 627 Squadrons was dispatched to attack the German cruiser Emden (squadron ORB, while other sources state Köln) at berth at Horten in Oslo Fjord. 106 Squadron supported the operation with twenty Lancasters, which took off at 15.30 as the main force element, carrying eleven 1,000 pounders each. They reached the target to find cloudless conditions and good visibility, but the target vessel could not be identified, possibly because it had been moved to a new location. Nine crews withheld their bombs after failing to positively identify the vessel, but eleven others bombed by the light of flares between 19.03 and 19.18 from an average of 8,000 feet in accordance with the raid controller's instructions. Some crews aimed at ships moored off Bluecher Quay, but no results were observed, and all of the participants returned safely home. F/O Stansfield brought back a photo of a cruiser, which was presumed to be the Köln, lying just north of Ostoya, an island a short distance to the north of Horten.

The main operation on the night of the 15/16th was directed at Ludwigshafen in southern Germany, home to a number of I.G.Farben factories, which were using slave workers in the production of synthetic oil. The attack was highly destructive, particularly in terms of the industrial damage inflicted, and was carried out without the assistance of 5 Group. 106 Squadron was the only 5 Group unit active on this night, providing fifteen Lancasters for a mining effort in the Spinach garden area off Danzig in the Baltic. They took off shortly after midnight, each carrying either five MkIV or four MkVI mines, and, after F/O Anderson turned back with a number of technical issues, the remainder arrived in the target area to find ten-tenths cloud with tops averaging out at 15,000 feet. Using H2S thirteen crews located their drop zones and successfully delivered their stores. ND682 failed to return to Metheringham after being brought down in the target area, and there were no survivors from the crew of F/O Barratt. It is interesting to note that the rear gunner, Sgt Green, was thirty-nine years old, and well beyond the normal age of aircrew.

The night of the 17/18th was another of heavy activity for the Command, in which more than thirteen hundred sorties were launched. The largest operation, which involved a 4 and 6 Group main force, was directed at Duisburg, while 1 Group almost obliterated the southern city of Ulm. 5 Group went to Munich with 280 Lancasters, thirteen of which were provided by 106 Squadron, led by W/C Stevens. They began to depart Metheringham at 16.30, and all arrived at the target to find almost cloudless skies and good visibility. The marking was accurate and concentrated upon the aiming points, the city centre and the railway installations, and they bombed a cluster of red TIs with a twenty-three-second overshoot in accordance with the Master Bomber's instructions. The Metheringham crews were over the target at 11,000 to 12,000 feet between 22.00 and 22.10, and only one failed to bomb after arriving too late. Returning crews claimed a highly destructive attack, which left the city centre and the railway targets devastated.

On the following night it was the turn of the distant Baltic port of Gdynia to play host to the Group, for which 106 Squadron put up fourteen Lancasters in an overall heavy force of 236. The targets were shipping generally, aiming-point A, and the cruiser Lützow in particular, aiming-point B, and the 106 Squadron crews were allotted in the ratio of twelve and two respectively. There was no cloud over the target, and visibility was good, but an effective smoke screen and intense light flak hampered identification of the aiming-points. The 106 Squadron crews were over the target either side of 22.00, and bombed in accordance with the Master Bomber's instructions from between 11,000 and 14,000 feet. It was not possible to make an accurate assessment of results, but bomb bursts were seen across the docks and quaysides. F/Os Arnott and Stansfield brought back aiming-point photos of the Lützow, and there were aiming-point A photos from Capt Pechey and F/O Newenham. Reconnaissance confirmed that damage had been inflicted upon shipping, port installations and residential property in the waterfront districts, at a cost of four Lancasters. Sadly, the squadron's NN726 was one of those failing to return, after being brought down in the target area. F/L Pritchard was killed with four of his crew, while both gunners escaped with their lives to become PoWs.

A particularly testing operation was mounted by the group on the night of the 21/22nd, which again involved a long round trip to Germany's north-eastern coast. The target was the oil refinery at Politz near Stettin, and, unusually for a standard operation, 617 Squadron was included on the order of battle[6]. The effort produced some damage to the plant, but it was by no means crippled, and the returning crews were faced with fogbound airfields at the end of their long and exhausting flights, causing five aircraft to be involved in crashes. 106 Squadron did not take part in the main operation, but sent two Lancasters to a railway junction at Schneidemühl (believed to lie between Berlin and Stettin) as a diversion, and ten others to lay mines in the Silverthorn garden area in the Kattegat. F/L Gilbert and F/O Scott took off in thick fog at 16.35 an 16.55 respectively, and found their way to the target area some three-and-a-half hours later, to deliver four 1,000 pounders and seven 500 pounders each from 15,000 feet. The gardeners were led away by W/C Stevens either side of 17.00, by which time only a quarter of the length of the runway was visible through the murk. They found ten-tenths cloud in the target area, which was not a problem as they were delivering their MkVI mines from high-level by means of H2S. W/C Stevens, however, having flown all the way to the waters off eastern Demark, found his H2S to be malfunctioning, and jettisoned his stores "safe". The others were all successful, and were diverted to Banff and Dallachy in Scotland on return.

Thereafter the group settled in at home for the Christmas period, probably more as a result of fog than of operational requirements, and was not called upon again until Boxing Day. It was then that elements from all of the groups were detailed to bomb enemy troop concentrations at St Vith, as the German breakout, known as the Battle of the Bulge, ground to a halt. 106 Squadron stayed at home on this occasion, and remained there until the night of the 28/29th, when it dispatched eleven Lancasters to lay mines in the Silverthorn and Yew Tree gardens in the Kattegat Channel between Denmark and Sweden. W/C Stevens was again the senior pilot on duty as they took off either side of 19.30, five bound for Silverthorn and six for Yew Tree. They all found their respective gardens in ideal weather conditions, and delivered between them a total of sixty-five mines by H2S from an average of 14,000 feet before returning safely home. The squadron operated for the final time in the year in the early hours of the 31st, when sending a dozen Lancasters as part of a 5 Group force to attack an enemy supply line at Houffalize in the Ardennes region of Belgium. They took off either side of 02.30, and found the target area under nine to ten-tenths cloud, which made identification very difficult. Five of the squadron's crews bombed on target indicators from an average of 10,000 feet, but seven others were unable to pick up the markers in time, and returned with their bombs. During the course of the month the squadron carried out operations on two days and ten nights, and dispatched 184 sorties for the loss of three aircraft and crews.

---

[6] This location is often wrongly spelled Pölitz, which is a town in Germany's Schleswig-Holstein region at the western end of the Baltic.

Confidence was high that the New Year would bring the long awaited victory, although no one knew how long the resistance of the tenacious enemy would last. What could be confidently stated, however, was that the Command had risen phoenix-like from the dark days of Berlin, and had contributed magnificently to the success of the land campaign, while maintaining a stranglehold on Germany's capacity to produce vital munitions and fuel stuffs.

January 1945

Flying Officer W Ted Hamilton and colleagues clearing snow in January 1945.

Although the tantalising scent of victory was in the air, much remained to be done, and despite chronic fuel shortages, the Luftwaffe continued to throw itself into battle, even though it was stretched beyond its capacity to defend every corner of the Reich. The New Year began with a flourish when the Luftwaffe launched its ill-conceived and ultimately ill-fated Operation Bodenplatte (Baseplate) at first light on the 1st, to catch the Allied air forces on the ground at the recently liberated airfields in France, Holland and Belgium. The modest success achieved was scant compensation for the loss of 250 front-line day fighters and fighter-bombers, around 150 of whose pilots were killed, wounded or became prisoners of the Allies, and it was a setback from which the Luftwaffe would never fully recover.

Later in the morning, ten 106 Squadron Lancasters joined ninety-two others and two Mosquitos of 5 Group to pay a visit to the Dortmund-Ems Canal at Ladbergen. They took off either side of 08.00, and were well on their way when LL748 lost an engine, forcing Lt Howes SAAF to turn back. The others reached the target without incident, and were able to identify it visually under cloudless skies and in good visibility. They bombed from an average of 11,000 feet between 11.16 and 11.18, aiming at the aqueduct section or the raised embankments, and returned safely to Metheringham with eight aiming-point photos. The operation was a success, which left the waterway breached again at a cost of two Lancasters. It was during this operation that F/S Thompson of 9 Squadron earned the award of the Victoria Cross, although sadly, it would have to be conferred posthumously, as he succumbed to his burns three weeks after his heroic actions. That evening 5 Group revisited the Mittelland Canal at Gravenhorst with 147 Lancasters and five Mosquitos, of which 106 Squadron provided nine of the former, led by W/C Stevens. The fine weather had persisted throughout the day, and the target was easily identified and marked for the main force element. The 106 Squadron crews bombed from an average of 10,000 feet between 19.13 and 19.16, and claimed good results, although an accurate assessment could not be made as most of the bombs contained delay fuses. Bad weather at Metheringham caused a diversion to northern stations on return either side of midnight, and when the photos were plotted, seven were found to be of the aiming point. Reconnaissance later confirmed that the operation had succeeded in causing further breaches.

A controversial operation took place in the early hours of the 5th against the French town of Royan, situated at the mouth of the River Gironde. The presence of a German garrison was preventing Allied access to the port of Bordeaux, and the operation was mounted in response to requests from Free French Forces, which were laying siege. The garrison commander magnanimously offered to evacuate the civilian population, but it seems that most declined, and many of these were to suffer the consequences in the ensuing bombing. 1 and 5 Group joined forces to provide 340 Lancasters, of which sixteen represented 106 Squadron. They began taking off at 00.10, led for the first time by S/L Bretherton, who had been promoted a week earlier and installed as A Flight commander in succession to S/L Allinson. It was approaching 04.00 as they lined up for the bombing run in cloudless skies and excellent visibility, but the start of the attack was delayed for two minutes to allow misplaced markers to be corrected. The 106 Squadron crews delivered their cookie and sixteen 500 pounders each from 8,500 to 11,200 feet on Pathfinder markers between 04.03 and 04.08, and witnessed an oil fire emitting volumes of black smoke. Four Lancasters crashed after becoming involved in mid-air collisions, and F/O A H Scott's PB617 was lost in this manner. It collided with 463 Squadron's PB695 in the target area, and all fourteen men lost their lives. F/O Scott was a member of the RAAF, as were the others in his crew with the exception of the RAF flight engineer. Over fifteen hundred tons of high explosives reduced around 85% of the town to rubble, and killed an estimated 30% of the civilian inhabitants. In the event, the French forces did not capture the town until mid-April.

While other elements of the Command were renewing acquaintances with Hanover on the night of the 5/6th, 140 Lancasters and Mosquitos of 5 Group attacked with great accuracy the previously mentioned enemy supply line at Houffalize in the Belgian Ardennes. 106 Squadron put up a dozen Lancasters, which departed Metheringham either side of 00.30, and one returned early with a coolant leak. The others found the target hidden beneath ten-tenths low cloud, which made the markers difficult to see. Three crews retained their bombs after failing to identify the aiming-point, but the others bombed from 9,000 to 11,400 feet between 03.04 and 03.10, and returned without incident. Hanau and Neuss were the main targets on the night of the 6/7th, neither of them involving 5 Group, but twenty Lancasters were sent mining off Baltic ports, and among these were five from 106 Squadron, whose crews were assigned to the Spinach garden, the approaches to the port of Gdynia in Danzig Bay. S/L Bretherton led them away either side of 16.00, and they all arrived in the target area some four-and-a-half-hours later to find good visibility above the complete cloud cover. They located their drop zones by H2S, and each delivered five mines as briefed from around 14,000 feet, before returning safely home.

The last major raid of the war on Munich took place on the night of the 7/8th, and was a two-phase attack conducted by over six hundred aircraft drawn from 1, 3, 5, 6 and 8 Groups. 5 Group went in first, dispatching 213 Lancasters, sixteen of which returned early. Sixteen Lancasters began to depart Metheringham at 16.40 led by W/C Stevens, and, after forming up, set out on the long journey across France to southern Germany. F/L Barron was forced back with technical issues, but the remainder arrived in the target area to encounter small amounts of medium-level broken cloud. The marking was assessed as accurate, and the 106 Squadron crews bombed on clusters of green TIs from 18,000 to 20,000 feet between 20.23 and 20.35. PB724 encountered a snow storm and severe icing conditions on the way home, and while trying to get underneath it, crashed at Meligny-le-Grand, thirty-five miles west of Nancy, after hitting trees. F/O J N Scott and four of the others on board were killed, while the wireless operator and rear gunner sustained severe injuries from which they ultimately recovered. Two hours after the 5 Group assault the second phase force arrived over the city, and inflicted further extensive damage on central and industrial districts.

After almost a week away from the operational scene the group prepared 218 Lancasters and seven Mosquitos on the 13th for a return that night to the oil refinery at Politz, which it had previously visited towards the end of December. Ten 106 Squadron Lancasters departed Metheringham between 16.15 and 16.30 led by F/L Barden, who was about to be promoted to take over as B Flight commander. A blind bombing attack had been planned to deal with the forecast weather conditions, but once at the target they turned out to be much clearer than anticipated, and this allowed for low-level marking to be carried out. Bombing took place in accordance with the Master Bomber's instructions from an average of 17,500 feet between 22.15 and 22.27, and all returned without incident with bombing photos plotted at 550 to 2,400 yards from the aiming-point. Photographic reconnaissance suggested that the plant was now in ruins. While this operation was in progress a further four Metheringham crews were laying mines in the Geraniums garden off Swinemünde. They found ten-tenths low cloud at the target, but employed H2S to establish their positions, and successfully delivered their stores from 14,000 feet shortly before 22.00.

Twenty-four hours later the oil offensive continued at Merseburg near Leuna in eastern Germany, for which a force of 573 Lancasters and fourteen Mosquitos was prepared, drawn from 1, 5, 6 and 8 Groups. The operation was carried out in two waves three hours apart, and 5 Group led the way with 210 Lancasters departing their stations either side of 16.00. A dozen took off from Metheringham led by S/L Bretherton, but F/O day returned early with an unserviceable rear turret. The remainder pushed on to find the target under clear skies, with some ground haze, and they bombed on green TIs with a fourteen second overshoot in accordance with the controller's instructions. *(The ORB summary describes ten-tenths cloud cover, and no bombing photos because of it. However, the individual crew statements all mention no cloud, and two reports specified bombing photos plotted at 1,600 yards from the aiming-point).* They were over the aiming-point at an average height of 15,000 feet between 21.02 and 21.07, and contributed to a highly successful attack. The second phase followed up with great accuracy and left the plant severely damaged. PB122 did not arrive home with the others, and it was learned later that it had flown into the ground at an acute angle near Vignacourt at 23.59. It was on the way home when it crashed, approaching Abbeville, and just forty miles from the coast and safety, and there were no survivors from the crew of F/O McIntosh RAAF.

Another long trek took over two hundred Lancasters and Mosquitos of 1 and 5 Groups to Brüx in Czechoslovakia, to attack the oil refinery on the night of the 16/17th. The operation involved fourteen 106 Squadron Lancasters, which took off either side of 18.00 for what would be a nine-hour round trip. They were each carrying a cookie and eight 500 pounders, one of which had a seventy-two-hour delay fuse. F/L Barden had to turn back with a failed starboard-inner engine, but the others all reached the target to find ten-tenths cloud and a smoke screen. The Pathfinder markers were accurate, and the squadron participants bombed them from 14,200 to 16,700 feet between 22.32 and 22.37, and all returned safely from what was confirmed to be an outstanding success, and another major setback to the enemy's oil production. The Group was involved in just one more operation before the end of the month, and this was a smallish area attack on Gelsenkirchen in company with elements of 4 and 8 Groups on the night of the 22/23rd. 106 Squadron was not involved in this operation, and finished the month with a tally of 108 sorties from operations on one day and eight nights, in return for the loss of three aircraft and crews. On the 24th the squadron was notified that it had won the coveted silver Lancaster trophy for the fewest avoidable accidents in the group during the final quarter of the year. There was not a single avoidable accident during the period, despite the squadron flying more hours than any other 5 Group unit. Having already held the trophy for the January to June period, the squadron had been "Top Dogs" in this category for nine months of 1944.

February 1945

February began with three main targets on the night of the 1/2nd, Ludwigshafen and Mainz for 1, 4, 6 and 8 Groups, and Siegen for 5 Group. 271 Lancaster crews were briefed to attack the town and its marshalling yards, situated some sixty miles east of Cologne. This would prove to be one of a number of failures during the first week of the month, caused largely by bad weather conditions in the vicinity of the targets. 106 Squadron provided fifteen aircraft for this operation, which began taking off shortly after 16.00 led by F/L Barden. They all reached the target area to find ten-tenths cloud with tops at 5,000 feet, and were instructed by the controller to aim at the skymarkers, which were being driven by the strong wind across the intended aiming-point. The glow of red target indicators was faintly visible through the clouds, but this was most likely the dummy site prepared by the Germans. It attracted many bomb loads, perhaps some from the 106 Squadron participants, who bombed from 8,000 to 12,000 feet between 19.29 and 19.33, and as a result, the target escaped serious damage, although the railway station was hit. Three Lancasters were shot down during the operation, and a fourth, 106 Squadron's LM215, crash-landed at Juvincourt airfield on the way home. This aircraft had been damaged by flak, but no injuries were reported among the crew of F/O Gray.

5 Group delivered the last major raid of the war on Karlsruhe on the night of the 2/3rd, when 250 Lancasters and eleven Mosquitos took off in mid-evening to head out across France. 106 Squadron put up fifteen aircraft, and those reaching the target encountered complete cloud cover, which thwarted any attempt by the Mosquito markers to find their aiming point. The Metheringham crews bombed on the glow of markers as instructed by the Master Bomber from 12,000 to 16,000 feet between 23.19 and 23.26, and all returned safely. The operation was a complete failure, and cost fourteen Lancasters, four of them from 189 Squadron stationed at Fulbeck, a dozen miles to the south-west of Metheringham.

There was little action for 5 Group thereafter until the evening of the 7th, when 177 Lancasters and eleven Mosquitos took off for the next attempt to disrupt the Dortmund-Ems Canal at Ladbergen. A dozen 106 Squadron Lancasters took off shortly after 21.00, each carrying twelve 1,000 pounders and a single 500 pounder, and, after one had turned back with excessive fuel consumption, the others reached the target to find seven to ten-tenths cloud. They bombed through gaps from 8,500 to 11,500 feet just after midnight on the controller's instructions, but could not assess the outcome as all bombs contained delay fuses. It turned out to be a rare unsuccessful attack on this target, photographic reconnaissance revealing that the bombs had fallen into fields, and had failed to cause any breach. While this operation was in progress, the frontier towns of Goch and Cleves were being pasted by the other Groups in support of an advance by the British XXX Corps.

The final attack on the oil refinery at Politz was delivered by 1, 5 and 8 Groups in two waves on the night of the 8/9th. The first phase was entirely a 5 Group affair employing low level marking, while a contingent of Pathfinders marked in standard fashion for the 1 Group second phase. The whole operation was conducted with great precision, and the refinery contributed no more oil to Germany's war effort. 106 Squadron was not involved in the main operation, but sent nine Lancasters to Neubrandenburg in north-eastern Germany as a diversion. They took off either side of 17.00, with F/O Laidlaw RAAF acting as raid controller, and set out for the target, which was only sixty miles short of Politz. They arrived at the target shortly before 21.00 and delivered flares and target markers from 12,500 feet to simulate a full raid. To add a little more realism they also dropped fifteen-and-a-half tons of bombs between them. The diversion was considered to be a success, and congratulatory messages were received on their safe return. While these crews were spoofing the enemy, six others from the squadron laid mines in the Geraniums garden off Swinemünde, led by S/L Bretherton. They picked up coastal pinpoints visually, confirmed by H2S, and F/O Hamilton used the now defunct rocket research site of Peenemünde on the island of Usedom as the starting point for his timed run. A total of twenty-four mines were successfully planted, and all aircraft returned safely home.

There was again relative inactivity for the Group between the above mentioned operation and the start of the Churchill-inspired series of heavy raids against Germany's eastern cities under Operation Thunderclap. These got underway at Dresden on the night of 13/14th in a two-phase attack led by 5 Group, which dispatched 246 Lancasters and nine Mosquitos. 106 Squadron contributed seventeen aircraft led by W/C Stevens, which took off in a ten-minute slot from 18.05. They all reached the target area to find a thin layer of ten-tenths cloud, through which they could make out the glow of red target indicators delivered by the low-level visual marking Mosquitos of 627 Squadron. The 106 Squadron crews bombed on the instructions of the Master Bomber from 13,000 to 15,250 feet with a thirty-second overshoot, and were on their way home by 22.30. They were among the 244 who delivered eight hundred tons of bombs into the city, and started fires which, not only could be seen from 150 miles into the return journey, but would also act as a beacon to the all-Lancaster force from 1, 3, 6 and 8 Groups following three hours behind. A further eighteen hundred tons of bombs from them would seal the fate of this ancient and historic city, and set off the same chain of events that had overwhelmed parts of Hamburg in July 1943. A firestorm developed, perhaps, of equal proportions to that at Hamburg, and the population, which was swelled by tens of thousands of refugees from the eastern front, underwent a terrifying ordeal. Various estimates of the death toll have been presented over the years, but it is now believed that around twenty-five thousand people lost their lives.

Ever since the above events, this operation has been held as the prime example of the unacceptable face of indiscriminate bombing of population centres, and has been used by the anti-war lobby to vilify Harris and his crews. There has also been much misinformation from German eyewitnesses, which has coloured opinions, not least of which is the assertion that RAF aircraft came down to rooftop height to strafe the helpless victims in the streets and open spaces. There is no basis in such claims, and it should be remembered that an American raid took place in daylight within hours of the RAF attack, and was covered by escort fighters, which might, in isolated cases, have flown low over the city. Curiously, no fingers have been wagged at them. Harris showed little interest in attacking Dresden, and carried out the raid in response to repeated urgings from Churchill via Chief of the Air Staff, Sir Charles Portal. Shortly afterwards, with a forthcoming election in mind, Churchill betrayed Harris by distancing himself from the area bombing policy.

On the night after Dresden a Thunderclap force of 499 aircraft drawn from 1, 3, 4, 6 and 8 Groups headed for Chemnitz, where unfavourable weather conditions led to a scattered attack, and a large proportion of the effort was wasted in open country. While this operation was in progress, a 230-strong 5 Group force was also active over eastern Germany, attacking an oil refinery at Rositz near Leipzig. 106 Squadron provided seventeen Lancasters, which took off either side of 17.00 led by S/L Bretherton. They arrived to

Crew of Wing Commander MMJ Stevens in front of Lancaster LM690, ZN-P, 'Come on Steve'.

find the target hidden beneath ten-tenths cloud, but the marking was assessed as accurate, and the Metheringham crews delivered their cookie and 500 pounders from 8,000 to 11,500 feet in accordance with the controller's instructions between 21.05 and 21.18. It was not possible to assess the outcome, but the glow of large fires through the clouds seemed to confirm the crews' belief that it was an effective attack. Photo-reconnaissance later confirmed damage to the southern end of the plant.

The squadron sent four Lancasters mining in the Silverthorn garden in the Kattegat Channel on the night of the 15/16th, led by S/L Bretherton. They took off at 16.45, and shortly afterwards S/L Bretherton lost his starboard-outer engine. Undaunted, he pressed on to the target, using H2S to pinpoint on Anholt Island, before making a timed run to the release point. The others were equally successful, pinpointing on Sjaellands Point or Hessel Island, and all returned safely having delivered six mines each. A return to the oil campaign on the night of the 19/20th saw seventeen of the squadron's Lancasters prepared as part of a 5 Group force of 260 aircraft bound for the refinery at Böhlen, some twelve miles south of Leipzig. It was a late take-off, in the twenty-five minutes before midnight, and W/C Stevens was the senior pilot on duty, supported by S/L Bretherton and the newly promoted S/L Barden. They all reached the target to find ten-tenths cloud with tops at 7,000 feet, and bombed on the glow of red TIs beneath the cloud in accordance with the controller's instructions. The Metheringham crews were over the target at an average of 16,500 feet between 04.19 and 04.41, and none was able to make an assessment of results. The plant escaped with only superficial damage, possibly as the result of the loss of the Master Bomber, W/C Benjamin DFC & Bar from 54 Base at Coningsby, who died alongside his navigator when their 627 Squadron Mosquito was shot down by flak over the target.

While elements from the other Groups were busy at Dortmund, Düsseldorf and Monheim on the night of the 20/21st, 5 Group made a further attempt on the Mittelland Canal at Gravenhorst, for which 106 Squadron contributed ten Lancasters. They took off either side of 22.00, and landed back at Metheringham six hours later with nothing to show for their efforts. Heavy cloud prevented accurate marking, and the Master Bomber decided to send the force home with its bombs. On the following night, however, while Duisburg and Worms provided the main fare, 5 Group set off to return to the canal, again with ten 106 Squadron Lancasters in attendance. They were airborne by 17.20, led by S/L Bretherton, and this time they found the target area to be cloud-free, and the visibility excellent. The marking was accurate and concentrated, and the 106 Squadron crews delivered their 1,000 and 500 pounders from 8,300 to 11,000 feet between 20.27 and 20.40, before returning home with eight aiming point photos. The night photos from the whole force suggested a concentrated attack, but as all of the bombs contained half-hour delay fuses, it was necessary to wait for reconnaissance to be carried out to gain confirmation. In the meantime, the group had time to lick its wounds after thirteen Lancasters failed to return home. Among the missing was the legendary personage of G/C "Tiny" Evans-Evans DFC, the wide-girthed station commander at Coningsby, and commander of 115 Squadron for a spell in 1941. The forty-three-year-old veteran could not shake off the desire to get at the enemy, despite the fact that his size must have been an impediment to fitting into the pilot's seat. He commandeered an 83 Squadron Lancaster, and gathered around him a scratch crew, which included the twenty-two-year-old navigator, S/L William Wishart DSO, DFC & Bar, formerly of 97 Squadron, who had flown seventy-nine operations, including eleven to Berlin. The bomb-aimer, F/L Fitch, was also the holder of a DFC and GM, and all but the rear gunner lost their lives after they were shot down by a night fighter to crash in a liberated region of Holland. One has to commend the courage and spirit of Evans-Evans, but these highly-decorated men making up his crew had already served their country with distinction, and perhaps, should not have been unnecessarily exposed to such danger so close to the end. When the PRU photos were examined, they confirmed that the canal had been breached again, and, according to Bomber Command, "rendered 100% unserviceable".

It was announced on the 23rd that W/C Stevens was to receive a DFC, a highly merited award in recognition of his determination to lead from the front, particularly on the more testing operations against heavily-defended targets. That night Pforzheim became the latest German town to become almost obliterated from the map following its one and only major encounter with Bomber Command. In a twenty-two-minute orgy of destruction 1, 6 and 8 Groups delivered eighteen hundred tons of bombs to reduce more than 80% of the built-up area to rubble and kill seventeen thousand inhabitants. 5 Group went north on this night with a modest force of seventy-three Lancasters, including a dozen from 106 Squadron, to attack what was believed to be a U-Boot base at Horten in Oslo Fjord. They were all safely in the air by 17.30, and they arrived in the target area to find clear skies and good visibility. The marking was accurate, and bombing took place from 10,000 to 11,500 feet in accordance with the Master Bomber's instructions between 20.45 and 20.54. Whether or not a U-Boot base existed is uncertain, but no shipping was seen by the crews, and a local report describes heavy damage in the port area and a shipyard, and the sinking of a tanker and floating crane. F/O Hamilton returned on three engines, and PB296 was ultimately declared a write-off, although there is no explanation in the ORB.

The squadron concluded its operational activities for the month on the night of the 24/25th, when sending nine Lancasters to lay mines in the Onions garden in Oslo Fjord, and was the only 5 Group unit operating. They took off shortly after 17.00, led by W/C Stevens, and found three to five-tenths cloud in the target area, but excellent visibility. H2S was used to locate the garden, and each crew planted six mines as briefed from around 11,500 feet. The presence of a seventy-mile-per-hour wind required the aircraft to be over land as the mines were released, and this demanded the crews' highest skills, while also exposing them to danger from the local defences, and seven of them were coned by searchlights. During the course of the month the squadron undertook ten bombing operations and three mining, and dispatched 153 sorties without loss.

March 1945

March was notable for a number of particular operations, which proved to be the last of the war on the targets concerned, and two of them were landmarks in another respect. The first of these was against Cologne on the morning of the 2nd, when over 850 aircraft were unleashed in two phases to pulverise what little was left standing in the once proud Rhineland capital city. The first wave of seven hundred aircraft bombed in clear conditions, and created further massive damage across the city on the western bank. The follow-up by 3 Group failed to add more than a pinprick after a GH station failed, and only fifteen aircraft bombed. Four days later the battered city fell to American forces. The new month began for 106 Squadron as the old one had ended, with participation by six of its Lancasters in a small mining effort in Oslo Fjord on the night of the 3/4th. They took off at 17.10, but F/L Simpson returned early with engine trouble, leaving the remainder to press on. They reached the target area to find visibility at twenty miles, and located their dropping points by means of H2S, before delivering thirty mines between them from around 10,000 feet. When they arrived home between 01.30 and 02.10 they were diverted to avoid a number of enemy intruders stooging around Metheringham. They ultimately shot the place up, but somehow inflicted no damage. More than two hundred other 5 Group aircraft were aloft on this night, attacking again the aqueduct section of the Dortmund-Ems Canal at Ladbergen, and breaching it in two places to put it permanently out of action. This operation finally brought to an end the group's long running association with this particular target.

Operation Thunderclap returned to Chemnitz on the night of the 5/6th, and rectified the earlier failure, while 5 Group continued the oil offensive with a return to Böhlen. 106 Squadron contributed fourteen Lancasters to the 248 of the type called into action, and they got away after 17.00 led by W/C Stevens, who was supported by S/Ls Barden and Bretherton. F/L Eakins turned back with a fuel leak, but the remainder reached the target to find ten-tenths cloud with tops at between 10,000 and 12,000 feet. The Pathfinders employed sky marking flares, and the 106 Squadron crews bombed from 11,100 to 13,200 feet in a seven-minute slot either side of 22.00 in accordance with instructions from the Master Bomber. A few explosions were noted through the clouds, along with the glow of fires, but no assessment was possible. PRU photographs later revealed some fresh damage to the site.

Briefings took place on the 6th for 191 crews of 5 Group for an operation that night against the small port of Sassnitz on the north-eastern corner of the island of Rügen, about fifty miles north of Peenemünde. 150 aircraft were to attack the port and its installations, while the remainder went for shipping in or near the harbour. 106 Squadron put up ten aircraft to attack shipping, and they were all safely off the ground by 18.30. They arrived in the target area to find four to seven-tenths cloud with tops at around 7,000 feet, but visibility was good, and the target easily identified. As F/O Penney ran up on a passenger liner, which he assessed at fifteen to twenty-five thousand tons, he saw it straddled by the bombs from two other aircraft. He followed up from 8,200 feet at 23.00, but cloud immediately obscured his view, and the results of his efforts were missed. F/O Roberts attacked the same vessel nine minutes later, and watched his bombs fall alongside, at which point the Lancaster sustained damage from an unknown cause, which included a large hole in the pilot's Perspex. F/O Barrow lost his hydraulics immediately after bombing, and flew all the way back to the emergency strip at Carnaby with his bomb doors open. F/O Hill reported a warship heading eastwards into open sea with a list to port, and F/O Kiesling spotted white smoke and flame issuing forth from a ship anchored amongst other ships offshore. Reconnaissance revealed later that three ships had been sunk, and part of the town had suffered extensive damage.

The oil refinery at Harburg, situated on the southern bank of the Elbe opposite Hamburg, was the target for 5 Group on the night of the 7/8th, for which 221 Lancasters were dispatched. 106 Squadron provided thirteen aircraft, which were off the ground by 18.30 led by S/L Barden. They arrived over the target to find eight-tenths cloud and red and yellow target indicators, which they bombed in accordance with the Master Bomber's instructions with a seven-second overshoot from 10,750 to 11,500 feet either side of 22.00. Bomb bursts were clearly seen, along with explosions and black smoke rising to 6,000 feet. All returned safely to Metheringham confident in the success of the operation, and this was confirmed by photographic reconnaissance, which revealed that a rubber factory had also been severely damaged.

The final raid of the war on Essen took place in the early afternoon of the 11th, when a new all time record force of 1,079 aircraft took off. 5 Group's contribution was 199 Lancasters, of which fourteen represented 106 Squadron, and a single Mosquito. The Metheringham contingent took off shortly after midday, led by W/C Stevens with S/L Bretherton in support. The city was covered by ten-tenths cloud, which required the Pathfinder element to employ skymarkers in the form of red and blue smoke puffs, and these were bombed by the 106 Squadron crews from 16,000 to 19,000 feet in a five-minute slot to 15.23. Over 4,600 tons of bombs left the city in a state of paralysis, from which there was no recovery, and American ground forces would capture it unopposed on the 10th of April.

The new record stood for just a little over twenty-four hours, and was surpassed when 1,108 aircraft departed their stations for the last raid of the war on Dortmund on the following afternoon, and delivered a record 4,800 tons of bombs. This time 5 Group provided 211 Lancasters, fourteen of them from 106 Squadron, which departed Metheringham at 13.30 led by S/L Barden, who had the station commander, G/C Heath, with him on board SW248. The Ruhr was still under a blanket of ten-tenths cloud, this time with tops at 6,000 feet, and the Pathfinders marked the target with green and blue smoke puffs. The 106 Squadron crews were directed by the Master Bomber to aim for the blues, which they did from 15,500 to 16,800 feet between 16.47 and 16.54, and returning crews spoke of brown smoke climbing through the clouds from the northern end of the city, and also a ring of smoke encircling the area. F/O Penney lost an engine while outbound, and arrived later than the others, to eventually bomb from 13,300 feet at 16.57. One 500 pounder hung-up, and he brought it back home on three engines, having contributed to another devastating attack, which left the city broken and in chaos. Just two aircraft failed to return, and one of them was the first to be posted missing by 106 Squadron for six weeks. RA508 was lost without trace, and it was a tragedy that P/O Baker and his crew should lose their lives so close to the end.

The night of the 14/15th took 244 Lancasters and eleven Mosquitos of 5 Group to Lutzkendorf, west of Leipzig, to attack the Wintershall synthetic oil refinery. Fifteen 106 Squadron aircraft lined up for take-off at 17.00, and they got away safely to rendezvous with the rest of the force. The conditions in the target area were described variously as ten-tenths cloud, no cloud, thin layer of cloud, thin banks of stratus with tops at 12,000 feet, a little medium cloud, poor visibility, good visibility, but there was unanimity with regard to the haze. Bombing was carried out on red and green target indicators in accordance with the Master Bomber's instructions from 8,000 to 11,000 feet between 22.02 and 22.07, and returning crews claimed an accurate attack, reporting explosions and fires, and thick black smoke ascending over the plant. Fourteen aircraft arrived safely in English air space, but conditions over Lincolnshire led to them being diverted to a number of airfields further south, including Silverstone, Chelveston and Gransden Lodge. Night fighters were out in force in the target area and on the return route, and the group lost eighteen Lancasters, 7.4% of the force. Among them was 106 Squadron's LL948, which came down near Karlsruhe, and from which only the rear gunner survived to be taken prisoner. The remainder of the crew of F/O Barrow RAAF have no known grave, and their names are commemorated on the Runnymede Memorial, having the sad distinction of being the last to lose their lives while operating on behalf of 106 Squadron.

Later that day, W/C Levis became the squadron's final wartime commanding officer on the departure of W/C Stevens, who was promoted to group captain and posted to Coningsby, presumably as station commander. George Levis was a fine sportsman, who had represented the RAF College at athletics, cross-country, boxing, football and cricket. He presided over his first operation on the night of the 16/17th, when the squadron provided a dozen Lancasters as part of an overall 5 Group heavy force of 225 aircraft, with eleven Mosquitos to carry out the marking. The target was Würzburg, a small city on the River Main, some ninety miles north-north-east of Stuttgart, where the railway infrastructure in the south was to be the point of focus for 106 Squadron. They were airborne from Metheringham by 18.00, and arrived in the target area to find clear skies and good visibility, and red and yellow target indicators already marking the aiming point. The Master Bomber called for a thirty-second overshoot, with which they complied, delivering their cookies and incendiaries from 12,000 to 12,300 feet in a seven-minute slot from 21.33. This was in the early stages of the attack, before fires had taken hold, but as the 106 Squadron crews turned for home, it was clear that fires were developing around the main aiming point further to the north. PRU photographs revealed that 89% of the city's built-up area had been reduced to ruins, and it was established later that at least four thousand people had been killed.

The synthetic oil plant at Böhlen was finally put out of action for good by a 5 Group attack on the night of the 20/21st, for which 106 Squadron put up sixteen Lancasters, in an overall heavy force of 224. The squadron was led for the first time by W/C Levis, and there was a late take-off between 23.30 and 23.50, which all accomplished safely. They found three-to-six-tenths thin cloud over the target, with tops up to 8,000 feet, but this was no impediment to the subsequent marking and bombing, which took place in the face of a moderate heavy and light flak defence, searchlights and a smoke screen. The squadron crews bombed on a cluster of red, yellow and green TIs in accordance with the Master Bomber's instructions from 11,100 to 12,800 feet, and they were on their way home before 04.00. Returning crews reported fires and explosions, and it was confirmed later that the plant was still out of action when captured by American forces a few weeks later.

A similar result followed a raid by the group on the Deutsche Erdölwerke refinery at Hamburg twenty-four hours later, for which 106 Squadron dispatched fifteen Lancasters as part of a 5 Group force of 151 plus eight Mosquitos. They took off either side of 01.30, and arrived at the target to find a small amount of thin cloud but good visibility, and the aiming point was easily identified by ground features and red and yellow target indicators. The squadron crews bombed from 15,500 to 18,000 feet between 04.07 and 04.13, and reported one very large explosion, followed by a sheet of flame rising to 4,000 feet. Many other explosions were observed, along with fires creating black smoke, and photo-reconnaissance revealed that twenty storage tanks had been destroyed. The plant was still out of action at the end of the war.

The small town of Wesel, situated on the border with Holland, had the misfortune to find itself in the front line as Allied ground forces advanced across the Rhine. It had become an important centre for enemy troops, and had been under attack from the air for some time to clear enemy resistance. Now, on the night of the 23/24th, elements of 5 and 8 Groups were called upon to deliver what would turn out to be the final blow. 106 Squadron put up fourteen Lancasters for this, its penultimate operation of the month, and they took off safely either side of 19.30, each carrying twelve 1,000 pounders and a single 500 pounder. They found the target under clear skies with slight ground haze, and they were able to identify it visually. The aiming point was well-marked by red and green TIs, which were bombed from 8,000 to 12,000 feet between 22.35 and 22.42 in accordance with the Master Bomber's instructions. The only incident of note was a bird-strike on NG397, which smashed the Perspex windscreen and caused injury to the pilot, F/O Richardson. The bird probably also sustained a headache! P/O Richardson landed at Manston, and was treated in the sick bay before being transferred to hospital. Reconnaissance confirmed the effectiveness of the attack, after which only 3% of Wesel's buildings remained standing. After the war it would claim to be the most completely destroyed town in Germany.

On the 25th it was announced that S/L Parry had been awarded a Bar to his DFC. The final operation of the month took place at lunchtime on the 27th, when ninety-five Lancasters from the group attacked an underground oil storage depot at Farge on the east bank of the Weser, north of Bremen. Fourteen 106 Squadron crews took part, taking off either side of 10.00 led by W/C Levis and S/L Barden. The target was identified visually by the river and railway lines, and F/L Gilbert also picked out a canal on the western bank and a PoW camp on the eastern bank. They aimed their bombs at marshalling yards or sidings, which were apparently concealing the storage tanks, releasing them from 15,700 to 17,000 feet shortly after 13.00. The results could not be immediately assessed, as delayed action bombs had been employed, but F/L Simpson remarked on a large plume of black, billowing smoke rising up from the centre of the target area. A simultaneous attack by 617 Squadron was mounted against the nearby Valentin Bunker U-Boot facility, the largest concrete structure then in existence, which was still under construction, and had just had its twenty-three-foot-thick roof concrete poured. Grand Slams and Tallboys penetrated the soft concrete, and the site was abandoned as unrepairable. During the course of the month the squadron operated on three days and nine nights, dispatching 157 sorties for the loss of two aircraft.

April 1945

The new month began for 106 Squadron with a rare accident involving ND501, which crashed on landing at Metheringham at 02.30 on the 3rd on return from a night training exercise. It was declared a write-off, but, happily, there were no injuries to F/O Smythe and his crew. The final month of the bombing war for the heavy brigade began for the group with an attack on what was believed to be a military barracks at Nordhausen, situated east of the Ruhr and some sixty miles south of Brunswick. The operation was mounted on the 4th, following up on a 1 and 8 Group raid on the previous afternoon. The 5 Group attack, by 243 Lancasters, was divided between the barracks and the town, ninety-three to the former and 150, including eighteen from Metheringham, to the latter, led by S/L Bretherton. They were safely airborne by 06.30, and arrived at the target to encounter five-to-seven-tenths cloud with tops as high as 7,000 feet. They were able to identify the target visually, and by red target indicators, and bombed from 12,000 to

Above and top: The crew of F/O Keith Richardson (Simon Sanders).

16,000 feet between 09.16 and 09.21. Some of the early bombing was seen to undershoot, but the Master Bomber corrected this by calling for a five-second overshoot, and, thereafter, the markers were soon obscured by smoke. Returning crews were able to report a concentrated attack on the town, and heavy damage was inflicted. The barracks were also hit, adding to the casualties already inflicted upon the unfortunate slave work force. F/O Boyd RAAF lost an engine outbound, and another on the way home, so opted to lob in at Brussels.

The benzol plant at Molbis near Leipzig was the target for a 5 Group force of 175 Lancasters and eleven Mosquitos on the night of the 7/8th. 106 Squadron provided nine aircraft led by W/C Levis, which departed Metheringham shortly after 18.00 and reached the target area some five hours later to find clear skies and excellent visibility. W/C Levis was among the first to arrive over the aiming-point, by which time he had already been coned in searchlights and damaged by flak as he turned to start his bombing run. He bombed on red and green TIs from 16,300 feet shortly after 23.00, and immediately thereupon he was attacked by a night fighter, which inflicted extensive damage to the starboard main-plane, inner fuel tank, fuselage, mid-upper turret and bomb sight. His gunners scored hits to drive the enemy off, and the Lancaster, RA567, made it home on dwindling fuel reserved to land at Wing. F/O Boyd was also coned by about twenty searchlights as he approached the target, and his crew spotted a BF109 lurking about nine hundred feet above. They took violent evasive action, which completely wrecked the bomb-run, and the load was ultimately jettisoned three miles west of the target. The remaining squadron participants delivered their cookies and 500 pounders from 16,200 to 17,000 feet between 23.03 and 23.07, and all production at the plant ceased for the remainder of the war.

The squadron contributed seventeen aircraft to a 5 Group force of 231 Lancasters and eleven Mosquitos for a return to the Wintershall synthetic oil refinery at Lutzkendorf on the night of the 8/9th. They began taking off at 18.00 led by S/L Bretherton, and found favourable conditions over the target, with clear skies, good visibility and just a little ground haze. They identified the aiming point by means of red and yellow target indicators, and the Master Bomber called for an eleven-second overshoot to compensate for a slight misplacement. The squadron crews bombed from 13,000 to 16,000 feet between 22.45 and 22.51, and returned safely to a diversion to Long Marston, an airfield just south of Stratford upon Avon in Warwickshire. At debriefing they reported explosions and fires at the target, and it was soon confirmed that the plant had been permanently put out of action. 1, 3, 6 and 8 Groups carried out a raid on Kiel on the night of the 13/14th, while a simultaneous mining effort involving over a hundred aircraft went ahead in Kiel Bay and the Kattegat. 106 Squadron contributed five aircraft to the former, Forget-me-not, led away by S/L Barden at 20.25. They found ten-tenths low cloud in the target area, but visibility was good higher up, and H2S enabled them to pinpoint their drop zones. F/O Gray had a mine shake off its carrier during take-off, and, thereafter, it rolled around in the bomb bay, threatening to push the doors open. This one was jettisoned safe, but the other five were delivered in anger from 10,500 feet at 23.19, and the remaining four crews followed up from similar altitudes between 23.27 and 23.41, each planting six mines.

Over 230 aircraft of 5 Group took off very late in the evening of the 16th for distant Pilsen in Czechoslovakia to attack the railway yards. 106 Squadron's NG414, one of eleven Lancasters departing Metheringham, swung out of control during its take-off run, and crashed. Happily, F/O Dean and his crew had scrambled clear before the bomb load went up and destroyed the aircraft. This proved to be the squadron's final aircraft casualty of the war. The incident forced the cancellation of two sorties, leaving eleven Lancasters to depart Metheringham either side of 23.30. They arrived in the target area to find clear skies and slight haze, and the target was identified by red and yellow markers, which the squadron crews

Wing Commander LG Levis and crew.

bombed from 15,100 to 16,000 feet between 04.00 and 04.09. Two large explosions were observed at 04.05, and other vivid explosions and smoke could be seen as they headed away from the target. F/O Harvey was confused by another operation on this night, taking place against railway yards at Schwandorf on the German side of the frontier, south-west of Pilsen, and by the time he identified the correct location, the Master Bomber had called a halt to proceedings. Metheringham remained unserviceable because of the accident, and returning aircraft landed at Harwell and Manston.

The squadron was not called into action when the group sent a small force on the long trek to Cham on the German border with Czechoslovakia on the night of the 17/18th, where the railway yards were completely destroyed. It remained at home also while elements of the group made up a force of over nine hundred aircraft, which reduced the island of Heligoland to the appearance of a cratered moonscape on the 18th. 114 Lancasters from the group returned to Czechoslovakia to deal with the railway yards at Komotau on the 18/19th, and this brought to an end the campaign against communications. It was the afternoon of the 23rd before the squadron next flew in anger, when seventeen Lancasters took off to attack the railway yards and port facilities at Flensburg on the Baltic side of the Schleswig-Holstein peninsular. W/C Levis and S/L Barden were the senior pilots on duty, but the operation was thwarted by cloud conditions during the bombing run, and the 149-strong force was recalled. The final major operation of the war to involve 5 Group took place on the 25th, when eighty-eight Lancasters joined elements of 1 and 8 Groups in an overall force of 359 Lancasters and sixteen Mosquitos to attack Hitler's 'Eagle's Nest' retreat at Berchtesgaden in the Bavarian mountains, and the nearby SS barracks.

106 Squadron was not invited to take part in that somewhat symbolic operation, but contributed fourteen Lancasters to the group's and, indeed, the Command's final offensive operation of the war by heavy bombers. It was an attack by 107 Lancasters and twelve Mosquitos on oil storage tanks at Tonsberg, in the mouth of Oslo Fjord, that same night. The 106 Squadron contingent was led by S/L Bretherton, and they got away from Metheringham in a ten-minute slot from 20.30. F/L Davis lost the use of his a.s.i., so turned back, and, unable to accurately assess his landing speed, decided to use the long runway at Carnaby. Twelve others found the target under eight to ten-tenths cloud, below which the visibility was excellent, and the controller called them down to bomb on clearly visible red and yellow TIs. They did so from 7,900 to 9,900 feet between 23.46 and 23.52, and reported many explosions and black smoke. F/O Smythe had to make a course correction and arrived over the target at 23.55, three minutes after the controller had called a halt, and he brought his bombs home. While this operation was in progress, S/L Barden and F/O Rowley RAAF delivered twelve mines between them into the waters of Oslo Fjord. Sadly, the ORB entry for this night is too corrupted to make out which crew had the honour to be the last to land after this final operation. During the course of the month the squadron operated on two days and five nights, dispatching ninety-three sorties without loss. The squadron learned that it had been awarded the silver Lancaster trophy

for the January to March 1945 quarter for the fewest avoidable accidents. This was the third time the squadron had been so honoured, and it reflected massively on the squadron and the Metheringham service community.

RAF Metheringham catering staff.

As soon as the bombing war concluded, elements of the Command were put on to humanitarian duties, the most urgent of which was Operation Manna, the delivery of food to the starving Dutch people still under enemy occupation. From the end of April through to the 8th of May hundreds of sorties were carried out, although 106 Squadron did not participate. Operation Exodus also began before the war had officially ended, to repatriate the many thousands of PoWs. 106 Squadron was involved in these flights on the 4th of May, when seventeen of its Lancasters brought home 402 former prisoners from Juvincourt, and on the 8th, the day on which the war officially ended, when six aircraft returned 144 men from Rheine. These operations would continue after the cessation of hostilities.

Once 106 Squadron entered the bombing war on the 9th of September 1940, it played a major role in all of the Command's campaigns, and produced a record of service equal to any and surpassed by none. A list of some of those personalities associated with 106 Squadron serves to justify its tremendous spirit. W/C Allen laid the foundations of efficiency, and this was built upon by his successors. W/C Guy Gibson went on to fame as a Dambuster and earned a Victoria Cross, and his 106 Squadron colleagues John Hopgood, who died at the Möhne Dam, and David Shannon, who served under Gibson and Cheshire at 617, and survived the war, went with him into bomber folklore. John Searby, who gained fame as the Master Bomber at Peenemünde, also enjoyed a glittering career, as did John (Dim) Wooldridge, whom Searby replaced as flight commander at 106 Squadron. W/Cs Baxter, Piercy and Stevens understood that effective leadership came from the front, and they were supported admirably by their flight commanders, many of whom paid the ultimate price for their devotion to duty. 106 Squadron was, without doubt, one of the finest in Bomber Command, and had Harris decided to take a squadron out of the line to tackle the dams operation, it seems likely that 106 would have been given the job. It carried out the fourth highest number of overall Lancaster operations in Bomber Command, and the third highest number of Lancaster overall operations and sorties in 5 Group.

.

The memory of this magnificent squadron and its final station is perpetuated by the Friends of Metheringham Association, based at the visitor's centre at Westmoor Farm, Martin Moor, Metheringham, Lincolnshire. It is a vibrant community of volunteer enthusiasts and members, who keep alive the memory of those who graced the squadron through five unrelenting years of war. Close by lies the former airfield, now returned to farmland, wherein stands a monument to the memory of all who served there.

They also served: WAAFs of the Intelligence Section brief aircrew.

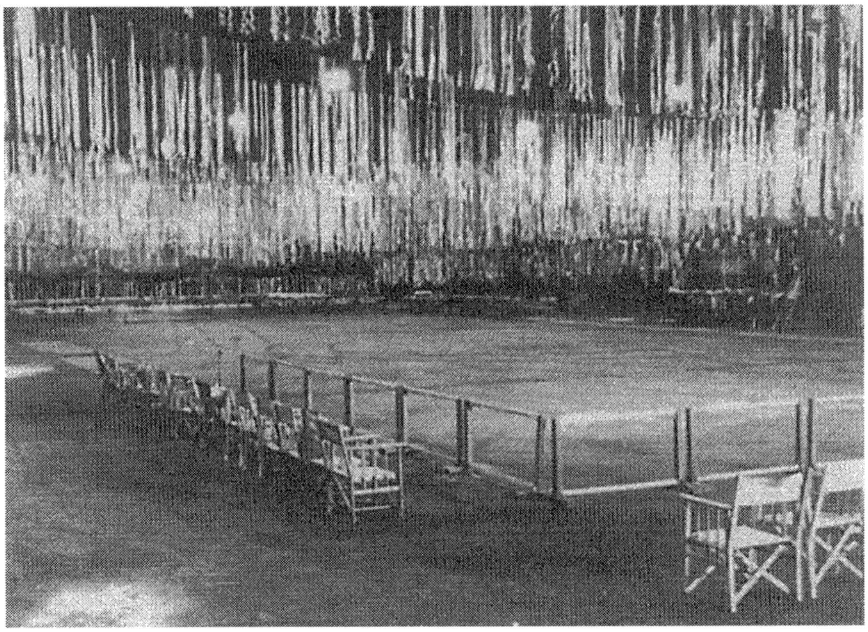

The party can start...Strips of 'Window' find a new purpose as bunting for the station's VE Day party.

Section Two: Key Facts about 106 Squadron

Stations

COTTESMORE	01.09.39. to 06.10.39.
FINNINGLEY	06.10.39. to 23.02.41.
CONINGSBY	23.02.41. to 01.10.42.
SYERSTON	01.10.42. to 11.11.43.
METHERINGHAM	11.11.43. to 18.02.46.

Commanding Officers

WING COMMANDER G R MONTGOMMERIE	08.10.38. to 16.06.40.
SQUADRON LEADER R D STUBBS DFC (Temp)	16.06.40. to 02.11.40.
WING COMMANDER W J H LINDLAY	02.11.40. to 28.02.41.
WING COMMANDER P J POLGLASE	01.03.41 to 05.04.41.
SQUADRON LEADER R.P. NELMS (Temp)	09.04.41. to 04.05.41.
WING COMMANDER R S ALLEN DFC	04.05.41. to 20.03.42.
WING COMMANDER G P GIBSON DSO DFC	20.03.42. to 14.03.43.
WING COMMANDER J H SEARBY DFC	14.03.43. to 09.05.43.
WING COMMANDER R E BAXTER DFC	09.05.43. to 30.03.44.
WING COMMANDER E K PIERCY DFC	30.03.44. to 25.08.44.
WING COMMANDER M M J STEVENS DFC	25.08.44. to 15.03.45.
WING COMMANDER L G LEVIS	15.03.45. to 18.02.46.

Aircraft

HAMPDEN	05.39. to 03.42.
MANCHESTER	02.42. to 06.42.
LANCASTER I/III	05.42. to 02.46.

Operational Record

OPERATIONS	SORTIES	AIRCRAFT LOSSES	% LOSSES
557	5745	169	2.9

CATEGORY OF OPERATIONS

BOMBING	MINING	OTHER
471	82	4

HAMPDEN

OPERATIONS	SORTIES	AIRCRAFT LOSSES	% LOSSES
150	1230	55	4.5

CATEGORY OF OPERATIONS

BOMBING	MINING
106	44

MANCHESTER

OPERATIONS	SORTIES	AIRCRAFT LOSSES	% LOSSES
36	151	9	6.0

CATEGORY OF OPERATIONS

BOMBING	MINING	OTHER
19	14	3

LANCASTER

OPERATIONS	SORTIES	AIRCRAFT LOSSES	% LOSSES
371	4364	105	2.4

CATEGORY OF OPERATIONS

BOMBING	MINING	OTHER
346	24	1

HEAVIEST SINGLE LOSS.

Schweinfurt 26/27.04.44. 5 Lancasters FTR.
St-Leu-d'Esserent 07/08.07.44. 5 Lancasters FTR.

Aircraft Histories

HAMPDEN.	To March 1942.
L4038	From 49Sqn. To 25 OTU.
L4042	From 44Sqn. To 408Sqn.
L4100	From 44Sqn. To 14 OTU.
L4103	From 61Sqn. Crashed in circuit at Finningley during night training 7.12.40.
L4120	From 61Sqn. Crashed at Finningley while training 16.12.40.
L4139	From 76Sqn. To 7Sqn.
L4149	From 76Sqn. To 50Sqn.
L4150	To 50Sqn.
L4174 ZN-A	Crashed near Finningley while training 31.5.40.
L4175 ZN-B	Crashed while trying to land at Finningley 24.10.39.
L4176	To 7Sqn.
L4177	To 7Sqn.
L4178	To 44Sqn.
L4180 ZN-F	FTR from mining sortie 29/30.10.40.
L4181	Crashed on landing at Finningley while training 6.7.40.
L4182 ZN-K	To 1 AAS.
L4183 ZN-P	Crashed on take-off at Finningley while training 29.11.40.
L4184 ZN-Q	Crashed on take-off at Finningley while training 13.10.40.
L4185 ZN-S	Crashed in the Thames Estuary on return from Dortmund 4/5.7.41.
L4186 ZN-T	Crashed in Lincolnshire while training 11.11.39.
L4187 ZN-U	Crashed in Lincolnshire while training 7/8.8.40.
L4188 ZN-V	Blew up over Buckinghamshire while training 1.9.40.
L4189	Crashed in Derbyshire while training 30.9.40.
L4194	From 195Sqn. FTR from mining sortie 22/23.11.40
P1198	To 144Sqn.
P1228 ZN-L	From 50Sqn. FTR Hamburg 30.11/1.12.41.
P1253	To 61Sqn.
P1254	To 14 OTU.
P1255	To BTU.
P1256	Crashed near Finningley during training 27.9.40.
P1258	To 25 OTU.
P1259	FTR from mining sortie 18/19.9.40.
P1290	FTR from mining sortie 7/8.11.41.
P1303	To 5Gp TF.
P1304 ZN-Y	Crashed in Yorkshire while training 21.12.40.
P1311	To 32 OTU.
P1320 ZN-B	Crashed in Lincolnshire during training 25.11.40.
P1321	To 50Sqn.
P1322	To 44Sqn.
P1336	Crashed at Coventry during training 24.5.40.

P1337	To 5Gp TF.
P1341	From 16 OTU. FTR Hamburg 15/16.1.42.
P2071	Abandoned over Shropshire while training 23.12.40.
P2073	To 408Sqn.
P2083	To 5Gp TF and back. Force-landed at Wellesbourne on return from mining sortie 27.5.41.
P2098	FTR from mining sortie 27/28.12.40.
P2099 ZN-K	Force-landed in Rutland during training 17.5.41.
P2129	To 16 OTU.
P4302	To 25 OTU.
P4314	From 14 OTU. Crashed near Finningley while training 3.1.41.
P4318	To 25 OTU.
P4323	From 16 OTU. FTR from mining sortie 23/24.2.42.
P4377	To 49Sqn.
P4398	From 83Sqn. FTR Münster 28/29.1.42.
P4413 ZN-J	Crashed while landing at Pocklington on return from Hamburg 16.9.41.
P4414	From 44Sqn. FTR from an intruder operation to the Cologne area 21/22.2.42.
P5323	From 7 AAU. Converted for use as torpedo bomber. To 455Sqn.
P5330	From 7 AAU. To 420Sqn.
X2914	Abandoned over Somerset on return from mining sortie 27.9.40.
X2921	To 44Sqn.
X2960	Force-landed near Finningley while training 18.9.40.
X2970	To 25 OTU.
X2986 ZN-F	FTR Cologne 20/21.4.41.
X3002	FTR Cologne 3/4.3.41.
X3021	From 49Sqn. FTR Schiphol 29/30.10.41.
X3058	From 61Sqn. FTR Münster 28/29.1.42.
X3131	From 83Sqn. Converted for use as torpedo bomber. To 455Sqn.
X3148 ZN-E	FTR Düsseldorf 10/11.4.41.
X3152	To 5BGS.
X3153	FTR Düsseldorf 10/11.4.41.
X3154 ZN-A	Crashed in Derbyshire during navigation exercise 21.12.40.
AD735 ZN-R	FTR Mönchengladbach (97Sqn crew) 7/8.7.41.
AD736	To 16 OTU.
AD738	FTR Brest 4/5.4.41.
AD743	To 25 OTU.
AD746 ZN-Z	Crashed on approach to Coningsby on return from Bremen 21.10.41.
AD749	To 14 OTU.
AD750	FTR from mining sortie 4/5.2.41.
AD756	FTR Düsseldorf 16/17.8.41.
AD758	To 44Sqn.
AD760 ZN-W	FTR from mining sortie 7/8.11.41.
AD763	Crashed on landing at Coningsby during a ferry flight 1.3.41.
AD765	To 144Sqn.
AD768	Abandoned over Ireland on return from Karlsruhe 1/2.10.41.
AD785	Blew up over Yorkshire on return from Hamburg 27.10.41.

AD790	Crashed on take-off at Coningsby while training 25.2.41.
AD799	To 49Sqn.
AD802	To 14 OTU.
AD803	To 455Sqn and back. To 408Sqn.
AD848	From 16 OTU. To 14 OTU.
AD855	To 44Sqn.
AD857	To 408Sqn.
AD861	Crashed off Plymouth on return from Brest (97Sqn crew) 7.7.41.
AD862	FTR Duisburg 2/3.7.41.
AD863	FTR Cologne 15/16.6.41.
AD873	FTR Duisburg 2/3.7.41.
AD895	FTR Bremen 29/30.6.41.
AD914	FTR Dortmund 4/5.7.41.
AD919	Force-landed soon after take-off from Coningsby when bound for Cologne 18.8.41.
AD925	To A&AEE.
AD929	To 50Sqn.
AD932	FTR from mining sortie 7/8.11.41.
AD970	Crashed off Skegness during air test 30.7.41.
AD984	FTR Bremen 20/21.10.41.
AD986	FTR Dortmund 4/5.7.41.
AD988	To 14 OTU.
AE120	FTR Mannheim 5/6.8.41.
AE123 ZN-D	From 49Sqn. FTR Bremen 21/22.1.42.
AE134	FTR Düsseldorf 16/17.8.41.
AE136	FTR Hamburg 26/27.10.41.
AE144	FTR Essen 10/11.10.41.
AE151 ZN-F	FTR from intruder sortie over Germany 21.12.41.
AE186	From 420Sqn. To 408Sqn.
AE193 ZN-A	FTR Duisburg 28/29.8.41.
AE220	FTR Mannheim 22/23.8.41.
AE232	FTR Hamburg 15/16.9.41.
AE246	To 420Sqn.
AE255	To 5 OTU.
AE261	To 49Sqn.
AE292	Crashed in Lincolnshire during training 14.1.42.
AE293	From 97Sqn. To 408Sqn.
AE299	From 207Sqn. FTR Berlin 7/8.9.41.
AE300	From 97Sqn. FTR Rostock 11/12.9.41.
AE301 ZN-N	From 97Sqn. FTR from mining sortie 26/27.8.41.
AE302	From 97Sqn. FTR Cologne 26/27.8.41.
AE307	Converted for use as torpedo bomber. To 455Sqn.
AE317	FTR Emden 26/27.11.41.
AE378	To 420Sqn.
AE391	FTR Gelsenkirchen 12.12.41.
AE425	Crashed on take-off from Coningsby en-route to Mannheim 11.2.42.

AE426	To 408Sqn.
AT115	FTR Hamburg 30.11/1.12.41.
AT121	FTR Münster 28/29.1.42.
AT122 ZN-A	FTR Münster 28/29.1.42.
AT123 ZN-K	FTR from mining sortie 3/4.1.42.
AT131	To 455Sqn.
AT141	To 408Sqn.
AT146	From 50Sqn. FTR from mining sortie 22/23.1.42.
AT178	To 49Sqn.
AT190	To 49Sqn.
AT191	To 49Sqn.
AT219	To 420Sqn.

MANCHESTER. From February 1942 to June 1942.

L7291	From 97Sqn. No operations. To 50Sqn.
L7301 ZN-D	FTR Cologne 30/31.5.42. 50Sqn crew Manser VC.
L7305	From 25 OTU. Became ground instruction machine.
L7315	From 61Sqn. No operations.
L7317	From 207Sqn. Force-landed near Lee-on-Solent on return from Dortmund 15.4.42. 21 operations total.
L7319	From 207Sqn. Completed at least 25 operations. Ultimate fate not recorded.
L7376	From 25 OTU. To 1654CU.
L7378	From 207Sqn. Completed 32 operations. To 1654CU
L7389	From 49Sqn. To Conversion Flight. Became ground instruction machine.
L7390	FTR Essen 25/26.3.42.
L7391 ZN-F	From 207Sqn. To 1485Flt.
L7394	From 83Sqn. FTR from mining sortie 29/30.3.42.
L7398	To 49Sqn.
L7399 ZN-X	FTR from mining sortie 2/3.5.42.
L7417 ZN-V	From 207Sqn. Crashed on cross-country excercise 19.5.42.
L7418	FTR from training flight, presumed lost in the Irish Sea 19.5.42.
L7434 ZN-U/J	To 1656CU.
L7456 ZN-T	FTR Cologne 30/31.5.42. 50Sqn crew.
L7457	From 97CF. To 83CF via 106CF.
L7461	From 97Sqn. To 1660CU.
L7463 ZN-L	From 97Sqn. FTR Rostock 23/24.4.42.
L7467	From 97CF. To 1661CU.
L7474	From 97Sqn. Abandoned over Lincolnshire while training 12.3.42.
L7485	From 207Sqn. FTR from mining sortie 16/17.4.42.
L7488 ZN-E	From 207Sqn. Became ground instruction machine.
L7515 ZN-O	From 207Sqn. To 49Sqn.
R5769	From 25 OTU. To 50Sqn.
R5770 ZN-G	From 25 OTU. To 1660CU.
R5780 ZN-G	From 83Sqn. Returned to 83Sqn.
R5796 ZN-K	From 207Sqn. 18 operations total. To 1654CU.

R5839	To 1661CU.
R5840 ZN-X	FTR from mining sortie 2/3.5.42.
R5841	To 1660CU.

LANCASTER. **From May 1942.**

L7569	From 44Sqn. Became ground instruction machine.
L7577	From 97Sqn on loan for one operation. Returned to 97Sqn. To 1660CU via 106CF.
L7579 ZN-Z	From A.V.Roe. To 1654CU via 106CF.
L7582 ZN-P	From 207Sqn. To 100Sqn.
R5492 ZN-S/Y	From 44Sqn. To 1661CU.
R5551 ZN-V	From 97Sqn. FTR Oberhausen 14/15.6.43.
R5572 ZN-M	From 97Sqn. FTR Gelsenkirchen 25/26.6.43.
R5573 ZN-B	FTR Cologne 8/9.7.43.
R5574 ZN-H	FTR Munich 21/22.12.42.
R5575	From 97Sqn. 106CF only. Returned to 97Sqn.
R5576 ZN-J	To 106CF. Crashed on take-off from Coningsby while training 21.7.42.
R5604 ZN-X	FTR Düsseldorf 31.7/1.8.42. Was carrying first 8,000lb bomb.
R5608 ZN-Y	FTR from mining sortie 25/26.7.42.
R5609 ZN-L	From 97Sqn. To 1LFS.
R5611 ZN-D/W	From R.A.E. FTR Pilsen 13/14.5.43.
R5614 ZN-Z	From 97Sqn. Crashed at Syerston while training 1.8.43.
R5631	From 44Sqn. 106CF only. To 1660CU.
R5637 ZN-D	FTR Düsseldorf 27/28.1.43.
R5638	FTR Düsseldorf 10/11.9.42.
R5665 ZN-D	From 44Sqn. FTR Remscheid 30/31.7.43.
R5668	To 207Sqn.
R5676 ZN-E	To 1660CU via 106CF.
R5677 ZN-B/A	FTR Wuppertal 29/30.5.43.
R5678	FTR Düsseldorf 15/16.8.42.
R5680 ZN-C/T	FTR Essen 13/14.1.43.
R5681 ZN-Y/O	Flown by W/C Gibson on his first Lancaster operation. FTR Essen 16/17.9.42.
R5683	Exploded over The Wash when bound for Duisburg 26.7.42.
R5684 ZN-P	FTR Frankfurt 24/25.8.42.
R5697 ZN-J	From 44Sqn. FTR Duisburg 20/21.12.42.
R5700 ZN-G	Completed 34 operations. To 9Sqn via 5MU.
R5702	From 50Sqn. To 460Sqn.
R5731 ZN-M	FTR Hamburg 3/4.3.43.
R5742	To 61Sqn.
R5748 ZN-R	FTR Hamburg 26/27.7.42.
R5749 ZN-G	FTR Essen 12/13.3.43.
R5750 ZN-Z	FTR Wilhelmshaven 18/19.2.43.
R5844 C4	From 50CF. Conversion Flight only. FTR Essen 1/2.6.42. First operational loss of 106Sqn Lancaster.
R5848 C7	From 207 via 106CF. To 1660CU.

R5854 C3	Conversion Flight only. To 97Sqn.
R5861 ZN-Q	FTR Wilhelmshaven 8/9.7.42.
R5864 ZN-K	To 61Sqn and back. Returned to 61Sqn.
R5899 ZN-F	FTR from mining sortie 18/19.9.42.
R5900 ZN-X	Crashed while landing at Syerston on return from Berlin 18.1.43.
R5901 ZN-U	To 44Sqn.
R5906	106CF only. To XVSqn.
R5910	To 61Sqn and back. To 1654CU.
R5914	FTR Munich 21/22.12.42.
W4102 ZN-E	Crashed on approach to Langar after early return from Aachen 5.10.42.
W4109	FTR Mainz 11/12.8.42.
W4118 ZN-Y/Z	FTR Turin 4/5.2.43.
W4127 C2	From 97Sqn. Conversion Flight only. To 619Sqn.
W4156 ZN-J	FTR Duisburg 8/9.4.43.
W4178	FTR Essen 16/17.9.42.
W4179	FTR Essen 16/17.9.42.
W4195 ZN-W	FTR Cologne 15/16.10.42.
W4238 ZN-C	Crashed at Newton following early return from Krefeld 2.10.42.
W4242 ZN-A/F	FTR Hanover 8/9.10.43.
W4253	To 1661CU.
W4256 ZN-V/D	FTR Gelsenkirchen 25/26.6.43.
W4261 ZN-C	FTR Essen 13/14.1.43.
W4302	FTR Cologne 15/16.10.42.
W4367 ZN-C	From 50Sqn. FTR Gelsenkirchen 25/26.6.43.
W4381	From 467Sqn. To 61Sqn.
W4768	FTR Krefeld 2/3.10.42.
W4770 ZN-O	FTR Hamburg 3/4.2.43.
W4771	FTR Cologne 15/16.10.42.
W4778	To 44Sqn via 106CF.
W4826 ZN-D	From 467Sqn. FTR Hamburg 30/31.1.43.
W4842 ZN-O/H	FTR Essen 27/28.5.43.
W4886 ZN-X	FTR Nuremberg 25/26.2.43.
W4897 ZN-X	From 156Sqn. To 463Sqn.
W4918 ZN-D	FTR Essen 5/6.3.43.
W4921 ZN-Z	To 617Sqn for training purposes.
W4922 ZN-J	From 156Sqn. FTR Mannheim 5/6.9.43.
DV181 ZN-E	FTR Turin 12/13.7.43.
DV182 ZN-S	FTR Mannheim 5/6.9.43.
DV195	FTR Nuremberg 10/11.8.43.
DV196 ZN-K	FTR Milan 7/8.8.43.
DV229 ZN-Z	Admiral Shyte-'Awk. To 463Sqn.
DV271	FTR Mannheim 23/24.9.43.
DV272 ZN-F	FTR Hanover 8/9.10.43.
DV273 ZN-L	To BDU.
DV274 ZN-K	To 463Sqn.
DV297 ZN-O	To 61Sqn.

DV339	To 61Sqn.
DV344 ZN-S	To 61Sqn.
ED303 ZN-A/J	From 467Sqn. FTR Hamburg 27/28.7.43.
ED358 ZN-T	From 50Sqn. FTR Leipzig 20/21.10.43.
ED360 ZN-K	From 467Sqn. Crashed near Wisbech on return from Cologne 9.7.43.
ED385	From 57Sqn. FTR Berlin 3/4.9.43.
ED409 ZN-B/E	From 50Sqn. FTR Berlin 31.8/1.9.43.
ED420	From 9Sqn. To 463Sqn.
ED451 ZN-O	FTR Essen 30.4/1.5.43.
ED542	FTR Essen 3/4.4.43.
ED593 ZN-T/Y	To 5LFS after many operations.
ED596 ZN-H	FTR Berlin 29/30.3.43.
ED649 ZN-X	FTR Oberhausen 14/15.6.43.
ED708	FTR Hamburg 27/28.7.43.
ED720 ZN-R	FTR Cologne 8/9.7.43.
ED752 ZN-H/P	FTR Stuttgart 14/15.4.43.
ED801 ZN-N	To 207Sqn via 1661CU.
ED819 ZN-U	FTR Munich 6/7.9.43.
ED873	From 97Sqn. Crashed while landing at Metheringham on return from aborted Berlin sortie 26.11.43.
ED874 ZN-O/D	From 97Sqn. FTR Berlin 2/3.12.43.
EE125 ZN-R	FTR Gelsenkirchen 25/26.6.43.
EE186	From 49Sqn. To 61Sqn.
EE191 ZN-R/G	To 463Sqn.
JA845	From SIU. No operations. To BDU.
JA871	FTR Leverkusen 22/23.8.43.
JA876 ZN-R	To 1661CU.
JA893 ZN-C	Ditched in North Sea on return from Berlin 3/4.9.43.
JA973 ZN-F/E	To 463Sqn.
JB146 ZN-F	Crash-landed at Romney Marsh on return from Berlin 1.9.43.
JB292 ZN-R	From 1660CU. FTR Salbris 7/8.5.44.
JB534 ZN-K	From 61Sqn. Crashed in Lincolnshire on return from Berlin 16.2.44.
JB562 ZN-M	Completed 11 operations to Berlin. FTR Schweinfurt 26/27.4.44.
JB566 ZN-C	Completed 10 operations to Berlin. FTR Nuremberg 30/31.3.44.
JB567 ZN-E	Completed 10 operations to Berlin. FTR Brunswick 22/23.4.44.
JB592 ZN-W	FTR Berlin 26/27.11.43.
JB593 ZN-T	Completed 13 operations to Berlin. FTR Königsburg 29/30.8.44.
JB601 ZN-V	Completed 11 operations to Berlin. FTR Schweinfurt 26/27.4.44.
JB612 ZN-U/G	FTR Salbris 7/8.5.44.
JB638 ZN-G	FTR Berlin 16/17.12.43.
JB641 ZN-X	Completed 11 operations to Berlin. FTR St Leu d'Esserent 7/8.7.44.
JB642 ZN-J	FTR Berlin 1/2.1.44.
JB645 ZN-F	FTR Berlin 1/2.1.44.
JB648 ZN-B	FTR Frankfurt 22/23.3.44.
JB663 ZN-A	Completed 111 operations. To 24MU.
JB664 ZN-N	FTR Vitry-le-Francois 27/28.6.44.

LL891 ZN-S/B	FTR Salbris 7/8.5.44.
LL948 ZN-V	FTR Lützkendorf 14/15.3.45.
LL953 ZN-C/O	FTR Gravenhorst 6/7.11.44.
LL955 ZN-E	FTR Gelsenkirchen 21/22.6.44.
LL974 ZN-F	FTR Vitry-le-Francois 27/28.6.44.
LL975 ZN-H	FTR Pommerval 24/25.6.44.
LM211 ZN-Z	To 7Sqn.
LM215 ZN-F	Crash-landed at Juvincourt on return from Siegen 1.2.45.
LM303 ZN-M	FTR Wilhelmshaven 11/12.2.43.
LM310	From 467Sqn. To 61Sqn.
LM377 ZN-F	To 61Sqn.
LM549 ZN-R	Crash-landed at Carnaby on return from Nantes 28.5.44.
LM570 ZN-Z	FTR Scholven-Buer 21/22.6.44.
LM641 ZN-D	FTR Secqueville 7/8.8.44.
LM690 ZN-P	To 7Sqn.
ME313	From 582Sqn via NTU.
ME324 ZN-R	To 1661CU.
ME355 ZN-P/S	From 514Sqn. To 50Sqn.
ME336	From 514Sqn.
ME630 ZN-P	From 97Sqn. FTR Leipzig 19/20.2.44.
ME668 ZN-L	FTR St Leu d'Esserent 7/8.7.44.
ME669 ZN-O	FTR Schweinfurt 26/27.4.44.
ME778 ZN-O	FTR Stuttgart 28/29.7.44.
ME789 ZN-B/R	FTR St Leu d'Esserent 7/8.7.44.
ME790 ZN-U	FTR Brunswick 22/23.5.44.
ME831 ZN-R	FTR St Leu d'Esserent 7/8.7.44.
ME832 ZN-J	FTR St Leu d'Esserent 4/5.7.44.
ND331 ZN-G/C	FTR Königsburg 29/30.8.44.
ND332 ZN-B	Crash-landed at Manston on return from Nuremberg 30/31.3.44.
ND333 ZN-R/S	From 83Sqn.
ND336 ZN-Q	FTR Berlin 30/31.1.44.
ND339 ZN-Z/U	Detached to 617Sqn. Returned to 106Sqn. FTR St Leu d'Esserent 4/5.7.44.
ND501 ZN-K/O	From 97Sqn. Crashed while landing at Metheringham during training 3.4.45.
ND511 ZN-N/E	FTR Gennevilliers 9/10.5.44.
ND535 ZN-Q	FTR Nuremberg 30/31.3.44.
ND585 ZN-J/Q	FTR Nuremberg 30/31.3.44.
ND680 ZN-P	FTR Coutances (Caen) 6/7.6.44.
ND682 ZN-X/K	FTR from mining sortie 15/16.12.44.
ND850 ZN-C	FTR Schweinfurt 26/27.4.44.
ND851 ZN-H	FTR Gennevilliers 9/10.5.44.
ND853 ZN-J	FTR Schweinfurt 26/27.4.44.
ND868 ZN-Q	FTR Dortmund Ems Canal 23/24.9.44.
ND870 ZN-S	FTR Salbris 7/8.5.44.
NE150 ZN-H	FTR Coutances (Caen) 6/7.6.44.
NG222 ZN-T	To 1654CU.
NG397 ZN-T	From 1661CU.

NG414 ZN-K	From 1661CU. Crashed on take-off at Metheringham bound for Pilsen 16.4.45.
NN719 ZN-Q	To 7Sqn.
NN725	To 7Sqn.
NN726 ZN-D	FTR Gdynia 18/19.12.44.
PA194 ZN-D	From 1661CU.
PA232 ZN-H	To RWA.
PA267 ZN-N	To 7Sqn.
PA310	To 7Sqn.
PA331	To 7Sqn.
PB122 ZN-Y	FTR Leuna 14/15.1.45.
PB144 ZN-P	FTR St Leu D'Esserent 7/8.7.44.
PB145 ZN-L/M	Damaged and written-off.
PB191 ZN-H	How's Hare.
PB203 ZN-M	FTR Darmstadt 11/12.9.44.
PB232 ZN-N	Twice damaged and written-off.
PB248 ZN-E	To 5LFS.
PB281 ZN-J	FTR Heilbronn 3/4.12.44.
PB284 ZN-U/S	To RAE for use in mine experiments.
PB296 ZN-X	Damaged beyond repair 23/24.2.45.
PB298 ZN-B	Force-landed near Fulbeck on return from Bremerhaven 19.9.44.
PB303 ZN-R	FTR Homburg 1.11.44.
PB304 ZN-Z/S	Crashed in Lancashire on return from operation to the Normandy battle area 30.7.44.
PB347 ZN-G	From 49Sqn. FTR Rheydt 19/20.9.44.
PB359 ZN-T	From 49sqn. FTR Rheydt 19/20.9.44.
PB617 ZN-B	FTR Royan 5.1.45.
PB618 ZN-G	
PB645	To 227Sqn.
PB676 ZN-E	From 35Sqn. To 189Sqn.
PB682	From 405Sqn.
PB724 ZN-L/M	FTR Munich 7/8.1.45.
PB732 ZN-K	From 189Sqn.
PB734 ZN-E	Crash-landed at Metheringham 1.2.45.
PD214 ZN-D	FTR Bremen 6/7.10.44.
PD429	To 186Sqn.
RA508 ZN-B	FTR Dortmund 12.3.45.
RA567	To 7Sqn.
RA581 ZN-B	To 35 Sqn.
RE130	To 7Sqn.
RF130 ZN-F	To 7Sqn.
RF151 ZN-E	From 189Sqn.
RF215	To 7Sqn.
RF235	Crashed at Rheine air base in Germany 9.5.45.
RF236 ZN-V	To the Middle East.
SW248 ZN-R	From 1661CU.
SW265 ZN-O	From 49Sqn.

Key to Abbreviations

A&AEE	Aeroplane and Armaments Experimental Establishment.
AA	Anti-Aircraft fire.
AACU	Anti-Aircraft Cooperation Unit.
AAS	Air Armament School.
AASF	Advance Air Striking Force.
AAU	Aircraft Assembly Unit.
ACM	Air Chief Marshal.
ACSEA	Air Command South-East Asia.
AFDU	Air Fighting Development Unit.
AFEE	Airborne Forces Experimental Unit.
AFTDU	Airborne Forces Tactical Development Unit.
AGS	Air Gunners School.
AMDP	Air Members for Development and Production.
AOC	Air Officer Commanding.
AOS	Air Observers School.
ASRTU	Air-Sea Rescue Training Unit.
ATTDU	Air Transport Tactical Development Unit.
AVM	Air Vice-Marshal.
BAT	Beam Approach Training.
BCBS	Bomber Command Bombing School.
BCDU	Bomber Command Development Unit.
BCFU	Bomber Command Film Unit.
BCIS	Bomber Command Instructors School.
BDU	Bombing Development Unit.
BSTU	Bomber Support Training Unit.
CF	Conversion Flight.
CFS	Central Flying School.
CGS	Central Gunnery School.
C-in-C	Commander in Chief.
CNS	Central Navigation School.
CO	Commanding Officer.
CRD	Controller of Research and Development.
CU	Conversion Unit.
DGRD	Director General for Research and Development.
EAAS	Empire Air Armament School.
EANS	Empire Air Navigation School.
ECDU	Electronic Countermeasures Development Unit.
ECFS	Empire Central Flying School.
ETPS	Empire Test Pilots School.
F/L	Flight Lieutenant.
Flt	Flight.
F/O	Flying Officer.
FPP	Ferry Pilots School.

F/S	Flight Sergeant.
FTR	Failed to Return.
FTU	Ferry Training Unit.
G/C	Group Captain.
Gp	Group.
HCU	Heavy Conversion Unit.
HGCU	Heavy Glider Conversion Unit.
LFS	Lancaster Finishing School.
MAC	Mediterranean Air Command.
MTU	Mosquito Training Unit.
MU	Maintenance Unit.
NTU	Navigation Training Unit.
OADU	Overseas Aircraft Delivery Unit.
OAPU	Overseas Aircraft Preparation Unit.
OTU	Operational Training Unit.
P/O	Pilot Officer.
PTS	Parachute Training School.
RAE	Royal Aircraft Establishment.
SGR	School of General Reconnaissance.
Sgt	Sergeant.
SHAEF	Supreme Headquarters Allied Expeditionary Force.
SIU	Signals Intelligence Unit.
S/L	Squadron Leader.
SOC	Struck off Charge.
SOE	Special Operations Executive.
Sqn	Squadron.
TF	Training Flight.
TFU	Telecommunications Flying Unit.
W/C	Wing Commander.
Wg	Wing.
WIDU	Wireless Intelligence Development Unit.
W/O	Warrant Officer.

69952905R00143

Made in the USA
Columbia, SC
30 April 2017